DATE DUE

MAY 0 2 1985		
MAY 0 1 1996		
OCT 0 6 1989		
SEP 24 '89		
SEP 30 '96 RT'L		
RT'D SEP 30 '96		
MAR 30 '97		
RT'D MAR 23 '97		
MAR 30 2001		
RECEIVED		
AUG 31 2000		

DEMCO 38-297

COMPARATIVE PSYCHOLOGY
IN THE
TWENTIETH CENTURY

Comparative Psychology in the Twentieth Century

Donald A. Dewsbury
University of Florida

Hutchinson Ross Publishing Company
Stroudsburg, Pennsylvania

Library of Congress Cataloging in Publication Data
Dewsbury, Donald A., 1939-
    Comparative psychology in the twentieth century.
    Includes bibliographical references and index.
    1. Psychology, Comparative.   2. Psychology,
Comparative—History—20th century.   I. Title.
II. Title: Comparative psychology in the 20th century.
[DNLM: 1. Psychology, Comparative—History.   BF 107.C6
D524c]
BF671.D48   1983   156   83-12649
1SBN 0-87933-108-9

Distributed worldwide by Van Nostrand Reinhold Company Inc.,
135 W. 50th Street, New York, NY 10020.

Contents

9: Conclusion / 331

Preface

Psychology is a science that has had few historians, and the special province of animal psychology has never been accorded the dignity of a full and thorough historical treatment.

Holmes (1916, 9)

Whoever aspires to write a definite history of comparative psychology and/or ethology will need the wisdom of Solomon to understand the human scientists and perhaps Solomon's ring to understand the scientists' animal subjects . . . .

Scott (1973, 52)

We are in a age when it is fashionable to trace one's roots. Although I have resisted the temptation to trace my genetic roots, the temptation to track my intellectual roots has proven irresistible. In reading accounts of the comparative psychologists that preceded my generation, I have been struck with their foresight and accomplishments. However, both the image and history of comparative psychology are generally perceived as poor. In this book I attempt to trace a consistent thread through the development of comparative psychology. By so doing, I hope to alter current perceptions of comparative psychology and thereby influence its future course. O'Donnell (1979) has criticized the late E. G. Boring for using history as a vehicle to effect change in his discipline. The present volume is an attempt to use history for precisely those aims. Thus my goals are best described as a cross between recording history and advocacy. I hope to escape some criticism by making my objectives and biases explicit.

The audience toward which the book is directed consists of professionals and graduate students in comparative psychology and related disciplines. I hope to provide a fairly comprehensive overview of the history of comparative psychology as I perceive it. The book may therefore be useful in graduate seminars concerned with such history. This book has not been conceived as a general textbook; any respectable textbook in this interdisciplinary field must incorporate the contributions of scientists from many disciplines—at least to some degree. Here, by contrast, I concentrate on the contributions only of psychologists, which produces a one-sided view of the animal-behavior field. However, it is the only way in which to tell the story I wish to tell. For example, I shall discuss the substantial contributions of comparative psychologists to the study of migration and orientation in birds and other animals. Although this contribution is considerable and often unrecognized, it is but a small part of the study of migration and orientation. The beginning student given only these materials would be poorly served.

I have long held that comparative psychology should exist in a state of intimate interaction with related disciplines such as ethology and sociobiology. Not all psychologists agree with this view (see, for example, Ratner, 1972). Burghardt (1980, 22) has written that my textbook, *Comparative Animal Behavior* (Dewsbury, 1978a) "owes far more to ethology than to Hull, Skinner, or Hebb." Erwin (1981, 15) criticized my selection of a title, wondering, "How are modern students ever to hear of comparative psychology?" In fact, I believe that comparative psychology has always been interdisciplinary, that the influences of Skinner, Hebb, and even Hull have been important for the field, and that the very best way in which the facts of comparative psychology can be made available to students in both comparative psychology and related fields is in a comprehensive, interdisciplinary text.

At first sight, this volume may appear to be a departure from my interdisciplinary approach to the study of animal behavior. Nothing could be further from my intentions. I believe that comparative psychologists and other scientists must cooperate in the study of animal behavior. However, I believe that they must do this as equal partners in the scientific endeavor. At one point psychology was viewed as the larger and more advanced discipline, with ethology as younger and less developed (see, for example, Schaffner, 1955). (See the list at the end of the book for all references cited in the Preface.) Today, by contrast, the pendulum has swung to the point where many behaviorists look down on comparative psychologists, and we often look down on ourselves. This book is, in part, an effort to restore balance. I strongly believe that representatives of the different disciplines should cooperate and interact—however, this should be done with a sense of respect for the accomplishments, strengths, and weaknesses of each.

A word about my style of writing history is in order. This is history written by an active, working scientist in moments stolen from teaching, research, and family responsibilities. I have observed less than one-fourth of the history I have tried to write. Further, my view of that history sometimes differs from the views of those that made the history. These factors produce both positive and negative effects. I believe that I possess a certain objectivity, perspective, and grasp of the relevance of events of the past for issues of the present. However, I lack both the firsthand knowledge of those who "were there" and the scholarly understanding of the history of science that is the hallmark of the trained historian. There is little that I can do about these matters except to point them out making the reader aware of them.

Psychology has now seen many historians, and animal psychology has seen some. I possess neither Solomon's wisdom nor his ring. However, I hope that this book will help to correct some misperceptions regarding the history of comparative psychology, to encourage others to correct the misperceptions that I promulgate, and to alter favorably the future course of my discipline. I hope this volume will serve in part as a sourcebook and encourage others to engage in more detailed and focused historical studies.

There are many people to thank for help given in the preparation of this book. Katherine J. O'Dea, Laura Sley, and Gerri Lennon typed the manuscript and made production of the manuscript pleasant. John A. Popplestone, Marion White McPherson, and John Miller extended hospitality during my visit to the Archives of the History of American Psychology at the University of Akron. Drs. Fred Stollnitz and Carol Diakow of the National Science Foundation (NSF) provided information beyond my expectations and made possible the analysis of NSF funding trends. Other helpful correspondents included Jay S. Rosenblatt of the Institute of Animal Behavior of Rutgers University; Dr. F. A. King and Nellie Johns of the Yerkes Regional Primate Research Center; Margaret Altmann of the University of Colorado; Frank A. Beach of the University of California, Berkeley; A. Keith Murray of the Psychobiology Study Section at the National Institutes of Health (NIH); Janet M. Cuca of the Research Analysis and Evaluation Branch of NIH; Robert Michel of McGill University; David Chiszar of the University of Colorado; Gilbert Gottlieb of the University of North Carolina; Darryl Bruce of Florida State University; and David Stevens of Clark University. Special thanks are due Douglas K. Candland, Jerry Hirsch, Stephen W. Porges, and Benjamin D. Sachs, who read the complete draft and provided many useful suggestions.

On a more long-term basis, I have to thank both my biological parents and my many teachers, who were my intellectual parents, for laying the foundations on which to build my work. As ever, the support of my family, Joyce, Bryan, and Laura, made completion of the book possible.

DONALD A. DEWSBURY

Twenty-six of the major works cited in this volume are to be reprinted in their entirety or as excerpts in a forthcoming volume entitled *Comparative Psychology*, edited by Donald A. Dewsbury. This volume will be published by Hutchinson Ross as part of the Benchmark Papers in Behavior series and will serve as a source book and companion volume for the present work.

COMPARATIVE PSYCHOLOGY
IN THE
TWENTIETH CENTURY

Chapter 1

The Nature and Assessment of Comparative Psychology

My goals in this book are a combination of writing history and advocacy. I believe that comparative psychology, viewed as a broadly based animal-behavior study conducted by psychologists, is a rich and exciting field with a history worthy of pride. However, as I shall illustrate in this chapter, most commentators on both the status and history of comparative psychology portray them as badly tarnished if not bleak. This book has been written in an effort to resolve the discrepancies between my image of comparative psychology and that which appears to prevail in the literature. I shall try to show that, as a result of both their own writings and those from related disciplines, the efforts of comparative psychologists have been badly misrepresented and their accomplishments sadly underestimated.

The image of comparative psychology is that of a human-oriented, laboratory-based, nonevolutionary study of trivial behavioral patterns in a few domesticated species. To caricature a typical historical outline, one typically learns first of the Greeks, classical philosophers, and the revolution started by Darwin. One then learns of a few noteworthy accomplishments by post-Darwinian scientists around the turn of the century, the decline of comparative psychology with the advent of behaviorism, and some rejuvenation with the development of classical ethology. Although I certainly did not originate this scenario, I regret that I must accept some share of responsibility for its perpetuation (Dewsbury, 1973a).

The story with which I should like to replace this tarnished image of comparative psychology is that of a historical continuity from the accomplishments of comparative psychologists around the turn of the century to those of the present. Comparative psychologists, as I shall define them, have never been many. However, throughout the twentieth century they have carved the continuous and rich history of a broad-based, evolution-oriented science of behavior. The ideals, goals, and tactics of these comparative psychologists have much more in common with those of the classical ethologists than has been generally recognized.

The notion that there is historical continuity in the history of comparative psychology is not new. The point has been made, for example, by Adler and Tobach (1971) in response to the scathing critique of comparative psychology by Lockard (1971). Schneirla (in Schaffner, 1955) departed from the norm in writing of a Whitman-Wheeler-Craig-Carr tradition in comparative psychology. However, the view that comparative psychology has a strong and continuous history has not become prevalent. I believe it has not because materials useful in documenting this history are scattered and fragmented. They have never been fully collected in a manner that permits a comprehensive understanding of the contributions of psychologists to the study of animal behavior. Although I do not believe that I can accomplish this in a single volume, my goal is to provide a major step in indicating how this can be done. I shall try to portray this rich history, at least superficially, and to point the way toward places where more detailed historical and analytical studies need to be conducted.

Chapter 1 deals with the problems of defining comparative psychology and classifying individuals as comparative psychologists. I will then document the overall negative image of comparative psychology that I believe generally prevails. In the remainder of the book, I will consider the history of comparative psychology, first from one perspective and then from another, in an effort to stimulate reassessment.

DEFINING COMPARATIVE PSYCHOLOGY

The problem of defining comparative psychology is a matter of no small importance. The ways in which one perceives certain trends and in which the field is perceived by those outside it are in part a function of one's definition. Comparative psychology has seen a number of definitions, and its practitioners are still not in agreement as to which is the most useful. As noted by Hess (1956, 305), "The problem of defining comparative psychology has not yet been solved." Demarest (1980, 988) conducted a survey of psychologists in an attempt to analyze the status and perception of comparative psychology. He noted "that no one seems to know what comparative psychology is, or more accurately, each individual has his or her own definition." In writing the editorial that helped reestablish the comparative content of the *Journal of Comparative and Physiological Psychology,* Thomas (1975, 3) noted the difficulties of defining comparative psychology and finally noted, "This Journal does not espouse a canonical definition of comparative psychology . . . ." I shall contrast some of the definitions that various authors have proposed and then explain my reasons for selecting one approach.

The Study of All Animal Behavior

The term *comparative psychology* has often been used to refer to all studies of nonhuman (often termed *sub*human or *infra*human) organisms. For example, Yerkes (1908, 271) noted the usage "in the commonly accepted sense of the psychology of all organisms excepting man." McConnell (1981, 3) noted that "anybody who worked with animal subjects was presumed to be a *comparative* psychologist, because that's what animal research of all kinds was called then."

The image of comparative psychology as including process-oriented studies of learning and learning theory is facilitated by implicit acceptance of such a broad definition in its textbooks. For example, six of the thirteen to fifteen chapters in the texts edited by Moss (1934, 1942) and Stone (1951) deal with learning. Even though a truly comparative psychology existed at that time, our own books tended to blur important distinctions.

Such a definition is inadequate in the 1980s. With it we should have to include most of the physiological psychology as well as process-oriented learning research of the sort that is generally not treated by individuals currently labeled comparative psychologists. A more restricted definition is required.

The Usage of C. Lloyd Morgan (1894)

In his landmark *An Introduction to Comparative Psychology* (1894, 36), C. Lloyd Morgan adopted an even broader definition. For Morgan, virtually all modern psychologists were comparative psychologists because the practice of psychology entailed the comparison and correlation of the results of various introspective observers. Clearly, that will not do for the 1980s.

Species Comparisons as the Hallmark of Comparative Psychology

In the most common variety of definition of comparative psychology, emphasis is placed on cross-species comparisons. Comparative psychologists compare the behavior of different species. For example, Gray (1973, 51) noted that "the purpose of comparative psychology is to compare the behavior of two species." For Schneirla (1952, 560), the objective of comparative psychology is "the study of similarities and differences in adjustive capacities and personality among the types of living organisms." Yerkes (1913a, 580) advocated the narrowing of the definition of comparative psychology to include study "by the method of comparison." Similar definitions have been provided by Davis (1907), Gottlieb (1976), Russell (1954), Hodos and Campbell (1969), and Schneirla (1962).

The method of comparing species has been of focal importance in the history of comparative psychology. The question now, however, is whether it should be its *sine qua non.* Many studies that are generally included within the rubric of comparative psychology are done with but one species and are valid in and of themselves without reference to other species. Are we to exclude them from the corpus of comparative psychology?

Some comparative psychologists appear to feel guilty for not making more explicit cross-species comparisons. However, I believe that comparative psychology must emerge from the straightjacket imposed on it by such limiting definitions. Marty Haraway has written perceptively:

> One unfortunate result of the name *comparative* psychology has been to place undue emphasis on making immediate and direct comparisons among species. Such comparisons have never been the main work of comparative psychologists, and I do not see why we must feel they should be. Our main work, it seems to me, has been to focus intensively on the behavior of a selected species, with a frank interest in that species for itself, or in its own right. . . . Direct comparisons among species are desirable, but we need not be obsessed with them simply because the word *comparative* occurs in the name of our science. (1981, 3)

Konrad Lorenz on the Comparative Method

Although not strictly providing a definition of comparative psychology, the usage of Konrad Lorenz requires some clarification. In a much quoted paper, Lorenz noted, "I strongly resent it . . . when an American journal masquerades under the title of 'comparative' psychology, although, to the best of my knowledge, no really comparative paper ever has been published in it" (1950, 239-240). American workers use the term *comparative* in a very general sense to mean only that comparisons are made across species or other taxa. For Lorenz (1960, 1981), by contrast, the term *comparative* implies the study of evolutionary history through the reconstruction of genealogies. The usage is derived from comparative anatomy. Lorenz and American psychologists are simply using the same word to mean different things.

It is unfortunate that such a misunderstanding arose through differential use of terms. Neither usage is right or wrong; they are simply different. Different words are needed. It is clear that American workers continue to use the term in a very broad sense. If different words cannot be found, we must at least recognize that some of our differences are not substantive but simply a result of using the same term in very different ways.

The Comparative Method of Stanley C. Ratner

One comparative psychologist who believed strongly in differentiating comparative psychology from other areas of animal behavior was the late Stanley C. Ratner. Ratner developed his own unique "comparative method" as the defining characteristic of comparative psychology (1972, 1980; Denny and Ratner, 1970). Ratner's comparative method entails six stages: background and perspective, classification of behavior, research preparations, variables, relations and comparisons, and general theory. Ratner had some keen insights into the scientific method. In my opinion, however, his method is useful outside of what we call "comparative psychology" and is too confining as a singular definition of comparative psychology.

Development and Evolution

It is possible to emphasize the study of development and evolution in the definition of comparative psychology. Thus, for example, Adler (1980, 956) treats comparative psychology as "defined as the integration of the evolution and development of behavior." A similar usage is proposed by Warden et al. (1935, 162).

There is merit in this approach as the study of development and evolution characterizes much of comparative psychology and is generally given minimal attention by animal psychologists outside the comparative tradition. In my judgment, comparative psychology is broader than this. Like others, I take as my starting point Niko Tinbergen's set of four questions to be asked in the study of behavior (1963). These are questions of evolutionary history, adaptive significance, development, and immediate control (Dewsbury, 1973*b*, 1978*a*). The complete study of behavior requires that all four classes of answers be provided in attempting to understand the causes of behavior.

A Pragmatic Approach

Having rejected the major definitions of comparative psychology, I find myself unable to provide a simple alternative. My solution, alas, is a pragmatic one. I believe that most comparative psychologists generally agree on what material does and does not fall within the rubric of comparative psychology. The problem, however, is that we cannot provide a simple definition; hence we suffer an identity crisis (see Dewsbury, 1968). The unanimity concerning the content of the field was apparent when Bermant (1965) surveyed the contents of the comparative courses taught at ten leading universities. There were obvious differences in emphasis, but the overall impression of the results is that the similarities among courses far outstrip the differences.

There are many psychologists studying nonhuman animals who fall outside the comparative tradition. I shall use the term *animal psychology* to refer to all work done by psychologists with nonhuman subjects. I shall treat comparative psychology as a subset of animal psychology. Pragmatically, the material of most physiological psychology, most process-oriented learning, and some studies of motivation are excluded from this tradition. In practice, then, comparative psychologists typically study either species other than those commonly used elsewhere in animal psychology or investigate a behavior that falls outside the usual domain. I have attempted to illustrate this in Table 1. Comparative psychologists typically study either unusual species or behavioral patterns that fall outside related areas of animal psychology, or both. With this usage, studies of hoarding in rats, learning in elephants, and orientation in birds would fall in the three different cells characterizing comparative psychology. Although this usage is not clean, I believe that it approximates that which has become prevalent. Further, it appears similar to the approach of C. Lloyd Morgan (1905) and to the "ecological psychology" of Morgan (1894).

I wish to return to the points made in the previous section. The objective of comparative psychology is to establish principles of generality. This point was underscored by Morgan (1905, 78), when he wrote, "Every piece of comparative and genetic work should be so planned as to contribute something to the estalishment or the support of the principles of psychology." Comparative psychologists develop principles of generality through addressing questions of the adaptive significance, evolutionary history, immediate control, and development of behavior. Comprehensive principles are developed when both proxi-

Table 1. A Conceptualization of the Subject Matter of Comparative Psychology as Distinguished from the Rest of Psychology

	Species Studied	
Behavior and Problems Studied	humans, lab rats, rhesus monkeys, white Carneaux pigeons	all others
Learning, motivation, physiology	other psychology	comparative psychology
All others	comparative psychology	comparative psychology

Source: Modified from D. A. Dewsbury, 1979a, Animal Behavior, in *Foundations of Contemporary Psychology,* M. E. Meyer, ed., Oxford, New York, p. 199.

mate and ultimate causation are the foci of study. Comparisons among species can be quite useful in developing general principles on some occasions and less useful in others. The comparative psychologist takes a broad, biologically oriented view of the study of behavior, makes comparisons when appropriate, and works to develop principles of generality.

Although the study of both proximate and ultimate causation is sometimes perceived as a new influence in psychology, it was understood by Morgan, as well as many other comparative psychologists. Morgan wrote:

> Why do animals begin to play and keep on playing? From the psychological point of view because they like it: from the biological view because they gain practice and preparation for the serious business of their after life. But why do they like it? Because, under natural selection, those who did not like it, and therefore did not undergo the preparatory training and discipline of play, proved unfit for life's sterner struggle, and have been therefore eliminated.

With minor modification, that passage could have been written today.

It should be noted again that the selection of a definition of comparative psychology has implications for the assessment of the field. Later in the chapter I will summarize various criticisms of comparative psychology. It must be remembered that different authors use different definitions, and thus some of their criticism may be more appropriate for the comparative psychology they envisage than for that which I envisage. Beer (1980, 19), for example, considers the possibility of splitting comparative psychology off from the rest of animal psychology but rejects it for the purposes for which he writes. The difficulty with such an approach is that the sins of other areas are attributed to comparative psychology. I apologize in advance for any misinterpretations resulting from such issues of definition.

Should the Term "Comparative Psychology" be Retained?

The continued use of *comparative psychology* to describe this area has received recent attention (for example, Demarest, 1980). Some authors believe that the term has outlived its usefulness. Thus Candland (1981, 2) has written that "the term comparative psychology no longer faithfully or suitably describes the activities of those whose research is with animal life."

I agree with Candland that the term is no longer descriptive and with Haraway that it is unfortunate. However, it is ours. I prefer to retain the term for two reasons. First, I am not sure what I would put in its place. My preference would be Morgan's (1894) "zoological psychology." However, I doubt that this would be widely adopted. Other terms such as *biopsychology* and Yerkes's *psychobiology* have come to have altered meanings. We appear stuck with the term.

I have outlined my other reason in an earlier publication (1973b). The tradition of comparative psychology is a long and illustrious one of which I am proud. A change of name would threaten to weaken our connection with that tradition. I have previously noted that, as a boy growing up around New York City, I frequently visited Madison Square Garden at Eighth Avenue and Fiftieth Street in New York. The tradition of being in or playing in "the Garden" is a long and rich one. The location of the arena has been moved several times so that it no longer is near Madison Square and bears little resemblance to a garden. However, the name moved with the arena even though it was no longer technically appropriate. Madison Square Garden and its tradition have endured, and I believe that comparative psychology will endure as well.

WHO IS A PSYCHOLOGIST?

My goal in this book is to single out the contributions of psychologists to the study of animal behavior. In order to do this, some ground rules must be established concerning who is and who is not to be considered a psychologist. Clearly, a "Grade A-certified" psychologist is one who received a Ph.D. from a department of psychology and spent most of his or her career working within a department of psychology. Typically, such individuals would be long-term members of the American Psychological Association. There are many such individuals whose stories I will tell. The difficulties stem from individuals who meet some or none of these criteria and yet made a substantial contribution to psychology. This is especially difficult with individuals working around the turn of the century. Many received their doctoral degrees before departments of psychology existed as independent entities. In addition, some who came along later met some but not all criteria. Who is a psychologist?

In classifying individuals as psychologists, I have made a number of decisions, some of which may appear arbitrary. I consider such workers as William James, James Mark Baldwin, and C. Lloyd Morgan psychologists since their primary identities appear to lie with psychology. Substantial contributions to comparative psychology were made by such workers as Jacques Loeb, H. S. Jennings, H. H. Donaldson, W. C. Allee, Charles O. Whitman, and Wallace Craig. Both Craig and Donaldson joined the American Psychological Association. However, all these distinguished workers were really biologists working with animal behavior. Their work is a necessary and important part of the history of comparative psychology. However, I believe I would bias the story of comparative psychology if I listed their achievements as those of psychology. A similar situation exists with regard to more recent workers such as John L. Fuller and John Paul Scott. Scott was a research professor of psychology at Bowling Green State University, and Fuller served as chair of the Department of Psychology at the State University of New York, Binghamton. Like the earlier workers, both contributed much to psychology. However, I feel it would be unfair to include their achievements; their work originated from other traditions.

Robert M. Yerkes, on the other hand, was identified with psychology throughout his career and meets most criteria for a bona fide psychologist. He preferred to call himself a "psychobiologist" (1932a) and even wrote: "Although never a psychologist myself, save by reason of the unprofitable identification or confusion of psychobiology with it, . . ." (1933, 211). I will unhesitatingly follow Yerkes (1910) and treat him as a psychologist. Similarly, I will follow Beach (1981) and the *New York Times* of November 1, 1962, in considering H. S. Liddell a psychologist, although only his master's degree was in psychology; Liddell's doctoral degree was in physiology.

A special problem appears with Karl S. Lashley, a pivotal individual in the development of psychology. Lashley received a master of science degree in bacteriology from the University of Pittsburgh in 1911. His doctoral degree was completed under Jennings at the Johns Hopkins University in 1914. It is not clear whether the Ph.D. was in zoology (Hebb, 1959; Beach, 1961) or genetics (Carmichael, 1959), but it clearly was not in psychology. However, Lashley completed a minor in psychology and was strongly influenced by John B. Watson and Adolf Meyer even before receiving his degree. Shepherd Ivory Franz, a physiological psychologist, was another strong early influence. Lashley then spent virtually his entire career in psychology departments and is strongly identified as a psychologist (for example, National Cyclopedia of American Biography 1962, 198). In 1929 he was president of the American Psychological Association. Writing of the influences on Lashley in graduate school, Hebb (1959, 144) noted, "He seems already to have been working more with Watson than with Jennings, but it was only in 1915 that he decided finally *to make his career psychology*" (italics mine). I unhesitatingly treat Lashley as a psychologist.

T. Wesley Mills presents another problem. Although teaching physiology in a School of Comparative Medicine, he was a pioneer comparative psychologist. Because he was one of the first five elected members of the American Psychological Association (with Titchener and Münsterburg) after the charter members, I shall consider Mills a psychologist.

Clearly, I have had to make some arbitrary decisions. I do not wish to make my task too easy. If I can persuade the reader that the accomplishments of psychologists have been considerable, I want it to be clear that the accomplishments truly are those of psychologists.

ETHOLOGY

Although in this book I am concerned expressly with comparative psychology, an important part of that story concerns its interaction with the related discipline of ethology. I will argue first that the overlap between contemporary comparative psychology and contemporary ethology is quite considerable and second that there always has been far more overlap between ethology and that part of animal psychology I am calling "comparative psychology" than many authors appear to believe. A very brief introduction to ethology must be presented if its relationship to comparative psychology is to be understood.

"Classical," or "core," ethology has the study of animal behavior as its focus. Ethologists have a long tradition of studying both *proximate causation* (that is, development and immediate control) and *ultimate causation* (that is, evolutionary history and adaptive significance). Ethologists emphasize the study of the naturally occurring behavioral patterns that are displayed by nondomesticated species behaving under natural conditions. In practice, however, many studies in classical ethology were conducted under laboratory or seminatural conditions. Classical ethologists were careful observers who were more concerned with the observation and description of behavior under natural conditions than with the formulation of complex theories. To use Tinbergen's title (1958), ethologists were "curious naturalists." Classical ethologists conducted a few studies on mammals; rather, studies of birds, fish, and insects dominated their literature.

In practice, classical ethology is strongly associated with Lorenz,

Tinbergen, and their associates and students. The ethological approach developed among this group of European zoologists during the 1930s and 1940s. It was transformed into modern ethology as the combined result of changes within ethology and of interaction with other disciplines during the 1950s and thereafter. A highlight in the history of ethology was the award of the Nobel Prize in Physiology or Medicine to Lorenz, Tinbergen, and Karl von Frisch in 1973 in recognition of their enormous contributions to science. The event provided inspiration for all animal behaviorists.

Ethology had several important forerunners in the twentieth century. Charles Otis Whitman, a biologist at the University of Chicago, is noted for proposing the study of behavioral homologies with methods similar to those used in comparative anatomy. American biologist Wallace Craig is noted for distinguishing between the variable, agitated behavioral patterns ("appetitive behavior") and more stereotyped "consummatory acts." Jakob von Uexküll is remembered especially for his concept of the *Umwelt,* or unique sensory-perceptual world of each organism. Oskar Heinroth, an early student of bird behavior, greatly influenced Lorenz.

"Ethology" has had many meanings over time. It is derived from a Greek word *ethos,* which may mean "character," "custom," "habit," or an "intrinsic property," depending on interpretation and the length of the *e.* John Stuart Mill practiced "ethology" as the science of character, and such an ethology gained some influence particularly at the University of California, Berkeley, around the turn of the century (see, for example, Bliss, 1899; Bailey, 1899). According to Lorenz, Heinroth used the term, and it was generally adopted over the objection of Lorenz, who was concerned about confusion with philosophers (see Lorenz in Schaffner, 1955, 76-77). Further discussion of the origins of the term can be found in Schaffner (1955, 76-77), Thorpe (1979, 9), and Jaynes (1969).

Other characteristics attributed to classical ethologists were an aesthetic sense and appreciation of their animals. Thus Beer (1980, 40) wrote that "comparative ethology, like comparative morphology, gives the impression of being sensitive to aesthetic, as well as to scientific values, combining portrayal of beauty with the recording of truth." As a graduate student, I was confused about the meaning of "ethology." The first prominent ethologist I met was the great Dutch ethologist, Gerard P. Baerends. I asked Professor Baerends how one could tell whether or not he was an ethologist. He asked me whether I liked the animals I was studying. At the time I was studying electric fish. Although it is hard to cuddle up to an electric fish, I found them fascinating and replied affirmatively. His response was that then I was an ethologist.

There are many good sources for the reader interested in learning more about ethology. Eibl-Eibesfeldt (1975) has written a comprehensive textbook in the more traditional German school, whereas Hinde (1982) has prepared a book more in the British tradition. Thorpe (1979) has described the history of ethology. Briefer introductions to ethology can be found in the writings of Beer (1973), Burghardt (1973), or Hess (1962). The reader really interested in capturing the spirit of ethology would do well to read some of the original writings by Lorenz and Tinbergen such as Lorenz's *The Foundations of Ethology* (1981) or Tinbergen's *The Study of Instinct* (1951).

THE IMAGE OF COMPARATIVE PSYCHOLOGY

The image of a discipline, as perceived from both inside and outside, is partly determined by what is written about it. Using this criterion one wonders how comparative psychology is as viable as it is what with an image that has undergone the beating that comparative psychology's has taken. In the pages of the *American Psychologist*, the *Annual Review of Psychology*, and other journals and books, the status of comparative psychology has been repeatedly assailed. I shall ignore for the time being the few positive things that have been written. If my quotations are excessive, it is because I do not think I am building a straw man, and I hope to convey some idea of the magnitude of the criticism comparative psychology has had to endure.

It is unclear who first lambasted comparative psychology; I will therefore begin with the proto-ethologist Whitman, who contrasted the methods of Charles Darwin with those of Mills, Romanes, and other comparative psychologists. According to Whitman (1898-1899, 525), Darwin's method was "too laborious and searching to be imitated by students ambitious to reach the heights of comparative psychology through a few hours of parlor diversion with caged animals, or by a few experiments on domestic animals." The game had begun.

Portrayals from Comparative Psychologists

Many of the most devastating portrayals of comparative psychology have been written by comparative psychologists themselves. McGill (1965) published a book of readings that was widely used in courses in comparative psychology and was important in establishing the image of the field. Much of this image was based on a table contrasting ethology and comparative psychology that was included in the introductory section of the book and is reproduced here as Table 2. As can be seen in the table, comparative psychologists are contrasted with ethologists and viewed as engaged in the study of learning and the development of theories of behavior by conducting laboratory work, controlling variables, utilizing statistics, and studying mammals, especially the laboratory rat.

Table 2. McGill's Conceptualization of the Difference Between Comparative Psychology and Ethology

	Comparative Psychologist	Ethologist
Geographical location	North America	Europe
Training	psychology	zoology
Typical subjects	mammals, especially the laboratory rat	birds, fish, insects
Emphasis	"learning," the development of theories of behavior	"instinct," the study of the evolution of behavior
Method	laboratory work, control of variables, statistical analysis	careful observation, field experimentation

Source: T. E. McGill, 1965, *Readings in Animal Behavior,* Holt, Rinehart, and Winston, New York, p. 20.

The "Big Three" Critiques.   Probably the three biggest critiques of comparative psychology by comparative psychologists have come from Beach (1950), Hodos and Campbell (1969), and Lockard (1971). In his classical "The Snark was a Boojum," Beach (1950) argued that throughout the century psychologists progressively restricted the range of species and problems under study. Beginning in about 1920, according to Beach, psychologists went "snark hunting" (that is, in search of animal behavior). Instead of a wide range of animals, they found but one, the laboratory rat, "and thereupon the Comparative Psychologist suddenly and softly vanished away" (Beach, 1950, 115). Beach's analysis was based on a classification and count of journal articles from 1911 to 1948. That procedure has played such an important role in the perception of comparative psychology that I will devote the next major section to it.

Hodos and Campbell (1969) began their paper by noting that since the appearance of the snark paper, psychologists had appeared to show renewed interest in the study of species other than laboratory rats. However, they contended that the selection of diverse species, such as teleost fish, reptiles, and carnivores, was a poor choice and that little could be learned from study of such diverse groups. They then proceeded to provide psychologists with an education regarding the study of evolutionary history and adaptation. Hodos and Campbell perceived a "widespread failure of comparative psychologists to take into account the zoological model of animal evolution" (1969, 337) and proceeded on the assumption that they needed education in this model. The subtitle of the paper was , "Why There Is No Theory in Comparative Psychology."

The third major critique was a paper by Robert B. Lockard entitled,

"Reflections on the Fall of Comparative Psychology: Is There a Message for Us All?" (1971). After a brief historical summary of comparative psychology, Lockard listed ten premises that he believed would have been widely accepted by comparative psychologists of the 1950s:

1. There exists a simple, linear phylogenetic scale of animal species from the unintelligent to the intelligent.
2. "Convenient" animals such as chickens, rats, cats, dogs, and monkeys can be arranged along the scale.
3. The comparative method is essentially a problem of scaling animals along the phylogenetic scale.
4. Animals lower on the scale are simpler than those higher on the scale but do not differ in kind.
5. Learning is the key to understanding animal behavior.
6. Evolution and genetics are irrelevant to psychology.
7. Species differences are few and unimportant.
8. Laws of behavior can be written in ways that do not include specific characteristics of the species under study.
9. The laboratory is the best place for the study of animal behavior.
10. Physical variables are the best ones to study.

Lockard spent the bulk of the paper demonstrating that all ten of these premises were false. He concluded with a consideration of the implications of these factors for psychology and emphasized the need for broad training for future comparative psychologists. The study of the evolutionary histories of behavior in closely related species and of analogous adaptations in ecologically similar species was emphasized.

Lockard's paper in particular produced much reaction. A flurry of letters appeared in the *American Psychologist*—some supporting Lockard and some defending comparative psychology. The most quoted reply was that of Boice (1971). Whereas Lockard had written of the "fall" of comparative psychology, Boice contended that "comparative psychology has never had the elevation from which to fall" (1971, 858). Another effect of Lockard's paper was to stimulate a consideration of "Comparative Psychology at Issue" at the International Congress of Psychology in Tokyo and the American Psychological Association meetings in Honolulu in 1972. With the aid of the New York Academy of Sciences, the proceedings were published by Tobach, et al. (1973).

It is notable that these papers appeared in journals that are widely read within psychology. Thus they affected not only comparative psychologists themselves but the perception of comparative psychology by influential psychologists throughout the discipline. Whatever their effects within the discipline, these and other papers appear to have had detrimental effects within the remainder of psychology.

Some Early Criticisms. Critiques of comparative psychology by comparative psychologists did not begin with the three papers I have singled out. For example, Yerkes wrote on the relationship of psychology to biology. He noted of psychologists that:

> As a group we lack the strength of faith in our aims, methods, and ability which alone makes for success in research. We lack enthusiasm; we are divided; we waver in our aims; we mistrust our methods as well as our assumptions; we question the value of every step forward, and, as an inevitable result, our subject lags at the very threshold to the kingdom of the sciences. (1910, 122).

Decades later Schneirla continued the trend:

> The fact is that at this stage we do not have a "comparative psychology," for the truly *comparative* aspects of the science have been progressively minimized the more investigators have focussed upon mammalian species and upon problems "close to the human level." (1964*a*, 314)

> Actually we have developed no discipline of comparative psychology, either in investigation or in theory, of any substantial proportions. (1952, 561)

Assessments by More Recent Psychologists. Younger comparative psychologists have followed in the tradition of harsh writing about comparative psychology. A few prime examples follow:

> Thus the traditional psychological approach to animal behavior can be characterized as nonevolutionary, nonecological, and narrowly anthropocentric. It is much less concerned with understanding the origin and nature of species-specific attributes involved in the adjustments of a given species to a complex, real-life situation than with describing and analyzing abstract traits or capacities of the isolated individual that have relevance to man. (Mason, 1968*a*, 403)

> Evolutionary theory has played an increasingly minor role in psychological theory and method, and American psychology has remained largely in the realm of being guided by *learning* theory. . . . It is now apparent that several decades of research in comparative psychology were limited in progress by the asking of inappropriate questions. (Eaton, 1970, 176, 187)

Daniel S. Lehrman described an incident in which Tinbergen introduced him noting that "Dr. Lehrman is a professor of psychology but he is really more of a zoologist." Lehrman wrote, "I took this as a compliment" (in Schaffner, 1955, 310).

Demarest (1980) published the results of a survey of the status of comparative psychology as perceived by members of the Division of Physiological and Comparative Psychology of the American Psychological Association. The paper appeared in the *American Psychologist.* One anonymous respondent was quoted as saying, "Comparative is an anachronistic field and should be absorbed into the main body of physiological and neuropsychology" (Demarest, 1980, 984).

Comments from Ethologists

Apparently following in the tradition of Whitman, ethologists have been as harsh on comparative psychologists as psychologists have been on themselves. Representative of the views of a number of ethologists is the perception of Crook and Goss-Custard (1972, 279), who portrayed comparative psychology as "highly controlled experimental testing of a range of alternative learning theories and animal training methodologies which . . . lack the breadth endowed by a firm base in biology." One of the leading pioneers of ethology, William H. Thorpe, has at times been especially harsh on psychologists:

> He has worked mainly with mammals—above all the white rat—and has devoted but little attention to interspecies differences or to the significance of his findings for behavior in its natural setting. Indeed one may surmise that the psychologist has chosen to work with animals rather than with men largely on account of their lesser complexity and greater tolerance of the indignities of the experiment! (Thorpe and Zangwill, 1963, x)
>
> Psychology tended to treat animals as if they were tiny men and so was subjective in approach. (Thorpe, 1979, ix)
>
> Comparative psychology, on the other hand, as the term has been used for the past fifty years or so, seems (temporarily one hopes) to have lost its identity and be on the wane. (Thorpe, 1979, 166)

Thorpe (1973) entitled a paper, "Is There a Comparative Psychology?. . ." Perhaps the most sharply worded comments came from R. F. Ewer:

> However, as long as the comparative psychologists brush aside the adaptive and evolutionary aspects of behavior, . . . so long will ethologists react by feeling that the comparative psychologists are a set of pig-heads who have merely progressed from studying what rats do in mazes to recording how many intromissions they make before ejaculation: and no synthesis will result. (1971, 805)

The View from Sociobiology

Perhaps the most exciting development in the study of animal behavior in the 1970s was the arrival of the field of "sociobiology." If comparative psychologists are to have any consolation from the treatment we received from sociobiologists, perhaps it is that classical ethology has been treated as harshly as have we. In the first chapter of the influential volume that congealed sociobiology, E. O. Wilson (1975a) included a

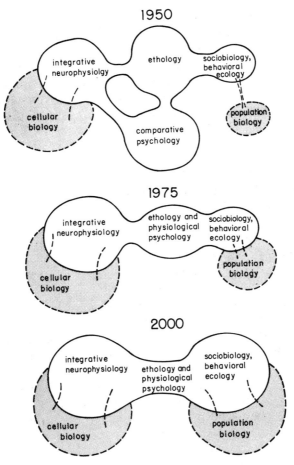

Figure 1. E. O. Wilson's conception of the relative number of ideas in various disciplines relating to behavioral biology as he believes they have changed and will change over time. Note Wilson's view on the cannibalization of comparative psychology (from Wilson, 1975a, 5).

diagram, shown here as Figure 1, that recorded the progressive demise and shrinking of comparative psychology and ethology. Wilson noted:

> The conventional wisdom also speaks of ethology . . . and its companion enterprise, comparative psychology, as the central unifying fields of behavioral biology. They are not; both are destined to be cannibalized by neurophysiology and sensory physiology from one end and sociobiology and behavioral ecology from the other. (1975a, 6)

Wilson's statements, stimulated replies at another symposium at the American Psychological Association meetings, the results of which were published in the the *American Psychologist* under the title, "The Sociobiological Challenge to Psychology: On the Proposal to 'Cannibalize' Comparative Psychology" (Wyers et al., 1980).

In an early textbook on sociobiology that had much influence on the field, Barash (1977a, 5) noted that comparative psychology "has become the study of maze running and bar pressing by white rats" and that "it may well be missing the forest for the trees."

ASSESSMENT OF COMPARATIVE PSYCHOLOGY BY COUNTING JOURNAL ARTICLES

One method of assessing the degree of attention paid to particular topics in a science is through an analysis of the relative frequency of papers fitting different categories and appearing in professional journals. For example, Bruner and Allport (1940) analyzed fifty years of change in psychology by counting the number of papers from fourteen psychological journals that fit each of thirty-two categories. They noted that, whereas in 1888/1898 just 3.5 percent of the papers dealt with nonhuman animals, 15.2 percent of the papers in 1938 dealt with nonhuman subjects. They noted that "perhaps the most significant feature in Table I is the uninterrupted rise in the use of animal subjects" (Bruner and Allport, 1940, 764). A similar rise in representation of animal papers was documented by Fernberger (1943) on the basis of a content analysis of papers presented at meetings of the American Psychological Association.

Schneirla's Analysis. Schneirla (1946) was probably the first to conduct an analysis specific to the field of comparative psychology. Schneirla compared the contents of the seven volumes of the *Journal of Animal Behavior* (*JAB*), which appeared just before World War I (1911-1917), with the volumes of the *Journal of Comparative Psychology* (*JCP*) that appeared just before World War II (1938-1941). He noted a number of striking differences. The most dramatic of these was the increase in the percentage of papers based on laboratory rats, from 19 percent in *JAB* to 66 percent in *JCP.* By contrast, the percentage of papers on invertebrate subjects dropped from 33 percent in *JAB* to 5 percent in *JCP.* Clearly, there were dramatic differences in the types of papers published in the two journals in their respective areas. Schneirla used these data to support his conclusions that comparative psychology was not really very comparative and that there had been change in comparative psychology during the period covered by his analysis.

However, Schneirla also noted something that has apparently been missed by most students who have conducted such analyses ever since. The *Journal of Animal Behavior* was very much an interdisciplinary journal, and many of the papers included in Schneirla's analysis were contributions not from comparative psychologists but from biologists studying animal behavior. Schneirla (1946, 310) noted, "In the earlier period a large proportion of the work on inframammalian subjects was contributed by zoologists, prominent among whom were Jennings, Wheeler, Mast, and Holmes." Schneirla further noted that even in this early period more of the research on problems of instinct came from zoologists; psychologists emphasized the study of learning and sensory function.

The Snark. Beach's paper "The Snark was a Boojum" (1950) extended Schneirla's analysis. Beach analyzed the contents of all odd-numbered volumes of the *Journal of Animal Behavior,* the *Journal of Comparative Psychology,* and the *Journal of Comparative and Physiological Psychology* from 1911 through 1948. He first categorized the contents of papers according to the species studied. Beach separated work done on Norway rats, all mammals except the rat, all vertebrates except mammals, and all invertebrates. The results are portrayed in Figure 2. It can be seen that research on Norway rats increased progressively throughout the period analyzed whereas there was only minimal research on nonmammalian species.

Beach next analyzed the type of "psychological function" studied in each of these papers. He utilized seven categories, but his graphic summary (see Figure 3) included only three. It is clear that the journal came to be dominated by studies of conditioning and learning.

Beach, and many students following him, concluded that comparative psychology changed between 1911 and 1948 and had become little more than the psychology of learning in rats.

Follow-Up Analyses. Since the publication of Beach's paper, numerous workers have completed follow-up studies of the content of these journals.

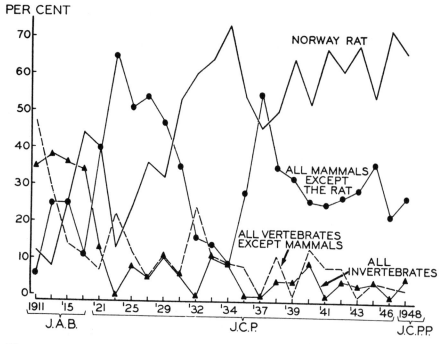

Figure 2. Beach's graph of the percent of all articles in various journals devoted to various phyla, classes, or species (from Beach, 1950, 117).

These analyses are relatively easy to do and can be fun. Notable anniversaries of the snark paper are celebrated with follow-up analyses.

The tenth anniversary of Beach's paper was commemorated by Dukes (1960), who analyzed the contents of the *Journal of Comparative and Physiological Psychology (JCPP)* for 1956-1958. He concluded, "Beach's message seems no less applicable today than in 1949" (Dukes, 1960, 157). Whalen (1961*a*, 84) analyzed the data from 1956-1959 and noted "the unfortunate possibility exists that animal psychology will remain the science of rat learning." Bitterman (1960) completed an unpublished analysis that brought Beach's analysis up to date and noted "no appreciable change." Bitterman (1965*a*, 396) published an updated graph that included information covering the decade following 1948 and again noted "no change in the pattern."

The twentieth anniversary was marked by Cassel (1971) who analyzed issues of *JCPP* from 1949-1970 and noted, "In 1970 as in 1950, the Snark is still a Boojum." Yeager (1973, 184) analyzed *JCPP* issues from 1968 through 1972 and suggested that "perhaps the editors of *JCPP* would do well to delete the word 'comparative' from the title . . ." Scott (1973, 31) examined data from 1960, 1965, 1969, 1970, and 1971

PER CENT

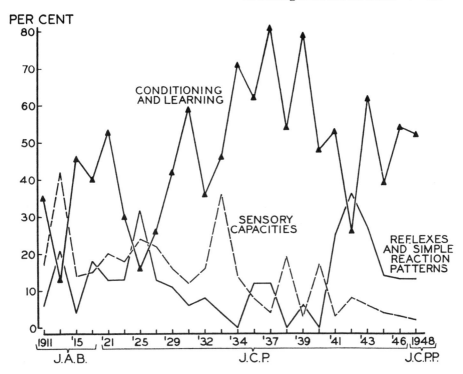

Figure 3. Beach's graph of the percent of all articles in various journals concerned with various psychological functions (from Beach, 1950, 119).

and noted that "the contents of the *JCPP* have changed not a bit in over 20 years."

Lown (1975, 858) marked the twenty-fifth anniversary of Beach's paper by noting "a resurgent interest in comparative psychology." His analysis included data from 1949 through 1973, and he was forced to admit that "over the past 25 years, the characteristics found by Beach do not seem to have changed a great deal" (Lown, 1975, 859). My modest contribution was an analysis of the first volume of *JCPP* under the editorship of Garth Thomas with Gilbert Gottlieb and William Wilson (Dewsbury, 1978*b*). I found 50 percent of the papers to deal exclusively with laboratory rats and noted that that "may be the lowest in this journal in my lifetime" (1978*b*, 108).

Now that thirty years have passed, three recent analyses have been published. Porter et al. (1981, 3) examined the even-numbered volumes from 1961 through 1976 and found that "the rat still dominates. . . ." Erwin (1982) examined four eras in comparative psychology and challenged the conclusion drawn by Porter et al. According to Erwin's analysis, the period of H. F. Harlow's editorship of *JCPP* showed a marked decrease in the domination of the journal by rat studies whereas rat research was more dominant under the editorships of Calvin P. Stone (1949-1950 sample) and William K. Estes and Elliot Stellar (1961-1975 sample). It should be noted, however, that, even under Harlow, the Norway rat accounted for 48 percent of the papers in *JCPP*. The anniversary analysis by Snowden (1982) will not be discussed here because it included no data from the *JCPP*.

The various follow-up analyses have revealed some minor perturbations in the content of *JCPP* since the period covered by Schneirla and Beach. However, there appears to have been no sustained reversal of the state that existed when their papers were written.

Importance.   One can never be certain of which factors enter into the shaping of the image of a discipline. However, it is clear that comparative psychology is widely perceived as the study of rat learning. Further, it is generally believed that this domination began since the 1920s. Thus, for example, Verplanck (1958, 101) noted the need for comparative psychology to return to biological emphases "familiar in the United States during the first decades of this century (but gone with the *Journal of Animal Behavior*)." Klopfer and Hailman (1967, 70) note "the decline of truly comparative psychology since the first quarter of this century." Snowden (1982, 5) wrote of the "golden days of *JCP* in the 1920s." Others have expressed similar views. In my judgment, journal frequency tabulations such as those under discussion have played a major role in shaping this image. Therefore, they are more than a trivial exercise; they have been vital to the image of comparative psychology as a science that has strayed from the "paths to truth."

Hidden Assumptions.   There are several hidden assumptions in the interpretation of data from journal frequency counts. The first is that absolute numbers are the critical factor (Dewsbury, 1973*b*). I have argued and shall argue that comparative psychology has always been a small part of the total psychological endeavor. Its success should be measured in terms of the quality of its research and its impact—not via frequency counts.

Gottlieb (1976) noted that *JCPP* includes many studies of physiological psychology. Physiological psychologists rely heavily on laboratory rats as experimental animals. To include such data in a journal frequency analysis generalized to comparative psychology is to seriously bias the data in the direction of rat research. Second, Gottlieb noted that "rat studies can be comparative" (1976, 295). He cited the work of Barnett, Boice, and Bolles as exemplars. His point was that studies of rats can relate to naturally occurring behavior and questions of broad biological significance.

Perhaps the major hidden assumption in these analyses is that comparative psychologists publish their comparative research in the *JCPP* (Dewsbury, 1973; Gottlieb, 1976). During many parts of the period prior to 1975, comparative research was less welcome in *JCPP* than more recently. Further, the readership of alternative journals has often been more responsive to comparative work than has that of *JCPP*.

Several researchers have assessed the contents of other journals in psychology and animal behavior, using the methods already discussed with respect to *JCPP*. Yeager (1973) analyzed *Behaviour;* Lown (1975) analyzed *Animal Behaviour;* Scott (1973) analyzed both *Behaviour* and *Animal Behaviour;* Millard (1976) analyzed the contents of the *Journal of the Experimental Analysis of Behavior;* Porter et al. (1981) analyzed seven additional psychological journals; Snowden (1982) analyzed *Developmental Psychobiology* and *Animal Behaviour;* and, not to be forgotten, Beach (1950) considered the *Journal of Experimental Psychology.* There are some differences in the results of these analyses. The general conclusion, however, is that the psychological journals tend to be as rat-dominated as *JCPP*, or more so, and the animal-behavior journals outside psychology are less dominated by rat research. This difference between *JCPP* and both *Behaviour* and *Animal Behaviour* is especially clear in the graphs presented by Scott (1973). Snowden (1982) concluded that snarks are boojums in "establishment circles." Many important comparative psychologists are simply publishing their comparative research elsewhere.

It is clear that content analyses of *JCPP* provide a serious underestimate of the extent and impact of research in comparative psychology.

A Second Look at Data from 1911-1923. The previous section dealt with matters relating to assessment of the current status of comparative psychology. There still remains the belief that the data of Beach and Schneirla indicate a substantial change from the period of 1911 through about 1923 to the present. What do the early data really tell us?

Beach (1950) plotted data from both *JAB* and *JCP*, using unbroken lines on a single set of axes. Examination of the results reveals that the differences between *JAB* and *JCP* are, in some respects, the biggest differences in the graph. For example, throughout the life of *JAB* about 35 percent of the studies were conducted on invertebrates; there is a precipitous drop with the advent of *JCP*. By contrast, there is a sharp increase in research on "all mammals except the rat." The latter trend is reversed permanently by the end of the 1920s.

The most serious error in interpreting these results is the failure of most students to recognize what Schneirla had first written—that these data include the contributions of biologists as well as of psychologists. *JAB* was truly an interdisciplinary journal with such biologists as

Samuel J. Holmes, H. S. Jennings, and William Morton Wheeler serving on the editorial board. Comparative psychologists published many excellent comparative studies in *JAB*. However, so did biologists. A count that fails to distinguish the contributions of biologists and psychologists presents a very misleading picture of *comparative psychology* in the era of this journal. Consider Volume 7, for example. It includes studies of crimson-spotted newts (A. M. Reese); fruit flies (W. H. Cole); and flatworms (J. M. D. Olmstead); *Pieris* butterfiles (P. Rau); earthworms (F. M. Baldwin); birds (T. C. Stephens; R. F. Hussey); amoeba (A. A. Schaeffer); Hessian fly larvae (McColloch and Yuasa); an infusorian (E. Shadall); and limpets (M. M. Wells). As best as I can determine, not one of these workers was a psychologist. The same volume includes papers by Walter Hunter, Karl Lashley, Harvey Carr, N. Utsurikawa, C. D. Reeves, and B. D. Pearce. All were psychologists, and all studies were with Norway rats. Robert Yerkes contributed a methodological paper. The most "comparative" papers by psychologists in the volume are by J. V. Yarbrough on delayed reaction in cats; on handedness in rhesus monkeys by Lashley, and on similarities in behavior between cows and humans by C. S. Yoakum. Earlier volumes of *JAB* contained more comparative papers by psychologists.

Clearly, an overall frequency count of papers in the 1917 *Journal of Animal Behavior* provides a very distorted view of the status of comparative psychology.

A Second Look at the *Journal of Comparative Psychology* in the 1920s. We turn next to the first three volumes of the *Journal of Comparative Psychology*. Beach's curves for the *JCP* of the 1920s show remarkable suppression of research on Norway rats compared to what came later and even to what came before. By contrast, there was much research on other mammalian species. What were these other mammalian species that dominated the journal and created the appearance of less emphasis on rats?

In examining Volume 1 (1921), I found only two papers dealing with invertebrates—one by G. C. Wheeler on land snails and one by W. F. Hamilton on starfish; neither author appears to have been a psychologist. There was a paper on the lateral line organs of the mudpuppy by W. J. P. Dye, a zoologist. I found only two papers by psychologists that dealt with neither rats nor humans; both deal with dogs. Stone studied light discrimination in dogs, and Elisabeth Gilman (1921) published a curious piece entitled "A Dog's Diary." Gilman summarized attempts to teach a dog to associate words with objects and wrote the paper in the first person from the standpoint of the dog. The paper begins, "I am a black-and-white cocker spaniel . . . ." (Gilman, 1921, 309)

Volume 2 of *JCP* includes two additional papers on starfish by W. F. Hamilton, one on mudminnows by F. Westerfield, one on guinea pigs by E. E. Nicholls, and a paper on loggerhead turtles by G. H. Parker. Apparently, not one of these authors was a psychologist. The contents of Volume 3 are similar to those of the second volume. Truly "comparative" papers by psychologists appear limited to one on delayed-response learning in cats by an E. A. Cowan and one on hearing in reptiles by the Japanese comparative psychologist Ryo Kuroda.

The most popular mammalian species beside rats in these three volumes appears to be none other than *Homo sapiens*. Throughout the 1920s *JCP* published a variety of papers on human behavior. Volume 2, for example, included a paper by Hunter and Sommermier on "The Relation of Degree of Indian Blood to Score on the Otis Intelligence Test." Three papers in Volume 2 were concerned with the effects of cigar and cigarette smoking on behavior. In his paper on the effects of smoking on dart throwing, Bates (1922) was careful to include a full-page, actual-size sketch of the dart! The page showing a diagram of the target showed it only to one-twelfth scale. It is papers on humans that inflate the number of non-rat papers and create the apparent decrease in rat research. Such is the "golden era" of *JCP* in the 1920s.

In my judgment, there were three important papers in the first three volumes of *JCP*. Biologist Holmes (1922) published a tentative classification of the forms of animal behavior, and Stone (1922, 1923) published two classic papers on the development of sexual behavior—both done with laboratory rats.

Conclusion. Frequency analyses of journal contents have played an important role in shaping the perceptions of both comparative psychologists and others about the nature of this field. However, because of hidden assumptions inherent in the method, it can produce results that are seriously misleading. Contemporary comparative psychologists have published research in a wide variety of journals and have impact well beyond that which can be measured in *JCPP*. By failing to separate the contributions of psychologists from those of other workers, authors have mistakenly created the impression that comparative psychologists from 1911 through the 1920s did far more comparative research than they actually did. The failure to note that many studies on "all mammals except the rat" were done on humans provided an illusion of comparative strength in the 1920s. I will argue that comparative psychologists always were a small part of the overall psychological picture. Nevertheless, their achievements have been noteworthy.

Beach's analysis (1950) served an important function in its time and certainly played a role in keeping comparative psychology as vibrant as I believe it to be. However, the time has come to recognize the limitations of such analyses. It matters not what percentage of research in comparative psychology was conducted using rats. What matters is what comparative psychologists did and found, and whether or not it is important. I will attempt to show that it was.

TEN MYTHS ABOUT COMPARATIVE PSYCHOLOGY

As a result of problems of definition, criticism regarding comparative psychology's image, misperceptions of the history of comparative psychology, and journal content analyses, various false impressions of the field have arisen. Thus far I have presented these somewhat unsystematically. I will try to make these more explicit so that they might ultimately by more effectively combatted. What follows are ten myths that I believe are held by enough people inside and outside comparative psychology so as to merit concern. Again, I will document these myths with direct quotations in order to make it clear that I am trying not to create a straw man.

Myth 1. The Rationale for Comparative Psychology Stems Directly from a Human Orientation.

Various authors have written that comparative psychology, unlike ethology, derives its research problems directly from matters relating to human behavior and that results are evaluated as they relate to human-related issues. A few representative quotations follow.

> The psychologists had looked for behavior, in animals, that conformed to the categories of learning patterns that had been worked out for humans, and had found little else . . . . (Beer, 1963, 170)

> They have always tended to look at man as the paradigm and to compare the performance and abilities of animals with his. (Thorpe, 1979, viii)

> Animals have traditionally been studied not for their own sakes, but, . . . as human stand-ins. . . . (Gould, 1982, 6)

> Usually investigated with the animal as a model of human behavior. (Immelmann, 1980, 2)

Similar passages could be quoted from such authors as Beach (1960); Beer (1980); Burghardt (1973); Lehrman (1962); Mason (1968); Schneirla (1946); and Thorpe (1961).

Myth 2. Psychologists Lack the Aesthetic Sense and Love for Animals that Characterize Ethology.

This characteristic is cited most clearly in the writings of Colin Beer. It is difficult to extract a simple quotation, as Beer generally describes ethology with an implicit contrast with comparative psychology. He noted that "aesthetic considerations and sheer curiosity also influenced the pursuit of natural history" by ethologists (Beer, 1980, 52). In a paper entitled "Was Professor Lehrman an Ethologist?," Beer concluded that indeed he was. A major reason for this conclusion was Lehrman's love of animals (Beer, 1975).

Schneirla (1946, 312) made a similar point about comparative psychology when he wrote that "American psychologists have become so preoccupied with their own functions in the experimental situation that the psychological distance between experimenter and animal subject has become alarmingly great."

Myth 3. Comparative Psychologists Are Not Concerned with the Study of Evolution.

It is frequently alleged that the study of evolution is a major interest in ethology but has not been prominent in comparative psychology.

> I believe that psychology neglects two other problems, . . . the problem of survival value, and that of evolution. (Tinbergen, 1955, 78)

> Comparative psychologists pay little attention to the relations between their data and evolutionary theory. (Deese and Morgan, 1951, 193)

> Evolutionary theory has played an increasingly minor role in psychological theory. . . . (Eaton, 1970, 176)

> Psychologists rarely make use of rigorous argument based upon the theory of natural selection. (McFarland, 1981, 153)

Similar passages can be found in the writings of Chiszar and Carpen (1980), Ewer (1971—see p. 805), Lockard (1971, point 6), and Verplanck (1955, 1958).

Myth 4. Comparative Psychologists Confine Themselves to Artificial Laboratory Situations Rather Than the Field.

It is generally acknowledged that comparative psychologists have made few contributions to understanding the natural lives of animals as they exist in nature. Rather, psychologists have confined themselves to the study of behavior under the artificially controlled conditions of the laboratory.

> The psychologist . . . has devoted but little attention . . . to the significance of his findings for behavior in its natural setting. (Thorpe and Zangwill, 1973, x)

> Comparative psychologists usually carry out their work in the laboratory. . . .(Wallace, 1973, 2)

> The obsession of behaviorism with controlling . . . the animal's physical environment . . . forced researchers to work in the laboratory rather than in what must have seemed the uncontrollable chaos of nature. (Gould, 1982, 7)

> Comparative psychology . . . never achieved an appreciation of the importance of naturalistic observation. (Crook and Goss-Custard, 1972, 279)

Similar statements have been made by Burghardt (1973), Lester (1973), Manning (1979), Lockard (1971, point 9), and Mason (1968).

Myth 5. Comparative Psychologists Study a Limited Range of Species.

It has frequently been asserted that comparative psychologists study a limited range of species—especially laboratory rats. Indeed, Thorpe (1956) estimated that 99 percent of the work of comparative psychology was based on laboratory rats. The basis for this calculation was not provided.

> Most psychologists have concentrated on . . . [a] surprisingly limited number of organisms . . . . (Burghardt, 1973, 336)

> "Comparative psychology" which became . . . less and less comparative until the casual reader, coming fresh to the subject, might have been led to conclude that the only animals in existence were the white rat and the cat! (Thorpe, 1979, 95)

Similar statements were made by Barash (1977*a*); Schneirla (1946); Thorpe and Zangwill (1963); and Verplanck (1955).

Myth 6. Comparative Psychologists Study Only Domesticated Species.

Related to the points made with respect to the preceding myth, it is asserted that comparative psychologists not only study a limited range of species but those they do study are highly domesticated.

> Comparative psychologists have primarily studied laboratory animals, species bred specifically for traits that would be useful in laboratory work and for genetic homogeneity. (Lester, 1973, 156)

> While nature often goes to great lengths to prevent creatures from mating with their immediate relatives, experimental animals have been domesticated and inbred for dozens of generations. (Gould, 1982, 7-8)

Similar points were made by Burghardt (1973); Thorpe (1979); and Whitman (1898-1899).

Myth 7. Comparative Psychologists Fail to Compare Closely Related Species.

It is asserted that comparative psychologists make only broad "phyletic-" level comparisons (see King, 1963) rather than the more "meaningful" comparisons of closely related species that typify ethological work. Among the characteristics cited by Burghardt (1973, 336) as characterizing the "ethological attitude" but relatively free of criticism by psychologists was the process of "comparing similar behaviors in closely related species."

Myth 8. Comparative Psychologists Are Preoccupied with Instrumentation.

It is often believed that comparative psychologists have become overly dependent on instrumentation and therefore have lost close touch with their animals. Schneirla (1946, 312) was concerned with this issue and noted that "Köhler has cautioned more than once against studying apparatus rather than the animal . . . ." Barash (1977a,5) wrote of the "wealth of sophisticated gadgetry, [and] elaborate data-gathering devices . . ." of comparative psychologists. Noting the range of psychologists' testing devices, many of which are named after their designers, Menzel wrote humorously:

Some day, if I can, I'm going to join the illustrious by patenting the tree as the Menzel Jumping Stand, the river as Menzel's Obstruction Apparatus, and the jungle as the Delta Primate Center General Test Apparatus. (1967, 171)

Myth 9. Psychologists Rarely Begin Their Studies with Description.

It is asserted that rather than beginning a research program by collecting systematic observational-descriptive data, psychologists typically rush in to ask complex questions without adequate background material. Thus, Burghardt (1973, 336) lists "beginning an analysis with descriptive studies" as one component of the ethological attitude not criticized by psychologists.

Myth 10. Psychologists Confine Their Studies to Learning Rather Than to a Wide Range of Ecologically Relevant Behavior.

It has often been asserted that comparative psychology has become the study of learning and that other problems have come to be ignored.

> In general, psychologists have concentrated on learned behavior, ethologists primarily with innate components of behavior. (Eaton, 1970, 182)

> In fact, comparative psychology has become the study of maze running and bar pressing by white rats. (Tinbergen, 1955, 86)

> The naive animal treated experimentally as a *tabula rasa* on which learned responses can be inscribed confident that no previous behavioral tendencies exist which may influence or render nugatory their results. (Thorpe, 1979, x)

Lorenz (1981) and Manning (1979) make similar statements.

CONCLUSION

In this chapter I have tried first to provide an understanding of the definition of comparative psychology in particular and of psychologists in general. I take a broad view that comparative psychologists study animals in order to ascertain principles of generality with respect to the evolution, control, adaptive significance, and development of behavior. Investigations in comparative psychology may or may not include explicit, cross-species comparisons.

The remainder of the chapter was devoted to a process of documenting what I believe to be both a poor contemporary image of comparative psychology and a general belief that the history of comparative psychology is not one of which we should be proud. I did this by quoting psychologists, ethologists, and sociobiologists and by analyzing the role of journal frequency counts in affecting our understanding of the history of comparative psychology. Finally, I proposed that the criticisms of comparative psychology can be summarized as ten myths about the field. The number is somewhat arbitrary and might well have been eight, or nine, or twelve.

Those outside comparative psychology may not appreciate the depth of criticism that has been made. Comparative psychologists are as much to blame for this as are those on the outside—probably more so. Lehrman (1970) noted that scientists have feelings and are troubled by misunderstandings that they take personally. Boice noted that "zoologists tend to be as accepting of us as we are of people with degrees in education" (1971, 859). As far back as 1904, Yerkes noted, "There is a tendency among physiologists—among natural scientists generally—to look upon psychology with distrust, if not with indifference or scorn . . . general distrust and ridicule of psychology. . . ." (1904*a*, 513) Comparative psychologists have made many errors. Nevertheless, the field has a history of excellence, a fact that I shall attempt to document in the remainder of this book.

Chapter 2

Chronological History of Comparative Psychology Through 1919

There are many ways to portray history. The most straightforward is to begin at the beginning and permit history to unfold chronologically. As an alternative approach, one can separate the total story into smaller pieces and discuss the history of each piece over time. Finally, history can be told through the stories of the people who made the history. Each approach has its strengths and weaknesses, and with each a slightly different picture emerges from the same set of events. The most comprehensive understanding should result when each of the perspectives can be used. I will first discuss the history of comparative psychology chronologically. This will be followed by three chapters in which I examine various aspects of comparative psychology as they have changed over time. Finally, I will present sketches of some of those who made the history of comparative psychology. The hope is that with such a three-pronged approach, the advantages of each of the three perspectives can be brought to bear on the problem of history.

My topic is "comparative psychology in the twentieth century." In the interest of continuity, however, I shall exercise poetic license and begin the twentieth century in 1894. The stage of 1894 will be set with a brief discussion of events occurring prior to that year as distilled from the sources cited. I shall then proceed to the main story—that of comparative psychology in the twentieth century.

ANIMAL-BEHAVIOR STUDY BEFORE 1894

Prehistory

We will begin the history with prehistory. This part of the story is best discussed by Warden (1927a, 1927b) and Singer (1981). Knowledge of this period comes largely from cave paintings. Nomadic hunters of the Upper Paleolithic period, roughly 34,000 to 10,500 years before the present, appear to have hunted in a land of plenty. Success in hunting required intimate knowledge of the prey. All indications are that early humans possessed such knowledge. The walls of cave dwellings and stone implements often were decorated with images of animals. The most common species portrayed in cave paintings were horses, bison, and oxen; these account for some 60 percent of the animals represented (Singer, 1981).

Domestication of animals and plants appears to have begun about 11,500 years ago in the Middle East and southwestern Asia (Singer, 1981). Although there has been much speculation about how domestication of common species occurred, there are few solid data. The extent of behavioral change occurring with domestication is controversial (see Boice and Ratner, 1975; Hale, 1969).

Early Civilizations

People of early civilizations lived in close contact with animals of many species. Ancient Egyptians, for example, practiced incubation of eggs. Animals are prominently depicted in Mesopotamian sculpture and in ancient Indian art. In the system of "levels" in ancient India, cows were ranked at the top, with horses and elephants close by. Some one hundred and twenty species of mammals, birds, and reptiles are referred to in the Christian Bible (Singer 1981). Animals were also prominent in a number of ancient animal cults that arose in various early civilizations (Warden, 1927a, 1927b).

Greek and Roman Civilizations

Animals were well known and much studied in Greek and Roman civilizations. Many species, both common and exotic, were maintained in aviaries and vivaries (Mountjoy, 1980; Singer, 1981).

Much philosophical reflection was directed at the problem of the relationships between human and non-human animals. Thus Alcmaeon (c. 520 B.C.) proposed that the powers of comprehension were greater in humans than in animals. Anaxagoras (500 B.C.) granted that animals possessed intelligence but proposed a superiority of human intelligence. The Cynics believed animals superior to humans because of their simplicity and lack of possessions. Although the Stoic philosopher Chrysippus believed that animals were able to reason, Seneca objected to such attribution (Singer, 1981). Similar debates occurred around the turn of the twentieth century. Beach (1955) dated the origin of a dichotomy between men and gods on the one hand and animals on the other with Heraclitus in the fourth century B.C. Only men and gods were the products of rational creation and possessed souls. Later Stoic philosophers such as Seneca maintained the man/god versus animal dichotomy and noted that animals lack the capacity to reason and to act from a moral sense (Warden, 1927a, 1927b; Singer, 1981).

The contributions of Aristotle (384-322 B.C.) far outshine any other Greek and Roman philosopher-naturalist. Warden (1927a, 1927b) proposed that Aristotle deserves to be known as "the founder of comparative psychology" (1927a, 68). The contributions of Aristotle are many and diverse. He wrote on the systematic classification of species, embryology, physiology, systematics, and, above all, behavior. He proposed a doctrine of five senses. Aristotle was a keen observer of behavior. For example, he is purported to have provided descriptions of copulatory behavior in more than thirty-six genera, including such species as lions, lynx, bears, hedgehogs, elephants, camels, eels, sharks, squid, lobsters, and ants (Coonen, 1977). He was also a vitalist and teleologist, believing in a life force, or soul, that guides the animal.

Among the most influential of Aristotle's proposals for comparative psychology was the notion of a great "chain of being," "ladder of life," or *Scala Naturae*. According to this notion, each species has a fixed place in the ladder of life, with humans at the top and various animals that are today classified as mammals, reptiles, crustaceans, arthropods, sponges, and other forms lying along a unidimensional continuum. These notions of man's place in the universe and of a unidimensional scale have been important in much writing on the relationships among humans, nonhumans, and the rest of the universe. A graphic *Scala Naturae*, based on Aristotle's descriptions, is portrayed by Singer (1981).

The Roman physiologist-physician Galen (c. A.D. 130-200) is credited with a conception of instinct similar to that of later eras. He observed the behavioral patterns of a young goat kid delivered by Caesarian section. The kid walked, scratched, and lapped up milk in the absence of any tutoring. It was concluded that the behavior of animals was present by design, not through tutoring (Holmes, 1916; Singer, 1981; Warden, 1927a, 1927b).

Pre-Nineteenth-Century Study

In many respects the long period between the classical Greek and Roman civilizations and the nineteenth century is less interesting for the student of comparative psychology than is what came before and after. There are three overlapping traditions of interest during this long period—natural history, applied animal behavior, and philosophy-theology.

The contributions of the early natural historians have been reviewed by Gray (1968-1969); Thorpe (1979); and Warden (1927a, 1927b). Among the leading natural historians of the sixteenth through the eighteenth century were the Swiss naturalist N. A. Gessner, together with John Ray, Gibert White (1720-1793); Francis Willughby (1635-1672); and Ferdinand Pernauer (1660-1731). Willughby, for example, is credited with discovering animal territoriality and with the belief that birds count clutch size. The point emphasized by Gray (1968-1969) is that these natural historians were amateurs, not professional zoologists. After reviewing the contributions of these and other amateur natural historians, Gray concluded "that zoologists pioneered the observational study of animal behavior while psychologists developed the laboratory approach is a generally held assumption which I have found impossible to verify" (1968-1969, 372).

This history of comparative psychology as affected by and affecting human utilization of nonhuman animals in portrayed beautifully by Mountjoy (1980). Throughout history humans have learned more and more about animals and have utilized this information in such activities as domestication and hunting. Mountjoy described horse-training manuals of the fourteenth century B.C., zoo management in the time of the Greeks, stud farms in Rome, the art of hunting with birds over the last 4,000 years, animal training in the time of Shakespeare, a duck decoy in which human and dog cooperated, the technology of bee-keeping, and the prevention of masturbation in horses. Among the conclusions that Mountjoy drew is that "there is a historical continuum of scientific work in comparative psychology from the earliest known documents up to the present" (1980, 151). The training of falcons provided an exercise in applied comparative psychology (Mountjoy et al., 1969).

The third major tradition during this period is the philosophical-theological. The history of this tradition is portrayed by such writers as Beach (1955), Gray (1968-1969), Holmes (1916), Singer (1981), and Warden (1927a, 1927b). Christian theology was dominated by the view that humans and nonhumans were sharply different. For example, the Christian natural historian Albertus Magnus (1206-1280) held that only humans possess the gift of reason and an immortal soul. Nonhumans exercise practical judgment at best. They cannot act freely as they are directed by their natural instincts. Thomas Aquinas extended this view, making a sharp distinction between the sensitive soul, possessed by "brutes" and the intellectual soul, possessed only by humans. "Animal and man are therefore separated by a broad and impassable barrier" (Holmes, 1916, 14). Although animals were presented as having sensations and sensory memories, they were thought to lack reason, freedom, and responsibility.

Philosopher René Descartes (1596-1650) interpreted animal behavior in terms of the action of the nervous system and studied nerve physiology. His view of animals was that they were virtual automata whose activities were driven solely by the actions of their bodily organization. Descartes maintained a "Cartesian" dualism and held that animals lacked the souls that humans possessed. Beach (1955, 402) quoted Descartes as writing, "After the error of atheism, there is nothing that leads weak minds further astray from the paths of virtue than the idea that the minds of other animals resemble our own."

The Cartesian separation of human and nonhuman was countered by such writers as Hermann S. Reimarus (1694-1768), David Hume (1711-1776), Julien de la Mettrie (1709-1751), and Georges Leroy (1723-1789). Gray placed particular emphasis on the contributions of Hume and Le Mettrie: "I believe that the cornerstone for a comparative science of behavior was laid by two contemporary realists who argued vividly that animals and men are not basically different" (1968-1969, 376).

The Cuvier Versus Geoffroy-Saint-Hilaire Debate

In the period around 1830, Baron Cuvier, the established apostle of the immutability of species, engaged in a series of debates with the younger and less influential Etienne Geoffroy-Saint-Hilaire. Jaynes (1969) portrayed Cuvier as the champion of "corpses reeking with formaldehyde" and Geoffroy-Saint-Hilaire as the champion of naturalistic observations of animals in the field. According to Jaynes, the seeds of the differentiation of comparative psychology as a laboratory science and ethology as a science of animals under natural conditions can be seen when one recognizes their derivation from Cuvier and Geoffroy-Saint-Hillaire, respectively.

A different view of these debates was presented by Chiszar and Carpen (1980). They pointed out that Geoffroy-Saint-Hilaire was also a defender of the view that all animals are built on a single structural plan and of the belief that ontogeny recapitulates phylogeny. Cuvier, on the other hand, was a believer in the view that organisms should be studied with a view toward their functioning, as designed for performance. The debate, according to Chiszar and Carpen, was less concerned with laboratory versus field approaches than with fundamental assumptions regarding ontogeny and structure. Both comparative psychology and ethology found origins in both sides of the debate. Chiszar and Carpen (1980, 959) concluded, "It will take a patient work of historical scholarship to untangle all of the threads that came together in the genesis of these two disciplines."

Darwin

Charles Darwin was certainly a pivotal individual in the development of the approach that led to comparative psychology. As noted by Howard (1927, 305), "We ought to speak of psychology as pre-Darwinian and post-Darwinian, since all that is in any essential degree new in the modern viewpoint is the result, directly or indirectly, of Darwinian influences." Far from being uninfluenced by Darwinian evolution, psychology was profoundly affected. James Rowland Angell (1909, 152) wrote about how "Darwin's radical theories succeeded in gaining such easy access to the psychological sanctuary." In reply to the question posed by Hodos and Campbell (1969) as to why there is no theory in comparative psychology, Warren (n.d.) noted that comparative psychology has a theory—the same synthetic theory of evolution that unifies all other biological sciences.

Darwin is best known for two books, *On the Origin of Species by Means of Natural Selection or the Preservation of Favoured Races in the Struggle for Life* (1859) and *The Descent of Man and Selection in Relation to Sex* (1871). Equally important in the development of the study of animal behavior, however, was *The Expression of the Emotions in Man and Animals* (1872). It was in the last-named work that Darwin reported many behavioral observations of direct influence on comparative psychology, especially the study of communication.

Angell (1909) listed three primary contributions of Darwin to psychology: his doctrine of instinct, the notion of continuity among the minds of animals, and the study of the expression of emotions. Darwin strove to overthrow the teleological notion of instinct and to show that instincts could evolve through natural selection (Angell, 1909; Ghiselin, 1973). With the notion that the minds (and behavior) of various species stem from common descent, the grounds for a comparative psychology became greatly solidified. Darwin noted, "There is no fundamental difference between man and the higher mammals in their mental faculties" (1871, 446). In *Expressions*, Darwin showed, as he had in other works, how careful, comparative observations of behavior could shed light on important principles of behavioral evolution. The evolution of behavioral patterns could be studied just as could the evolution of structure.

Darwin was well aware of the implications for psychology. He wrote, "Psychology will be securely based on the foundation . . . of the necessary acquirement of each mental power and capacity by gradation. Much light will be thrown on the origin of man and his history" (1859, 373).

For further discussion of Darwin's influence, see Angell (1909), Burghardt (1973), Baldwin (1909), Carter (1898), Ghiselin (1973), and Howard (1927*a*).

The Post-Darwin Era

Jaynes (1969) described the extent to which comparative psychology came into vogue, especially in Europe, just after the appearance of Darwin's works. Jaynes credited a book by Flourens in 1864 as having "founded comparative psychology in name" (Jaynes, 1969, 602). In the 1870s there were no fewer than five textbooks called "Comparative Psychology." The term was used by John Lubbock, G. J. Romanes, Herbert Spencer, Douglas Spalding, and others.

Perhaps the most profound implication of Darwin's views was the conclusion that the higher mental, moral, and spiritual faculties of humans could be accounted for with evolutionary principles. Attacks on this view led to vehement defenses on the part of those in the "anecdotal movement" (Warden, 1928; Warden et al. 1935). The anecdotalists set out to prove that animals possessed a rudimentary human mind and collected three kinds of evidence in support of the proposition: (1) Animals can reason; (2) animals show complex social behavior; and (3) animals display human emotions (Warden, 1928). Among the leading anecdotalists, Warden lists Buchner, Lindsay, and Perty.

Foremost in this connection was George John Romanes (1848-1894). Romanes's *Animal Intelligence* (1882) is a classic of the genre. Like Darwin and others of his time, Romanes was forced to rely heavily on anecdotes as the empirical basis for his writings on animal behavior. Romanes was not unaware of the risks inherent in relying on anecdotal evidence. In his preface, he wrote, "I have fished the seas of popular literature as well as the rivers of scientific writing" and encountered an "endless multitude of alleged facts" (Romanes, 1882, vii). Romanes laid down three principles to guide his selection: alleged facts should be (1) from some authority; (2) observable unmistakably; or (3) corroborated by similar observations. The book is organized by taxa and contains a wealth of such anecdotes. Regrettably, Romanes's application of his three principles was insufficient, and he is generally written of unfavorably because of his reliance on the anecdotal method. That Romanes was well aware of the principles of the scientific method, however, is demonstrated in his *Jelly-fish, Starfish, and Sea-urchins* (1885). Such methods were not generally useful in the study of mental continuity in 1882, however.

Two other noteworthy books by Romanes were *Mental Evolution in Animals* (1883) and *Mental Evolution in Man* (1888). In these works Romanes developed his own doctrine of "levels," somewhat reminiscent of Aristotle. Echinodermata were at level 17; birds at level 25, and

George John Romanes, 1848–1894.
Photograph courtesy of the Archives of the History of American Psychology.

anthropoid apes and dogs at level 28. Whereas the emotional development at level 18 is characterized by surprise and fear, that at level 28 includes shame, remorse, and deceitfulness. The developing human is born at level 16, reaches the level of insects and spiders at ten weeks, and is ranked with anthropoid apes and dogs at fifteen months. Carter (1899) notes that Romanes was a mental monist throughout.

In the 1880s Romanes and Morgan engaged in a controversy concerning the possibility of a comparative science of psychology, the definition of instinct, and the automatism doctrine of consciousness (see Gray, 1963*b*). The former two topics have been with us ever since.

Forerunners of Ethology and Comparative Psychology

In the late nineteenth and early twentieth centuries, there existed a group of animal behaviorists whose work had important influences on the development of both ethology and comparative psychology. Although not psychologists, their work must be mentioned at least in passing.

Douglas Alexander Spalding (c. 1840-1877) has been called the "first experimental behaviorist" (Gray, 1962, 299). He is most remembered for his work on the ontogeny of instinctive behavior as exemplified in his papers of 1873 and 1875. Spalding wrote on visual and auditory development, the release of instinctive reactions, the embryology of behavior, the maturation of behavioral function, and imprinting (see Gray, 1967a). Although working primarily with young chicks, Spalding also worked with other species of birds and observed mammalian behavior as well. He wrote, "Many of the very greatest authorities in science refused to believe in those instructive performances of young animals about which the less learned multitude have never had any doubt" (1875, 507). Various aspects of Spalding's career have been summarized by Gray (1962, 1967a, 1967b) and Robinson (1977).

Beginning in 1888 Jacques Loeb published a series of papers in which he proclaimed the importance of the objective study of behavior. Loeb is best known for developing his theory of tropisms, according to which behavior can be explained as forced movements resulting from physico-chemical reactions occurring in animals as they occur in plants. The behavior of "lower" organisms was to be understood as controlled in a deterministic manner by such reactions. The view drew strong criticism as from Jennings and von Buddenbrock (1916). Hirsch (1973) credits Loeb with first proclaiming the importance of the objective study of behavior and decrying the futility of subjectivism and anthropomorphism. Loeb wrote extensively, as in his *Comparative Physiology of the Brain and Comparative Psychology* (1900); *The Mechanistic Conception of Life* (1912); and *Forced Movements, Tropisms, and Animal Conduct* (1918). Hirsch (1973) has discussed various aspects of Loeb's career.

Sir John Lubbock was an early student of learning as well as other behavior and natural history in insects. His *Ants, Bees, and Wasps* (1882) brought together the results of his various studies. Warden (1928, 490) called Lubbock "the founder of the modern laboratory method of approach." He is credited with originating the use of mazes in the study of learning, with first using puzzle devices and the problem method under laboratory conditions, and with inventing a glass-covered ant nest that permitted long-term observation. Lubbock also used a "preference method," later criticized by Loeb, in studying the sensory capacities of insects. Lubbock (1882, 247) wrote, "In order to test their intelligence, it has always seemed to me that there was no better way than to ascertain some object which they would clearly desire, and then to interpose some obstacle which a little ingenuity would enable them to overcome." Such has been the rationale for an enormous number of studies in the last hundred years.

According to Gray (1968-1969, 381), Lewis Henry Morgan (1818-1881) was the "first ethologist in the sense in which we presently use the word." Morgan was an American lawyer and naturalist who is best known for his *The American Beaver and His Works* (1868). Gray quoted Morgan's report of an anecdote that appears to represent an early case of Pavlovian conditioning. Morgan called for a series of monographs on the habits, modes of life, and mutual relations among the major animal species — an early-day ethogram. Darwin (1871, 447) praised Morgan's as "excellent work."

There are many others whose contributions to the study of animal behavior merit at least some mention. For example, J. Henri Fabre, August Forel, Albrecht Bethe, G. Peckham, and E. Peckham were early students of insect behavior. Max Verworn advocated an objective approach in the study of invertebrate behavior (Carmichael, 1969). Karl Groos's studies of the significance of play were influential. However, a complete treatment of this era is outside the range of this work.

Beginnings of American Psychology

This same period saw the development of psychology as an experimental science and the establishment of a firm base for psychology in North America. Credit for opening the first psychology laboratory is given to Wilhelm Wundt at Leipzig in 1879. In that same year Wundt's first American student, G. Stanley Hall arrived in Leipzig. Wundt was to have great influence on the development of American comparative psychology through such students as Hall, Hugo Münsterburg, James McKeen Cattell, E. B. Titchener, and others.

In 1885 T. Wesley Mills, trained as a physiologist and teaching in the Veterinary College of McGill University in Montreal, founded the Association for the Study of Comparative Psychology. Although membership was open to everyone, the society was composed mainly of students and teachers in McGill's School of Comparative Medicine. In his presidential address of 1887, Mills noted "The term comparative psychology, in its modern sense, gives us the widest desirable scope as including all that pertains to the mind and soul of the animal kingdom" (1898, 17).

Harvard psychologist William James played an important role in the establishment of psychology in North America. His *Principles of Psychology* (1890) became the standard textbook in the field for many

T. Wesley Mills, 1847–1915.
*Photograph courtesy of Notman
Photographic Archives.*

years. Perhaps the most important section for comparative psychology was the entire chapter James devoted to instinct. James defined instinct as "the faculty of acting in such a way as to produce certain ends, without previous education in the performance" (1880, 383). He is quoted as having written to President Eliot of Harvard as early as 1875, "A real science of man is now being built out of the *theory of evolution* and the facts of archeology, the nervous system, and the senses" (Misiak and Sexton, 1966, 130, italics mine).

In 1887 Hall founded the first American psychological journal, the

American Journal of Psychology. This journal provided an outlet for some of the most important early papers in comparative psychology.

The American Psychological Association (APA) was founded in 1892. Among special scientific societies, only the American Chemical Society (1876) and societies formed by mathematicians and geologists in 1888 appear older. The initial meeting at which the APA was founded occurred on July 8, 1892, at Clark University. There were twenty-six charter members, including James, Hall, Cattell, and James Mark Baldwin. The group elected twenty-four additional members and decided to hold their first formal meeting on December 27 at the University of Pennsylvania. At the Philadelphia meeting, five additional members were elected, including Titchener, Münsterburg, and Mills. Accounts of these events are provided by Cattell (1917; 1943), Dennis and Boring (1952), and Fernberger 91943*a*).

1894–1899: THE BEGINNING OF AMERICAN COMPARATIVE PSYCHOLOGY

I have chosen to begin the story in 1894. The choice is somewhat arbitrary, but 1894 is as good a year as any and somewhat better than most. It was an interesting year (see Langfeld, 1944). In 1894 von Helmholtz and Romanes both died; Margaret Floy Washburn received her doctoral degree from Cornell University under Titchener. John Dewey went to the University of Chicago and Münsterburg was in the midst of a trial period at Harvard. Hall, a firm advocate of evolutionary psychology, was in his sixth year as president of Clark University; Baldwin was on the faculty at Princeton. Meanwhile William McDougall was finishing his fourth year of study at Cambridge; Edward Lee Thorndike was an undergraduate at Wesleyan; Robert Mearns Yerkes was an undergraduate at Ursinus; and the young John Broadus Watson was a freshman at home in Greenville, South Carolina, at Furman University.

In 1894 a considerable group of psychologists was distressed with the progress of the *American Journal of Psychology,* feeling that it had become too much a house organ for Hall and Clark University. Led by James McKeen Cattell and James Mark Baldwin, they proposed either buying the journal from Hall or at least securing the appointment of a broad-based board of editors; Hall refused. Cattell and Baldwin then founded the *Psychological Review,* a journal destined to publish many of the most important papers in the history of comparative psychology. Langfeld (1944) listed among the cooperating "psychologists" such individuals as Binet, Dewey, Donaldson, James, and Münsterburg.

The year 1894 saw the first publication in English of Wilhelm Wundt's *Lectures on Human and Animal Psychology.* The translation from German was by J. E. E. Creighton and E. B. Titchener. The book was important in establishing the legitimacy of animal psychology in "establishment" circles and in fostering the growing movement toward the objective analysis of behavior. Wundt noted that there are two perspectives from which we can approach the study of animal psychology. With the first,

> We may set out from the notion of a kind of comparative physiology of mind, a universal history of the development of mental life in the organic world. Then the observation of animals is the more important matter; man is only considered as one, though, of course, the highest, of the developmental stages to be examined. (1894, 340)

Wundt went on to present the alternative approach to animal psychology —that in which human psychology is the principal object of investigation. With that approach, the study of animals becomes of interest only as it relates to understanding the human mind. Wundt prefers this latter approach. However, Wundt's recognition and implicit acceptance of the former approach as a viable alternative was important in establishing the legitimacy for the study of animal psychology in and of itself without immediate concern for its relevance to humans. Thus, Warden (1928, 514) noted, "Even so conservative a writer as Wundt . . . recognized the right of comparative psychology to develop a content independent of human reference in the same sense as zoology is independent of human morphology and physiology."

In another section of the lectures, Wundt assailed the use of the anecdotal method, the "inclination of animal psychologists to see the intellectual achievements of animals in the most brilliant light" (Wundt, 342), and Romanes himself. Wundt considered the nature of instinct and the various definitions of instinct that had been proposed. He noted, "Still even today the *theories* of instinct form a regular museum of conflicting opinions" (Wundt, 389). Still even today indeed! Later Wundt discussed animal social behavior, touching on social instincts, temporary associations and friendships, and "animal marriage."

Boring (1957, 345) calculated that at the rate Wundt published, he wrote or revised at a rate of 2.2 pages per day or about one word every two minutes, day and night for sixty-eight years!

Of course, the most memorable event in the eventful year of 1894 was the publication in England of C. Lloyd Morgan's *An Introduction to Comparative Psychology.* I have reviewed that book previously (Dewsbury, 1979*b*; see also Adler, 1973). Among the highlights of

C. Lloyd Morgan, 1852–1936.
*Photograph courtesy of the Archives of the
History of American Psychology.*

Morgan's book are a description of trial-and-error learning, an early suggestion of "constraints" on learning, suggestion of an *Umwelt*-like view of perceptual works, and rejection of Lamarckian inheritance of acquired traits. Morgan defined instinct in terms of stereotypy, appearance in all appropriate individuals of a species, and the absence of a need for learning (Morgan, 1894, 207). Although individuals may have an innate capacity for motor responses, such responses may be perfected with practice. Adler (1973) finds in Morgan's work interests that presaged current research on migration, behavioral development, social distance, and surrogate mothers. Morgan would later address the problem of instinct repeatedly in his writings on animal behavior (Richards, 1977).

Morgan's *An Introduction to Comparative Psychology* is most frequently referred to in relation to his famous canon:

> In no case may we interpret an action as the outcome of the exercise of a higher psychical faculty, if it can be interpreted as the outcome of the exercise of one which stands lower in the psychological scale. (Morgan, 1894, 53)

I shall have more to say about the impact of the canon later. Earlier I suggested, "For those who would be ashamed of the heritage of comparative psychology, I would suggest an excursion with C. Lloyd Morgan" (Dewsbury, 1979, 679-680).

Comparative psychology has been a discipline with its controversies. One of them raged in the pages of *Science* in 1896. It was triggered by Wesley Mills. Mills noted a report in *Science* that Morgan had reported that young chicks peck at food instinctively but have to be taught to drink. Mills questioned the implication that there are instincts with no need of perfection with practice on the one hand and learned responses on the other. Mills triggered a barrage of letters from both professional comparative psychologists and amateurs (1896a, 1896b, 1896c, 1896d; "The Writer of the Note," 1896; Lucas, 1896; Baldwin, 1896a, 1896b; Elliott, 1896; Morgan, 1896a; Buchanan, 1896). The issue appeared to hinge, in part, on whether the authors referred to a response to water in the mouth, as occurs after pecking at a droplet, or a response to standing water, as in a trough. At any rate, the exchange brought out issues relating to the nature of instinctive behavior, the perfectability of instinctive behavior, the separability of nature and nurture, the implications of Lamarckian versus other forms of inheritance, "social inheritance," the nature of "environmental" influences on behavior, and the utility of testing hypotheses about adaptive behavior with domesticated species.

One of the many contributions by psychologists to the study of evolution was the proposal of "organic selection" by James Mark Baldwin in 1896. Recall that Baldwin was a charter member of APA and the co-founder of the *Psychological Review*. He was APA president in 1897. In actuality, similar proposals were made in the same year by Baldwin (1896c), Morgan (1896b), and H. F. Osborn (1896), although the process has come to be known as the "Baldwin effect" (Simpson, 1953) or genetic assimilation (Waddington, 1953). The Baldwin effect was a means of explaining the inheritance of "acquired" traits without accepting a Lamarckian interpretation. Three steps would be involved. Different individuals would first develop different phenotypes for nongenetic reasons. Second, hereditary characteristics having similar adaptive advantages would develop in the population. Finally, selection would favor genes leading to the progressively more channelized development producing a phenotype similar to that of the original nongenetic characteristic. In essence, an adaptation that was initially nongenetic and individual would become hereditary. That such a process was feasible was best demonstrated by Waddington (1953) in an experiment dealing with heat shock and wing morphology in fruit flies. The story is told in more detail by Gottlieb (1979). Broughton (1981) discusses the reasons for the virtual disappearance of Baldwin from contemporary discussions of psychology despite his considerable early influence, twenty-one books, and 150 articles.

James Mark Baldwin, 1861–1934.
Photograph courtesy of the Archives of the History of American Psychology.

In 1898 Mills published *The Nature and Development of Animal Intelligence.* Like a surprising number of books of that time, this is a recasting and republication of earlier works. Mills summarized his work on such behavior patterns as hibernation and death feigning, and research on such species as dogs, squirrels, cats, rabbits, guinea pigs, pigeons, and domestic fowl. Mills was especially interested in the study of behavioral development. Writing on the development of dogs, Mills (1898, 167) noted, "The two great periods are: that before the eyes are open, and that succeeding this one. The time between the opening of the eyes, and the establishment of real vision and hearing, constitutes a transition or intermediate period." This resembles the later development of critical periods in dogs by J. P. Scott (1962). Mills was optimistic about the development of comparative psychology, noting, "Comparative psychology is now beyond the stage of neglect and contempt . . ." (1898, 49). Mills occasionally wrote with a "forked tongue." He was contemptuous of those who failed to make detailed and careful studies of their animals under reasonable normal conditions. Gottlieb (1979) indicated that Mills's statement, "Filling up books and periodicals is one thing, and reaching truth another" (Mills, 1898, viii) was directed at Baldwin.

Meanwhile events were occurring at Clark University that would set the pace for much of animal psychology in the twentieth century. Linus Kline and Willard S. Small began work that would lead to the first psychological studies of rats and the development of the first mazes. The story of the first use of rats and mazes was pieced together through correspondence with various participants by Miles (1930) and Warden (1930). Kline entered Clark in 1896 to study "zoological psychology" (Miles, 1930). His three papers during this period are of great interest and will be discussed shortly. Kline was interested at the time in homing in pigeons, bees, and other species. He had hoped to find a way to study what we would term *home sickness.* While working with chicks and reading Morgan's *An Introduction to Comparative Psychology,* "the idea occurred to me of using little boxes somewhat as harmless traps to study the ways by which rats search for food on out-of-the-way places" (Kline in Miles, 1930, 326). The notion of using rats came from work being done in the Biology Department at Clark by Colin C. Stewart. Stewart was studying the effects of alcohol, diet, and barometric pressure on the behavior of rats in revolving cages. Stewart began with wild, "gray" rats; he wrote, "If anyone wants to know why I changed from wild gray rats to *white rats* in 1895, let him work with gray rats for a year" (Miles, 1930, 334).

In the fall of 1898 Kline planned his research. Kline wrote, "I was impressed with the importance of working with animals in as natural moods as conditions permitted" (Miles, 1930, 326). Noting that the rat is a gnawer and that gnawing should be done under conditions of hunger but

Linus W. Kline, born 1866.
*Photograph courtesy of the
Clark University Archives.*

without fear, Kline in 1898 devised some "mouse boxes," from which rats could learn to get food. On December 3, 1898, he began what appears to be the first study of learning in rats. Comparative psychologists have always been interested in social interactions; on January 9, 1899, Kline began a study in which two rats were jointly engaged in securing food from a box.

Both Small and Kline agree that Edmund C. Sanford deserves credit for first suggesting the use of mazes. Kline noted that he had described to Sanford "runways which I had observed several years ago made by large feral rats to their nests under the porch of an old cabin on my father's farm in Virginia" (Miles, 1930, 331). Sanford immediately suggested the use of the Hampton Court maze. Kline then copied the pattern from an encyclopedia, although it appears that Small actually constructed the first maze. In his classical publication on rat-maze learning, Small (1901) noted that the rat's propensity for winding passages was one major factor in the adoption of the maze method. Like Kline, Small was concerned that his experimental situation be as natural as possible. He noted the resemblence between his maze and the home burrows constructed by kangaroo rats, a different species, as drawn by Ernest Seton Thompson. It is clear that the Kline-Small research was quite independent of that of Thorndike; whereas the former drew inspiration from Morgan and Wundt, the latter cites Lubbock. Also beginning independent systematic research on learning during this period was L. T. Hobhouse in England.

With regard to the first use of white rats as subjects, it appears that Stewart got his first animals from C. F. Hodge at Clark. At about the same time, H. H. Donaldson, a neurologist listed as a cooperating "psychologist" in the founding of *Psychological Review*, began a colony at the University of Chicago. Donaldson and others later developed rats into the famous Wistar strain at the Wistar Institute of Anatomy in Philadelphia. Further information on Donaldson and his relationship to psychology is provided by McMurrich and Jackson (1938) and Dallenbach (1938). One of his most unusual contributions to psychology was his postmortem analysis of the brain of Hall (Donaldson and Canavan, 1928).

Having established the origin of rat work and mazes at Clark and elsewhere, we can return to Small and Kline and their publications during this period. Small (1899) published a paper on the development of behavior in rats designed to parallel Mills's work on other species. He carefully documented the development of behavior and sensory function in young rats. Small's remaining two rat publications were published in the next century.

Linus Kline is one of comparative psychology's forgotten men. An ethologist interested in understanding the spirit behind the early comparative psychology would do well to consult Kline's three papers in *American Journal of Psychology* published in 1898 and 1899. The first, "The Migratory Impulse vs. Love of Home," is frankly human based. However, in an effort to understand the evolution of migratory behavior, Kline provided a comprehensive review of the literature at the time and covered a wide range of species beginning with crustaceans, insects, fish, and birds. In his conclusion, Kline contrasted the migrant with the lover

Willard S. Small, 1870–1943.
Photograph courtesy of the
Clark University Archives.

of home. The migrant is portrayed as "finding profitable objects and kindred spirits in a variety of situations" (1898, 80). The lover of home, by contrast, "is provincial, plodding, and timid" (1898, 81).

Kline's two papers in 1899 were largely methodological and illustrate the broad base of comparative psychology. In "Methods in Animal Psychology," (1899a), he summarized methods and discussed results of his research on *Vorticella* wasps, chickens, and rats. Kline discussed the advantages and disadvantages of both field research and experimental studies. He noted that "both methods are necessary to a more abundant ingathering of facts . . . . Both have their share of errors and abuses" (1898a, 257). Kline proceeded to describe research that covered not only learning, but sensory function, reproductive behavior, and behavioral development.

Perhaps Kline's most fascinating paper is "Suggestions Toward a Laboratory Course in Comparative Psychology" (1899b). In constructing a laboratory course in comparative psychology, Kline recommended research on amoeba, vorticella, paramecia, hydra, earthworms, slugs, fish (including sticklebacks, 1899b, 413), chicks, white rats, and cats. Kline laid out a wide range of studies of sensory function and various behavioral patterns. In designing the laboratory course, Kline noted:

> A careful study of the instincts, dominant traits and habits of animal as expressed in its free life—in brief its natural history should precede as far as possible any experimental study. . . . In setting any task for an animal to learn and perform, two questions should be asked: (1) Does it appeal to some strong instinct? (2) Is it adapted to the animals range of customary activities? (1898b, 399)

In these passages Kline sounds very much like an ethologist of a much later era.

Edward Lee Thorndike began graduate work at Harvard in 1896. In his research on the behavior of young chicks, he encountered difficulties in that his landlord refused to permit them in his room, and James was unable to obtain laboratory space for him at Harvard. Thorndike's early studies were therefore conducted in the cellar of William James's home. His Harvard work was published in 1899 and primarily dealt with instinctive reactions in the pecking behavior of chicks (Thorndike, 1899a). Thorndike noted that while there are some instincts that are characterized by the "regularity and precision with which the needle approaches the magnet," others are just as instinctive but "vague" and "irregular" (1899a, 290). For a variety of personal and financial reasons, Thorndike left Harvard in 1897 to complete his doctoral degree at Columbia, "bringing in a basket my two most educated chickens" (1936, 265). Joncich (1968) described many of these events.

Thorndike's thesis, completed in 1898, is a classic entitled "Animal Intelligence: An Experimental Study of the Associative Processes in Animals." Thorndike began with a blast at the anecdotal method and the one-sided reports provided noting, "Dogs get lost hundreds of times and no one ever notices it or sends an account of it to a scientific magazine. But let one find his way from Brooklyn to Yonkers and the fact immediately becomes a circulating anecdote" (1898a, 24). The bulk of the thesis dealt with learning in cats, dogs, and chicks. Thorndike constructed his

Edward L. Thorndike, 1874–1949.
*Photograph by Harris & Ewing, courtesy of
the National Academy of Sciences.*

famous puzzle boxes that required cats to trip a latch or other device in order to escape and secure food. He concluded that in solving the problem, the animals do not display reason but simply hit on the solution through trial and error. Further, Thorndike was unable to find any beneficial effect of either imitation, seeing another animal solve the problem, or of being "put through" the problem having the human experimenter move the animal's limbs through the requisite motions. His results were summarized for wider audiences in *Science* (1898*b*) and in a paper entitled, "Do Animals Reason?" in *Popular Science Monthly*

(1899*b*). An opportunity to lecture at Woods Hole provided Thorndike the opportunity to conduct one of the earliest studies of learning in fishes (1899*c*). He demonstrated escape learning in *Fundulus.*

Perhaps it was inevitable that two writers on "animal intelligence" as different as Mills and Thorndike would come to blows, but come to blows they did. Thorndike (1898*c*) reviewed Mills's book and cast high praise on Mills's observations on development in a variety of species. Thorndike liked little else about the book, however. He noted that Mills "refuses the moderate attitude of Lloyd Morgan and reverts to a position comparable to that of Romanes" (1898*c*, 520). Thorndike called for more carefully designed experiments and less "mixing up opinion with observation" (1898*c*, 520).

The forked tongue was unleashed by Mills:

> This investigator claims to have swept away, at one fell swoop, almost the entire fabric of comparative psychology. . . . Dr. Thorndike has not been hampered in his researches by any of that respect for workers of the past . . . Comparative psychologists are readily and simply classified — they are all insane — the only difference being one of degree. . . . (1899, 263)

Mills objected to the unnatural conditions of Thorndike's experiments, his lack of observations, and his failure to recognize individual differences. Mills's argument regarding the importance of natural conditions is typical of many later debates:

> As well enclose a living man in a coffin, lower him, against his will, into the earth, and attempt to deduce normal psychology from his conduct. (1899, 266)

> [These] associations bear about the same relation to the normal psychic evolution of animals as the behavior of more or less panic-stricken or otherwise abnormal human beings does to their natural conduct. (1899, 274)

Mills had some interesting views on the kinds of data needed in comparative psychology. He wrote, "At the present stage of comparative psychology we are in need of observations down to the minutest details" (1899, 267), and "It is important to make observations on wild animals, and there seems to be room for the worker in comparative psychology in zoological gardens as well as in the field or forest" (1899, 273).

Thorndike resented Mills's personal attack: "I cannot see that the presence or absence of megalomania in me is of any interest to comparative psychology" (1899*d*, 416). Thorndike noted that he himself had "long since criticized my method" (1899*d*, 413) on grounds of its unnaturalness. However, he defended his experiments against the criticisms of Mills (and Kline) because such experiments provided the only way "to give us an explanatory psychology and not fragments of natural history" (1899d, 415). Mills (1904) saw no reason to change his view.

There were other events occurring during this period both in the United States and elsewhere. Hobhouse, in England, had independently begun experiments on learning similar in some respect to those of his American counterparts. In Germany Th. Beer, A. Bethe, and J. Von Uexküll published in 1899 an influential paper in which they adopted a strong mechanistic position in interpreting invertebrate behavior. To the best of my knowledge, this often-cited paper has never been published in an English translation. In the *American Journal of Psychology*, Triplett (1898) published a paper that Zajonc (1969) regards as the first experiment in social psychology. Although dealing with humans, the paper was important for psychological studies of animal behavior as it dealt with the phenomenon of social facilitation—a topic important in later studies. Meanwhile Yerkes had entered graduate school at Harvard and in 1899 transferred from the zoological laboratory to psychology. Watson remained at home in Greenville, less than a year away from his fateful move to the University of Chicago.

As should be evident, this six-year period was one of great development in comparative psychology. In 1899 courses in comparative psychology were initiated at Chicago by G. H. Mead and at Clark by E. C. Sanford. Warden and Warner (1927) place the first two comparative-psychology research laboratories at Clark, under Sanford, and Harvard, under Yerkes.

Bruner and Allport (1940) characterize this period as predominantly optimistic. Psychology was breaking away from philosophy and building a house of its own. The evolutionary influence was strong as was the growth of the scientific method as derived from Wundt and the other German laboratories. The stage was set for the twentieth-century growth of this discipline.

1900-1909: COMPARATIVE PSYCHOLOGY BLOSSOMS

The beginning of the twentieth century saw a continuation of the optimism that began with the end of the nineteenth. In 1907 C. Judson Herrick would write, "Comparative psychology has arrived" (1907, 76). According to Yerkes (1908, 271), "More important contributions to our knowledge of comparative psychology, animal behavior, and of certain aspects of the physiology of the nervous system have been made during the past two years than ever before in a like period." According to Mills (1904, 755), "Probably in no direction has more solid advance been made within the last ten years than in the psychology of instinct, impulse, habit and kindred subjects." Yerkes (1943a) later remembered that period as a time when psychology became experimental rather than naturalistic and reasonably controlled rather than anecdotal. It was a time when the study of learning became prominent in comparative psychology. However, comparative psychologists remembered the importance of relatively natural testing conditions and of the study of other aspects of the animal's life and behavior.

Learning

The study of learning in the decade began with publication by Small (1900) of studies done with Kline's food-puzzle boxes. Whereas Thorndike put the animal in a box and food on the outside, the Clark workers put food inside and the animal on the outside. Small was concerned that the animal do things "only in the line of its inherent abilities" (1900, 133). The rats had to dig through sawdust or gnaw through paper strips to get to the food. Digging (and gnawing) were selected as being a "characteristic activity in the free life of the rat" (1900, 135). By testing two rats simultaneously, Small was able to look at social interactions and imitation. Small explicitly recognized the disadvantage of working with an "albino sport" that would differ from its wild congeners but felt that, at this stage in its development, psychology needed "careful description of the psychic life of special animal forms. Generalization will come in due time" (1900, 133). Small's hungry rats often stopped to carry off pieces of paper left from the solution of the problem — perhaps an early example of "instinctive drift" (see Breland and Breland, 1961). Small noted, "The nest-building instinct is so strong, that the mere sight of a bit of available material serves to distract the unstable attention of the rat from her quest of food" (1900, 152). Again, in his famous study in the Hampton Court maze, Small (1901) stressed the relevance of the task to the animal's natural life. Small had originally planned to work with wild rats, but the "difficulties were considerable" (1901, 209), and he worked mainly with the domesticated form. Small found that domestication appeared to reduce the disparity in performance between the sexes and wondered whether domestication "operates similarly with the human species" (1901, 212).

The year 1901 saw publication of *Mind in Evolution* by English researcher Leonard Trelawney Hobhouse. Hobhouse's results were collected in experiments on his own dog and cat and then with zoo animals, including several species of monkeys, an elephant, and an otter, all of whom lived at the Belle Vue Gardens in Manchester, England. Like the Clark workers,

Hobhouse tended to put food inside a container and the animal outside rather than the reverse. He used a variety of tasks including some with tool use and box stacking similar to those later used by Wolfgang Köhler. Although Hobhouse acknowledged the priority and importance of Thorndike in stimulating this research (in Warden, 1930), his results were very different. Whereas Thorndike believed he had seen the gradual growth of habits, Hobhouse believed that "the method of learning does not ordinarily . . . conform to the notion of the gradual growth or inhibition of a habit" (Warden, 1930, 206). Rather, Hobhouse felt that his animals formed ideas, "at first perhaps dimly grasped; then clearly seen; for a while waveringly held, but soon definitely established" (Warden, 1930, 206). Hobhouse also found positive effects of animals being "put through" a task. Although subjective and teleological in places, Hobhouse's work had a strong evolutionary flavor (see Razran, 1971; Gottlieb, 1979).

Sir John Lubbock added to his earlier work with insects and extended them to mammals in *Intelligence of Animals* (1904). Washburn and Bentley (1906) found rapid learning of a color discrimination in fish, and Triplett (1901) believed he observed imitation in fish.

In 1899 Thorndike had begun research with three cebus monkeys housed in his flat on West 123rd Street in New York (Joncich, 1968; Bitterman, 1969). He devised a variety of problem boxes for use with the monkeys but reported, "We find no evidence of reasoning" (1901a, 184). Neither did he find evidence of imitation. There was no question that the monkeys were able to learn problems that other species appeared unable to master. However, Thorndike believed the difference to be one of degree, not kind. He concluded, "The only demonstrable intellectual advantage of the monkeys over the mammals in general is the change from a few, narrowly confined, practical associations to a multitude of all sorts, for that may turn out to be at the bottom the only demonstrable advance of man . . ." (1901a, 240). Thorndike's conclusion that the learning process did not differ qualitatively across a wide range of species (1901a, 1901b, 1901c) was to have great impact on the comparative study of learning throughout much of animal psychology for much of the century (see Bitterman, 1969).

The first two decades of the century, however, were a period of great activity in the comparative study of learning. Research emanated primarily from Harvard, Clark, and Chicago. Robert Yerkes finished his doctorate at Harvard in 1902 and remained there, carving out the beginning of a reputation that would make him a leading figure in comparative psychology for many years. Yerkes was interested in a whole range of behavioral patterns besides learning. His comparative studies of learning in the decade, however, include research on turtles (1901); green crabs (1902); frogs (1903); crawfish (Yerkes and Huggins, 1903); and dancing mice

Robert M. Yerkes, 1876–1956.
*Photograph by Dellenbeck, courtesy of the
National Academy of Sciences.*

(Yerkes, 1907). His student L. W. Cole (1907) added raccoons to the list, while C. S. Berry and M. E. Haggerty studied rats, cats, and monkeys.

Although he knew there was also a lively interest in comparative psychology at Clark, Yerkes was given to understand that it was "either indiscreet or bad form for a Harvard psychologist to try to cultivate friendly professional relations with Hall and his Clark associates" (1943*a*, 75). Whereas the Harvard workers tended to publish relatively brief papers confined to the learning performance of their animals, the Clark workers wrote long introductions and discussed points of methodology and the life history of the species under study. A. J. Kinnaman (1902*a*, 1902*b*) appears to have been the first to study rhesus macaques under laboratory conditions. He gave credit to Thorndike, however, for the first use of monkeys. It is not clear whether Thorndike or Hobhouse began first; the difference probably was a matter of days. Kinnaman discussed five basic approaches to the study of behavior: free observation in the natural habitat; developmental analysis; training; free observation in captivity; and experiment in captivity. Kinnaman saw problems with the use of both training and free observation in captivity but wrote favorably of field, developmental, and experimental research. Kinnaman's monkeys learned to manipulate a number of devices and appeared to show signs of both reasoning and imitation.

James P. Porter's study of learning in spiders included not only studies of modifications of behavior that "seem to be intelligent" (1906a, 352) but of web building, feeding, mating, and tropisms. Porter (1904, 1906b) also studied learning in English sparrows, vesper sparrows, and cowbirds. H. B. Davis (1907) of Clark studied intelligence in raccoons but began his paper with a discussion of feeding, vocalization, play, hibernation, washing behavior, and a variety of other instinctive patterns. He noted the importance of work both in the laboratory and in the field and that "nowhere is it more essential that these two sorts of observation should go hand in hand" (1907, 447-448).

Meanwhile John B. Watson completed his dissertation at the University of Chicago and remained there after completing the Ph.D. Although Watson's work at Chicago was primarily on rats, he did persuade the university to buy him four monkeys in 1906. The monkeys were used in a study of imitation (1908a). Watson (1904) called for more research on imitation. During 1905 and 1906 a lasting correspondence between Watson and Yerkes developed. The careers of these two giants of comparative psychology were to parallel each other for some years before diverging in sharply different directions. Watson's dissertation at the University of Chicago (1903) was a study of behavioral development in white rats. He began working with rats through caring for for Donaldson's colony. Watson studied the changes with age in the young rat's ability to solve various kinds of problem boxes and mazes. He correlated this with neural development; The monograph includes page after page of histological sections of the developing-rat nervous system. Yerkes (1904b) reviewed the work quite favorably.

Watson's dissertation was well received, and his meteoric rise in psychology began. However, the procedure of sacrificing rats for brain study drew the ire of antivivesectionists and *Life* magazine, and Watson was caricatured as a killer of baby rats.

Although Watson did little in the way of species comparison while at Chicago, his student C. S. Yoakum (1909) did publish some research in which learning in squirrels was compared to that in other species.

Early comparative psychologists both in this decade and the next

John B. Watson, 1878-1958.
Photograph courtesy of the
Archives of the History of American Psychology.

appeared obsessed with the role of imitation in learning. Failures to find beneficial effects of imitation on learning were reported in cats, dogs, and chicks (Thorndike, 1898*a*), monkeys (Thorndike, 1901*a*), and raccoons (Davis, 1907, Cole, 1907). On the other hand, some evidence of imitation was found in rats (Small, 1900; Berry, 1906), English sparrows (Porter, 1904), rhesus macaques (Kinnaman, 1902*b*), several species (Hobhouse, 1902), cats (Berry, 1908), and several species of monkeys (Haggerty, 1909; Watson; 1908).

It was during this decade that American psychologists became familiar with the phenomenon of conditioning. The story of Edwin Burket Twitmyer's doctoral dissertation "A Study of the Knee Jerk" is a case in point. Twitmyer used a bell as a signal and stimulating hammers to trigger the reflex. One day the apparatus failed, and the knee jerk was observed to occur in the absence of the hammer. Seizing on this chance occurrence, Twitmyer shifted his emphasis to this paradigm. As Twitmyer was unaware of the research by Pavlov and Bekhterev at this time, this is clearly an independent discovery of the conditioned reflex. Twitmyer presented the paper at the APA meetings in 1904 (1905). William James chaired the session and Twitmyer's paper was the last before lunch. After Twitmyer presented his paper, James is quoted as saying, "This is another interesting example of learning. If there are no comments, I shall declare this session adjourned" (Fernberger, 1943b, 347-348); he then rushed off to lunch. The lack of discussion may, together with other factors, have inhibited later American research on the conditioned reflex (see Irwin, 1943; Fernberger, 1943b; Coon, 1982).

Interest in classical conditioning grew during this decade. Thorndike also is reported to have developed a classical conditioning paradigm by clapping his hands just before throwing food on top of an animal's cage (Bitterman, 1969). Systematic introduction to American workers of Pavlov's research on classical conditioning was through a paper by Yerkes and Morgulis (1909).

Another notable learning study of the decade was that of Yerkes and Dodson (1908). They studied the learning of black-white discrimination as a function of the intensity of the electric shock used to motivate the animals. I do not know whether this was the first use of shock in such an experiment. They found that the effect of shock intensity depended on the degree of difficulty of the problem; stronger shock improved performance for simple tasks but not for more difficult discriminations. The Yerkes-Dodson law is often cited throughout psychology.

Field Studies

Although studies of learning were prominent during the decade, there were other important developments in comparative psychology as well. Among the persistent trends in comparative psychology that were to be important throughout its history, advances were made in this decade with respect to field research, study of a wide range of behavioral patterns, primatology, behavioral ontogeny, evolution, and methodology. Psychologists have generally been cognizant of the advantages of field studies and sympathetic toward their execution. For other reasons, many psychologists have preferred laboratory work. That does not bear, however, on their regard for the value of field research. Kinnaman (1902a), in the introduction to his laboratory study of learning in primates, noted of the field method, "This method can be made to bear first-class fruit. It has the advantage of seeing the real animal in his natural, unhampered reactions" (1902a, 99). Davis (1907, 448) noted, "The two sorts of observations should go hand in hand." The driving force behind psychology at Clark, Hall, cautioned that the results of the laboratory research being done "are narrower in scope and less characteristic than are the data that come from patient investigation of life histories in natural habitats from birth to death" (1908, 201). When Watson was able to release his monkeys on an island in Florida, he wrote to Yerkes, "There is a spontaneity which I have never seen in the north" (Cohen, 1979, 45).

Of course, there is a big difference between sympathy toward field research and execution of same. In 1907 Watson, the "founder of behaviorism," obtained funds from the Carnegie Institution for field research on the behavior of birds in the Dry Tortugas, islands off the tip of Florida near Key West. Thus began the first of three summers Watson would spend on the Dry Tortugas. The resulting work is simply first-class ethology. In his report in *Bird-Lore* Watson (1907a) dealt primarily with the status and population characteristics of noddy terns, sooty terns, and some other species. In a monograph, however, Watson (1908b) dealt with a wide range of behavioral problems relating to the life history of the two closely related species of terns in true ethological tradition. Watson studied eating and drinking, the nesting cycle, mating behavior, mate and egg recognition, development, orientation, and even maze learning. In a manner similar to that later discussed by D. S. Lehrman (for example, 1965), Watson noted the dramatic changes in behavior after the egg is laid (1908b, 208). He was sensitive to important differences between the species; for example, nest shifting was displayed every two hours in noddy terns and every twenty-four hours in sooty terns. Watson found no evidence of egg recognition in either species. He dyed the eggs and noted that the behavior of the noddy tern was not affected at all by such alteration. Watson similarly exchanged the nests of different individuals and found little effect on behavior; location rather than other characteristics, was critical to recognition. His attempts at studying orientation with birds released in Key West, Havana, and New York were a prelude to his later research on homing in birds.

Yerkes (1903) studied frogs in nature. He was interested in their responses to sound, and he utilized a variety of different stimuli to determine which would cause a frog to leave the bank and jump into the water. He concluded that frogs respond to the splash of other frogs.

Study of a Wide Range of Behavioral Patterns

The extent to which Watson was interested in a wide range of behavioral patterns is apparent from the preceding discussion. However, it was already apparent in his doctoral dissertation (1903). A keen observer Watson noted that his rats often went through the same passage in a maze as had a previous rat. Watson devised an apparatus made of wood and wire netting and lined with paper to study the ability of his rats to detect and move toward odors from their conspecifics. He first found no evidence that young rats track the odors of each other through the maze. However, he later altered his conditions and demonstrated that "adult rats show a preference for entrances that contain the odor of the opposite sex" (1903, 53). This surely must have been one of the earliest experimental demonstrations of detection and preference of a mammalian pheromone. Watson's early work is a nice example of how rat research can be "comparative" (see Gottlieb, 1976). Other examples of the broad behavioral interests of comparative psychologists of this period are found in the papers of Davis (1907) on the behavior of raccoons; Porter (1906) on spiders; and Yerkes (1903) on frogs.

Primatology

As might be expected in a science so closely associated with human behavior, the study of primates has played an important part in the development of psychology. The work during this decade of Thorndike (1901a), Hobhouse (1902), Kinnaman (1902a, 1902b), Watson (1908), and Haggerty (1909) provided a start toward the long tradition of primate research in comparative psychology.

The "Father of Clinical Psychology" (Zusne, 1975), Lightner Witmer, became interested in primate behavior during this decade. Witmer (1909) studied a chimpanzee, Peter, who was being exhibited in a theatrical act, and he wrote of "A Monkey with a Mind." In his stage performance, Peter skated, rode a bicycle, drank from a tumbler, and smoked a cigarette. Witmer believed that Peter was well aware that he was giving a stage performance: "He knows what he is doing, he delights in it, he varies it from time to time, he understands the succession of tricks which are being called for . . ." (1909, 182). Witmer then tested Peter privately and at the Psychological Clinic of the University of Pennsylvania on several occasions. Peter's performance was impressive as he solved various problems and displayed an ability to imitate. Witmer was critical of animal psychologists' attempts at studying imitation.

Witmer was especially interested in communication. Peter was able to comprehend language and to articulate the word *mama*. Witmer noted, "If Peter had a human form and were brought to me as a backward child and this child responded to my tests as credibly as Peter did, I should unhesitatingly say that I could teach him to speak, to write, and to read, within a year's time" (1909, 199). Witmer's concluding prediction erred only in anticipating home rearing of chimpanzees sooner than it occurred: "I venture to predict that within a few years chimpanzees will be taken early in life and subjected for purposes of scientific investigation to a course of procedure more closely resembling that which is accorded the human child" (1909, 205). The work of the Hayeses, Kelloggs, and Gardners would come much later.

Behavioral Ontogeny

Another recurrent theme in comparative psychology is the importance of studying behavior as it develops in the individual and the ways in which genes and environment interact in development. Mills noted:

> The most fruitful work thus far done has been the observation of the development of animals from birth upward by the consecutive or (fairly) continuous method . . . . It is important that similar observations and experiments be made on other of our domestic animals and especially on wild animals. (1904, 756)

The work of Watson (1903) in *Animal Education* and Watson (1908b) in studying the development of behavior of two species of terns in the field is consistent with that approach, as is that of Small (1899).

Two other remarkable pieces of developmental work appeared during the decade. Yerkes's *The Dancing Mouse* (1907) is a classic. Yerkes described the "dancing" behavior of these mutant mice as well as their genetics, sensory capabilities, and ability to learn. Although he found that the tendency to display the dancing movements (actually bouts of repeated whirling) was inherited, there was no evidence of transmission of the learning of a black-white discrimination. Jennings called the work "doubtless the fullest, most satisfactory, and most suggestive experimental account that we have of the behavior of any higher animal" (1908, 93-94).

The other major developmental paper of interest is that of Edward Conradi (1905), of Clark University, on song learning in the English sparrow. Conradi had canaries rear English sparrows in a way in which the sparrows never heard calls of their own species. He found evidence of both instinctive bases for song and of remarkable flexibility. In one instance he noted, "In due time this bird developed his sparrow chirp when calling for food, though he heard no sparrow note and was in a room with about twenty or more canaries" (1905, 195). The sparrow call later gave way to the song of a canary. Of two birds studied later, Conradi noted:

> Here we have, then, two young sparrows which in about nine months not only imitated some of the song of the canary but also adopted the canary's call-note, and which upon removal from the canaries and again hearing sparrow notes very freely, rather rapidly dropped back in the ways of the sparrow, but upon renewed instruction rapidly regained all they had lost. (1905, 198)

In other work Allen (1904) chose guinea pigs as subjects because of the advanced developmental status of their nervous system at birth. She found that two-day-old guinea pigs could learn a simple maze to get to their mothers.

Evolution

As already apparent, the study of evolution provided a primary impetus for the development of comparative psychology and interest continued during this decade. Recall that Hobhouse's *Mind in Evolution* appeared in 1902. Baldwin (1902) published a collection of his earlier essays under the title of *Development and Evolution*. The driving force behind the work at Clark, Hall published his "A Glance at the Phyletic Background of Genetic Psychology" in 1908. In 1909 Hall extolled Darwin's contribution to psychology in a AAAS symposium on "Fifty Years of Darwinism" (Hall, 1909).

Methodology

A strong emphasis on methodological rigor has always been a part of the laboratory approach in animal psychology. If there is a consistent trend in the decade, it is the extent to which psychologists were using more objective terms in the study of behavior and efforts to infer consciousness were gradually disappearing. However, during this period psychologists were still struggling with these issues and the extent to which consciousness was within the realm of study in comparative psychology. The use of objective nomenclature and the problem of animal consciousness remained much discussed (for example, Kirkpatrick, 1907; Washburn, 1904, 1908a; Yerkes, 1906).

Other Events

There were some other things happening in the first decade of the century that require at least some comment. Scientists outside psychology were, of course, making great advances in the study of behavior as well. Their de-emphasis herein does not imply that they were not important. This is the story of comparative *psychology*. Loeb during this decade was continuing his research on tropisms at the University of Chicago. He influenced Watson, although Watson was advised not to do his dissertation under Loeb. Meanwhile Jennings was studying the behavior of lower organisms at The Johns Hopkins University (1904, 1906). When Watson moved to Johns Hopkins in 1908, he would take Jennings's course and be otherwise influenced by him as well. At the same time Loeb and Jennings became embroiled in a bitter scientific controversy (see Pauly, 1981). Whereas

Jennings emphasized variability and internal factors in the regulation of behavior, Loeb emphasized stereotypy and external control. Watson appears generally to have sided with Loeb (Pauly, 1981). Watson (1907*b*) criticized Jennings's approach for its reliance on behavioral definitions of perception and overemphasis on continuity in the determination of behavior in "higher" versus "lower" organisms (see also Jensen, 1963). Watson even introduced evidence from introspection (1907*b*, 290).

In 1908 Margaret Floy Washburn published *The Animal Mind: A Text-Book of Comparative Psychology,* a book that would go through

Margaret Floy Washburn, 1871–1939.
Photograph courtesy of the Archives of the History of American Psychology.

several editions and be a standard in comparative psychology for many years. She covered a variety of topics, dealing generally with sensory function and learning. Although Karl T. Waugh (1908) from Chicago wrote a generally positive review of this book from the Titchener tradition, Washburn (1908b) felt it necessary to defend the volume.

Comparative psychologists continued to grapple with the problem of instinct. Kline concluded, "No problem of psychology has created such a Babel of tongues and been treated with more meager results; surely he would be a bold man who should even now attempt to write the last word on the subject" (1904, 778). In fact, the battle had barely begun.

Comparative psychology continued to spread. By 1909 there were new courses in comparative psychology at Cornell, Drake, Harvard, Ohio State, Iowa, Johns Hopkins, Michigan, Mount Holyoke, Oklahoma, and Texas, and new research laboratories in comparative psychology at Chicago, Cornell, Johns Hopkins, Michigan, and Texas (Warden and Warner, 1927).

Watson considered the status of comparative psychology at this time. He noted that "comparative psychology has completely justified its existence" (1906, 155), but he was concerned about its future development. Having broken the surface of many problems, there was a need for further refinement—especially in the study of mammalian behavior. Watson surveyed the available facilities and found them wanting. If comparative psychologists were to study the broad range of problems that Watson thought they should (for example, development, imitation, learning, homing), they would need better facilities. Watson proposed an experimental station for the study of animal behavior:

> The need to the psychologist of an experimental station for the study of the evolution of the mind is as great as is the need to the biologist of an experimental station for the study of the evolution of the body and its functions. (1906, 156)

The idea was endorsed by Baldwin (1906) with the addition that such a station should be built in cooperation with zoologists.

1910-1919: A DECADE OF ELABORATION, BEHAVIORISM, AND WAR

Much of what happened in the second decade of the century can be seen as an elaboration and extension of that which occurred in the first. The study of learning remained prominent, but there were developments with respect to methodology, instinctive behavior, primatology, behavioral development, and fieldwork that provided balance and built on the foundation of the previous periods. The rise of behaviorism, under Watson, and the onset of a devastating war were the two major new events of the decade. The study of sensory function became greatly emphasized, and Karl Lashley arrived.

Although the work of the decade is to be found in many journals and books, that in the *Journal of Animal Behavior* (*JAB*) was particularly important. With the expansion of work in comparative psychology, the *Journal of Comparative Neurology* became the *Journal of Comparative Neurology and Psychology* during the period of 1904-1910 (compare Pfaffman, 1973). It then, not *JAB*, is properly the first journal of comparative psychology. In 1910, however, the journal included an announcement of a new publication (Anonymous, *Journal of Comparative Neurology*, 1910, 20, 625-626):

> The Journal of Animal Behavior will accept for publication field studies of the habits, instincts, social relations, etc., of animals as well as laboratory studies of animal behavior or animal psychology. It is hoped that the organ may serve to bring into more sympathetic and mutually helpful relations the "naturalists" and the "experimentalists" of America. . . . (1910, 625)

The editorial board included nine individuals of whom six (Madison Bentley, Harvey Carr, Edward Thorndike, Margaret F. Washburn, John Watson, and Robert Yerkes) were psychologists. S. J. Holmes, H. S. Jennings, and W. M. Wheeler completed the board; Yerkes served as managing editor. Volume 6, No. 6, included a notice that the price would be raised from the initial three dollars to five dollars per volume. Volume 7 (p. 385) carried the brief notice, "The Board of Editors has decided to discontinue publication of the Journal of Animal Behavior until the unfavorable conditions created by the war shall have ceased to exist." *Psychobiology*, edited by Knight Dunlap of Johns Hopkins, published two volumes from 1917-1920.

Learning

Thorndike's *Animal Intelligence* was published in 1911. The book consisted mainly of reprinted copies of Thorndike's earlier work; only two chapters were new. In an introductory chapter Thorndike called for comparative psychology to study behavior for its own sake and without reference to consciousness. Harvey Carr noted that Thorndike's research constituted "a conspicuous landmark in the development of comparative psychology" (1912, 441). Henceforth, Thorndike would move progressively more into educational psychology and make few contributions to comparative psychology.

The comparative study of learning continued. In the study of invertebrates, Day and Bentley (1911) reported a study that purported to demonstrate learning in paramecia based on their improved turning in a narrow capillary tube. Yerkes (1912) conditioned earthworms, and Stevens (1913) studied "acquired chromotropisms" in spider crabs. John F. Shepard (1911, 1914) published abstracts of two studies of maze learning in humans, rats, cats, and ants. Shepard would have a long and productive career at the University of Michigan. Sadly, however, he would publish little of his work, and much of it appears lost (see Raphelson, 1980). Shepard had much influence through his students; one of his students in particular, Schneirla, would greatly expand Shepard's work with ants.

Among the studies of learning in birds were those by Cole (1911) on the rate of learning in chicks; by Hunter (1911) on maze learning in pigeons; and those on crows by Coburn (1914) and by Coburn and Yerkes (1915). Other species studied included pigs (Yerkes and Coburn, 1915), cats and dogs (Shepherd, 1915a), and primates (for example, Yerkes, 1916a).

Much of the interest in the study of learning in the decade centered on higher processes and the abilities of animals to learn complex problems.

John F. Shepard, 1881–1965.
Shepard is pictured leading a laboratory class in a
field study of ant behavior in Michigan in 1912.
Students are examining an ant hill between Ann
Arbor and Ypsilanti. *Photograph from the
Z. Pauline (Buck) Hoakley collection, courtesy of
the Archives of the History of American Psychology.*

John F. Shepard shown leading a laboratory class in
a field study of ant behavior in Michigan in 1912.
Dr. Shepard has a student smell the formic acid from
an ant. *Photograph from the Z. Pauline (Buck)
Hoakley collection, courtesy of the Archives of the
History of American Psychology.*

Walter S. Hunter, a student of Carr in the functionalist school of the
University of Chicago, proposed use of the delayed-response test as a
measure of the "functional presence of a representative factor" (1913). He
proposed that it was better than tests of tool use or imitation because the
nature of the controlling stimuli could be determined more precisely. A
stimulus would be made to first appear then disappear in one of three
boxes. The animal had to select the correct box after varying periods of

Walter S. Hunter, 1889–1954.
*Photograph courtesy of the
National Academy of Sciences.*

delay following removal of the stimulus. Maximum delays tolerated were ten seconds for rats, twenty-five seconds for raccoons, five minutes for dogs, and twenty-five minutes for human children. Hunter proposed various ways through which the delay might be mediated.

Lawrence W. Cole, a product of the Harvard laboratory, got into a bit of a scuffle with the Chicago functionalists over the behavior of raccoons. Cole (1912) followed up Davis's earlier paper treating the senses and instinctive behavior of raccoons. Chicago's Gregg and McPheeters (1913) criticized the procedures used in Cole's study of raccoon intelligence

(1907). Cole (1915) replied with what Hunter called a "deplorable tone" (1915, 406) and in a manner that Hubbart and Johnson called "somewhat polemic" (1916, 318). The basic issue involved Cole's view that raccoons used images in solving complex problems and Hunter's preference to postulate mere "sensory thought." Cole tended to play down the differences between the results of the two laboratories and was pleased to see the debate related to the behavior of raccoons. "The psychology of mammals must now cease to be a mere generalization of the psychology of cats . . . . Experimental animal psychology is now sixteen years old . . .; it must cease to be a generalization of the behavior of cats . . ." (1915, 159).

Progress was also being made in the study of higher processes in primates. In 1913 the German Wolfgang Köhler was appointed director of the anthropoid station on Tenerife, Canary Islands, by the Prussian Academy of Sciences. World War I left Köhler confined on the island until 1920. There he would conduct a series of important studies of problem solving in chimpanzees using various detour problems, problems in making of implements from sticks, tool using, and tests of box manipulation and stacking. The results were published in German in 1917 and in English in revised form as *The Mentality of Apes* by Köhler (1925).

Yerkes had planned to spend a sabbatical year in 1915 on Tenerife working with, or next to, Köhler. When the war intervened, Yerkes was unable to go there. Instead, he spent 1915, in Montecito, California, studying the private collection of primates that belonged to a physician, G. V. Hamilton—who himself made various contributions to the study of animal behavior (for example, 1916). The collection included ten monkeys and one orangutan. The result of Yerkes's effort was *The Mental Life of Monkeys and Apes* (1916). Yerkes, who must have been infatuated with floorplans and photographs of facilities, included complete information about the facility. Köhler concluded that "the chimpanzee can *possibly* show insight" (1925, 236). Yerkes used similar problems and drew similar conclusions. He believed that the orangutan Julius solved problems ideationally (1916, 68). He provided four criteria that led to this conclusion (1916, 131). Yerkes believed that the processes that anthropoid apes used in learning these problems were fundamentally different from those used in other species. This meant that quantitative comparison with other species was meaningless. *"Where very different methods of learning appear, the number of trials is not a safe criterion of intelligence.* The importance of this conclusion for comparative and genetic psychology needs no emphasis" (1916, 68). Comparison of trials to learn in different species was subsequently used frequently in learning studies. There appears to have been some misunderstanding between Yerkes and Köhler as the latter had described some of his results in correspondence with Yerkes and felt that they were underrepresented in Yerkes's book (Haslerud 1979).

Interest in imitation continued, with Witmer (1910) reporting imitation in macaques; Porter (1910) providing evidence of imitation in birds; and Shepherd (1911) reporting negative results with raccoons.

Field Studies

Watson returned to the Dry Tortugas for two more summers—in 1910 and 1913. His goal was primarily to study orientation in the noody and sooty terns. He (1910*a*) reported the results of homing by birds from several release sites.

On his third trip to the Tortugas, in the summer of 1913, Watson brought along Karl Lashley. Lashley was graduated from the University of Virginia in 1910, received an M.S. in bacteriology from the University of Pittsburgh in 1911, and was a graduate student at Johns Hopkins, receiving the Ph.D. in 1915. With Lashley handling the transportation and release of the birds for studies of orientation, the problems that had plagued the earlier work suddenly disappeared. Birds released from Mobile, Alabama, and Galveston, Texas, were able to return to the Tortugas in as little as four days. The remarkable aspect of the results was *"large numbers of birds returning over open water from all distances up to approximately nine hundred miles"* (1915, 464). In the introduction to their monograph, Watson and Lashley (1915) described alternative theories of homing. Although visual cues appeared to be used around the islands, they calculated that they could not have been used from distances as great as those to Mobile and Galveston. They postulated some form of distance orientation but could not explain the mechanism. Watson (1915, 464) noted "It is unbelievable that the problems connected with homing and migration can long resist the combined attacks of scientific students." Unbelievable it may be, but they are still not well understood.

Watson and Lashley had time for other studies of the terns as well. Confining the terns in cages over water, they found that the noddies survived well and appeared well adapted to the water. The sooties, however, appeared unable to swim, and one died. Watson and Lashley puzzled as to how the sooties could have stayed days over open water unless there was more driftwood than appeared likely. In the two concluding sections of the monograph, Lashley followed up Watson's earlier work with a report on "Notes on the Nesting Activities of the Noddy and Sooty Terns," and Watson reported on "Studies of the Spectral Sensitivity of Birds." In the same issue Lashley published the results of his work on the Tortugas relating to the acquisition of skill in archery. Lashley was versatile!

Karl S. Lashley, 1890–1958.
Photograph courtesy of the
National Academy of Sciences.

Study of a Wide Range of Behavioral Patterns

Examples of the work of comparative psychologists with a wide range
of behavioral patterns can be found in the observations of Cole (1912)
on play, the following response, and food washing in raccoons, Hamilton
(1914) on primate sexual behavior, and Yerkes (1915a) on maternal
behavior in primates. The topics of handedness and the modifiability
of handedness in primates were studied by Shepherd Ivory Franz (1913),
Yerkes (1916), and Lashley (1917). The abnormal persistence of a sucking response in cats was recorded by Lashley (1914).

Perry F. Swindle (1919*a*) published a paper on the analysis of nest building in birds and other species that was widely cited in its time and anticipated some themes that were developed by later workers such as Lorenz and Lehrman. Instinctive behavior for Swindle consisted of "very simple responses consisting of one or a very short series of elements" (1919*a*, 173). Swindle believed that "nest construction is the result of an interplay of instinct-groups" (1919*a*, 174), which became blended together into a biologically appropriate act through the effects of natural selection. Swindle emphasized that the observed movements were "purposeless"; indeed, sometimes even harmful. Elaborate nests are built as birds learn to utilize these instinctive response clusters in ways that produce a complex final product.

Swindle also emphasized the changes in behavior as birds progress through the nesting cycle so that "new group-complexes manifest themselves" (1919*a*, 181) at different times. The reaction of a bird to an intruder, for example, was found to vary with the degree of completion of the nest.

Primatology

Interest in the study of primates continued to grow during this decade. Yerkes's monograph (1916) and the research of Köhler were landmarks. Shepherd studied intelligence in two chimpanzees and concluded that they are "the most intelligent sub-humans of which we have knowledge" (1915*b*, 396). Witmer (1910) studied imitation in macaques; Hamilton (1914) studied sexual behavior; and Yerkes (1915) reported on maternal behavior. The contributions of Hamilton and Yerkes to primatology in this era have recently been reviewed by Marshall (1982). The work of Lashley and Watson will be discussed below.

By this time Yerkes was fully convinced of the importance of primate research and would devote most of the rest of his career to it. In ways that will be elaborated as I proceed, Yerkes was more responsible than any other individual for the broad knowledge of primate behavior we have today. Recognizing the potential of primate research and the kind of facilities needed, Yerkes (1916*b*) called for the development of a field station for primate studies. He followed Watson's earlier lead in pointing to the advantages of such a central facility. Ever the practical organizer, Yerkes considered several potential sites in warm climates and estimated that, were it built in southern California, a $50,000 annual budget and endowment of $1 million would be required. He did not have in mind a narrow range of research problems but rather a broad-based study of primates to include important forms of behavior, social relations, physiological activity, life history, genetics, comparative anatomy, and histology.

Behavioral Ontogeny

Some excellent developmental work was conducted during this decade as the study of behavioral ontogeny matured into one of the primary interests in comparative psychology. One of the leading facilitators of such work was one Watson, who noted that we should

> take our animal subjects into the laboratory, preferably when they are young (very often at birth), and watch the gradual way in which their instinctive life develops. This gives us a key to what all animals of a particular species naturally and instinctively do—i.e., the acts which they perform without training, tuition, or social contact with their fellow animals. (1910*b*, 348)

In his paper, "Instinctive Activity in Animals," Watson tells us how we can analyze instincts—through the use of the deprivation experiment.

> We must bring up certain members of a given species in isolation from their kind in order to watch the development of activity without tuition, and compare the results with those obtained from a set of similar experiments in which the animals are brought up in social contact with fellows of their own age and with adults of the same species. (1912*a*, 376)

> Experiment shows that young animals without previous tuition from parents or from their mates and without assistance from the human observer can and do perform the correct act the very first time they are in a situation which calls for such an act. (1912*a*, 377)

Watson proposed that there are three classes of responses: inherited fixed modes of responding; those that are partially congenital but not completely so; and random activities.

Watson (1914, 114) recommended two methods for the study of instinct—field observations and the deprivation experiment. In the latter book, as in the other two papers just cited (1910*b*, 1912*a*), Watson reviewed a wide range of studies of the development of instinctive behavior.

In their 1915 monograph on terns, Watson and Lashley considered several developmental problems. They also provided (1913) an empirical record of behavioral development in two rhesus macaques from birth through fifteen weeks and included descriptions of a wide range of behavioral patterns. Lashley (1913) studied the ability of a parrot to reproduce inarticulate sounds.

The first of a long series of studies on the development of mouse killing in cats was completed by Berry (1908) in his work on imitation. Berry concluded that cats learn to kill mice through imitation. The problem was re-examined by Yerkes and Bloomfield, who concluded "Kittens possess the instinct to kill mice" (1910, 262).

Young chickens have long been favored subjects in the study of behavioral development. Breed noted the degree to which the behavior of the young animal lies along a continuum with that before hatching:

> The early post-embryonic life of the chicks continued the scope of activities already begun in the egg. The alternations of passivity and activity, the lifting movements of the head combined with stretching movements of the legs, the occasional reflex forward thrust of the bill followed usually by movements of the mandibles, loud chirping along with other violent activity, —all these were common aspects of the behavior of chicks just before as well as immediately after hatching. (1911, 75)

Shepard and Breed (1913) followed up the earlier work on the development of pecking accuracy. The title of their paper, "Maturation and Use in the Development of an Instinct," anticipates the later colorful titles of J. P. Hailman (that is, "The Ontogeny of an Instinct" and "How an Instinct is Learned"). Fletcher (1916) studied the development of behavior in chicks hatched from alcoholized eggs. Haggerty (1912) reported observations on the development of instinctive behavior in a young sparrow hawk.

Some credit must be given Yerkes for his early work in behavior genetics—a field that has been very active in comparative psychology for many years. The Harvard laboratories produced four studies in the *Journal of Animal Behavior* during the decade. Yerkes compared wild and domesticated rats and concluded that "savageness, wildness, and timidity are heritable behavior-complexes" (1913b, 296). Ada Yerkes (1916) compared stock and inbred rats with respect to both learning and neuroanatomy. Utsurikawa (1917) compared the reactions of inbred and outbred albino rats to a variety of stimuli. Coburn (1912) described a "singing" mouse discovered in New York City, and Coburn (1913) sought additional examples so that breeding studies might be conducted.

Evolution

Swindle (1917) considered the biological significance of various eye appendages and marking on a variety of species. He considered various adaptive correlations such as the presence of white whiskers in nocturnal animals and dark whiskers in diurnal species. Swindle concluded that such appendages facilitate fixation and retention of fixation on objects. In his 1919 paper on nesting behavior, Swindle noted, "A preponderence of useful groups of movements where such exists, may be attributed to the biological factor of natural selection" (1919, 175). Watson (1911) reviewed the work of C. Judson Herrick on the evolution of brood parasitism in birds. Watson defined instincts as "phylogenetic modes of responses" (1914, 106-107) and devoted a whole chapter to a discussion of warning coloration, sexual selection, and related topics.

Methodology

Two classics in methodology appeared during this decade. Yerkes and Watson (1911) collaborated on a monograph on methods of studying vision in animals. The study of sensory function in animals was developing rapidly during this period. There was a need for careful consideration of the kinds of stimuli that could be properly used in the study of light vision and color vision. Yerkes and Watson considered all these problems and provided directions for constructing various kinds of preferred apparatus. Mast noted that this monograph showed "how we have outgrown the purely qualitative stage in this branch of science and have actually entered upon the quantitative phase" (1913, 147).

The other major event regarding methodology was the publication in English translation of Oskar Pfungst's *Clever Hans* in 1911. The horse Clever Hans had been purported to be able to perform various arithmetical feats. After various experimental manipulations, Pfungst determined that the horse was cueing in on slight movements of the head in the questioner. Pfungst then took the problem into the laboratory and showed that he himself could baffle observers by using the same cues on which the horse had relied (Clever Oskar?).

Yerkes (1917a) compared and contrasted the methods of Hunter and Hamilton with his own for the study of reactive tendencies in various ontogenetic and phylogenetic stages. He also published a note (1915b) discussing "unnaturalness" in psychological experiments and called for more automated recording devices as a means of eliminating experimental error. Hunter (1916) noted the need for comparative psychologists to include the names of the species studied in the titles of their papers.

Sensory Function

The study of animal sensory systems blossomed in this decade. The last issue of each of the seven volumes of the *Journal of Animal Behavior* included a series of review papers covering advances in the study of different taxa in the preceding year. Perusal of these reviews reveals the extent of interest in sensory function. For example, Watson (1911) devoted more than half of his review of progress in the study of vertebrates in 1910 to sensory function. Representative studies of visual function in chickens include those of Bingham (1913) and Breed (1912).

The Yerkes-Watson paper on methodology (1911) was a major advance. Representative studies of the period include those of Yerkes and Eisenberg (1915) on color vision in ring doves and Lashley (1916) on color vision in fowl.

Watson came close to von Uexküll's view of the *Umwelt* when he wrote, "Apparatus and methods are at hand for forcing the animal to tell us about the kind of world he lives in. If it is a smell world, we shall find it out. If it is a world of vision in which there are no colors, we shall not long remain ignorant" (1910, 350*b*).

Behaviorism

On February 24, 1913, John B. Watson delivered the first of a series of lectures at Columbia University that are generally marked as the beginning of the school of psychology known as "behaviorism." The series was completed on March 26. The first lecture was published as "Psychology as the Behaviorist Views It" in the *Psychological Review* (1913). The paper began, "Psychology as the behaviorist views it is a purely objective experimental branch of natural science" (1913, 158). Watson wrote, "The time seems to have come when psychology must discard all reference to consciousness; when it need no longer delude itself into thinking that it is making mental states the object of observation" (1913, 163).

Watson's goal was to remove consciousness from the realm of problems studied by psychologists and to replace it with an emphasis on behavior. What was new was the attempt to develop a complete program and to extend this approach to human behavior. The essence of behaviorism then is that we should study behavior. Extreme environmentalism is not and never has been a *fundamental* tenet of behaviorism. It did characterize one form — *later*-Watsonian behaviorism. In the 1913 paper Watson noted that organisms "adjust themselves to their environment by means of hereditary and habit equipments" (1913, 167). The same Watson who delivered the Columbia lectures in February, 1913, spent the summer of 1913 in the Dry Tortugas studying terns as noted previously.

The paper was followed in 1914 by a more complete version of the lectures, *Behavior, An Introduction to Comparative Psychology.* The book begins with the 1913 paper as Chapter 1. What was Watson's image of comparative psychology in this classic text of behaviorism?

> Unquestionably it is a mistake to neglect field work. . . . No one who has ever used monkeys as subjects can help feeling how handicapped we are at

the present times in our laboratory studies of simian life through lack of systematic knowledge of their life in the open. (1914, 30)

The student of behavior has come to look upon instinct as a combination of congenital responses unfolding serially under appropriate stimulation: the series as a whole may be "adaptive" in character (always adaptive from the Darwinian standpoint) or it may be wholly lacking in adaptiveness. (1914, 106)

In all, Watson devoted two chapters to instincts. He provided a list of eleven instincts that are characteristic of all vertebrate species (for example, sex, vocalization, defense, and attack); reviewed instinctive activity in reptiles, fish, and other organisms; and devoted special attention to the developmental "serial unfolding" of instincts. Watson also discussed Yerkes's work in behavior genetics.

At one point Watson noted, "Certain scientific writers are inclined to doubt even the existence of instincts" (1914, 125). He took Berry to task for his work on mouse killing by cats. Two pages later the work of Wallace Craig was cited in support of Watson's view.

An entire chapter of the book was devoted to the evolutionary origins of instincts. Watson discussed heredity, mutations, variation, the Darwinian concept of selection, changing views of selection, protective resemblence, warning coloration, sexual selection, Lamarck's views, and the direct adaptation theory.

In reviewing the book, Thorndike noted, "For students of objective behavior to regard themselves as martyrs, heroes, or prophets is now unnecessary" (1915, 467). However, Thorndike did feel Watson spent too much time discussing sexual selection. Thorndike also thought that Watson might have included more on microorganisms as well as "some concrete cases of the phylogeny of behavior such as Whitman's story of incubation or the course of the scratch reflex . . ." (1915, 463). Thorndike called these "among the most stimulating facts of animal psychology" (1915, 463).

Watson developed these ideas in textbook form in *Psychology from the Standpoint of a Behaviorist* in 1919. C. Judson Herrick (1920, 451) called the chapter on instinct "an important original contribution." The book has recently been discussed in detail by Amsel (1982).

Watson's primary contributions appear to have been his organization, systematization, and extension of what was already a prevalent approach in the study of behavior. Claims have been made for the title of the "founder" of behaviorism on behalf of numerous psychologists, including Jennings (Jensen, 1962), Loeb (Hirsch, 1973), Watson (Cohen, 1979), Thorndike (Joncich, 1968), and Knight Dunlap (Dunlap, 1932). Each contributed to the development of an objective approach in behaviorism, as did others (see Burnham, 1968).

Miscellaneous

Various other developments in the decade are of interest. In July of 1910 a joint meeting was held in London of the Aristotelian Society, the British Psychological Association, and the *Mind* Association to discuss instinct and intelligence (Washburn, 1911). The symposium featured talks by Lloyd Morgan (1910) and McDougall (1910). For McDougall, "instincts are essentially differentiations of the will to live that animates all organisms" (1910, 258).

Dunlap (1919) published a paper, "Are There any Instincts?," that would begin to set the tone for the 1920s.

Comparative psychology continued to grow, both in size and stature. During the decade there were seventeen universities offering new courses in comparative psychology and seven new research laboratories (Warden and Warner, 1927). Among those honored as president of the American Psychological Association were Baldwin (1897), Thorndike (1912), Watson (1915), and Yerkes (1917).

On April 6, 1917, Yerkes was hosting a meeting of Titchener's Society of Experimental Psychologists when word came that the United States had entered World War I. A committee was formed to consider how psychology could be of service in time of war. APA President Yerkes chaired the committee. He played a leading role in organizing psychologists and developing mental tests for use in World War I (see Evans, 1975). By November, 1918, over four hundred psychologists were in uniform, and many were involved in the mental-testing effort. Boring (1961) published a photograph of the First Company of Commissioned Psychologists at Camp Greenleaf, Georgia, in 1918. It shows Hunter, Stone, J. J. B. Morgan, K. M. Dallenbach, Boring, and other prominent psychologists; Major Yerkes is shown in an inset. For a critical opinion of the role of Yerkes in World War I, see Gould (1981).

It had been an active decade. However, the war would have a great impact on the activities of the next decade and the course of the development of comparative psychology.

Chapter 3

Chronological History of Comparative Psychology, 1920 to 1949

1920-1929: A DECADE OF CONTROVERSY AND TRANSITION

Views regarding comparative psychology in the 1920s vary. According to Beach (1974, 57) "During the first 15 years of the century it flourished and then fell into desuetude." Hunter (1952) wrote that in 1919 he was advised to leave animal psychology as there was no future in it. However, in Hunter's view, "the most prolific period in animal behavior studies was just getting under way" (1952, 174). Bruner and Allport (1940) and Misiak and Sexton (1966) treat the decade as one of controversy. O'Donnell (1979) considers it a period of crisis for experimentalism in the face of a growing challenge from applied psychology. In a way, it was all of these. According to Samelson (1980a, 468), "The decade of the twenties was an interregnum in psychology." I believe this description fits comparative psychology the best; it was indeed an interval between two reigns.

The comparative psychology of the teens was dominated by Yerkes and Watson. The level of activity declined in the second half of the decade and was greatly reduced by the war. During the period immediately after the war, neither Watson nor Yerkes was a major force in comparative psychology. The students they had trained generally did not establish sustained careers in comparative psychology. The new generation of comparative psychologists had not yet arrived. Recovery occurred slowly in the late twenties and was full in the 1930s and 40s. The twenties, however, are remembered as a decade of controversy and of transition.

While Yerkes served in various capacities in the army from 1917-1919, eventually rising to the rank of lieutenant colonel, his leaving Harvard along with several others, decimated that faculty (see O'Donnell, 1979). Yerkes's major efforts related to psychological testing. At the close of the war, he decided to resign the post he had accepted at the University of Minnesota and remain in Washington. He served as chair of the Research Information Service for the National Research Council (NRC), director of the Science Service, and chairman of the NRC Committee on Scientific Problems of Human Migration. In 1921 Yerkes edited a report summarizing the efforts in psychological testing in World War I. One of his administrative efforts was to be of considerable importance for the future of comparative psychology. In 1921 the NRC organized the Committee for Research in Problems of Sex. This organization would be a major source of funding for the new generation of comparative psychologists for many years (see Aberle and Corner 1953). Yerkes chaired the committee from 1921 to 1947. It was not until 1924 that he returned to the academic community at the Institute of Psychology of Yale University.

John B. Watson, the other giant of the period, had problems of his own. Watson had progressively directed his attention more and more to the study of human behavior in the last half of the previous decade and thus was already somewhat removed from *comparative* psychology. Watson and J. J. B. Morgan (1917) published a paper suggesting that many emotional responses were based on conditioning. The paper was important in the history of the study of motivation (see Remley, 1980). In work with a graduate student at Johns Hopkins, Rosalie Rayner, Watson conducted the much-cited research with "Little Albert." A conditioned fear of a white rat was created by providing an aversive noise, made by striking a steel bar just behind Albert B.'s head, just as Albert reached for the rat (Watson and Rayner, 1920).

During this time Watson and Rayner began an extramarital affair that was eventually discovered by Watson's wife. Both the Rayners and Mary Ickes Watson were socially prominent, and the resulting divorce created a major scandal in the national newspapers. Even before the scandal and without serious question, Watson was removed from his faculty position. Faculty members were expected to be pillars of virtue, and such behavior could not be tolerated. Comparative psychology thus lost its second prominent Johns Hopkins researcher as Watson, like Baldwin before him, was driven from the academic world for reasons relating to such concerns. Watson was never to return fully, although he found consolation in a very successful career in advertising (see Cohen, 1979; Buckley,

1982).There is some evidence that Watson and Rosalie did some of their love making connected to various devices to conduct early studies of the physiology of human sexual behavior (McConnell, 1974; Magoun, 1981). Although Watson and Rayner were happily married and Watson was successful in his business career, comparative psychology had lost a major force. Lashley was to write that "any one who knows American psychology today knows that its value derives from biology and from Watson" (Beach, 1961, 171).

In 1920 Lashley joined the faculty at the University of Minnesota; in 1926 he went to Chicago, and from there he went to Harvard in 1935. During this period he continued to influence and facilitate studies in comparative psychology. His own primary efforts, however, were directed at the study of the physiological bases of behavior—often of maze learning by rats.

The advance guard of the new generation of comparative psychologists arrived during the 1920s. Calvin P. Stone completed his doctorate under Lashley in 1921. On March 21, 1920, Lashley wrote to prospective graduate student Stone suggesting possible research topics. The letter provides an excellent idea of the range of Lashley's interests and the problems confronting Stone; it was reprinted in full by Beach (1961). Among his interests Lashley listed comparative studies of sensory function; effects of drugs, diet, and the like on learning; "the experimental control of instincts"; physiology of the nervous syusystem in relation to learning; and the general functional anatomy of the brain. Lashley advised Stone, "Decide what animals you want to work with and get as familiar with the normal behavior as you can" (Beach 1961, 177). In 1922 Stone joined the faculty at Stanford where he would have a long and productive career, eventually being elected to the National Academy of Sciences and as president of the American Psychological Association.

The new faces arrived from diverse places. H. C. Bingham earned a Ph.D. from Johns Hopkins. Carl J. Warden completed his degree at Chicago in 1922 and went to Columbia University in 1924. He would be a major force in the study of motivation and an important historian of comparative psychology. Henry Nissen completed his degree under Warden in 1928 and went to work with Yerkes at Yale. Zing-Yang Kuo was a graduate student at the University of California in Berkeley, finishing in 1923. Leonard Carmichael received the Ph.D. from Harvard in 1924; Curt P. Richter completed his doctoral degree under John Watson at Johns Hopkins.

It was during this period, in 1920, that William McDougall, already very influential in a variety of areas of psychology, left England for Harvard. Later he would write, "In America I was known as a writer who had flourished in the later middle ages and had written out a list of alleged

Calvin P. Stone, 1892–1954.
Photograph courtesy of the
Archives of the History of American Psychology.

instincts of the human species" (1930, 216). McDougall was an influential and widely read psychologist; his *Outline of Psychology* (1923) sold around 100,000 copies.

With the demise of the *Journal of Animal Behavior* in 1917 and *Psychobiology* in 1920, comparative psychology was served primarily by the *Journal of Comparative Psychology,* edited by Knight Dunlap and Yerkes and founded in 1921, and by *Comparative Psychology Monographs,* begun under the editorship of Hunter in 1923.

Carl J. Warden, 1890–1961.
Photograph courtesy of the Columbiana Collection,
Low Memorial Library, Columbia University.

The Controversy over Behaviorism

The two big controversies of the decade were related to behaviorism and the study of instinct. Although Watson was out of formal academic circles, he retained some ties and continued to do some writing (see Cohen, 1979). Two articles in *Harper's* were entitled "What Is Behaviorism?" (1926) and "The Behaviorist Looks at Instincts" (1927). His book *Behaviorism* was published in 1924 and revised in 1930. This book was

William McDougall, 1872–1938.
Photograph courtesy of the
Archives of the History of American Psychology.

reprinted in paperback in 1959 and became widely available. Unfortunately, it is through the latter book, rather than the earlier works, that most people know Watson. The book was hastily written. Of it Watson wrote, "This book still shows its hasty origin" (1936, 280). Watson reports that he "polished it" for the 1930 edition, but it is not clear how he regarded the final version. Watson's thinking during this period changed in two parallel ways. First, he came to write almost exclusively about humans. Second, he became strongly environmentalistic. The two trends were interrelated. As Watson studied human behavior more, he became convinced that instinctive behavior was less important than in nonhumans. He wrote the famous sentence:

> I should like to go one step further now and say, "Give me a dozen healthy infants, well-formed, and my own specified world to bring them up in and I'll guarantee to take any one at random and train him to become any type of specialist I might select—doctor, lawyer, artist, merchant-chief and, yes, even beggar-man and thief, regardless of his talents, abilities, vocations, and race of his ancestors. (1930, 104)

He also wrote, "Is there nothing then in heredity? How absurd. Certainly there is. We are born men not kangaroos" (1927, 231).

Watson wrote little about nonhumans during this period; his position is not clear. However, he never forgot the extent to which specific behavioral patterns could develop in nonhuman animals in the absence of specific tutoring (for example, 1927, 228). Late-Watsonian behaviorism was indeed strongly environmentalistic. However, such strong environmentalism characterized neither earlier Watsonian behaviorism nor those forms promulgated by other authors (for example, Skinner). It is unfortunate that behaviorism has come to stand for environmentalism in the views of so many readers.

In 1923 Watson wrote a scathing review of McDougalls's *Outline of Psychology* in the *New Republic* entitled, "Professor McDougall Returns to Religion." Watson wrote, "It seems almost unthinkable that Mr. McDougall can be sincere in this development" (1923, 12); "Mr. McDougall's purpose . . . is an insult to the corporate body of facts and deductions we call science" (1923,12). "From his earliest writing he, like many Englishmen, has been a telepathist at heart" (1923, 13), and "The book is unsafe to put in the hands of elementary students or even of the general public" (1923, 13).Watson's primary objection was to McDougall's attribution of "purpose" in the control of behavior.

After years of debate in print, Watson and McDougall finally met in a face-to-face debate at the D.A.R. Memorial Constitutional Hall in Washington, D.C., under the sponsorship of the Washington Psychological Society on February 5, 1924. The story is told by Larson (1979) and Cohen (1979), and the results were published by W. W. Norton (Watson and McDougall, 1929). A thousand people, including intellectual elite, political figures, jurists, and socialites packed the hall. Watson used most of his time not railing at McDougall but describing behaviorism. He wrote, "Behaviorism is new wine that cannot be put into old bottles" (Watson and McDougall, 1929, 39). For his part, McDougall attacked what he regarded the simplistic nature of behaviorism: "Dr. Watson's views are attractive to those who are born tired, no less than to those who are born Bolshevists" (1929, 42). Both the audience and the panel of three federal judges declared McDougall the winner. This may have been as close to a "media event" as psychology has known.

The Controversy over Instinct

The debate over instinct was as acrimonious as that over behaviorism—indeed, it was an outgrowth of the development of behaviorism. It appears that several different concepts had become confused in the literature. "Instinctive responses" were taken to be specific responses to specific stimuli that were displayed as the result of the inheritance of certain structures. The emphasis was on the specific stimulus-responses relationships. "Instincts," on the other hand, were taken to be more global and often overtly teleological. McDougall would define an instinct as "an inherited or innate psycho-physical disposition which determines its possessor to perceive, and pay attention to objects of a certain class, to experience an emotional excitement of a particular quality upon perceiving such an object, and to act in regard to it in a particular manner, or at least, to experience an impulse to such action" (1911, 29).

Dunlap (1919) and Bernard (1921) initiated this round of the controversy. Both came out strongly against the notion that there were global instincts of the sort proposed by Thorndike and McDougall. However, both accepted the view that there were inherited instinctive reactions. Dunlap (1922) underscored the latter point.

A more radical position was taken by Kuo in "Giving Up Instincts in Psychology" (1921) and "How Our Instincts Are Acquired" (1922). Kuo went further than either Dunlap or Bernard to propose that the only inherited responses were reflexes (that is, "units of reaction"). In "A Psychology without Heredity" (1924) and later (for example, 1929, 1967), Kuo modified his position. In his later position, Kuo held that one could not deny the existence of instincts because the organism and its environment interacted so closely and so continuously in development that the distinction between inherited and acquired responses could not even be made. He argued, therefore, not that acquired responses did not exist but that "unless we are willing to accept the vitalistic or mentalistic program in psychology, in which program heredity can be justly dealt with in the abstract, the entire concept of heredity should be dismissed from our science" (1924, 446).

In the view of many, behavioristic students of the evolution of behavior in the 1980s, behavioral patterns have come to adapt the organism to the environment as the result of the past operation of natural selection. This is not teleological because there is no implication that the organism understands or strives toward goals. Rather, the organism inherits the

Zing-Yang Kuo, 1898–1970.
Photograph courtesy of Gilbert Gottlieb.

tendency to build structure that, if it develops in appropriate environment, leads the animal to display certain behavioral patterns in certain situations. Differences among species appear to be the result of genetic differences. Kuo appears to have regarded all such thinking as teleological. He noted:

> For the constant variations of the environmental context in a given ecological niche the different developmental histories of different individuals are sufficient to explain how the evolution of behavior takes place. In other words, behavioral variations are merely variations of behavioral phenotypes actualized from among numerous behavioral potentials, the genotypes of the species remain unchanged. (1967, 200)

It is clear that Kuo's version of behaviorism was even more radically antihereditary than was Watson's later version. It must be emphasized, however, that this was not true of all forms of behaviorism.

Various authors defended the existence of instincts and/or of instinctive behavior. Carmichael (1925) pointed out that Kuo had not acted out of logical necessity in denying heredity once he asserted that heredity and learning were inseparable. Kuo could equally well have rejected the acquired. Geiger (1922) believed that Kuo's own early position implied acceptance of some form of instinct. Hunter (1920) was concerned mainly with the modification of instincts. McDougall (1921-1922) summarized all the various criticisms of instinct theory, especially as they related to human behavior, and attempted to defend his position. He noted that Kuo "out-Watson's Mr. Watson" (McDougall, 1921-1922, 299). "Forced" to either give up instinct in psychology, with Kuo, or to give up the idea that "an instinct is merely a motor mechanism" (1921-1922, 310), McDougall opted for the latter.

Edward C. Tolman, Kuo's academic advisor, dismantled the underlying assumptions of Kuo's position and came to the conclusion that *"instincts cannot be given up in psychology"* (Tolman, 1922, 152). Tolman (1923) compared and contrasted various versions of instinct theory and wrote in favor of a teleologically based approach. His views on instinct and their hierarchical structure are interesting in light of the later instinct theories promulgated by the ethologists such as Tinbergen. There were three levels in Tolman's hierarchies: independent reflexes, subordinate acts, and "determining adjustments." The determining adjustments set the subordinate acts in readiness and are themselves organized in hierarchies. Tolman wrote, "In the case of such a hierarchy of adjustments it is obvious that the function of all, save the lowest one in the sequence, consists in a *release* of a lower determing adjustment rather than in a release of actual subordinate acts" (1920, 220, italics mine). Tolman used Swindle's (1919a) analysis of nest building as an example of the hierarchical nature of instincts. He noted that;

> The individual random responses continue *until* some one of them presents a new stimulus, the final response to *which,* removes the condition or stimulus which was the original cause of the determining adjustment itself. In the case of the bird, the activity continues until a nest eventually gets built. (Tolman, 1920, p. 226)

Thus Tolman's model includes not only a hierarchy of acts and determinants but a role for feedback in the termination of instinctive activity. Tolman believed that with such a model he could build instincts, purpose, and thoughts into a behavioristic approach. Tolmanian behaviorism clearly differed markedly from that of either Watson or Kuo.

There would be periodic outbreaks of the instinct debate throughout the history of comparative psychology to the present time—particularly in the 1950s.

Motivation

The twenties was a period of much interest in the study of motivation in animals. Much use was made of indirect and easily measured aspects of behavior rather than the occurrence of instinctive patterns. The most typical apparatus was the Columbia Obstruction Box, introduced by Moss (1924). An animal was introduced into one end of a long chamber separated from some incentive by a grid that was wired to deliver electric shock. Both the strength of the shock and the motivational level of the organism could be varied. This permitted an analysis of the effect of various antecedent conditions on the crossing response, as well as a comparison of the "strengths" of different drives. Moss (1924) reported a total of eleven experiments in which the relative strength of a hunger drive and sex drive were manipulated. He also introduced apparatus in which animals could choose between two incentives. Both kinds of apparatus were developed further by Jenkins et al. (1926). Subsequent studies of such drives were conducted by Warner (1927), Tsai (1925), and Nissen (1929). Nissen studied the effects of gonadectomy, vasectomy, and the injection of various substances on performance.

Another favorite apparatus of the time was the running wheel. A rat was confined in a cage with access to a standardized wheel in which it could run; the number of revolutions could be recorded as a function of various experimental treatments. Wang (1923, 1924) studied "spontaneous" activity as a function of the estrous cycle of female rats as well as during pregnancy and lactation. Richter (1922) studied diurnal cycles and the relationship between running and such variables as food, temperature, illumination, and age.

Richter (1927) utilized running wheels and also constructed a "multiple-activity cage" in which he could record the amount of time spent per day by the rat in climbing, running, burrowing, gnawing, eating, drinking, and mating. The approach is significant because it relied on naturally occurring behavioral patterns and permitted study of a variety of behavioral patterns as they unfolded in a natural order controlled by the rat. The method is much less unnatural than imposition of an electric shock between the animal and the incentive. It is unfortunate that it was not utilized more widely.

Behavior Genetics

The field of behavior genetics was slowly growing. A landmark study appeared when Tolman (1924) published the results of his selection study on maze learning in rats. This appears to be the first use of the genetic method of artificial selection for a behavioral trait under such controlled conditions. Tolman reported a response to selection after just one generation. The reliability of Tolman's maze was low, and the study appears flawed in a number of repects. Nevertheless, it was a notable pioneering study that would lead the way for many more selection studies in laboratories of comparative psychology. Tryon began his selection study in 1927 (see Tryon, 1940). When Burlingame (1927) reviewed the available literature on the effects of heredity of behavior in animals, she was able to find just twelve studies—more than half of them by psychologists. Meanwhile McDougall (1927) was attempting to demonstrate the genetic transmission of acquired traits.

Behavioral Development

Studies of behavioral development continued. Working under Lashley, Charles Bird (1925, 1926) completed two studies of the development of pecking in young chicks. Bird attempted to dissociate maturation from practice during the first three days of life and emphasized the importance of maturational factors. Moseley (1925) conducted a similar study. McDougall and McDougall (1927) reported observations suggesting that a kitten may have killed mice instinctively. Griffith (1920) believed that rats' reponses to cats are instinctive.

Various pioneering studies of the development of reproductive behavior were completed in the 1920s. Stone (1922) completed a major study of the sexual behavior in rats, part of which dealt with development. The first complete copulations were observed at sixty-four days of age. Stone (1924a) analyzed the effect of defective diets on the development of sexual behavior in rats. In his study of the development of copulatory behavior in apes, Bingham (1928) emphasized the role of experience and copulatory play. Working under Yerkes at Yale, Chauncy McKinley Louttit (1929a) studied the ontogeny of sexual behavior in guinea pigs. He concluded that maturation was more important than experience.

Probably the most significant event of the decade in the study of development was the publication of Leonard Carmichael's three studies (1926, 1927, 1928) of the development of motor patterns in the embryos of frogs and salamanders. By rearing the embryos under the anesthetic, chloretone, Carmichael eliminated all motor movement and presumably reduced sensory input. When the drug was removed, the experimental

Leonard Carmichael, 1898–1973.
*Smithsonian Institution photograph No. 76-17992,
courtesy of the Smithsonian Institution.*

animals swam with the same coordination and vigor as control animals
that had been permitted to swim throughout the period. The two sets of
follow-up observations confirmed the result. Carmichael (1926, 57) concluded
after discussing the proposals of Kuo, "It seems to the writer that the
facts observed cannot be explained without any reference to heredity."
Carmichael (1928, 259) noted that "heredity and environment are
interdependently involved in the perfection of behavior." Later he wrote,
"At the time, the results of these experiments surprised me and almost
shocked me. They did not support my then strongly held belief in the
determining influence of the environment at every stage in the growth of
behavior" (1967, 37).

Reproductive Behavior

There were considerable advances in the study of reproductive behavior during the decade. Stone's study (1922) is a classic. Stone wanted to study the natural behavior of animals. However, he wanted to do so under conditions that would permit the collection of systematic data and the manipulation of variables in a controlled way. Copulatory behavior in rats appeared to be an ideal focus for study. He wrote:

> Interest is shifting . . . [to] defining units of response and analyzing the stimuli by which they are activated . . . . Investigations of congenital behavior have not been sufficiently intensive to give a complete account of either the overt patterns of activity or the activating stimuli . . . . For this reason there is need, at the present time, of comprehensive studies of fundamental types of native behavior . . . to ascertain the life histories of both the constituent elements and the patterns as wholes. (1922, 95)

Stone's study was a comprehensive one, including basic descriptive data, developmental considerations, and an analysis of the sensory regulation of copulatory behavior. Stone (1923) followed up the analysis of sensory control with more refined methods. He reported (1924b) the occurrence of "female" behavior in male rats and thus initiated a long sequence of studies of the occurrence of male behavior in females and female behavior in males. He also analyzed the retention of copulatory behavior in male rats after castration (1927b). Sturman-Hulbe and Stone (1929) studied the maternal behavior of rats, including nest building, behavior associated with parturition, and the effects of various manipulations.

Guniea pigs first became popular subjects for the study of reproductive behavior during the 1920s with the work of Avery (1925) and Louttit (1927, 1929a, 1929b). Louttit's analyses included study of the description, development, and modification of sexual behavior. Progress was also made in the study of primate reproductive behavior, as will be noted below.

Individual Behavioral Patterns

Although there is some overlap among categories, it is sometimes useful to divide behavioral patterns into those generally displayed by the individual animal, reproductive behavior, and social behavior (see Dewsbury, 1978a). The Columbia group made several advances in the study of individual behavior. Warner (1928) presented a detailed analysis of the facts and theories of bird flight. The various forms of flight were compared and contrasted.

Warden and Warner (1928) studied the bases of an ability to respond to verbal stimuli in a German Shepherd dog. "Fellow" was "widely known on stage and screen" and is pictured in the frontpiece. Warden and Warner considered the sensory capacity and intelligence of Fellow and other dogs. They warned, "The attitude of the modern comparative psychologist is one of healthy skepticism toward supposed cases of animal genius and human-like levels of animal intelligence" (1928, 1). Times had changed since Romanes. The authors were cautious in their conclusion "that the dog has learned to associate certain sounds, rather than words in the human sense, with the proper objects and commands" (1928, 19).

Elaine Kinder (1927), a student of Richter, studied the effects of age, reproductive condition, and temperature on nest building in rats.

Stone (1927, 36) reviewed recent research on studies of "native or *fundamentally* native behavior in vertebrates," including behavioral development, appetites, hibernation, migration, and reproductive behavior.

Sensory Systems

The study of sensory and perceptual processes continued throughout the decade. Representative interests include those in color vision in dogs, cats, and raccoons (Gregg et al., 1929) and in the discrimination of brightness by ring doves (Warden and Rowley, 1929). Warden and Baar (1929) demonstrated a Müller-Lyer illusion effect in ring doves.

Learning

Several notable learning studies appeared during the decade. Norman R. F. Maier (1929) published his first study of reasoning in white rats. T. C. Schneirla published his first study of learning and orientation in ants in 1929. The numerous studies of primate learning will be discussed in the next section. H. S. Liddell (1925, 1926) described procedures and results of studies of both classical conditioning and maze learning in sheep and goats. Donald K. Adams (1929) studied cats in a variety of patterned-string, delayed-response, and puzzle-box problems. Adams maintained that the existence of higher mental processes can be inferred from behavior (1928, 1929). He believed that his results yielded conclusions closer to those of Hobhouse than to those of Thorndike and that cats possess "practical ideas" in the sense of Hobhouse.

Primatology

The study of primate behavior was somewhat quiescent during the first part of the decade. Shepherd (1923) published a study of a chimpanzee and an orangutan at the National Zoo in Washington, D.C. Köhler's *The*

Mentality of Apes was finally published in English translation in 1925. O. L. Tinklepaugh (1920), working at the University of California, Berkeley, completed a study of problem solving in four macaques.

The situation changed with the return of the energetic Robert Yerkes to the academic world in 1924. Yerkes had always made great use of any opportunities to study primates. He had earlier studied Hamilton's collection in California and then converted the family's summer farm in New Hampshire into the "Franklin Field Station" (Yerkes, 1914). Prior to World War I, Yerkes had corresponded with a Madam Rosalia Abreu, of Havana, Cuba, the first person reported to manage the conception and birth of a chimpanzee in the Western Hemisphere. After the war Madam Abreu invited Yerkes to visit. After an initial trip he decided that a full-scale investigation of Madam Abreu's animals would be useful. During the summer of 1924, Yerkes and three assistants spent several weeks in Havana studying Madam Abreu's colony. One result was Yerkes's *Almost Human* (1925). Yerkes wrote:

> Naturalistic observations and laboratory experiments have each their peculiar values . . . the person, whether layman or scientist, who depends wholly on rigidly controlled laboratory studies for his knowledge of the anthropoid apes or of man is naive indeed, and to be pitied rather than abused. (1925, xv)

> In studying the primates, the sympathetic attitude, patience, and leisureliness of the naturalist should be combined with the critical attitude and demand for rigid checks and controls which are characteristic of the experimentalist. (1925, 103)

Madam Abreu's collection included marmosets, various New World monkeys, macaques, mangabeys, baboons, mandrills, black apes, one gibbon, three organutans, and fourteen chimpanzees. Yerkes and his associates studied intelligence, communication, emotional behavior, and the maintenance of the primates.

As another example of Yerkes's skill in developing opportunities to study primate behavior, he arranged to spend six to eight weeks each winter for three years in Sarasota, Florida, studying the female mountain gorilla, Congo, who belonged to the Ringling Brothers Circus (1927a, 1927b, 1928). Yerkes was able to travel to Africa in 1929.

In 1929 Robert and Ada Yerkes published *The Great Apes: A Study of Anthropoid Life*. The volume is a comprehensive survey of the habits, life histories, nervous systems, social behavior, and many other behavioral patterns in gibbons, orangutans, chimpanzees, and gorillas.

H. C. Bingham, an associate of Yerkes, published "Sex Development in Apes" in 1928 and two studies of box-stacking in chimpanzees (1929a, 1929b). Bingham (1927) studied parental play in chimpanzees.

Field Studies

The decade was a period of dormancy for comparative psychologists doing field studies. Near the end of the decade, however, Yerkes's organizational skills enabled his associates to embark on two historic trips to conduct field studies of primate behavior. On June 7, 1929, Bingham sailed for the Congo and a study of gorilla behavior; on December 26 Henry Nissen sailed for French Guinea and a study of chimpanzees. Yerkes was back! The age of scientific field studies was begun and probably owes more to Robert M. Yerkes than to any other single individual.

Conclusion

It had been a decade of turmoil, as in the controversies over beaviorism and instinct. World War I and other events slowed progress, especially during the first half of the decade. By the end of the decade, however, Yerkes was back and at full speed. By 1927 ten more unversities had added courses in comparative psychology, and nine more had started research laboratories in the area (Warden and Warner, 1927). A new generation of comparative psychologists was either preparing to begin to or beginning to develop the field in new and exciting ways. Comparative psychology was again healthy and growing.

1930-1939: A NEW GENERATION

In the opinion of many, including many of those who forged the history of comparative psychology, the thirties lie in the midst of a period of progressive decline. Misiak and Sexton (1966) see it as a period during which clinical psychology developed and the fields of psychology became progressively more specialized. The thirties was a decade in which the grand learning theories were first conceived; it becomes important in this decade to differentiate what I am calling "comparative psychology" from the rest of "animal psychology," which became dominated by learning theories in the 1940s.

I view the thirties as an outstanding decade in comparative psychology. Yerkes was in full gear and would soon get his Florida primate facility. A new generation of younger comparative psychologists had either just completed graduate school or would do so in the decade. This new generation would lead a resurgence of activity with foci in fieldwork, behavioral development, behavior genetics, comparative sensory systems, and reproductive behavior. The new generation would be more effective at launching long-term, stable research programs. New textbooks would appear. Perhaps most important of all, the new generation would be more effective than the old at replicating themselves, albeit with mutations. As a result of their own teaching skills, the burst of population growth, and improved funding, these comparative psychologists would train an unprecedented number of fine younger students. In this way they appear to have ensured the healthy status of comparative psychology for some time to come.

Comparative Psychologists in 1930

Yerkes, Stone, Lashley, and Warden were the leading figures in comparative psychology in 1930. Yerkes had returned from Europe and was busy with the development of the Orange Park facility and the development of a primate-research program that would bear great fruit during the decade. Lashley was at the University of Chicago; he would move to Harvard in 1935. Stone was firmly entrenched at Stanford as was Warden at Columbia.

Meanwhile Kuo had returned to China after receiving his doctoral degree in 1923. Political instability created several interruptions of his efforts at a sustained research program (see Gottlieb, 1972). Carmichael was active at Brown; he would become a dean at the University of Rochester in 1936 and president of Tufts in 1938. In 1927 McDougall had moved from Harvard to Duke, where he would work not only on the inheritance of acquired traits but on psychical research as well.

But it was the new contingent of comparative psychologists that created much of the excitement in the thirties. T. C. Schnierla was attracted to psychology and the study of ants, as both an undergraduate and graduate student at Michigan, by the venerable John F. Shepard. He received a Sc.D. in 1928; his research was on learning and orientation in ants. He then moved to New York University. In 1930 Schneirla spent a year as a National Research Council Fellow in Lashley's laboratory at Chicago. Norman R. F. Maier received a Ph.D. under Shepard in 1928 and spent time in the late twenties at the University of Berlin and Long Island University. His friendship with Schneirla would develop as he too was an NRC Fellow at Chicago. Maier would then return to the University of Michigan. After receiving his doctorate from Warden in 1929, Nissen joined Yerkes at Yale. O. L. Tinklepaugh, a 1927 California Ph.D., and Bingham, a 1923 Ph.D. of Johns Hopkins, were already there. Josephine Ball, who had worked in Lashley's laboratory as an undergraduate, completed her degree at Berkeley in 1929. Winthrop N. Kellogg completed a Ph.D. under Robert Woodworth at Columbia in 1929 and joined the faculty of his undergraduate institution, Indiana University. He was a Social Science Research Council Fellow at the Yale Laboratory in 1931-1932.

Henry W. Nissen, 1901-1958.
Photograph courtesy of the
National Acadamy of Sciences.

An equally prominent cadre of scientists would complete graudate school in the financially troubled 1930s. Harry F. Harlow completed his degree with Stone at Stanford in 1930 and moved directly to the University of Wisconsin. Stone followed that up when C. Ray Carpenter completed graduate study at Stanford two years later. Carpenter moved to the Yale laboratories as a National Research Council Fellow. He apparently was assigned the task of doing his first primate field study; Carpenter would take it from there. He moved to Bard College of Columbia in 1934 and Penn State in 1940. Frank A. Beach did not take his first psychology course until the 1930/31 academic year at Kansas State Teachers College in Emporia, where he was an English major. Beach completed his thesis work at the University of Chicago in 1936 (after several false starts) and moved to Harvard to work with Lashley for a year. Beach would move to the American Museum of Natural History in New York in 1937 and complete Ph.D. oral examinations at Chicago in 1940.

Although not really a comparative psychologist, I must include B. F. Skinner who completed graduate study at Harvard in 1931. D. O. Hebb completed a Ph.D. under Lashley at Harvard in 1936; Clifford T. Morgan at Rochester in 1939. Kenneth Spence, David Krech, A. H. Maslow, Robert Tryon, Calvin Hall, and Meredith Crawford, all of whom contributed to the discipline, appeared in this period.

The maturation of this generation of comparative psychologists in a

Harry F. Harlow, 1905–1981.
Photograph courtesy of the
Department of Psychology, University of Wisconsin.

relatively short period of time was to lead to the advances of the thirties
and ensure survival in the forties.

Facilities

The major advance of the period in the availability of research facilities
related to Yerkes and the Yale laboratories. Fortunately, the history of
the founding of the Yerkes Laboratories is well documented (Gray, 1955;
Hahn, 1971; Yerkes, 1932*b*, 1943*b*). Yerkes viewed his operation as three
pronged with bases in New Haven, Orange Park, and in overseas field
research. The seeds of the Orange Park operation go back to Yerkes's
paper in *Science* (1916*b*), calling for such a facility. A two-hundred acre

tract of land was selected in Orange Park, Florida, about fifteen miles south of Jacksonville. The Rockefeller Foundation provided funds, and the buildings were completed and turned over to Yale on June 9, 1930. Four chimps moved in from Yale the next day, and the first birth occurred on September 11. By 1941 there would be forty-five chimps at Orange Park—the largest collection in the world. The facility was named in honor of Yerkes in 1942. Some researchers would also work at the nearby marine facility at Marineland. Maslow (1936) would study primates in a zoo; Cooper (1942) studied lions under the seminatural conditions of a lion park. Thus psychologists could be found in the field, in zoos, in animal parks, and museums—as well as on the more traditional university campuses.

Field Research

Nissen's report of his field study of chimpanzees appeared in 1931. He had made three trips of ten to thirty-three days each into the field and spent the intervening periods in Pastoria. Nissen's report includes descriptions of the area, social organization, activity distribution, nests, feeding, and social behavior of chimpanzees. Bingham's report on gorillas appeared in 1932. Like Nissen, he reported on a wide range of aspects of primate biology, including feeding, nesting, and social behavior. W. C. Allee (1933, 370) noted, "At last such field studies have been put on a sound basis which should result in the hunting of information rather than of specimens." The results of these two trips appear somewhat incomplete by contemporary standards. The studies were important, however, because they extended the Yerkes program beyond Yale, Orange Park, New Hampshire, Madam Abreu's, California, and the Ringling Brothers's Circus, and initiated an era of primate fieldwork.

The story of Carpenter's work is detailed by Price (1968). Working out of the Yale laboratories, Carpenter started his career of monkey watching on December 25, 1931, on Barro Colorado, an island in Gatun Lake in what was then the Panama Canal Zone. It was Carpenter's work that would set a new standard for completeness, accuracy, and detail, and it was Carpenter who would become the major driving force behind primate field biology (see DeVore, 1965). In his report of his field study of howler monkeys on Barro Colorado, Carpenter (1934) reported on the motor patterns, territoriality, social organization, and general ecology of howlers. Later a film he made would introduce many students to the howlers of Barro Colorado. Carpenter would be a leader in the field of educational films and television. Carpenter (1935) also reported on the behavior of red spider monkeys in western Panama.

The project that Carpenter regarded as his most productive (Price,

C. Ray Carpenter, 1905–1975.
Photograph courtesy of the Pennsylvania State University.

1969) entailed the collection of a hundred rhesus macaques from Southeast Asia for release on Cayo Santiago Island near Puerto Rico in 1938. The original plan was to establish a colony of gibbons in the New World, but the presence of gibbons proved incompatible with that of humans when the wives of two scientists were attacked and bitten (Windle, 1980). The colony is thriving today and has been the target of many studies of rhesus behavior (see Windle, 1980). Carpenter spent much of 1938 and 1939 observing the monkeys.

In the summer of 1932, Schneirla traveled to Barro Colorado to begin his career as a field psychologist studying the behavior of ants. He would make a total of eight trips to Barro Colorado, typically for about six months at a time, and a total of at least fifteen major field trips to Panama, the Phillipines, Thailand, southwestern United States, and elsewhere. Schneirla (1938) reported the results of his third trip to Barro Colorado. He had already solved his basic research problem of finding the immediate cause underlying the alternation of army ant colonies between

T. C. Schnierla, 1902–1968.
Photograph courtesy of Gilbert Gottlieb.

migratory and nonmigratory phases. The key lay in the status of the larval brood. An active brood stimulates raids and migration; a passive brood decreases the activity of workers. Schneirla noted: "Only in consequence of detailed observational and experimental study may we hope to work out the causal factors which underlie the characteristic behavior of a given animal; a self-evident rule which is frequently ignored by impatient theorists" (1938, 53).

Textbooks

Margaret Floy Washburn's *The Animal Mind* was published in 1908, with subsequent editions in 1917, 1926, and 1936. The book "served as the standard comparative psychology text for the next twenty-five years"

(Zusne, 1975, 296). That changed in the 1930s as the field produced the first new textbooks in a generation. F. A. Moss edited *Comparative Psychology* for Prentice-Hall in 1934. The book was an edited volume with a total of fifteen chapters contributed by twelve authors. It opened with a chapter by Throndike entitled "Why Study Animal Psychology?" This was followed by chapters on history (R. H. Waters); maturation and "instinctive" functions (Stone); motivation (Stone); drugs and internal secretions (Moss); and sensory systems (D. M. Purdy): There were six chapters on various aspects of learning (P. E. Fields, S. I. Franz, H. S. Liddell, W. T. Heron, and E. C. Tolman). The book concluded with a chapter on individual differences by Tryon and chapters on social psychology and "gifted" animals by Tinklepaugh.

Maier and Schneirla (1935) collaborated on *Principles of Animal Psychology*. It was to become a classic, reissued in paperback form in 1964. The first part of the book consists of a taxon-by-taxon treatment of the behavior of nonmammalian species. The parallel organization of the chapters and the summary tables make the material easy to follow. Part II includes chapters on natively determined behavior, reactions to stimuli, and neural mechanisms. Part III concerns learned behavior in mammals. The authors appear to have written for the Senator Proxmires of the day:

> When a science has matured in its theories intelligent prediction of further advances is possible. It is then that science may make a distinct social contribution . . . . The emphasis of practical application at the expense of theoretical contributions is the long route to scientific progress and therefore to social progress. . . . Unless the investigation has been planned upon the broad basis of theoretical understanding the results are almost certain to have a very limited scope of application. (1935, 6)

The third major text was a three-volume work, *Comparative Psychology: A Comprehensive Treatise* by C. J. Warden, T. N. Jenkins, and L. H. Warner. Volume 1 appeared in 1935 and included material on history (see Warden, 1928) and a variety of general biological and other foundation material. Volume III, dealing with vertebrates, was published in 1936 and contains six chapters, one each on Pisces, Amphibia, Reptilia, Aves, Mammalia, and Primates. Volume II, dealing with plants and invertebrates, was not published until 1940. It too was organized taxon by taxon. In the introductory volume the authors noted, "If comparative psychology is to develop along natural science lines, a broad biological viewpoint must be adopted without reserve" (1935, 91). The book helped establish that viewpoint.

Norman L. Munn published *An Introduction to Animal Psychology* in 1933. Although the subtitle, "The Behavior of the Rat," was more

Norman R. F. Maier, 1900–1977.
Photograph courtesy of the
Archives of the History of American Psychology.

descriptive than the title, the book did contain a general review of unlearned behavior, general activity, sensory processes, and learning. W.C. Allee (1936) reviewed the Warden et al. book, writing:

> There is, however, nothing in print known to me which so completely and fairly appraises the historical combined with the general biological background of behavior . . . . To a much greater degree than usual, I find myself seriously impressed by the accuracy, skill and good judgment used in the selection and presentation of this material. (1933, 295, 298)

McAllister (1935) wrote a joint review of the books by Moss, Munn, and Warden et al. He criticized the lack of consistency in the edited volume of Moss. The struggle between the consistency of a single-authored work and the expertise available in a multiauthored book is still with us (see Chiszar, 1972).

Individual Behavioral Patterns

Comparative psychologists retained their interest in a variety of behavioral patterns displayed by the individual animal. Interest in orientation continued. Ralph Gundlach, a psychologist at the University of Washington, studied the sense of direction in cats and pigeons (1931) and conducted a field study of homing in pigeons (1932). He concluded that visual cues were necessary for homing in pigeons. Warner (1931a) reviewed the literature on orientation and homing in birds and contrasted four hypotheses for their explanation. Warner favored a learning-theory explanation.

It was during the 1930s that P. T. Young began a long series of studies of the control of ingestive behavior in rats and the factors that affect food preferences (for example, 1932). Although the study of food hoarding would not become prominent until the 1940s and 1950s, some research was conducted in the 1930s (for example, Wolfe, 1939).

There were some rather unusual studies as well. Walter Miles (1931) studied the behavior of fish in elevated water bridges connecting adjoining aquaria. He proposed that such water bridges might be useful "in this day of commercialized and polluted water courses" (1931, 131). More fun to complete must have been Stone's study of sex differences in running ability in thoroughbred horses (1935). Stone examined purchase prices, weight allowances, record running times, racing forms, and other sources of data and concluded that males are generally faster than females.

Interest in tropisms had not died completely within psychology as indicated by a paper coauthored by a young Harvard psychologist named B. F. Skinner (Barnes and Skinner 1930).

Reproductive Behavior

Stone's interest in the study of sexual behavior continued, as, for example, in a study conducted with the Columbia Obstruction Box (Stone et al., 1935). Stone (1932) studied the effects of castration in rabbits. Meanwhile Frank Beach published his first seven papers, dealing generally with sexual behavior, maternal behavior, and the effects of cortical lesions. Beach (1939) also studied maternal behavior in the pouchless marsupial *Marmosa cinera.*

Frank A. Beach, born 1911.
*Photograph by the author at his
sixty-fifth birthday celebration, 1976.*

Working at John Hopkins, Josephine Ball was an active researcher on reproductive behavior during this decade. In representative studies she found an increase in the sexual behavior of castrated male rats with estrin administration (1937*a*) and refined the methods of measuring sexual activity in female rats (1937*b*). By removing the uterus and vagina, Ball (1934*a*) tested the notion that afferent impulses from these structures were necessary for sexual activity; she found normal sexual behavior after the operations. In a landmark study, Ball (1934*b*) also demonstrated a quantitative relationship between the pseudopregnancy response in female rats and the amount of copulatory behavior in which they engaged. She manipulated both the amount of copulation and other factors. The results were important in beginning the process of revealing the extent to which male sexual behavior and female responsivity have evolved in conjunction with each other.

Carpenter studied reproductive behavior in much of his primate research. While still at Stanford, however, he had studied behavioral effects of gonadectomy in pigeons (1932, 1933). In the footnote to his first paper on pigeons the Duke University alumnus thanked Stone for his wise counsel and "Dr. William McDougall of Duke University for initially encouraging and assisting me in the study of social behavior of animals" (1933a, 25).

Securely established in Orange Park, Yerkes and his associates devoted much attention to the study of reproductive behavior. In his biography of Yerkes, Hilgard (1965) noted Yerkes's contributions to the study of sensory systems, habit formation, and problem solving. His contributions to the study of reproductive behavior surely belong next to Yerkes's other fine achievements. The study of sexual behavior in chimpanzees by Yerkes (1939) provides as clear and useful a description of mammalian copulatory behavior as can be found in any decade. Yerkes and Elder (1936) published a classic study of fluctuations in female receptivity correlated with the chimpanzee menstrual cycle. In conjunction with Carl G. Hartman, O. L. Tinklepaugh, who was an associate of Yerkes, published two papers on behavioral aspects of parturition (Hartman and Tinklepaugh, 1930; Tinklepaugh and Hartman, 1930).

In other representative research Causey and Waters (1936) studied parental carrying behavior in rats, including extended observations on 1,262 instances of carrying by female rats. In an extensive literature review, they considered a wide range of mammals including echidnas, marsupials, carnivores, and other species. Anderson (1936) studied the reliability of measures of copulatory behavior, and Bruner and Cunningham (1936) studied the effect of thymus extracts on female sexual behavior.

Social Behavior

The broad-based studies of the Yerkes group extended into the social behavior of chimpanzees as well as to other behavioral patterns. In a "naturalistic" study Yerkes (1936) analyzed social relationships in a chimpanzee "family" at Orange Park. Yerkes (1933a) recognized the importance of social grooming in maintaining social relationships in primates, noting that chimpanzee grooming "represents a genetically important pattern of primate social response, from which have evolved incomparably useful forms of social service; that it represents a step in the socialization of primate behavior . . ." (1933*a*, 21). Anticipating later field research by Geza Teleki, Nissen and Crawford (1936) reported the occurrence of food sharing among chimpanzees.

In Harlow's laboratory at Wisconsin, A. H. Maslow, who would later gain fame as a humanistic psychologist, conducted important early studies of the role of dominance in primate social behavior (Maslow, 1936; Maslow and Flanzbaum, 1936).

The other major development lay in the area of what might be called experimental animal social psychology. Social psychologist Robert B. Zajonc (1969) performed a service to comparative psychology when he organized and reprinted representative studies of social behavior conducted by comparative psycologists. In most studies experimental manipulations were conducted under laboratory conditions. The research shows how systematic laboratory work can be done even on behavior as complex as social interaction. The categories of behavior used by Zajonc include coaction, imitation, social stimulation and deprivation, affiliation, aggressive behavior, communication, cooperation, competition, and dominance and social organization. The book deserves more attention that it has received. Many of the foundation studies in this often-neglected area were done in th 1930s. The first study reprinted in the Zajonc book is that of H. F. Harlow (1932) on the social facilitation of feeding in albino rats. Satiated rats were found to resume feeding on introduction of a food-deprived rat that ate in their presence. Crawford and Spence (1939) studied imitation by chimpanzees in a discrimination-learning situation. Bayroff (1939) studied competition in a swimming response in white rats. Lepley (1937) analyzed the effects of social facilitation and competition on rats running to food in a straight alley. Although the presence of a second animal produced some facilitation, competition led to a deterioration in performance in the animal that consistently lost. Crawford (1937) studied cooperation among chimpanzees in the solution of box-pulling, two-cord, and double-handle problems. Carl Murchison (1935) studied the effect of food deprivation in chickens as a function of social dominance.

Behavior Genetics

The study of behavior genetics during this period was dominated, as one might expect, by studies relating to maze learning. Heron (1935) used the "Minnesota automatic maze" in a selection study. A classic was the long-term selection study of Robert C. Tryon, a student of Tolman. Tryon was especially careful to select a measuring procedure with good reliability (for example, 1930). The selection study was begun in 1927 and was a long-term effort; the most complete report is that of Tryon (1940). Using an artificial-selection procedure, Tryon was able to develop "maze-bright" and "maze-dull" lines of rats. Although it is unlikely that the lines differed from each other in a manner as implied by those titles (Searle, 1949), the response to selection for the phenotype as measured was clear cut. Ivan Krechevsky (1933) reported on the hereditary basis of "hypotheses" in Tryon's F_7-generation rats. The contemporary reader may not care for the maze-learning task as a basis for study. Nevertheless, these were important efforts in bringing the genetic basis of behavior under careful, quantitative, laboratory study.

E. A. Rundquist (1933), working under Heron at Minnesota, reported results of a successful selection study of spontaneous activity in rats and analyzed some of the correlated responses in his strains. Stone (1932b) followed up the earlier work of Yerkes, Coburn, and others on the inheritance of wildness and savageness in rats. Stone studied albino Wistar rats, yellow-hooded rats, wild animals, and some crosses. Animals were rated on an eleven-item scale; hiding behavior and maze learning also were studied. Consistent differences were found.

Meanwhile, McDougall (1938) published his fourth report on his Lamarckian experiment. The matter was, it is hoped, put to rest by Agar et al. (1954).

A genetic study on maze learning in mice, published by E. Vicari, drew a response from the young B. F. Skinner. Contrary to the understanding of many, Skinner consistently recognized the importance of genetic factors in behavior. He wrote, "The mere inheritance of behavioral traits is so patent that there would seem to be no necessity for an experimental demostration of the fact . . ." (1930, 344). Comparative psychologists were well on their way to demonstrating the importance of genetics as one factor in the development of behavior.

Development

Some studies of behavioral development were basically normative in nature. Working in the Yale laboratories, Jacobsen et al. (1932) studied physical development, physiological maturation, and behavioral development of chimpanzees, during their first year. Carmichael (1934; Warkentin and Carmichael, 1939) studied the development of the righting reflex in cats and rabbits. In work that anticipated the detailed studies of the 1970s, Tsai (1931) studied the sucking preferences of young rats, showing that there are decided nipple preferences.

Kuo published a number of developmental studies relating to the ontogeny of instincts. In studies of rat-cat interactions (for example, Kuo, 1930, 1938), he emphasized the complexity of developmental pathways. A kitten raised in the same cage as a rat would appear to become "attached" to it; raised with a litter mate and a cat, however, attachment was greater to the litter mate. In his studies of embryonic behavior as an antecedent of posthatching behavior (for example, 1932*a*, 1932*b*), Kuo again emphasized the complexity of development. He noted the number of behavioral patterns of the independent animal that could be seen in some form before hatching.

> Are we to accept . . . that the so-called instincts are really prenatally acquired responses?
> *Far from this!* Recently I have maintained that the concepts of both instinct and habit must be abandoned . . . . Behavior is neither prenatally nor postnatally acquired, nor is it hereditary. The development of behavior is an absolutely gradual and continuous process. (1932, 120)

Despite Kuo's use of italics and exclamation points, his point would be missed by many.

Cruze (1935) and Padilla (1935) returned to the problem of the maturation of pecking in chicks — a problem inherited from Spalding, Breed, Shepard and Breed, Bird, and Moseley. They found little effect of practice on pecking accuracy. Cruze concluded that learning is involved in the response of swallowing.

Kellogg (1931) studied fear in young rats, mice, and birds. He believed that fear of snakes is learned in the species studied.

Studies of early experience would become especially popular in the 1950s. The role of Lashley in initiating this approach is not always recognized. Lashley and Russell (1934) found that rats reared to the age of a hundred days in darkness showed indications of normal distance perception in a jumping task. Working under Lashley, Hebb (1937) studied aspects of discrimination learning by rats reared in darkness.

Among the more remarkable papers on behavioral development during the period is that on the acquisition of bird song by Herbert C. Sanborn (1932), an American psychologist who had studied in Germany. Sanborn first reviewed the earlier work, including that of W. E. D. Scott and E. Conradi. Sanborn hand-raised birds of various species, including orioles, cardinals, brown thrashers, robins, bluebirds, and goldfinches. Summer after summer, Sanborn raised a new group of birds. His conclusion would presage the later conclusions of Nottebohm and others who have worked with bird song:

> I am inclined to think that the problem in question has been perhaps oversimplified in the belief that birds *either* imitate *or* learn their songs . . . . Certain birds inherit their song in a fairly typical form in every species, while others are so gifted with the capacity for imitation that they add other notes and songs to their repertoire. (1932, 362)

Certainly the most widely cited developmental study of the period was that reported by W. N. Kellogg and L. A Kellogg (1933) in *The Ape and the Child*. In the summer of 1931, the Kelloggs obtained the loan of a young female chimpanzee, Gua, from the Yale laboratories. Gua was two and one-half months younger than the Kellogg's son, Donald, who had been born August 31, 1930. The Kelloggs would rear Donald and Gua, as if they were two human children, for a period of nine months. They were treated as similarly as possible, and detailed records were kept of the comparative development of the boy and the chimpanzee. Kellogg and Kellogg (1933) noted the similarities and differences between the two in favor of both Donald and Gua. Although Gua was younger than Donald, she was developmentally more advanced and progressed more rapidly in some respects. She showed little tendency to vocalize, however. Like other authors, Kellogg and Kellogg emphasized the importance of both hereditary and environmental influences in the development of behavior. *Time* [**21**(25) (1933), p. 44] called the work a "curious stunt."

Sensory Processes

Investigation of sensory processes continued as an active endeavor in comparative psychology; detailed discussion lies beyong the realm of emphasis of this book. Representative studies include color vision in chimpanzees by Grether (1939*a*, 1939*b*) and a review of color vision in fishes by Warner (1931*b*). Lashley remained active in this area, as in his fifteenth study of the mechanisms of vision in rats (1938*a*).

Motivation

Studies in the Columbia Obstruction Box were still prevalent in the 1930s, as exemplified in Stone's work, cited earlier, and Nissen's study (1930) of maternal behavior. Leuba (1931) criticized the method and its unrecognized sources of error. Disenchantment with the method would grow.

E. E. Anderson (1938) studied the interrelationship of forty-seven different measures relating to drives, including copulation, sand digging, maze learning, activity, and defecation.

Calvin S. Hall (1934) suggested that defecation and urination may provide a useful measure of individual differences in rats. The method would be much used in the future as the "open field" test in which both activity and defecation are measured.

Physiological Analyses

In his APA presidential address, Lashley (1930) reviewed some "Basic Neural Mechanisms in Behavior." He noted inadequacy of the theories of the day and attempted an alternative to reflex theory. In his APA presidential address, W. S. Hunter (1932) tried to distinguish psychology from other sciences—especially physiology.

There were many analyses of the neural and endocrine bases of behavior. Foci were the study of reproductive behavior, as discussed earlier, and learning.

In the chapter of his textbook dealing with the physiological bases of instinctive behavior, Morgan (1943) included material on perceptual factors, obstacle avoidance, migration, hoarding, hibernation, nest building, and maternal behavior. A whole chapter of the book was devoted to mating behavior. Morgan dedicated his book to Lashley and Richter.

Learning

Comparative psychologists continued to study learning in a variety of species including goldfish (Perkins and Wheeler, 1930); turtles (Tinklepaugh, 1932*a*); water snakes (Kellogg and Pomeroy, 1936); larval frogs (Munn, 1939); and cats (Carmichael and Marks, 1932). Liddell et al. (1934) compared conditioned motor reflexes in pigs, dogs, sheep, goats, and rabbits. Meanwhile Schneirla (for example, 1933) continued his investigation of learning in ants. Maier came into prominence with some studies of problem solving in rats using some original problems he devised (for example, 1938).

The study of learning in primates was emphasized in several laboratories. Harry Harlow's laboratory was quite active during this period, with much of the effort directed at the study of complex learning in various primates, some of which were housed in zoos (for example, Harlow et al. 1932; Maslow and Harlow, 1932). Analyses of learning in chimpanzees were stressed, as might be expected, in the Yale laboratories. Spence (1939), for example, studied multiple-choice problems, and Tinklepaugh (1932*b*) studied multiple delayed reactions. The two classical studies demonstrating the effectiveness of token rewards in learning were conducted in the Yale laboratories by Wolfe (1936) and Cowles (1937). In a study entitled "Pre-Linguistic Sign Behavior in Chimpanzee," Yerkes and Nissen (1939) noted the occasional occurrence of rudimentary symbolic processes in chimpanzees. They regarded delayed-response learning in the absence of spatial cues as particularly relevant.

Theory

The emphasis on polemical theoretical exchanges that characterized the 1920s had given way to a strong empirical trend in the 1930s. The theoretical activity that dominated animal psychology at this time related to learning theory, not to comparative psychology. There were a few developments of note, however. Schneirla (1939) introduced his approach-withdrawal theory of behavior. His view was that young organisms tend to approach mild sources of stimulation and withdraw from more intense stimuli. Schneirla believed that with this rather simple principle, he could integrate many phenomena that had been viewed as fundamentally different.

Yerkes (1933*b*) maintained that anthropocentrism and introspection were both important to psychology. He maintained that he himself, by contrast, was a psychobiologist and hence would have none of it.

Karl Lashley's presidential address to the Eastern Psychological Association, "Experimental Analysis of Instinctive Behavior" (1938*b*), is a classic. Lashley cited many examples in an effort to develop a modern view of instinct. He noted, "I am well aware that instincts were banished from psychology some years ago, but that purge seems to have failed of its chief objective" (1938*b*, 447). Lashley maintained that a model of instinct, free of "finalistic speculations," (p. 449) could be developed. As exemplars of instinctive behavior, in 1938 he cited courtship in birds, construction of spider webs, and von Frisch's studies of dances in honeybees. Lashley approached the ethological idea of a *Sollwert* when he wrote that nest-building behavior might be found to terminate when "it presents a satisfactory sensory pattern" (Lashley, 1938*b*, 450). He rejected the notion that instinctive behavior is controlled by relatively simple stimuli of the sort ethologists would later call "sign stimuli." "The accumulated observations suggest that instinctive behavior is dependent upon a complex of stimuli," wrote Lashley (1938*b*, 456). Lashley further rejected Dunlap's notion (1919) that although there may be instinctive responses, there are no instincts with what Lashley called "physiological coherence." Using evidence from the study of maternal behavior as being in opposition to such a view, Lashley noted, "There is good evidence that animals without previous experience may give specific reactions to biologically significant objects and that the recognition or discrimination of these objects may be quite precise." (1938*b*, 452). Twenty-five years later and many laboratory experiments after his studies in the Dry Tortugas, Lashley had not forgotten the lessons he had learned there. According to Thorpe (1979; 47), this paper "independently of Lorenz, but almost exactly at the same time, expressed almost every point of importance which came to characterize the ethological view of instinct."

Conclusion

The 1930s saw the arrival of an unprecedented crop of gifted young comparative psychologists, the development of new research facilities, the publication of major new textbooks, and advances in the study of a wide range of research problems. Comparative psychologists were studying primates, social behavior, reproductive behavior, and behavior genetics. Major efforts at field research were being made by workers such as Schneirla and Carpenter. The physiological analysis of instinctive behavior was beginning. Was this a period of decline?

1940-1949: A DECADE OF SUSTAINED VIGOR

The peaceful and affluent conditions during the approximate period from 1927 to 1932 had yielded a bumper crop of young comparative psychologists. The period of transition from the 1930s to the 1940s contrasts sharply with that from the 1920s to the 1930s. The thirties were a decade of economic depression. By the end of the decade and through the first half of the next, the world was at war. Probably due to the combined effect of troubled financial conditions, the call to military service, and the attractiveness of such areas of psychology as learning theory, there was a noticeable drop in the number of productive comparative psychologists entering the field during this period. A similar decrease had occurred when the world had last gone to war. World War I was devastating to comparative psychology. Although many believe that the forties was a period of decline in comparative psychology (for example, Schneirla, 1946a; Scott, 1973), I believe that the vigor that was generated in the 1930s was sustained in the 1940s. The forties saw fewer new faces and few developments whose roots could not have been seen in the thirties. However, that bumper crop of comparative psychologists had matured and, unlike their predecessors of the previous war, had somehow managed to sustain their level of activity. The forties, in my view then, was a period of relatively little innovation but of some major achievements that grew from the maturation and full flowering of the comparative psychologists who had arrived in the previous decade.

Practical Matters

The Yale laboratories continued to flourish during the 1940s. Many of the best comparative psychologists of the time passed through Orange Park at some time in their careers. Beginning July 1, 1942, the facility was operated jointly by Yale and Harvard with Lashley succeeding Yerkes as director and Nissen as assistant director. At this time the facility was renamed in honor of Yerkes. The accomplishments of the Orange Park facility were summarized by Yerkes (1943b) in *Chimpanzees: A Laboratory Colony*. The book includes a description of the facility and its development and a discussion of such aspects of chimpanzee behavior as sensory worlds, reproductive behavior, social behavior, learning, and higher processes.

The other major facility of the time was located at the American Museum of Natural History in New York City. Beach had joined the staff of the museum on leaving Lashley's laboratory. When G. K. Noble, head of the Department of Experimental Biology, died in 1940, there was an attempt by the administration of the museum to terminate the department. After many machinations and with the help of Yerkes and Lashley, the Department of Animal Behavior was founded, with Frank Beach as curator and departmental chairman, in 1942 (see Beach 1974). With Lester Aronson already on the staff, Beach persuaded Schneirla to join on a half-time basis. Schneirla succeeded Beach as curator when the latter moved to Yale in 1946. The museum would be influential in research and training with such names as Tobach, Lehrman, and Rosenblatt among the more prominent workers at various times.

Two events of the decade are of interest with respect to professional journals. Beginning in 1947, with Volume 40, the *Journal of Comparative Psychology* would become the *Journal of Comparative and Physiological Psychology*, with Stone as editor. The move has caused much discussion ever since, with the journal reverting to the former title in 1983. The second event will be discussed more fully in the next decade; in 1948 the international journal of animal behavior, *Behaviour,* was founded. There have always been psychologists among the board of editors; in fact, Beach and Carpenter served on the original board.

At the meeting of the APA in Detroit in 1947, it was decided that the Division of Physiological and Comparative Psychology would be merged with the Division of Experimental Psychology. The current Division of Physiological and Comparative Psychology was not established until 1964 (Scott, 1973).

The second edition of Moss's *Comparative Psychology* appeared in 1942. It was updated from 1934, but it was otherwise similar to the earlier edition. The final volume of the Warden, Jenkins, and Warner set, Volume II, appeared in 1940.

Comparative Psychologists

Yerkes became involved in government administration in World War II, as he had in World War I. Again he helped to coordinate the efforts of psychologists in the war effort (see Hilgard 1965). Although retired as emeritus professor in 1944, Yerkes remained in important force for years thereafter. Lashley moved to Orange Park, where he would remain as director of the Yerkes Laboratories until 1955. Stone continued at Stanford and became the editor of the *Journal of Comparative and Physiological Psychology*.

As noted earlier, Beach moved from the American Museum of Natrual History to Yale in 1946, and Schneirla assumed leadership of that institution's Department of Animal Behavior. Harlow maintained his active laboratory at Wisconsin while Nissen remained as assistant director in Orange Park. Carmichael continued some activity despite his administrative position at Tufts. Carpenter moved to Penn State in 1940.

Among the new faces were William S Verplanck, who completed his doctorate at Brown in 1941; M. E. Bitterman, who finished a Ph.D. at Cornell in 1945; and Eckhard Hess, who finished at Johns Hopkins in 1948.

Major Events

During the 1940s Carmichael and Stone followed Baldwin, Thorndike, Watson, Yerkes, Washburn, Dunlap, Köhler, Lashley, and Hunter as comparative psychologists elected president of the APA. In his presidential address, "The Experimental Embryology of Mind" (1941), Carmichael discussed the nature of the development of sensory and motor capacity in the fetus.

Stone's address, "Multiply, Vary, Let the Strongest Live and the Weakest Die—Charles Darwin" (1943) appears to have been forgotten generally but should be remembered as a classic in comparative psychology. Stone provided a general review of a century of progress in the study of evolution. He first discussed Lamarck and the problem of inheritance of acquired traits. Stone was critical of Lamarck, as might be expected. However, as he pointed out, Lamarck did a service to psychobiology by "according to behavioral evolution a place no less prominent than form and structure, an evaluation no one has rejected" (1943, 4). Stone noted that Lamarck had perceived that "no theory of descent could win adherents unless it gave a plausible account of the evolution of animal instincts" (1943, 4). Stone proceeded to a discussion of the evolution of instincts by natural selection. He noted that the term "instinct" has been greatly misused and has suffered from multiple definitions. Believing that recent attempts to banish the term had accomplished little, Stone said "Unfortunately, these attempts are working to our disadvantage by diverting the attention of young researchers from a wealth of behavioral phenomena which are known to have great, although not yet fully evaluated, theoretical and practical implications" (1943, 7). Stone next discussed variation, quoting extensively from Darwin. He then went on to discuss sexual selection and reproductive isolating mechanisms. His conclusion merits reprinting in full:

Behavioral Ecology

Animal psychologists have neglected the study and appraisal of this important topic. Therefore, I can think of no better attitude with which to indoctrinate our colleagues of tommorow who would make animal psychology their specialty than one of constant vigilance for opportunities to study the instincts as they are related to the subject of behavioral ecology. (1943, 24)

In this passage the prescient Stone anticipates the development of behavioral ecology as it occurred much later. It is worth noting that this was the APA presidential address, not a zoology colloquium, and that it was written in 1943. It has to be one of the gems of the literature in comparative psychology. Regrettably, the address was not delivered orally because of a cancellation of the year's scientific program at APA due to the war.

The "Conference on Genetics and Social Behavior" was held at the Jackson Laboratory, Bar Harbor, Maine, on September 10-13, 1946 (Scott, 1973, 1976). The purpose was to develop plans for a new research project headed by Scott and supported by the Rockefeller Foundation. Conferees included those who had demonstrated an interest in behavior genetics. The group photograph, published by Scott (1973) and reprinted here, shows the following comparative psychologists (as defined in Chapter 1): H. S. Liddell, C. P. Stone, R. M. Yerkes, F. A. Beach, T. C. Schneirla, C. T. Morgan, C. R. Carpenter, and C. S. Hall. This was one of several meetings that would bring psychologists, biologists, and others together, eventually leading to formal organization.

On April 10, 1947, the "Symposium on Heredity and Environment" was held in conjunction with the meetings of the Society of Experimental Psychologists at Princeton University. The papers were published in *Psychological Review.* Speakers included Beach, Carmichael, Lashley, Morgan, Stone, and Hunter. Beach (1947a) discussed apparent evolutionary changes in the control of mammalian mating behavior. He suggested that in the course of mammalian evolution, the cerebral cortex came to exert more influence, and lower structures and hormones, less influence, in the control of mating behavior. Beach noted the importance of both genetically determined neuromuscular factors and experiential influences.

In his contribution to the symposium, Carmichael (1947) considered the growth of sensory control before birth and urged a re-evaluation of the antihereditarian view he felt was dominant in recent psychology. Carmichael discussed the anti-instinct revolt of the 1920s and proposed that the pendulum had swung too far in the anti-instinct direction. He also noted that the research he reviewed showed how mistaken Watson and other anti-instinct theorists of the 1930s had been.

Morgan (1947) reviewed the literature on "The Hoarding Instinct,"

**Conference on Genetics and Social Behavior
held at the Jackson Laboratory in 1946.**
Front row (left to right): B. E. Ginsburg, N. E. Miller,
G. Murphy, C. E. Keller, H. S. Liddell, C. P. Stone,
L. V. Searle. *Second row:* D. Twitchell-Allen,
L. B. Murphy, E. M. Vicari, A. Gregg, R. M. Yerkes,
G. B. Lal, A. Scheinfeld, H. H. Strandskov, L. O'Neill.
Back row: W. M. Dawson, F. A. Beach, T. C. Schneirla,
C. T. Morgan, W. C. Young, R. C. Cook, J. L. Fuller,
H. J. Bagg, J. P. Scott, O. H. Mowrer, D. M. Levy,
E. A. Beeman, C. R. Carpenter, D. H. Dietz,
W. Kaempffert, C. S. Hall, G. W. Woolley,
M. A. Kennard, C. C. Little.
Photograph courtesy of J. P. Scott.

and discussed a variety of determinants of hoarding. He qualified his answer to the question of whether hoarding was learned or innate but noted, "Since it comes out spontaneously without training, it is plainly instinctive" (1947, 336).

Lashley (1947) produced another gem! The first paragraph of the paper demonstrated the ethological attitude displayed throughout Lashley's career. It consisted of a description of the webs of two crab-bellied spiders of the genus *Gasteracantha* that he had observed outside his window a few days previously. He noted:

The ornamented web perhaps the most beautiful of those spun by the orb-weavers, is as characteristic of the genus as is the body form, and the activities by which it is constructed are as certainly determined by heredity as is the body structure.

The student of animal behavior, who sees on every hand the genetic determination of such elaborate physical and behavioral patterns, is naturally prejudiced toward stressing hereditary factors in behavior. (1947, 325).

Lashley then considered species and individual differences in the anatomy of nervous systems and their genetic influences and the problem of relating function to structure.

Stone (1947, 342) considered four methods useful in "the experimental study of innate behavior as related to environmental factors." These included (1) uniform heredity and varied environment, (2) uniform environment and varied heredity, (3) genetic analysis, and (4) cytological analysis. He recommended the combined use of all four methods.

Hunter served as discussant. He said, "Historically, the interesting thing is that all of the speakers place their emphasis on heredity" (1947, 348). Hunter also mentioned that the anti-instinct revolt of the 1920s had all but purged the term from the psychological vocabulary. He then went on to make a very important point. Despite the anti-instinct revolt and the disappearance of the words *evolution* and *instinct* from the psychological vocabulary during this twenty-five-year period, *empirical research* on instinctive behavior had continued in comparative psychology. Hunter noted nine areas in which significant progress had been made during the preceding twenty-five-year period, including pecking behavior in chicks, hoarding and maternal behavior in rats, neural and hormonal factors in emotional behavior, patterns of sexual behavior, selective breeding of maze-bright and maze-dull rats, studies of genes and human intelligence, unlearned pattern organization in afferent neural centers, fetal and neonatal behavior, and the study of tropisms. As Hunter noted and as can be seen from the preceding historical review, comparative psychologists continued to study these forms of behavior and their genetic and environmental determinants throughout this period, as in other parts of the century. Other authors have not always understood the activities of comparative psychologists with the clarity displayed by Hunter—the same individual who had started studying delayed-response learning in 1913 and scuffled with Cole over raccoon behavior in the 1915 *Journal of Animal Behavior*.

Throughout these major events we see that the trend that had been continuous, but hidden, was emerging from the shadows. In the next decade the influence of ethology would interact with these trends already apparent in psychology.

Field Research

The 1940s saw the peak of field research by Carpenter (see Carpenter, 1964). The decade began with his "A Field Study in Siam of the Behavior and Social Relations of the Gibbon" (1940a). Carpenter's two papers on the sexual behavior of rhesus monkeys on Cayo Santiago (1942a, 1942b) are among the best descriptions of such behavior under such conditions and cover a broad range of behavioral patterns related to sex. I recently reprinted sections of the first of the papers as the first selection in a collection of classical papers in the study of sexual behavior (Dewsbury, 1981). Carpenter also made various efforts to integrate the empirical data in order to develop a coherent picture of primate ecology and social behavior. He (1940b) sounded an early warning regarding the conservation of rhesus macaques and the potential problems in availability for American laboratories.

Schneirla's field research on army ants continued. Schneirla and Piel (1948) summarized Schneirla's field research over the previous sixteen years for a *Scientific American* audience. In September of 1944, Schneirla traveled to the Tehuantepec region of Mexico to study the social behavior of army ants under conditions of the dry season. On this trip he developed tinnitus as a side-effect to an antimalaria drug; the disorder would never fully leave him (Tobach and Aronson, 1970).

Individual Behavior

Beach (1945a) reviewed the literature on "play" behavior and attempted to generate a useful definition. Schlosberg (1947) found little value in the concept of play.

McBride and Hebb (1948) conducted a study of the behavior of bottle-nosed dolphins at Marineland, Florida, that included individual behavior (sleep, play, fear), reproductive behavior, and social activities.

Much effort was directed during the 1940s at the study of hoarding (for example, Bindra, 1948; G. A. Miller, 1945; Morgan, 1947). Siegel and Stuckey (1947) delineated the diurnal patter of eating and drinking in rats.

Schneirla and Maier (1940) responded to criticism and reviewed developments in the study of locomotion and the control of behavior in starfish. French (1940a) studied the reactions of paramecia to chemical stimuli.

Reproductive Behavior

Beach was active during the decade, publishing both original research and synthetic papers. The original research related to the development of copulatory behavior, neural mechanisms, endocrine regulation, and stimulus factors. His analysis of the multisensory basis of sexual arousal revealed that no single sense is necessary for the initiation of sexual activity (Beach, 1942a); as more senses are eliminated, the less likely is the initiation of copulation. The paper is still cited frequently. Beach's skill in synthesizing and integrating material was at least as important as his original research. He wrote a number of papers bringing together diverse aspects of the control of reproductive behavior. Beach (1942b) reviewed central-nervous mechanisms and reproductive behavior in fish, amphibians, birds, and mammals. In reviewing physiological and psychological studies of sexual behavior in mammals, Beach (1947b) included some three hundred and thirty-five references.

Stone remained active, as with his study of the temporal relationships in copulatory behavior (Stone and Ferguson, 1940) and of precocial sexual behavior induced by hormone injections (Stone, 1940).

Many workers included information about reproductive behavior in their more general papers, as in the work of McBride and Hebb (1948) on dolphins, Yerkes (1943) on chimpanzees, and Carpenter on primates observed in the field.

Other researchers contributed to the growth of the area. J. P. Seward and G. H. Seward studies sexual and maternal behavior in guinea pigs (J. P. Seward, 1940; Seward and Seward, 1940), and Margaret Altmann (1941a) studied the sexual cycle of the sow. C. A. Reed not only studied copulatory behavior in hamsters but wrote a very useful comparative review paper describing the copulatory patterns of a variety of species of small mammals (Reed, 1946; Reed and Reed, 1946). Cooper (1944) described parturition in cats.

Social Behavior

In addition to the information on social behavior that came from studies conducted in the field and under seminatural conditions, experimental animal psychology flourished. Whereas the occurrence of imitation or observational learning in animals had been controversial in the days of Thorndike and Hobhouse, there were now many demonstrations of its occurrence, and interest shifted to understanding the processes involved. Herbert and Harsh (1944) studied imitation in cats and noted that observation of an animal learning provided more benefit than watching a skilled performer. Warden et al. (1940) studied imitation in two species of monkeys. Bayroff and Laird (1944) found that rats would learn to follow trained animals through a maze under some conditions.

Cooperative problem solving was studied in rats by Daniel (1942, 1943) and in chimpanzees by Crawford (1941). In Crawford's study two chimpanzees were first trained to choose a set of four colored panels in a predetermined order in order to obtain a food reward. They were then placed in separate cages so that each had access to two of the panels and the correct sequence had to be generated by the two chimpanzees working cooperatively. Not only did the two animals watch each other and respond appropriately, but they gestured to and virtually pushed the partner in the direction of the appropriate stimulus.

Studies of the effect of competition by Winslow (1940, 1944a, 1944b) revealed a variety of social interactions when either cats or rats had to perform in a competitive situation in which only one animal received the reward.

Dominance was studied by Ross and Scott (1947) and by workers at the Yerkes Laboratories (Crawford, 1942a, 1942b; Nowlis, 1941; Yerkes, 1940, 1941). Individual differences seemed more important than sex or other variables in determining dominance in chimpanzees. Hebb (1949a) devised a system to study the determinants of individual differences in the temperaments of chimpanzees.

Schneirla (1946b) reviewed a number of problems in the study of the biopsychology of social organization. He cautioned against facile generalization across widely divergent taxonomic groups or "levels." The concept of levels and the danger of generalizing across them would become a major theme in much of Schneirla's writing. Schneirla also cautioned against overreliance on the concept of dominance in explaining social organization.

Behavior Genetics

Tryon (1940) published a fairly complete summary of his long-term selection study and also summarized the results in the book edited by Moss (1942). The genetic basis of audiogenic seizures in mice became an active topic of research in the area and first became prominent in the 1940s (Hall, 1947; Witt and Hall, 1949). Finger (1943) studied the effect of heredity on audiogenic seizures in rats. Hall and Klein (1942) observed individual differences in aggression in rats and noted that those selectively bred for fearlessness in a strange situation were more aggressive than were rats selectively bred for timidity. Mowrer (1940) noted a hereditary basis for an abnormal "tumbler" mutation in pigeons. The Bar Harbor conference on genetics and social behavior was discussed earlier.

Development

G. H. Seward (1940) studied the determinants of filial behavior in suckling guinea pigs. Hall and Whiteman (1951) conducted a study of the effects of early experience in mice, reporting that mice exposed to intense noise early in life were more "emotionally unstable" as adults than were controls. Daniel and Smith (1947) analyzed the behavior in which newly hatched loggerhead turtles orient and move toward the sea rather than back toward the beaches on which they hatch. Dennis (1941) repeated Spalding's old study of effects of restraint during maturation on the ability of birds to fly—this time using buzzards as subjects. Although the rudiments of flight were present, movements were awkward, and Dennis stressed the importance of practice in the development of flying ability.

The Yerkes Laboratory workers continued their interest in development. Procedures used in studying chimpanzee development were described by Nissen (1942). The most widely cited developmental study of the period was begun in 1947 when Keith J. Hayes, having just received a Ph.D. from Stanford, moved to Orange Park and, together with his wife Cathy, reared chimpanzee Viki in their home. The Hayeses found much evidence of imitation during the six years of rearing Viki but were successful in teaching her to say only a few rudimentary words. The results were published in the next decade (Hayes, 1951; Hayes and Hayes, 1952).

Learning

The 1940s was a period in which learning theories were in their prime; the field of learning was dominated, for the most part, by the theories of Hull, Tolman, and Guthrie. Many of the best students of learning concentrated on theoretical questions. Nevertheless, there was some comparative research as well. It should be noted that in the primary empirical study related to his theory, Guthrie utilized cats in a puzzle box in a manner reminiscent in some respects of the method used by Thorndike (Guthrie and Horton, 1946). The authors provided many sketches from photographs of the exact topography of responses made as cats escaped from the confinement of the box by brushing a vertical stick.

French (1940b) reported evidence of an apparently learned response in paramecia escaping from a capillary tube. Learning was also studied in species such as minnows (Schiller, 1948a); octopuses (Schiller, 1948b); and ants (Schneirla, 1946c).

Perhaps the most notable studies of learned responses were conducted in the Harlow and Orange Park laboratories. Harlow published approximately thirty studies of primate learning, as well as a couple of papers on cats, during the decade. Many entailed physiological manipulations and their effects on problem solving. Andrew and Harlow (1948) studied the concept of generalized triangularity in macaques.

Perhaps the most significant of Harlow's papers in the decade was that "The Formation of Learning Sets" (1949). In that paper Harlow showed than when given several hundred different, but similar, problems, the macaques's ability to learn to make discriminations improved. In essence, they "learned to learn." Harlow also included data on children and on the effects of brain lesions in macaques. A wider audience became exposed to Harlow's work in a *Scientific American* paper, "Learning to Think" (Harlow and Kuenne, 1940).

Representative studies from the Yerkes group included the role of motivational factors in insightful problem solving (Birch, 1945); discrimination learning with delayed reward (Riesen, 1940); and simple discrimination learning in young chimpanzees (Gardner and Nissen, 1948). Gardner and Nissen compared the rate of learning simple discriminations in horses, cows, sheep, and human aments with their chimpanzee data. They supported the conclusion that "there is no regular increase in the rate of simple habit formation at progressively higher levels of the mammalian series" (1948, 163). The conclusion had been drawn before and would be drawn many times in the future. The search for species differences in learning ability and/or process focused on more complex problems, including Harlow's learning-set task, as few orderly differences could be generated with simple problems.

Physiological Bases of Behavior

Lashley remained as active as ever in studying the neural bases of behavior—particularly learned behavior and visual function. However, physiological psychology had suffered greatly under the effects of the same factors that had affected the growth of comparative psychology. The redevelopment of physiological psychology is generally dated as occurring in the 1940s. Particularly notable was Donald O. Hebb's *The Organization of Behavior* (1949b). Although ostensibly a neuropsychological theory, Hebb relied heavily on comparative research on development, perception, and related phenomena. In his section on instinct, for example, Hebb discussed Lorenz and Tinbergen on vacuum activities, Kinder on nest building, Beach on sexual behavior, and Daniel and Smith on orientation in loggerhead turtles.

Research on hormones and behavior was directed primarily at the study of reproductive behavior and was discussed under that subheading. The major event in this area was the publication of Beach's *Hormones and Behavior* in 1948. The book was a well-organized overview of the information available at the time. Beach considered gonadal cycles, effects of gonadal removal, and effects of hormone administration on males and females among fishes, amphibia, reptiles, birds, and mammals.

He discussed such behavioral patterns as migration, aggression, activity, learning, and emotion, as well as a variety of other issues relating to the interpretation of endocrine effects on behavior. Allee (1948) reviewed the book positively and heartily recommended it to both beginning and mature students.

Abnormal Behavior

Comparative psychologists of the 1940s developed an interest in behavioral patterns that may be labeled "abnormal" because they share certain characteristics with behavioral patterns so labeled in humans. It was an era of the study of convulsions, experimental neuroses, and regression (for example, Altmann, 1941b; Maier and Glaser, 1940a; Morgan and Waldman, 1940; O'Kelly, 1940).

Issues of Theory

There were a number of other events of interest in the decade that generally relate to matters of theory to one degree of another. Conflicts among psychologists and others regarding terminology occurred in the 1940s and anticipated the same debates that would occur with the advent of sociobiology in the 1970s. The controversies related to "angry mosquitoes" and "cruel ants." Beach (1945b) criticized a report in which possible effects of the sounds produced by the mosquitoes were interpreted using terms derived from human behavior. Beach noted, "Serious students of animal behavior have long been aware of the dangers of interpreting the reactions of a lower species in terms of psychological experiences characteristic of human beings" (1945b, 610).

The conflict between Schneirla and Laurence J. LaFleur was more prolonged (LaFleur, 1942, 1943, 1944; Schneirla, 1942, 1943). Schneirla was critical of several aspects of LaFleur's original report in which the latter described "antisocial" behavior in ants. Schneirla particularly criticized the use of anthropomorphic terminology, writing that the "time-worn pre-scientific habit should not be confused with the more serious attempts at comparative study encouraged by the Darwinian movement (1943, p. 245). LaFleur, for his part, felt that such terms could be linked "to types of behavior objectively verifiable in man and in many species of animals" (1943, p. 97). The similarities with the debates over sociobiology in the seventies are striking. The journal editor terminated the debate after each author had fired two shots.

C. P. Richter (1947) summarized his views on the nature of biological drives. He proposed that the body acts to maintain homeostasis, as discussed by earlier workers, and that behavioral mechanisms enter in when physiological mechanisms cannot maintain proper internal conditions.

Schneirla was active in various theoretical and related endeavors. In 1949 he wrote the first version of his article "Psychology, Comparative" for the *Encyclopaedia Britanica*. It went through revisions in 1959 and 1962 (see Schneirla, 1962) and became a standard reference source as an introduction to comparative psychology.

Schneirla (1949) elaborated his views on the concept of levels as related to the comparative study of behavior. He believed that fundamentally different processes may govern the behavior of widely divergent species and the labeling of such processes with simple names tends to obscure the very divergent underlying mechanisms that may be involved. He wrote, "The terms 'levels' is a convenient conceptual device for developing a systematic theory of different patterns of adaptation to the given conditions of existence in different organisms" (1949, 244). He cautioned against the use of anecdotalism, analogy, "purpose," and related concepts.

Lashley's "Persistent Problems in the Evolution of Mind" (1949) provided an excellent summary and overview of his position regarding comparative psychology, instinct, behavioral evolution, and related matters. He noted that instinctive behavior often can be plastic and adaptive. The importance of studying the sensory factors involved in triggering instinctive behavior was emphasized. A genetic determination of some specific types of behavior was noted. Lashley noted, "Evolutionary changes between marsupials and man have been almost exclusively an increase in the capacity to discover significant relations among the elements of a situation and to adjust behavior in terms of a maximum number of such relations (Lashley, 1949, 41)." As ever, Lashley's work was wide ranging.

Ethology

Toward the end of the decade ethology became apparent in comparative psychology. In 1948 the journal *Behaviour* was founded, with Beach and Carpenter on its editorial board. References to ethological work began to creep into American papers as in the citations of Tinbergen's work by Schneirla (1946a) and Hebb (1949b). The first International Ethological Conference was held in 1947; psychologists would later play a role in attending and in the administration of the U.S. Ethological Conference Committee. In July of 1949 the Society for Experimental Biology held a symposium on "Physiological Mechanisms in Animal Behavior" at Cambridge University (Danielli and Brown, 1950). Both Lashley and prominent ethologists (for example, Lorenz, Tinbergen, Baerends, and Thorpe) were present. The published book would increase the access of American workers to European ethology. The interaction would dominate the 1950s.

Conclusion

It had been a decade of war followed by peace, with a dearth of young comparative psychologists coupled with vigor by established workers. One cannot use the number of publications to gauge impact. Nevertheless, the numbers are impressive. Lashley published eighteen papers in the decade, and the aging Yerkes published twenty-three. Schneirla published thirty-one papers; Harlow, thirty-six; and Beach, forty-one. Many of these were significant and served either to increase the empirical foundation of comparative psychology or to solidify with integration and theory. It is true that comparative psychology could not match the rapid growth and prosperity that characterized learning theory during this time. Nevertheless, it remained very active. At the risk of repetition, it is difficult for me to see how this can be called a decade of "decline."

Chapter 4

Chronological History of Comparative Psychology, 1950 to the Present

1950-1959: THE ARRIVAL OF ETHOLOGY

Classical ethology developed among a group of European zoologists during the 1930s and 1940s. American comparative psychologists gradually became more aware of European ethology during this period. However, it was in the fifties that ethology and comparative psychology made full contact. Interactions were often strained. Comparative psychology in the 1950s was indeed dominated by the interaction of comparative psychologists with ethologists. That interaction triggered, among other thing, a second postwar anti-instinct revolt in American comparative psychology. The pyrotechnics over ethology and instinct tended to mask other major events occurring in comparative psychology at the time. Increased attention was being devoted to developmental studies—especially the effects of early experience in both mammals and birds. There was a minor revival of the study of invertebrates. Exploratory behavior attracted much attention. With increased federal funding for research, relative peace, and a sound economy, graduate students returned to comparative psychology. In many respects, then, the postwar 1950s showed some similarities to the postwar 1920s: Both were periods of transition.

Comparative Psychologists

Three generations of psychologists reached different landmark events in the 1950s. For the stalwarts who had built and maintained the field, it was death. Stone died in 1954 in Palo Alto; Hunter in the same year in Providence. Yerkes died in New Haven in 1956. In 1958 we lost Lashley (Poitiers, France), Nissen (Orange Park), and Watson (New York). The giants of the field—Hunter, Lashley, Nissen, Stone, Watson, and Yerkes—were all lost in a single decade.

Comparative psychology was sustained by that "bumper crop" of comparative psychologists of the twenties and thirties who had reached full scientific maturity. Beach moved from Yale to a new facility at the University of California, Berkeley, in 1958. Kellogg left Indiana for Florida State and research on dolphins in 1950. Others maintained stability: Schneirla in New York, Harlow in Wisconsin, and Carpenter at Penn State.

The major occurrence in comparative psychology during the 1950s, however, was the resumption of the production of young comparative psychologists. With the return of stable times, the leaders of comparative psychology began to attract, train, and stimulate the new generation necessary to assure continuation of the field. That process has continued to an unprecedented degree to the present. E. Tobach, D. S. Lehrman, and J. S. Rosenblatt came from Schneirla's laboratory in the 1950s. C. Rogers, R. G. Rabedeau, and R. E. Whalen came from Beach's laboratory. Harlow's students of the 1950s included R. A. Butler, G. M. French, G. E. McClearn, W. A. Mason, D. R. Meyer, K. M. Michels, A. M. Schrier, and J. M. Warren. Also arriving in the 1950s were such workers as M. E. Bitterman, J. Hirsch, J. V. McConnell, W. R. Thompson, and H. Moltz. Thus, although the fifties was a period of tragic loss, it was also a period that saw a multitude of new and important faces.

Interaction with Ethology

The growth of awareness by psychologists of ethological work was gradual. Much of ethology was published in European languages, and Americans are not noted for foreign language fluency. The founding of *Behaviour*, the publication of the Symposium of the Society for Experimental Biology (Danielli and Brown, 1950), and the beginning of various international meetings helped to bring comparative psychologists and ethologists together. In the 1950s more and more ethological work appeared in English. Lorenz's *King Solomon's Ring* appeared in 1952. Tinbergen's excellent synthesis, *The Study of Instinct,* was published in 1951; his *Curious Naturalists* appeared in 1958. In a very important development, Claire

Schiller (1957) published *Instinctive Behavior: The Development of a Modern Concept*. It included English translations of some of the classic papers of Lorenz, Tinbergen, and von Uexküll. There was an introduction by Lashley and a preface by Tinbergen.

Ethology arrived on American shores presenting a relatively unified front with a coherent theoretical view of behavior written by skilled naturalists who were also highly skilled and appealing writers. By contrast, American psychologists were vigorous and active but disorganized and fragmented—each going in his or her own direction. Instead of a coherent theory, there was controversy. Few writers could appeal to a broad audience with the style and substance displayed by Lorenz and Tinbergen.

Psychologists had a history of ambivalence toward the concept of instinct; they were greatly concerned with the details of the developmental processes that lead to behavior. Ethologists had many misconceptions about comparative psychology; often they saw little but late Watsonian behaviorism. This was understandable given the lack of a coherent source. However, it magnified and exacerbated the other differences between the groups. Psychologists were perceived as radical environmentalists, and their suggestions that environment was important to development appeared to confirm this perception. Psychologists tended to perceive the ethologists as fuzzy-thinking vitalists utterly lacking in an understanding of the scientific method. Ethologists sometimes thought of psychologists as interested in nothing but the immediate determinants of maze learning in rats. Both were wrong; mutual recognition of this fact occurred gradually.

The "shot heard round the world" of the controversy was Daniel Lehrman's "A Critique of Konrad Lorenz's Theory of Instinctive Behavior" (1953). Although toned down somewhat from his initial draft, the paper remained a stinging attack on Lorenz's theory. Lehrman was especially critical of Lorenz's views on development; he called them finalistic and preformationistic. He believed that preconceived ideas of the rigidity of the development of behavior would stifle future research. Whereas ethologists relied heavily on the "deprivation" experiment, wherein animals are reared in the absence of conspecifics or other important environmental input, Lehrman had reservations about the kinds of conclusions one could draw from such studies. He applied Schneirla's concept of levels and criticized the ethologists for merging processes in widely divergent organisms that may have very different underlying mechanisms with a single label. He believed that Lorenz relied too heavily on analogical reasoning. Lehrman had little use for Lorenz's views on motivation or of the view that there is a simple isomorphism between overt behavior and correlated neural events. As examples of the kind of developmental research needed, he cited Kuo's work on embryonic behavior, American research on maternal behavior, and Schneirla's various studies.

Daniel S. Lehrman, 1919–1972.
Photograph by Rae Silver, courtesy of Rae Silver.

Lehrman's critique seemed to sting ethology. Its major effect, however, appears to have been the baring in a clear manner of exactly what major differences needed further discussion and development. Over the ensuing years, ethologists and comparative psychologists were to meet face to face many times. Both fields would be changed by these meetings; in my judgment both were changed for the better.

One of the major meetings between ethologists and comparative psychologists occurred at a conference sponsored by the Macy Foundation and held in Ithaca, New York, September 26-30, 1954 (Schaffner, 1955). The published work is a transcript that shows the various interruptions and digressions, enabling the reader to follow the thinking and approaches of the participants in a manner not possible with neatly finished papers. Beach, Schneirla, and Lehrman led the psychological forces; Lorenz and Tinbergen represented ethology. There were also a variety of participants from related disciplines.

Tinbergen referred to Lehrman's paper as a "blast" and "sniping" but interpreted it as revealing real differences and showing a keen interest in ethological work. Although he felt that the pendulum had swung too far in the paper, Tinbergen accepted some of Lehrman's criticisms. He noted that "use of the term 'innate' can now be forgotten. I have accepted Dr. Lehrman's . . . criticism on this point, and I believe we can build constructively from here on" (in Schaffner, 1955, 111).

Although there were differences, there were common interests and goodwill on both sides. Beer (1975) relates a story according to which soon after publication of Lehrman's critique, Lehrman, Gerard Baerends, and Jan van Iersel met to discuss the paper in a Montreal hotel. The meeting began stiffly. Then van Iersel's attention was drawn by a bird singing in the garden. The three went off in pursuit of the hermit thrush and discovered a common bond in bird watching. When they returned to their discussion, the atmosphere had changed.

The interaction continues to this day. Contacts increased as American workers attended and participated in the organization of the International Ethological Conferences. In addition, a number of American workers studied in Europe. In 1953 an English-language ethology journal was founded, the *British Journal of Animal Behaviour*. In his opening editorial in the journal, W. H. Thorpe began, "Previous to Lorenz the idea of instinct, while accepted as an inescapable fact by field naturalists, was in general highly repugnant both to experimental zoologists and to psychologists" (1953, 3).

Some areas of empirical research became foci in the ethological debate. In discussing the complexities of behavioral development, Lehrman cited the work of Kuo on embryonic head movements as an antecedent of pecking in developing birds. Lehrman's statement was unfortunately interpreted as meaning that he thought pecking to be learned. Riess (1954) raised female rats deprived of experience in manipulating objects and found their nest-building behavior to be deficient. One might conclude that this shows nest building is not instinctive. However, Eibl-Eibesfeldt raised deprived rats and found nest building to be normal (see Eibl-Eibesfeldt and Kramer, 1958). The difference lay in the testing conditions; Riess had tested his females in an unfamiliar environment. Birch (1956) placed wide rubber collars around rats' necks to prevent them from licking themselves. Such treated females showed deficits in maternal behavior. Other researchers were unable to confirm this result, although the reasons why they could not are unclear.

Tinbergen (1948) described research wherein the behavior of young birds to a moving stimulus varied with the direction in which the stimulus was moved—an example of a "configurational stimulus." When pulled in one direction, the model resembled a goose and drew little response from the young birds. When moved the other way, it resembled a hawk and elicited escape responses. Hirsch et al. (1955, 280) tested the effect with domesticated chicks and found the hypothesis to be "untenable under controlled laboratory conditions." In his reply Tinbergen (1957) emphasized that Hirsch et al. had used domesticated animals and that the hypothesis might not hold for them. Tinbergen noted, *"Facts found in one species, or hypotheses formed about one species, simply cannot be disproved by testing another species"* (1957, 412). Hirsch (1957) replied, emphasizing that various qualifications regarding the generality of conclusions drawn from their results were cited in the Hirsch et al. paper. Melzack et al. (1959) conducted a similar experiment with mallard ducks and found influences of both heredity and environment. Gray (1966) later reviewed the entire history of the study of the innateness of antipredator responses from Spalding and Mills onward.

Clearly, some of the differences between ethologists and comparative psychologists of the time resulted from the ways in which they conducted and interpreted experiments and could not be readily resolved with a few additional data. Time and goodwill have healed most of the wounds.

The Second Postwar Anti-Instinct Revolt

Input from ethology triggered renewed consideration of the role of instinct in explaining behavior and elicited critical papers from, among others, Beach (1955), Hebb (1953), Schneirla (1956), and Verplanck (1955). Psychologists contended (1) that there are many environmental determinants of behavior, not just associative learning; (2) both genes and environment are necessary for all behavior; (3) only genes and cytoplasm, not behavior, are inherited; (4) the concept of instinct is difficult to define and must be defined by exclusion; (5) deprivation experiments cannot demonstrate innateness; (6) only *differences* between organisms can be explained on the basis of heredity; (7) different mechanisms may operate at different phyletic levels; and (8) premature categorization may choke off further research. According to Hebb, asking how much of a particular behavioral pattern is learned and how much innate "is exactly like asking how much of the area of a field is due to its length, how much to its width" (1953, 44).

Comparative psychologists remain hesitant in using the instinct construct. However, increasing numbers appear willing to use the term as long as it is recognized that important environmental antecedents may be necessary for the occurrence of the behavior. Instinctive patterns arise in the absence of *specific* learning. If the use of the instinct construct grows, we can look forward to a third anti-instinct revolt.

Self-Criticism

Ethologists were not alone in criticizing comparative psychologists during this period; the psychologists did a good job on themselves. For example, Beach's "The Snark was a Boojum" appeared in 1950 and received more discussion than had some of the earlier works of the genre. Schneirla (1952) published a critical evaluation of conceptual trends in comparative psychology and opened with a section entitled, "Have We a Comparative Psychology?" The process would continue in later decades.

Symposia

The decade saw an increase in the number of symposia functioning to bring together various scientists for discussion of controversial issues. The Macy Symposium has already been discussed. With support from the New York Zoological Society and the New York Academy of Sciences, J. P. Scott convened a conference on the "Methodology and Techniques for the Study of Animal Societies." Among the contributors were psychologists C. R. Carpenter, B. F. Riess, and T. C. Schneirla. The proceedings were edited by Scott (1950).

A second Bar Harbor conference at the Jackson Laboratory dealt with the "Effects of Early Experience on Mental Health" (see Scott, 1973, 1976). Psychologists H. S. Liddell, D. O. Hebb, S. Ross, L. Carmichael, W. T. James, J. McV. Hunt, C. S. Hall, R. L. Solomon, T. C. Schneirla, and F. A. Beach were among those present.

In April of 1952 the Florida Psychological Association brought together W. C Allee, H. W. Nissen, and Meyer Nimkoff for "A Re-Examination of the Concept of Instinct." The conference was interesting because it brought together a biologist, a psychologist, and a sociologist; it was published in *Psychological Review* (Allee, 1953; Nissen, 1953; Nimkoff, 1953). Particularly significant was the presence of Allee, who did much for the study of behavior, especially social behavior (see Schmidt, 1957). Nissen noted, "Many animals exhibit complex patterns of behavior, constant for the species and apparently unlearned, which need a name to set them off descriptively from other behaviors" (1953, 291). It is such a loose framework for instinct that has proven attractive to so many psychologists.

A unique cooperative venture between the Society for the Study of Evolution and the American Psychological Association began in 1953 with plans for conferences on behavior and evolution. Conferences were held in Harriman, New York, in April of 1955, and in Princeton, New Jersey, in April of 1956. The publication stemming from the conferences was edited by Anne Roe and George Gaylord Simpson (1958) and was entitled *Behavior and Evolution;* it became a classic. Beach, Nissen, Carpenter, Harlow, W. R. Thompson, and Roger Sperry, contributed valuable chapters. Other important chapters were contributed by Hinde and Tinbergen, Ernst Caspari, and Colin Pittendrigh. Pittendrigh (1958) used the term *teleonomy* to differentiate careful analyses of the adaptive significance of behavior from teleology; the two are often confused.

A conference on "Biological and Biochemical Bases of Behavior" (Harlow

Conference on the Effects of Early Experience on Mental Health, held at the Jackson Laboratory, 1951.
Front row (left to right): J. P. Scott, K. H. Pribram, H. S. Liddell, D. O. Hebb. *Second row:* P. Rabe, S. Ross, L. Carmichael, J. E. Anderson. *Third row:* J. Tee-van, W. T. James, J. L. Fuller, J. McV. Hunt, E. Fredericson, J. Antonitis, C. S. Hall, R. Morison, C. Henry. *Fourth row:* F. C. Evans, J. W. M. Whiting, A. J. Brodbeck, D. M. Levy, J. B. Calhoun, R. L. Solomon. *Back row:* J. A. King, T. C. Schneirla, J. C. Eberhart, F. A. Beach, P. V. Lemkau, P. F. D. Seitz. *Photograph courtesy of J. P. Scott.*

and Woolsey, 1958) was held in Madison, Wisconsin, and included contributions by Harlow, D. R. Meyer, Beach, Riesen, and Hebb. Comparative psychologists also participated significantly in the Nebraska Symposium on Motivation, held annually in Lincoln (for example, Beach, 1956; Schneirla, 1959*a*).

Publishing Events

Various other publishing events are worth noting. The third edition of the edited textbook, *Comparative Psychology,* appeared in 1951, this time edited by Stone. The format resembles the Moss volumes closely. Norman L. Munn's *Handbook of Psychological Research on the Rat* (1950) was an expansion of his 1933 text and is still a useful reference.

The *British Journal of Animal Behaviour* began in 1953. McConnell began the *Worm Runner's Digest* in 1959. It carried a delightful mix of comparative psychology and humor. In 1967 it split to become half *Digest* and half the *Journal of Biological Psychology*—allegedly because some scientists could not tell the humor from the science. Regrettably, publication of this delightful journal ceased in 1979.

In an effort to improve communication and reduce ambiguity, Verplanck (1957) published "A Glossary of Some Terms Used in the Objective Science of Behavior." The volume includes definitions of many terms, mainly from ethology, comparative psychology, and operant psychology.

The landmark publication of the decade in experimental psychology was S. S. Steven's *Handbook of Experimental Psychology* (1951), which was required reading for a large crop of graduate students in psychology for years. Featured were chapters by Carmichael (Ontogenetic Development); Hall (The Genetics of Behavior); Nissen (Phylogenetic Comparison); and Beach (Instinctive Behavior: Reproductive Activities).

Annual Review of Psychology

The *Annual Review of Psychology* began its annual evaluation of the various fields of psychology in 1950 with Stone as editor. A brief survey of the decade's chapters is illustrative of the impact of ethology and other trends in the 1950s. Hebb (1950) devoted just two and a half of his fifteen pages on "Animal and Physiological Psychology" to comparative studies. Deese and Morgan (1951) devoted most of their paper on "Comparative and Physiological Psychology" to physiological studies. They opined that comparative psychologists devote little attention to evolutionary theory and do not attempt to see relations between their data and comparative biological information. Deese and Morgan noted that they could not synthesize comparative psychological information because the field lacked an established framework. Nissen and Semmes (1952) reviewed comparative and physiological psychology and were more sanguine about the status of comparative psychology. Much of the comparative literature reviewed, however, was from European workers.

Hess opened his "Comparative Psychology" by noting, "This has been a good year for comparative psychology" (1953a, 239). He provided a balanced chapter noting progress in both comparative psychology and ethology. Russell's chapter (1954) on "Comparative Psychology" emphasized such topics as sensory processes, audiogenic seizures, effects of electroshock convulsions on behavior, and studies of conflict and behavior disorders. Meyer (1955) presented a balanced analysis of progress in the field but made some remarks about ethology that were challenged by his successor, Hess (1956). According to Bindra, "If American comparative psychologists have a fixation on the rat, the European ethologists are spreading their libido too thinly on too many species" (1957, 399). Bindra presented a balanced and moderate approach to instinctive behavior consistent with that of Nissen (1953). Bindra proposed that "the adjective 'instinctive' serves merely to identify this rough class of behavior, leaving open the question of the exact role of learning and other mechanisms in determining the specific behavior patterns" (1957, 401). Verplanck (1958) was more critical of comparative psychology than of ethology.

Despite several balanced presentations, the overall impression one gets from these papers is not overly favorable to comparative psychology. The intervals between successive chapters on comparative psychology in this publication have increased progressively since the 1950s.

Field Studies

After prolonged illness, Schneirla returned for more fieldwork on Barro Colorado in 1955. Carpenter completed a survey of howlers on Barro Colorado in 1959 (see Carpenter, 1962). Broadly trained in behavior at Cornell, Margaret Altmann began a program of field research on moose and elk (for example, 1952).

Individual Behavior

Much research continued in the context of motivational theory and dealing with eating and drinking behavior. Hoarding continued to be a popular topic and was studied in both rats (for example, Licklider and Licklider, 1950) and hamsters (Smith and Ross, 1950). Hess (1953b) analyzed the role of "shyness" in hoarding, and Ross et al. (1955) wrote a useful review of experimental studies of hoarding. Both Beach (1950) and Ross et al. (1955) emphasized the value of studying hoarding in a species of "natural " hoarders rather than with laboratory rats.

In 1954 Schneirla edited the proceedings of a conference on animal orientation; his contributions were systematic reviews of the status of orientation research in ants and mammals (1954a, 1954b).

Reproductive Behavior

The highlight of the decade in the study of reproductive behavior was the publication of Ford and Beach's *Patterns of Sexual Behavior* (1951).

As the combined work of an anthropologist and a comparative-physiological psychologist, the book is a broad survey of sexual behavior in both human and nonhuman animals. Material from both is blended in discussions of such material as types of sexual stimulation, self-stimulation, homosexuality, and female-fertility cycles.

The study of copulatory behavior in rats underwent a major shift in 1956 with the publication of descriptive papers by Beach and Jordan (1956) and Larsson (1956). After this time workers became more careful about discriminating mounts, intromissions, and ejaculations when studying copulatory behavior. Failure to do this can greatly affect the conclusions drawn from an experiment. After 1956 such studies would be rare. The study by Larsson, a Swedish psychologist, is especially notable as it is a comprehensive monograph including information on development and the effects of a variety of temporal manipulations on copulatory behavior. Such an experimental approach would dominate much of the research on copulatory behavior for the rest of the decade (for example, Beach and Whalen 1959).

The stimulus for many studies of copulatory behavior of the era was a theoretical model proposed by Beach (1956) and Beach and Jordan (1956). Building on earlier proposals, Beach hypothesized two processes regulating sexual behavior—an *arousal mechanism,* responsible for the initiation of behavior, and a *copulatory mechanism,* responsible for execution.

During this period biologist W. C. Young was building an important program of research on reproductive behavior in guinea pigs. A number of psychologists worked with Young during their training. Some of the best early behavior-genetic work was done with guinea pigs during this time (for example, Goy and Jakway, 1959).

Social Behavior

Several important review papers appeared in the 1950s. Thompson's and Carpenter's reviews in *Behavior and Evolution (*1958) found broad audiences and appreciable influence. Hebb and Thompson (1954) reviewed research on animals, with special attention directed to social behavior, in the *Handbook of Social Psychology.* This paper was important because it attempted to present research in comparative psychology to other psychologists in a positive, rather than the usual negative, light.

The decade saw a flurry of studies in experimental animal social psychology. Social facilitation was studied in eating by dogs by James (1953), in copulatory behavior of rats by Larsson (1956), and in learning by Angermeier et al. (1959). Hypothesized emotional reactions to the pain of other rats was studied by Church (1959). Smith and Hale (1959) used a conditioning procedure to modify the social rank of domestic fowl. Darby and Riopelle (1959) studied observational learning in rhesus monkeys. In the Darby-Riopelle study it was found that animals profit more from the errors of the performing animals than from the correct responses.

Behavior Genetics

A long-term program for the study of the behavior of the geneticist's "white rat," fruit flies, was begun in the 1950s by Jerry Hirsch. The program is especially significant because manipulations of genotype can be made with *Drosophila* that are not possible with mammalian species. It has therefore been possible to study gene-behavior relationships with a greater degree of precision than has been possible with mammals. The program is also significant as another instance of psychologists' studying invertebrates. The research represents a continuation of the Tolman-Tryon-Hirsch tradition. Hirsch and Tryon (1956) demonstrated the advantages of a procedure of mass screening with reliable individual measurement. They stressed the importance of reliable measurement in selection studies and demonstrated the advantages of quick tests that could be conducted with large numbers of animals. Hirsch and Boudreau (1958) completed a study of artificial selection for phototaxis in *Drosophila melanogaster,* and Hirsch (1959) used a ten-unit maze in the study of geotaxis.

Studies with mammals continued such as those of Stamm (1956) on hoarding in rats, Thompson (1953a) on exploratory behavior in "bright" and "dull" rats, and Lindzey (1951) on audiogenic-seizure susceptibility in inbred strains of mice.

Hall's chapter in the *Handbook of Experimental Psychology* (1951) provided major impetus for the growth of behavior genetics.

Development

The study of development showed more than the usual expansion during the decade and became a major field of investigation. Much attention was devoted to the study of early experience. The combination of the developmental tradition in comparative psychology, Freudian theory, ethological studies in imprinting, Hebb's theories, and social concerns converged to initiate a boom in research with a developmental orientation. Particularly influential was a review by Beach and Jaynes (1954) of the effects of early experience on sensory function, feeding, reproductive behavior, social behavior, temperament, and learning; they appear to have helped coalesce the dispersed literature into a major research focus.

Workers from the Yerkes Laboratories became especially interested in the role of restricted sensory input on sensory and perceptual function (for example, Riesen, 1958a; Riesen and Aarons, 1959; Nissen et al., 1951). Deficits in sensory-perceptual function were generally found to follow restricted experience in a given sensory modality. Effects of early experience on the response to pain by dogs were studied by Melzack and Scott (1957).

Many studies of early experience were directed at what may be labeled "temperament," as, for example, the occurrence of defecation and activity in an open field and other measures of "emotionality" and "activity." Examples are the work of Melzack (1954) and Thompson and Heron (1954). Levine (1957) found effects of early experience on drinking in rats.

The ethological influence stimulated a series of major research programs by laboratory psychologists on imprinting in fowl (for example, Hess, 1959; Jaynes, 1956; Moltz and Rosenblum, 1958). Another area of research on birds was the study of innate form preferences in young animals (for example, Fantz, 1957; Rheingold and Hess, 1957). Fantz completed his dissertation with Hess and then moved to Orange Park.

The results of the Hayes's studies with Viki, begun in the last decade, were published in the 1950s (for example, K. Hayes, 1950; C. Hayes, 1951; Hayes and Hayes, 1952).

During the 1950s Harlow's interests gradually shifted from neuropsychology and the study of learning to the study of social and reproductive behavior and the developmental influences on both. Harlow raised rhesus monkeys in the absence of their mothers but in the presence of inanimate surrogate mothers. In the 1950s he found that the young monkeys responded to the surrogate as they would to a live mother, clinging to it and going to it when stressed. The texture of the surrogate was found to be more important than whether or not the animal suckled from the particular object. This had implications for drive theories. Harlow's research was summarized in *Scientific American* (1959) and in his presidential address to APA (1958a). The thrust of the latter was the implications of the studies and of "contact comfort" for drive theory. Harlow had developed an entertaining writing and speaking style that was filled with quips and statements of double meaning. His presidential address even included poetry:

The Hippopotamus

This is the skin some babies feel
Replete with hippo love appeal.
Each contact, cuddle, push, and shove
Elicits tons of baby love.
(1958a, 677)

Schneirla (1957a) reviewed the concept of development in comparative psychology, emphasizing the importance of developmental analysis and his views on the implications of his levels concept for developmental studies.

Schiller (1952) reviewed the development of complex responses in primates. He noted that the motor components are often innate. Experiential factors were seen as especially important in determining the stimuli that evoke these patterns. Such naturally occurring behavioral sequences were viewed as extremely important in the performance of complex tasks such as manipulating sticks.

The growth of comparative developmental psychology during this period was masked to some degree by the overwhelming input of the ethologists. However, it was an important phenomenon in the history of comparative psyhology and should be recognized as such.

Sensory Function

As discussed earlier, much of the interest in the study of sensory function revolved around developmental questions. For example, Siegel (1953), working under Schneirla, studied visual deprivation in ring doves. Other sensory studies included Towe's study (1954) of figural equivalence in pigeons and Kellogg's study (1959) of size discrimination in bottle-nosed dolphins; Adler and Dalland's study (1959) on spectral thresholds in starlings; and Riley and Rosenzweig's study (1957) on echolocation in rats.

Learning

The 1950s saw a renaissance of interest in studies of learning in invertebrates. The studies that received most publicity were those of James V. McConnell and his associates on classical conditioning in flatworms (planarians). Thompson and McConnell (1955) reported the occurrence of classical conditioning using a light-shock paradigm. McConnell et al. (1959) cut flatworms in half and found that when heads regenerated a new tail and tails regenerated a new head, both showed retention. Many of McConnell's studies would become controversial.

Also controversial were Beatrice Gelber's studies of learning in paramecia. Gelber attempted to condition paramecia to approach a thin wire that was associated with food. She succeeded in demonstrating behavioral change in a variety of studies (for example, 1952). The interpretations of these behavioral modifications were debated hotly in the literature (for example, Gelber, 1957; Katz and Deterline, 1958; Jensen, 1957a, 1957b).

In my judgment, the issue was never resolved. Lepley and Rice (1951) studied spontaneous alternation in paramecia.

Although they received less publicity than the studies of flatworms and paramecia, comparative psychologists studied other species of invertebrates as well. These included studies of learning or spontaneous alternation in earthworms (Ratner and Miller, 1959; Robinson, 1953; Wayner and Zellner, 1958), mealworms (Grosslight and Ticknor, 1953), and octopuses (Sutherland, 1959).

Students of learning in fish included Cole and Caldwell (1956) and Munn (1958); M. E. Bitterman began a long-term program of comparative studies of learning with research on fish. In a much-cited paper, Bitterman et al. (1958) compared the performance of fish and rats in several situations.

Among students of learning in carnivores were Warren and Barron (1956) working with cats and Michels and Brown (1959) working with raccoons.

The study of primate learning continued, as with Warren's study (1959) of discrimination learning in rhesus monkeys and many other studies from Harlow's laboratory. The work of Paul Schiller, a Hungarian psychologist who has moved to the Yerkes Laboratories and who was killed in 1949, was published by C. H. Schiller (1957). P. H. Schiller (1957) interpreted much of the "insight" reported in chimpanzees as the outgrowth of naturally occurring play in these animals.

In his paper in the Roe and Simpson book, Harlow (1958*b*) reviewed the evolution of learning. He cautioned researchers about the difficulties of developing tasks with which to make meaningful comparisons of learning across species. He speculated on the adaptive significance of the ability to learn complex problems in nature. Harlow noted that there are certain problems that have been solved by primates and no other animals. In his most sweeping conclusion, Harlow proposed that all learning could be explained in terms of a single process that was common across species. He favored a "uniprocess inhibition theory" according to which ineffective responses are gradually eliminated. He noted a "fundamental unity of learning and the continuity of its developing complexity throughout phylogenesis" (1958*b*, 288). Harlow concluded, "There is no evidence of an intellectual gulf at any point, and there are no existing data that would justify the assumption that there is a greater gap between men and monkeys than there is between monkeys and their closest kin . . ." (1958*b*, 282).

Physiological Analyses

Physiological psychology grew considerably during the 1950s, and some of the research overlapped with the comparative approach. That reported in the volume edited by Harlow and Woolsey (1958) is representative. Lashley approached the end of a long career of looking for the basis of learning and, in a paper entitled "In Search of the Engram," concluded, "I sometimes feel . . . that the necessary conclusion is that learning just is not possible" (1950, 478).

It was during the 1950s that Lehrman began his influential research on endocrine and other determinants of reproductive behavior in ring doves (for example, Lehrman, 1958). Beach (1958) reviewed literature on the evolution of endocrine control of behavior and noted that there is little change in the nature of the hormones themselves across species; that is, the hormones of a bird are nearly identical chemically to those of a rat. What changes in evolution are the uses to which hormones are put. Thus injection of the same hormone into different animals can produce very different behavioral responses.

Motivation

Nissen (1954) delineated his version of a drive theory of motivation. The major event of the 1950s with respect to the study of motivation was, however, the reevaluation of drive theory. Harlow led the attack. He was especially critical of drive-reduction theory. Research in Harlow's laboratory had shown that monkeys would readily perform an operant task in order to engage in visual exploration of various stimuli (for example, Butler and Harlow, 1954). Further, they would learn to operate puzzle devices with no extrinsic motivational manipulations. Where was the primary drive reduction? Similar results were found with rodents. The opportunity to explore was found to be reinforcing, and there were many studies of curiosity (for example, Berlyne, 1955). Data from sexual behavior and ingestive behavior, in what Harlow called the "rodentological" literature, led to similar conclusions. Harlow (1953, 27) noted, "These data suggest that, following the example of the monkey, even the rats are abandoning the sinking ship of reinforcement theory." He continued, "A key to the real learning theory of any animal species is knowledge of the nature and organization of the unlearned patterns of response" (1953, 29).

Conclusion

By the end of the decade comparative psychology had changed. Resolution of some of the differences with ethologists had begun, and the interactions of comparative psychologists with others interested in animal behavior were expanding. Dominance of animal psychology by learning theory appeared to show some signs of weakening, and increasing numbers of young comparative psychologists were becoming active in the field. The prognosis looked good.

1960 TO THE PRESENT: A PERIOD OF UNPRECEDENTED GROWTH

The period from 1960 to the present has been one of unprecedented, explosive growth. Many new scientists have entered the field of comparative psychology and have advanced it in a number of significant directions. With an increasing population size and a sustained period of substantial federal funding, the field developed rapidly.

The task of writing a history for this period is doubly difficult. The first problem is one of sheer magnitude; a history written in the same style used in previous sections would occupy a large portion of the book and make it approach the status of a contemporary textbook. The second problem is that time has not yet been permitted to act so as to separate the wheat from the chaff. It is difficult to detect the trends in contemporary events that will match those of historians writing with the benefit of hindsight. My solution to this problem is to try to sketch only a few of the major trends in the last twenty-two years as I see them. Thus I will omit the contributions of some contemporary scientists who have done more than some of those earlier workers. I apologize for doing so in advance. My goal is to delineate history—not to write a contemporary text. I will attempt to show that the trends we have seen in the earlier work have been carried through to the present.

As comparative psychology has grown in the last two decades, it has proliferated in all directions. Although comparative psychologists have always interacted with biologists and other scientists, such interaction became more intense in the past twenty-two years. Further, within the field there has been great diversification, with those sharing restricted interests forming their own organizations and often publishing their own journals. We thus see a pattern of increased fragmentation within the field together with a reaching out from it. The combined effect of these phenomena is to make trends in comparative psychology more difficult to isolate—indeed, it becomes increasingly more difficult to identify comparative psychology itself. However, both trends are a sign of the health and vigor of contemporary comparative psychology.

The period has been an active one. Major trends have included increased levels of self-evaluation and self-criticism by comparative psychologists and finally, very recently, increased organization of comparative psychologists. We have seen a new challenge to the field—that from the approach of sociobiology. As a result of increasing interaction with biologists, we have seen an increase in the use of ecological approaches as in the ecological approach to the study of learning and foraging strategies. The rise of behavioral ecology has been as anticipated by C. P. Stone in 1943. Comparative psychologists have increasingly escaped the grasp of behaviorism to become more cognitive, and one sees a return of titles that include "consciousness," "mind," and such. Related to this has been the controversy over the possibility that apes can be taught to use language. The extent to which these trends will appear significant to historians of the future is unpredictable.

Comparative Psychologists

As might have been expected from actuarial considerations, although this provides little consolation, the field has lost some of its brightest lights. Included are Schneirla (1968), Kuo (1970), Lehrman (1972), Carmichael (1973), Carpenter (1975), Stanley Ratner (1975), Clifford Morgan (1976), and Harlow (1981). It is a testimony to the work of these comparative psychologists that so many new faces can be seen in the field and that comparative psychology seems healthy despite such major losses.

Societies

The American Psychological Association (APA) reactivated Division 6, the Division of Physiological and Comparative Psychology, in 1964. This once more gave comparative psychologists a home in APA more suited to their interests than was the Division on Experimental Psychology. There are many, however, who feel that the division remains dominated by physiological psychologists and that a separate division is required (see Boice, 1971; Demarest, 1980).

At its 1977 business meeting, Division 6 of APA decided to establish the Committee on the Status of Comparative Psychology, with Ethel Tobach as chair. In addition, the committee, which was restricted to a limited geographical region for logistical reasons, established the Committee of Correspondent Members in 1978. The membership list of November, 1978, included forty-four names; most of the leading comparative psychologists were recruited.

As a partial outgrowth of this committee and the growing concern that comparative psychologists take positive steps toward increased organization, the *Comparative Psychology Newsletter* began publication in December, 1980, with Jack Demarest as editor. The newsletter has provided a means for effective informal communication among comparative psychologists.

Another organization of psychologists providing an outlet for comparative psychologists has been the Psychonomic Society. The origins of the society can be traced to December of 1958, with the first meeting held at the University of Chicago in September of 1960 (Garner, 1976). Although not noted by Garner, the term *psychonomic* was used by Baldwin in *Development and Evolution* (1902).

The major organizations functioning to bring comparative psychologists into contact with other animal behaviorists have been the Animal

Behavior Society in the United States and the Association for the Study of Animal Behavior in Great Britain. Although it had antecedents as part of other organizations, the Animal Behavior Society itself was founded in Montreal on December 27, 1964 (see Guhl and Schein, 1976). The organization had benefited comparative psychologists by facilitating their interactions with other scientists, thus both widening the audience for their work and broadening the range of work to which they are exposed. Psychologists have been active in the administration and scientific program of the Animal Behavior Society.

Other organizations serve those with relatively specialized interests. An informal West Coast Sex Group served as the model for the Conference on Reproductive Behavior. This group, founded as the Eastern Regional Conference on Reproductive Behavior in East Lansing, Michigan, in 1969, provides a meeting place for students of reproductive behavior and its neural and endocrine determinants. I have written an informal history of this organization (Dewsbury, 1979c).

Organizations serving clientele that are apparent from their names are the International Society for Research on Aggression, the International Society for Developmental Psychobiology, the International Primatological Society, and the Behavior Genetics Association.

Journals

An explosion of journals has parelleled that of organizations; often the two go hand in hand. Members of the Animal Behavior Society, for example, automatically receive *Animal Behaviour.*

There are various journals within psychology. Little change occurred in the *Journal of Comparative and Physiological Psychology* during this period. The entertaining editorial written by Harlow (1962) on the occasion of his retirement as editor is one that should be read by all comparative psychologists. That of Thomas (1975) marked some change in emphasis in the journal. In 1983 the journal split into a new journal in physiological psychology (*Behavioral Neuroscience*) and a new *Journal of Comparative Psychology,* thus repeating the process that occurred in 1910.

The Psychonomic Society publishes several journals, some of which serve comparative psychologists, among others. *Psychonomic Science* was begun in 1964 and became the *Bulletin of the Psychonomic Society* in 1973; *Animal Learning & Behavior* was begun in 1973. Another journal catering primarily to psychologists began as *Communications in Behavioral Biology* in 1968, became *Behavioral Biology* in 1972, and has been *Behavioral and Neural Biology* since 1979.

Various new specialty journals are of interest to comparative psychologists. *Developmental Psychobiology* was founded in 1968, and

Hormones and Behavior in 1969. Other specialty journals include *Behavior Genetics* (1970), *Aggressive Behavior* (1974), *Sleep* (1978), and *Behaviour Analysis Letters* (1980). Other journals are restricted to particular taxa but have major behavioral content; they include *Primates* (1957), *Folia Primatologica* (1963), and *Carnivore* (1978).

Among journals facilitating the interaction of comparative psychologists with ethologists and other animal behaviorists are *Zeitschrift für Tierpsychologie* (1937), *Behaviour* (1948), and *Animal Behaviour*. *Animal Behaviour* began formal publication as the *British Journal of Animal Behaviour* in 1953 but became *Animal Behaviour* in 1958 as the result of cooperation between English and American animal behaviorists. *Animal Behaviour Monographs* was published from 1968 to 1973.

An array of new journals cater to animal behaviorists of varying background. These include *Applied Animal Ethology* (1974), *Behavioral Ecology and Sociobiology* (1976), *Behavioural Processes* (1976), *Biology of Behaviour* (1976), *Behavioral and Brain Sciences* (1978), and *Ethology and Sociobiology* (1979).

One aid to keeping up with this massive increase in the literature is the appearance of *Animal Behaviour Abstracts,* begun as *Behavioural Biology Abstracts* in 1973.

Another serial publication, *Advances in the Study of Behavior,* began publication in 1965 under the editorship of Lehrman, R. A. Hinde, and Evelyn Shaw. It includes approximately six review papers per volume; Volume 11 was published in 1980.

Textbooks

Two books have essentially continued the series begun by Moss and Stone: Waters et al.'s *Principles of Comparative Psychology* (1960), and Dewsbury and Rethlingshafer's *Comparative Psychology: A Modern Survey* (1973).

Several books of readings, consisting of reprinted journal articles, appeared during this period. One that was widely used was Thomas E. McGill's *Readings in Animal Behavior,* first published in 1965 and revised in 1973 and 1977.

In a book that combined original material and reprinted papers, Ratner and Denny published *Comparative Psychology: Research in Animal Behavior* in 1964 and revised it in 1970. This was followed up by Denny's *Comparative Psychology: An Evolutionary Analysis of Behavior* (1980).

Another edited book that appeared during the period was Gordon Bermant's *Perspective on Animal Behavior* (1973). Although not intended as a text, E. L. Bliss's *Roots of Behavior* (1962) was popular in some schools.

Books authored by one or two writers included Breland and Breland's *Animal Behavior* (1966), Maier and Maier's *Comparative Animal Behavior* (1970), Joseph Cooper's *Comparative Psychology* (1972), David Lester's *Comparative Psychology: Phyletic Differences in Behavior* (1973), F. J. Mortenson's *Animal Behavior: Theory and Research* (1975), and Dewsbury's *Comparative Animal Behavior* (1978a).

Despite all these titles, textbooks in animal behavior were written predominately by zoologists during this period. Most deserving of mention in a book about psychology is Hinde's *Animal Behaviour: A Synthesis of Ethology and Comparative Psychology*, which was published in 1966 and revised in 1970. The book includes numerous citations from comparative psychology.

Clearly, growth in the area of textbooks had paralleled that in other areas.

Facilities

The major characteristic in the development of facilities was the founding of numerous laboratories in colleges and universities, both large and small, throughout North America. Although a few major facilities have been developed, the more typical pattern is for one or two comparative psychologists to locate at each of a large number of universities rather than to become concentrated in centers.

The major development in facilities lay in the area of primate research. In 1960 the U.S. Congress authorized funding for the first of seven primate-research centers that would eventually come under the authority of the National Institutes of Health (see Bourne, 1973; Goodwin and Augustine, 1975). These include the Oregon Regional Primate Research Center, Washington Regional Primate Research Center, Delta Regional Primate Research Center, Yerkes Primate Research Center, Wisconsin Regional Primate Research Center, New England Regional Primate Research Center, and the California Primate Research Center. The Yerkes Primate Research Center resulted from the transfer of the Yerkes Laboratory from Orange Park to Emory University in Atlanta as part of the Primate Center program (Anonymous, 1965; Bourne, 1965).

A major new effort was the development of the Institute of Animal Behavior at Rutgers University in Newark, New Jersey. Lehrman was its first director, with Jay S. Rosenblatt assuming the directorship on Lehrman's death in 1972. The Institute was formally established by vote of the Rutgers faculty and its board of governors in 1966. It grew organically from the interests of its faculty and brings together students of animal behavior from diverse approaches (Rosenblatt, 1982).

The saddest development of the period was the decision of the board of trustees of the American Museum of Natural History to dissolve the

Department of Animal Behavior in 1980. The department had been an important center of training and research in the field.

Self-Assessments

The past two decades have seen increased self-assessment and criticism—some might say self-flagellation—in comparative psychology. A few evaluations have been positive as when Carmichael wrote of "the present healthy and active state of the scientific study of the behavior of infrahuman organisms" (1968, 47).

Anin et al. (1968) asked a panel of nine psychologists to determine the 538 most important psychologists of all times. Comparative psychologists were generally rated well, with Köhler, Lashley, Thorndike, Watson, and Yerkes among the fifty-three persons receiving the highest possible score. The most obvious omissions from the list are the forgotten Linus Kline and Wesley Mills.

The literature of self-criticism will be discussed briefly to complete perspective; it has been discussed in more detail in Chapter 1. Lockard criticized comparative psychologists for overuse of albino rats (1968) and wrote of the "decline and fall" of comparative psychology (1971). Both papers elicited numerous replies in the *American Psychologist*. The conferences sponsored by the New York Academy of Sciences were held in response to Lockard (Tobach et al., 1973).

The paper by Hodos and Campbell (1969) focused more specifically on the kinds of evolutionary comparisons psychologists tend to use. The paper helped set the occasion for a conference on Brain, Behavior, and Evolution in Tallahassee, Florida, in February of 1973 (Masterton et al., 1976a, 1976b). This conference brought together numerous behaviorists, anatomists, and paleontologists to consider the problems encountered in the study of brain, evolution, and behavior.

The many other examples of self-criticism (see Chapter 1) stimulated a survey of the status of comparative psychology in the APA (Demarest, 1980). The survey revealed a wide divergence of opinion regarding not only the status of comparative psycholoy but also its basic definition. The problem of definition was a major factor in stimulating me to write this book.

Perhaps partly as a result of the negative evaluations they kept writing about themselves, comparative psychologists became less frequently represented in the *Annual Review of Psychology* during the 1960s and 1970s. Frequently ethologists were chosen to write chapters on comparative psychology, and many of the chapters emphasized ethological considerations. Chapters were prepared by Thorpe (1961), Wood-Gush (1963), Mason and Riopelle (1964), Scott (1967), Crook and Goss-Custard

(1972), and Mason and Lott (1976). Thorpe contrasted, for our colleagues, ethology with comparative psychology noting the broad range of species studied in ethology and "the rather narrow range adopted by the psychologist who seldom deals with species other than rat, monkey, pigeon, ape, and man" (1961, 28). Although the paper by Mason and Riopelle (1964) was confined to primates, it covers the broad range of problems that typifies comparative psychology. The paper by Mason and Lott (1976) also exemplifies the best of comparative psychology, discussing in some depth the problem of comparison, social behavior, and learning. They discussed the broad basis of comparative psychology and the many urgent calls for a rapprochement between ethology and comparative psychology. They noted, "Today it appears that the synthesis is essentially complete" (Mason and Lott, 1976, 150).

Field Studies

Considering the tradition of Watson, Lashley, Carpenter, Schneirla, Bingham, and Nissen, it should come as no surprise that comparative psychologists have continued to be active in field research. Much of this activity was reviewed by Miller (1977a), who delineated five important roles that naturalistic observation can play in comparative psychology. Like previous writers, he noted "the importance of balancing controlled laboratory experiments with systematic, quantified field observations" (1977a, 211).

Gottlieb (1963a) stated that most observations on imprinting that had been made by ethologists were the result of research with captive animals—generally animals reared in incubators. It was psychologist Gottlieb who initiated a program of naturalistic research on imprinting (1963a, 1963b). Gottlieb not only considered imprinting in nature but also worked with two ecologically different species of ducks—one hole nesting and one surface nesting. Hess (1972) also studied imprinting in a natural habitat and noted differences regarding the reversibility of imprinting in the field as compared with that observed in the laboratory.

Given the long tradition of primate field research one would expect psychologists to study primates in their natural habitat. William Mason, a graduate of Harlow's laboratory, has long conducted a program that features both laboratory analyses and field studies, particularly of *Callicebus* monkeys (1968a, 1968b). Field studies by Irwin Bernstein include one of the lutong of Kuala Selangor (1968) and one of pigtailed macaques (1967). Emil Menzel has conducted field experiments with Japanese macaques (1966, 1967, 1968). Menzel writes particularly effectively on the value and advantages of fieldwork. Analyses of communication in South American primates have been conducted by Charles Snowden and his associates (Hodun et al., 1981; Snowden and Hodun, 1981).

Field studies by psychologists have not been confined to a few species. Petrinovich et al. (1976), for example, studied communication in white-crowned sparrows. Howard Topoff (1976) described graphically the experiences one has in conducting fieldwork such as his studies of army ants in tropical rain forests.

Given the interest of psychologists in rodent behavior, field studies of rodents are to be expected. Lockard (1975) studied the effects of illumination on the behvior of kangaroo rats in the field. Glickman (1980) is studying social behavior in desert rodents in the field.

Other mammalian species have been studied by psychologists: moose and elk (Altmann, 1963); bison social and sexual behavior (Lott, 1974); analyses of sexual selection in elephant seals (LeBoeuf, 1974); and attempts to use methods from taste-aversion studies to control coyotes (Gustavson et al., 1974). The tradition of field research is alive and well in psychology.

Individual Behavior

Studies of the behavior of individual animals have continued but generally have been less publicized than those of reproductive and social behavior. The long history of interest in animal orientation has been continued by such workers as Merle Meyer (1964a, 1964b) and Helmut Adler (for example, Adler, 1970). Carmichael (1963) summarized the results of a symposium on orientation held in Munich in a column called "Psychology in Action."

Biological rhythms have become a popular topic (for example, Morin et al., 1977; Rusak and Zucker, 1975). Nearly fifty years after his first publication, C. P. Richter (1971) described the inborn nature of the rat's twenty-four hour clock. The study of sleep has aroused much interest and generated its own organization and journal, *Sleep.* Various efforts have been made to consider the adaptive significance of sleeping behavior (for example, Webb, 1974).

A variety of other behavioral patterns have interested comparative psychologists. Many have studied ingestive behavior, as did Beatrice Gardner (1964) in her study of hunting and ingestive behavior in salticid spiders and Goldstein (1960) who studied feeding in salamanders. Glickman and Sroges (1966) used the resources of a collection of zoo animals to conduct a broad comparative study of exploratory behavior that has implications for evolution and adaptive significance. Donald Jensen (1959) completed a study of feeding, fission, and related behavior in paramecia.

Reproductive Behavior

The founding of the Conference on Reproductive Behavior and of *Hormones and Behavior* are but two signs of the growth of the study of reproductive behavior in the past two decades. Psychologists have contributed to a host of books that have appeared during these years; some have been edited by psychologists. Most notable was the volume edited by Beach (1965), which stemmed from two conferences held in Berkeley in 1961 and 1962 and included many of the leading workers in ethology, comparative psychology, and other discplines. The results of another Berkeley conference, held in honor of Beach's sixty-fifth birthday, were published by McGill et al., (1978). Adler (1981) edited a general book on reproductive function and behavior; Dewsbury (1981) traced the history of the study of reproductive behavior in this century; Rheingold (1963) published an excellent set of studies of maternal behavior in a variety of species; and Bermant and Davidson (1974) wrote a textbook on the topic of reproductive behavior.

It is difficult to detect a few trends in this massive activity. The study of reproductive behavior has become closely linked to analyses of its physiological bases, and many studies have entailed manipulations of neural and endocrine processes. Analysis of hormonal effects have become quite sophisticated with state-of-the-art techniques rapidly being developed and applied. The hormonal effects found in adults have been quite different from those of critical developmental periods (see Beach, 1975). Beach (1967) developed a physiological model according to which sexual behavior is organized in lower-brain centers and the spinal cord and inhibited from above.

Other trends relate to the behavior itself. I have reviewed copulatory behavior in a wide range of mammalian species (Dewsbury, 1972) and conducted research on forty-three species of muroid rodents (Dewsbury, 1975). An excellent example of the potential for reproductive behavior to provide a focus for the integration of research on stimuli, social factors, endocrine effects, and other influences can be seen in the research program of Lehrman on ring doves (for example, 1965).

Social Behavior

Zajonc (1965, 1969) synthesized research in the area of experimental animal social psychology, emphasizing such topics as social facilitation, competition, and cooperation. Much effort has been devoted to the study of communication as psychologists have played a major role in the study of ultrasonic communication (for example, Nyby and Whitney, 1978) and olfactory communication through pheromones (Brown, 1979; Doty, 1976;

Thiessen and Rice, 1976). A new perspective on the definition and study of aggressive behavior was provided by Moyer (1968). Psychologists have been interested in population density and the effects of crowding (for example, Thiessen and Rodgers, 1961). Many of the field studies (for example, Topoff, 1976; LeBoeuf, 1974; Lott, 1974) and studies of primate behavior (for example, Bernstein and Mason, 1963) have dealt with social behavior. With the advent of sociobiology, more and more psychologists, like other scientists, have been drawn to the study of social behavior.

Behavior Genetics

The textbook written by John L. Fuller and W. R. Thompson (1960) is generally credited with having brought the fragments of behavior genetics together to formulate an integrated subdiscipline. The book is wide ranging, dealing with methods and a variety of behaviors in both human and nonhuman animals. The text by Fuller and Thompson has been succeeded by those written by Thiessen (1972); McClearn and DeFries (1973); and Vale (1980). A book edited by Jerry Hirsch (1967) brought together state-of-the-art work in behavior genetics and was a major influence on the development of the field.

There are other signs of the development of behavior genetics in the time since Fuller and Thompson. The Institute of Behavioral Genetics has been established at the University of Colorado, and such schools as the University of Texas and the University of Minnesota have become major centers of behavior-genetic research. An entire journal, *Behavior Genetics*, is devoted to research in this field. The literature on behavioral studies in genetically defined lines of house mice has become so massive that a 1,222-item bibliography was published by Sprott and Staats (1975) and has been periodically updated in *Behavior Genetics* since that time.

Development

Like other areas of comparative psychology, the study of behavioral development has seen the beginning of its own journal, *Developmental Psychobiology*, and a flurry of books. Representative books include Fiske and Maddi's *Functions of Varied Experience* (1961); Newton and Levine's *Early Experience and Behavior* (1968); Stevenson et al.'s *Early Behavior: Comparative and Developmental Approaches;* Moltz's *The Ontogeny of Vertebrate Behavior* (1971); Tobach et al.'s *The Biopsychology of Development* (1971); Burghardt and Bekoff's *The Development of Behavior: Comparative and Evolutionary Aspects* (1978); and Spear and Campbell's *Ontogeny of Learning and Memory* (1979). Gottlieb has edited a series of volumes on *Studies on the Development of Behavior and the Nervous System* (1973, 1974, 1976).

With so much research on behavioral development, it is difficult to isolate trends, but a few highlights can be noted. After a prolonged absence, Kuo returned to the literature with studies of the development of interspecies coexistence and development of embryonic behavior (Gottlieb and Kuo, 1965; Kuo, 1967). Gottlieb (1968) reviewed literature on prenatal behavior in birds. The study of imprinting continued with classic papers published by Moltz (1960) and Hess (1964). Research on effects of early experience on mammalian behavior peaked in the late 1950s and 1960s; progress was reviewed critically by Daly (1973). Along with effects of early experience on behavior, psychologists found changes in neuroanatomy and neurochemistry (for example, Bennett et al., 1964). Writings by J. P. Scott (1962, 1963) triggered an exchange between him and Schneirla and Rosenblatt (1963) regarding critical periods and continuous processes in behavioral development. Research on effects of manipulation of early hormones revealed critical periods very much like those proposed by Lorenz for imprinting (Beach, 1975). No account of behavioral development is complete without mention of the influential studies of experience and the development of behavior in rhesus macaques by Harlow and his associates (for example, Harlow et al., 1971).

Instinct

Debate over the concept of instinct and its application surfaced periodically since the general resolution of the 1950s. The earlier papers were summarized and excerpted by Birney and Teevan (1961). Moltz's critique (1965) and Jensen's paper (1961) were extensions of the earlier debate.

A new round of skirmishes was triggered by the publication of Lorenz's *Evolution and the Modification of Behavior* (1965). Lehrman (1970) replied as many of the issues thought to have been resolved in the 1950s resurfaced.

Sensory Function

Many psychologists considered sensory function as it relates to behavior. In the study of orientation, for example, Adler and Dalland (1959) and Meyer (1964a) studied the sensory capacities of birds in relation to the demands required for orientation. Much of the research on communication has led to considerations of the functioning of the auditory system, olfactory mechanisms, or other sensory systems in animals. Kellogg (1961) summarized research on echolocation in bottlenosed dolphins. A few other examples of the wide range of sensory studies by comparative psychologists include the review of the development of sensory systems by Gottlieb (1968) and the study of the evolution of auditory function as exemplified by Heffner et al., (1969).

Physiological Bases of Behavior

It is probably true that growth in the study of physiological bases of behavior has occurred more rapidly in the past two decades than has comparative psychology. Although much of this research has drifted away from comparative behavioral studies in the direction of "behavioral neuroscience," there have also been many physiological studies of the kinds of behavior discussed here. For example, textbooks of physiological psychology (for example, Carlson, 1981) typically include chapters on the physiological bases of sexual behavior, ingestive behavior, sleep, aggression, and learning. There have been many review papers of the physiological bases of sexual behavior, maternal behavior, and related naturally occurring behavioral patterns. I shall not attempt to review this active area in a short space.

A notable effort for the comparative study of behavior is the work of Jerison (1970, 1973) and others on the evolution of brain size in vertebrates. The work has important implications for the study of the evolution of behavior.

The field of hormones and behavior produced its first elementary textbook with the publication of A. I. Leshner's *An Introduction to Behavioral Endocrinology* (1978).

Evolution

The long tradition of evolutionary theorizing in comparative psychology was manifested on a number of fronts. Particularly evident was the attempt to tie together studies of brain evolution and behavior, as noted in the paper of Hodos and Campbell (1969), in the Tallahassee conference, and in the work of Jerison (1970, 1973).

Much research on domestication and its effects on behavior was reviewed and synthesized by Boice (1973). At least in rodents, the "degenerative" effects of domestication appear greatly exaggerated. Similar conclusions were drawn when domesticated strains of ducks were tested under appropriate conditions (Miller, 1977b).

A theory of reinforcement developed by Glickman and Schiff (1967) was based on the premise that reinforcement mechanisms function to ensure occurrence of instinctive behavior patterns critical to the survival and reproductive success of organisms.

Many psychologists have speculated on the evolution of various aspects of behavior, as in Whitney's paper (1976) on the spread of human sociality and Dewsbury's proposals (1982) regarding the cost of ejaculates and sexual selection. Skinner, not usually thought of as an evolutionary theorist, published two significant and relevant papers during this period. In "The Phylogeny and Ontogeny of Behavior" (1966), he considered some apparent similarities between the shaping of behavior in the individual and the evolution of species-typical patterns of behavior. In this paper Skinner quoted Watson's famous passage about the lack of genetic influence on behavior and categorically denied that such a position is held by many behaviorists. Skinner (1975) explicitly considered the manner in which "phylogenic behavior" can be shaped throughout evolution. For example, he considered how green turtles might come to home on a small island in the middle of an ocean and invoked continental drift to show how the behavior might evolve through a gradual process with some resemblance to the shaping of behavior in the individual organism.

Learning

A major development in the study of learning in invertebrates was the publication of the three-volume set edited by Corning et al., (1973) entitled *Invertebrate Learning*. With chapters covering many invertebrate taxa, diverse material was reviewed within three sets of covers. In July of 1964 a major conference was held in Cambridge, England, dealing with "Learning and Associated Phenomena in Invertebrates" (Thorpe and Davenport, 1965). The conference brought together such adversaries as McConnell, Gelber, and Jensen, as well as others engaged in the study of invertebrate learning. In another development, Jacobson et al. (1967) published what appears to be a definitive demonstration of classical conditioning in flatworms.

The conclusion that species differences in vertebrate learning cannot be meaningfully studied using simple tasks was generally confirmed in a comprehensive review by Brookshire (1970). However, many workers held out hope that quantitative comparisons among species might reveal meaningful differences when more complex learning tasks were used. Although Warren (1965a) expressed some hope that orderly phyletic differences might be found, by 1973, he was less sanguine (1973). The many factors that can influence behavior in such situations render quantitative comparisons difficult (Harlow, 1958b; Warren, 1973).

In an effort to study evolutionary changes in learning that are correlated with the evolution of brain structures, Masterton and Skeen (1972) compared hedgehogs, tree shrews, and bush babies with respect to delayed alternation learning. They concluded that the development of the prefrontal system and its behavioral correlates may have been important in anthropoid evolution.

An alternative approach was taken by M. E. Bitterman (1960, 1965a, 1965b) who developed a testable model based on the assumption that qualitatively different processes may act in different taxa. Bitterman relied primarily on reversal learning and probability learning with spatial and visual cues to differentiate animals of different taxa. The system received criticism (for example, Warren, 1973) and was later defended and modified (Bitterman, 1975, 1976). The system is particularly appreciated for being explicit and testable.

The major trend in the last twenty years appears to be a consideration of learning in relation to the naturally occurring behavioral patterns and ecological adaptations of the species under study. This approach was stimulated by several notable papers. In "The Misbehavior of Organisms," Breland and Breland (1961) wrote of their experiences in training animals in a commercial venture and challenged some of the general principles of various behavior theories. They concluded, "The notion of instinct has now become one of our basic concepts in an effort to make sense of the welter of observations which confront us" (1961, 684). Garcia and Koelling (1966) reported results on conditioned taste aversion, demonstrating that organisms learned some associations more readily than others. This was followed by more research (for example, Garcia et al., 1974) and by some controversy (for example, Bitterman, 1975). Seligman (1970) questioned the very existence of general laws of learning and noted that organisms appear "prepared" to learn some things and "contraprepared" to learn others. This approach has led to a considerable spurt of learning studies that were done in relation to ecological considerations and constraints (for example, Seligman and Hager, 1972; Hinde and Stevenson-Hinde, 1973). More recently students of learning have related their results to models of foraging strategies and optimality (for example, Kamil and Sargent, 1981). Many of these considerations have appeared in another new journal, *Behaviour Analysis Letters*.

Examination of learning in relation to instinctive behavior and ecological consideration has led to re-evaluation of earlier work as well. For example, Moore and Stuttard (1979) interpreted the escape from puzzle boxes by the cats of Guthrie and Horton (1946) as largely an instance of naturally occurring greeting response of cats.

The ecological approach to learning has helped to unify the study of learning and to relate it to work by other students of animal behavior.

Language in Apes?

Perhaps the most publicized research in recent comparative psychology has been that devoted to the attempts to demonstrate the occurrence of language in chimpanzees (and gorillas). The work follows that of the Kelloggs, the Hayeses, and Kohts (see Kellogg, 1968).

Gardner and Gardner (for example, 1969) began with Washoe, teaching her American Sign Language while rearing her in a trailer in their back yard. Washoe learned to use and to recognize a variety of signs. David Premack (for example, 1970) used a set of plastic objects that could be attached to a board with each object functioning as a word. The chimpanzee Sarah learned to recognize and build sentences that could be seen as instances of various logical categories. Rumbaugh (for example, Rumbaugh and Gill, 1976) used a copmputerized system and a "language" ("Yerkish") in which the chimpanzee Lana could build or respond to sequences of geometric-form stimuli on back-lighted panels.

Much controversy has surrounded the interpretation of these experiments, with the focal issue revolving about the extent to which the systems exemplify the defining attributes of human language (for example, Limber, 1977). More recently, Terrace (1979a) used sign language and some procedures differing from those of Gardner and Gardner in training the chimpanzee Nim Chimpsky. The more modest performance levels of Nim helped to spark the controversy (see Marx, 1980).

Later workers have now entered the debate and other chimpanzees have been trained by the original workers and their associates. It is clear that very complex communication systems have been taught to these animals. The extent to which these systems resemble human language hinges on a set of rather complex issues that cannot be resolved within the context of a history.

Comparative Cognitive Psychology

The 1970s saw great growth of the cognitive approach throughout much of psychology; it comes as no surprise that such growth occurred in comparative psychology as well. Premack and Woodruff (1978a) argued that chimpanzees may have a theory of mind. Shown videotapes of human actors struggling with various problems, chimpanzees were able to select a photograph that was indicative of an appropriate solution. They argued that such performance implies the existence of various mental states in the chimpanzee. Premack and Woodruff believe that the chimpanzee is a mentalist; "he is not intelligent enough to be a behaviorist" (1978a, 526). Herrnstein (1979) trained pigeons to respond differentially to pictures containing or not containing trees of various sorts and argued that the various responses imply an ability to use concepts.

Gallup (1977, 1979) found that chimpanzees with experience looking into mirrors responded to facial alterations, made by painting a spot on an anesthetized animal, by immediately manipulating the area of the spot. Gallup argues that such self-recognition implies self-awareness in apes. He further argues that no comparable behavior has been observed in species other than apes. Epstein et al. (1981), however, argued that similar behavior can be shaped in pigeons and can be explained in terms of environmental history.

The question of animal awareness was again raised by zoologist Donald R. Griffin. Griffin (1976) believes that such behaviors as communication in honeybees and the chimpanzee language studies imply conscious intent to communicate. Although critical of this approach, Mason (1976a, 1980) emphasized the importance of a concept of "mind" in contemporary animal behavior.

Sociobiology

Among the most exciting occurrences in the last two decades has been the emergence of sociobiology. The basic foundation of sociobiology, as with most such movements, grew gradually with the work of many researchers such as Hamilton and Trivers. The field was coalesced, however, with the publication of E. O. Wilson's *Sociobiology: The New Synthesis* (1975a). Sociobiologists generally have emphasized explanation of the ultimate causation of social behavior as the result of natural selection acting to change gene frequencies. It is assumed that selection works at the level of the individual or gene, as opposed to the group, and that apparently altruistic behavior can evolve if it fosters the reproductive success of close relatives of the donor.

Some sociobiologists have misused analogies in searching for explanations of behavioral phenomena; such methodological excesses often occur with the spread of a new approach. Terms taken from human experience have sometimes been applied carelessly to nonhumans. Some psychologists (for example, Beach, 1978; Tobach, 1978) have criticized such methodological excesses; others have embraced sociobiological theory (for example, Campbell, 1975).

Wilson's book (1975a) challenged comparative psychology by predicting its eventual disappearance. In reaction to this proposal, a symposium was held at the Toronto meetings of the APA in 1978 (Wyers et al., 1980). The participating authors displayed diverse reactions to sociobiology. A middle-of-the-road position was taken by Glickman, whose response was "to teach and incorporate the best of evolutionary-ecological thought, while discouraging the glib uses of analogy and terminology found in much sociobiological writing" (1980, 962). It would seem that with its methodological rigor, comparative psychology is in an ideal position to conduct careful research stimulated by the exciting principles stemming from sociobiology.

Honorary Volumes

The remarkable progress made by contemporary comparative psychologists has been built on the foundation provided by earlier workers. It is therefore fitting that the contributions of those earlier workers be appropriately recognized. Recently, as various milestones have approached, efforts were made in their honor. A volume planned as a Festschrift for Schneirla became, instead, a memorial volume (Aronson et al., 1970). Aronson et al. (1972) published selected writings of Schneirla. A memorial symposium for Lehrman was published by Rosenblatt and Komisaruk (1977). The proceedings of a "Beach Party," held on the occasion of Beach's sixty-fifth birthday were published by McGill et al. (1978). These important events have helped tie the present to the past.

A CHRONOLOGY OF COMPARATIVE PSYCHOLOGY

One useful way to summarize history is through chronology. Selection of items for inclusion in a chronology must be somewhat arbitrary; nevertheless, it does provide some basis for effective summary.

Animal Behavior Before 1894

1859   Charles Darwin publishes *The Origin of Species.*
1864   Pierre Flourens publishes *Psychologie Comparée.*
1871   Charles Darwin publishes *The Descent of Man and Selection in Relation to Sex.*
1872   Charles Darwin publishes *The Expression of the Emotions in Man and Animals.*
1879   Wilhelm Wundt founds the first psychology laboratory at Leipzig.
1882   George J. Romanes publishes *Animal Intelligence.*
1885   T. Wesley Mills founds the Association for the Study of Comparative Psychology.
1892   The American Psychological Association is founded.

1894–1899: The Beginnings of American Comparative Psychology

1894   Baldwin and Cattell found the *Psychological Review.*
         C. Lloyd Morgan publishes *An Introduction to Comparative Psychology*
         Wilhelm Wundt's *Lectures on Human and Animal Psychology* appears in English.

1896 James Mark Baldwin proposes the "Baldwin effect"—a major proposal in evolutionary theory.

1898 Wesley Mills publishes *The Nature and Development of Animal Intelligence.*

   Linus Kline conducts the first study of learning in rats.

   Edward L. Thorndike publishes *Animal Intelligence, An Experimental Study of the Associative Processes in Animals.*

1899 Willard S. Small constructs the first maze for use with rats.

   Linus Kline publishes two landmark papers on broad comparative methodology.

   Thorndike and Mills debate the value of observation versus experimentation.

1900-1909: The Blossoming of Comparative Psychology

1900 Willard S. Small publishes "An Experimental Study of the Mental Processes of the Rat."

1901 Small publishes the first study of rats learning a maze.

   E. L. Thorndike publishes "The Mental Life of Monkeys: An Experimental Study."

1902 L. T. Hobhouse publishes *Mind in Evolution.*

   A. J. Kinnaman publishes the first laboratory study of the behavior of rhesus macaques.

1903 John B. Watson publishes his doctoral dissertation, *Animal Education.*

1905 Edward Conradi publishes his work on the role of experience in the ontogeny of bird song.

   Edwin B. Twitmyer publishes his work on classical conditioning of the patellar reflex.

1907 Robert M. Yerkes publishes *The Dancing Mouse.*

   John B. Watson spends a summer on the Dry Tortugas studying the behavior of noddy and sooty terns.

1908 Margaret Floy Washburn publishes her textbook, *The Animal Mind.*

1909 Yerkes and Morgulis publish a paper introducing the work of Pavlov to American psychology.

1910-1919: A Decade of Elaboration, Behaviorism, and War

1910 A symposium on instinct and intelligence, featuring Lloyd Morgan and Wiliam McDougall, is held in London.

1911   Edward L. Thorndike publishes *Animal Intelligence. The Journal of Animal Behavior* begins publication.

Yerkes and Watson publish *Methods of Studying Vision in Animals.*

Pfungst's *Clever Hans* is published in English.

1913   Watson publishes "Psychology as the Behaviorist Views It."

W. S. Hunter introduces the delayed-response test.

Wolfgang Köhler goes to the island of Tenerife to study chimpanzees.

1914   Watson publishes *Behavior: An Introduction to Comparative Psychology.*

1915   Watson and Lashley publish evidence of distance orientation in birds flying over open water.

1916   Yerkes publishes *The Mental Life of Monkeys and Apes.*

1917   Psychologists serve in World War I.

1919   Knight Dunlap publishes "Are There Any Instincts?"

P. F. Swindle publishes an innovative analysis of nest building.

1920-1929: A Decade of Controversy and Transition

1920   Edward C. Tolman proposes a hierarchical theory of instinct.

1921   The National Research Council Committee for Research in Problems of Sex is founded.

The *Journal of Comparative Psychology* is founded.

Zing-Yang Kuo publishes "Giving Up Instincts in Psychology."

1922   Calvin P. Stone publishes "The Congenital Sexual Behavior of the Young Male Albino Rat."

1924   Tolman publishes the first study of artificial selection for a behavioral trait in psychology.

Yerkes studies Madam Rosalia Abreu's primates in Havana.

1925   Köhler's *The Mentality of Apes* appears in English.

1926   Leonard Carmichael publishes his first study of the development of behavior in frog and salamander embryos.

1927   Robert C. Tryon begins his study of the genetic bases of maze learning using the method of artificial selection.

1929   T. C. Schnierla publishes his first study of learning and orientation in ants.

H. C. Bingham and H. W. Nissen sail for Africa to conduct pioneering field studies of primate behavior.

1930-1939: The Arrival of a New Generation

1930   The facility to be known as the Yerkes Laboratories of Primate Biology is opened.

1931   C. R. Carpenter begins a study of howler monkeys on Barro Colorado.
1932   T. C. Schneirla begins field research on ants on Barro Colorado.
1933   The Kelloggs publish *The Ape and the Child.*
1934   F. A. Moss publishes *Comparative Psychology.*
1935   N. R. F. Maier and T. C. Schneirla publish *Principles of Animal Psychology.*
        Warden, Jenkins, and Warner publish the first volume of their three-volume treatise on comparative psychology.
1938   Carpenter establishes a breeding colony of rhesus macaques on Cayo Santiago.
        Lashley publishes "Experimental Analyses of Instinctive Behavior."
1939   Yerkes publishes important studies of sexual behavior, life history,social dominance, and prelinguistic sign behavior in chimpanzees.

1940-1949: A Decade of Sustained Vigor

1940   Carpenter publishes his field study of gibbons in Siam.
        Tryon publishes "Genetic Differences in Maze-learning Ability in Rats."
1942   Frank Beach publishes eleven important papers on sexual behavior.
        The Department of Animal Behavior of the American Museum of Natural History is founded.
1943   Stone publishes his APA presidential address, "Multiply, Vary, Let the Strongest Live and the Weakest Die—Charles Darwin."
1946   The Conference on Genetics and Social Behavior is held in Bar Harbor, Maine.
1947   A Symposium on Heredity and Environment is held at Princeton University featuring Beach, Carmichael, Morgan, Lashley, Stone, and Hunter.
        The *Journal of Comparative Psychology* becomes the *Journal of Comparative and Physiological Psychology,* and the APA Division of Physiological and Comparative Psychology merges with the Division of Experimental Psychology.
1948   Schneirla prepares his first *Encyclopaedia Britannica* article on "Psychology, Comparative."
        The journal *Behaviour* is founded with Beach and Carpenter on the editorial board.
        Beach publishes *Hormones and Behavior.*

1949   H. F. Harlow publishes "The Formation of Learning Sets."
D. O. Hebb publishes *The Organization of Behavior.*
Schneirla elaborates the concept of "levels" in the comparative study of behavior.
Lashley publishes "Persistent Problems in the Evolution of Mind."

1950-1959: The Arrival of Ethology

1950   Beach publishes "The Snark was a Boojum."
1951   S. S. Stevens's *Handbook of Experimental Psychology* is published.
Catherine H. Hayes publishes *The Ape in Our House.*
Ford and Beach publish *Patterns of Sexual Behavior.*
1953   D. S. Lehrman publishes "A Critique of Konrad Lorenz's Theory of Instinctive Behavior."
The Daytona Beach Instinct Symposium features Nissen and Allee.
Harlow publishes "Mice, Monkeys, Men, and Motives."
1954   Beach and Jaynes review "Effects of Early Experience upon the Behavior of Animals."
The Macy Conference on Group Processes features Lehrman, Schneirla, Beach, Tinbergen, and Lorenz.
Hebb and Thompson publish "The Social Significance of Animal Studies" in the *Handbook of Social Psychology.*
1957   C. H. Schiller edits *Instinctive Behavior.*
W. S. Verplanck publishes a glossary of terms.
1958   H. F. Harlow publishes his APA presidential address, "The Nature of Love."
The interdisciplinary *Behavior and Evolution* is published.
Hirsch and Boudreau publish their study of artificial selection for phototaxis in fruit flies.

1960-1969

1960   The National Institute of Health's Primate Research Centers Program begins.
Fuller and Thompson publish *Behavior Genetics.*
Breland and Breland publish "The Misbehavior of Organisms."
1962   Harlow publishes "Fundamental Principles of Preparing Psychology Journal Articles."
1964   The APA Division of Physiological and Comparative Psychology is reformed.
The Animal Behavior Society is founded.

1965   Beach publishes *Sex and Behavior,* based on the 1961 and 1962 Berkeley conferences.

       The Yerkes Laboratories are moved to Atlanta.

       M. E. Bitterman publishes a testable model of the evolution of learning.

1966   Garcia and Koelling publish their first paper on learned taste aversions ("Garcia effect").

       B. F. Skinner publishes "The Phylogeny and Ontogeny of Behaivor."

1969   Gardner and Gardner publish "Teaching Sign Language to a Chimpanzee."

       Hodos and Campbell publish *"Scala Naturae:* Why There is No Theory in Comparative Psychology."

1970-1982

1970   *Development and Evolution of Behavior* is published in memory of Schneirla.

1971   Robert Lockard publishes "Reflections on the Fall of Comparative Psychology: Is There a Message for Us All?"

1972   The New York Academy of Sciences Conferences on Comparative Psychology at Issue are held in Tokyo and Honolulu.

1973   The Tallahassee Conference on Evolution, Brain, and Behavior is held.

1976   A Berkeley "Beach Party" celebrates Beach's sixty-fifth birthday.

1977   Division 6 of APA appoints the Committee on the Status of Comparative Psychology chaired by Ethel Tobach.

1978   An APA symposium is held on "The Sociobiological Challenge to Psychology."

1980   Jack Demarest starts *Comparative Psychology Newsletter.*

1983   The *Journal of Comparative Psychology* resumes independent publication.

Chapter 5

Problems of Method in Comparative Psychology

In Chapters 2, 3, and 4 we progressed through the history of comparative psychology in chronological order, an ideal method for studying the trends in history as they unfolded over time. However, with such an organization, continuity with respect to any one problem area is lost. Thus to gain continuity, the various problem areas in comparative psychology need to be considered problem by problem, rather than chronologically, as they will be in Chapters 5, 6, and 7. Some of the persistent methodological problems will be discussed in this chapter.

SPECIES USED IN COMPARATIVE PSYCHOLOGY

Selection of Species

A persistent problem throughout the century has been the selection of species for study. Problems encountered include whether comparisons should be made, choice of species, and the problem of domestication.

Should We Compare? As noted in Chapter 1, for many authors comparison among species is the essence of comparative psychology.

Yerkes (1913a) proposed limiting the term *comparative psychology* to studies in which there is explicit comparison of species. Others have indicated that the central objective of comparative psychology is the comparison of behavior across species (for example, Russell, 1954; Schneirla, 1952). I shall pursue a different approach here; thus, for purposes of this book, the objective of comparative psychology is considered to be the development of functional relationships, laws, and theories regarding the control, development, evolutionary history, and adaptive significance of behavior. Comparative psychologists strive to develop principles of generality. With this approach, comparisons across species are frequently considered necessary and/or important in answering the questions posed. However, for other questions comparative methods may not be called for and may waste effort.

Earlier, I addressed the issue of when and where species comparisons are needed (Dewsbury, 1973b). When studying evolutionary history, it is almost always necessary to make comparisons across species. When studying problems of immediate control or development, comparisons can often be quite instructive, but they are not essential for many purposes. When studying adaptive significance, the role of comparison changes with the method. With the behavior-genetic method, the experimental method, or the method of within-species comparison, between-species comparisons are not essential. When, however, one uses the method of adaptive correlation, cross-species comparisons are necessary. Thus explicit cross-species comparisons are seen herein not as essential to the definition or conduct of comparative psychology but rather as one methodological tool that may be useful and/or necessary for some problems.

What Species Should We Study If We Choose Just One? There are many advantages to single-species research; these were fully understood by Beach (1950) and elaborated on by Skinner (1966). Major advances have been made by geneticists concentrating on fruit flies, for example. There are many cases in which a single species possesses characteristics that make it uniquely appropriate for certain kinds of research. Research on the squid giant axon and the nervous system of *Aplysia* can be taken as representative examples. Where other things are equal, such factors as cost, availability, ease of maintenance, and the existence of a substantial literature are all relevant. In essence, then, the species should be selected on the basis of the ease and effectiveness with which the particular question under consideration can be answered.

With the approach advocated here, proximity to humans is not a major factor in the selection of species. As noted by Beach:

> If we remove man from the central point in a comparative science of
> behavior, this may, in the long run, prove to be the very best way of

reaching a better understanding of his place in nature and of the behavioral characteristics which he shares with other animals as well as those which he possesses alone or which are in him developed to a unique degree. (1960, 17)

What Species Should We Select for Comparison?   Many of the issues discussed with respect to single-species research apply equally well to cross-species work. In addition, however, one must choose a level at which to compare. King (1963) delineated three levels at which comparisons can be made—the genetic level, the species level, and the phyletic level. When working at the genetic level one compares the behavior of different strains, breeds, or subspecies of a single species. When working at the species level, one works with closely related species—typically within a genus, family, or superfamily. Work at the phyletic level entails comparisons across a broader range of species—often across orders or classes. Although there is some overlap among these three levels of comparison, they provide a useful structure within which to consider types of comparison made.

The level of comparison chosen will vary with the problem under study. Ethologists have often focused on the tracing of homologies and the delineation of evolutionary history. Often this is best done at the species level so that changes in the fine structure of behavior occurring through evolution can be seen. Even when studying adaptive significance, the species level can permit the observer to see behavior-ecology relationships more precisely than with the phyletic level because the species under study generally differ in fewer ways that are extraneous to the problem under study (King, 1962).

The student of behavior who is interested in understanding the broad sweep of evolutionary history will often be unsatisfied with species-level comparisons since they lack the sweeping generality being sought. That student may prefer work at the phyletic level. Even the student of adaptive significance may gain by studying species that are taxonomically quite diverse but ecologically similar. Some students of behavior are interested not in questions of adaptive significance or evolutionary history but simply in delineating the generality of a phenomenon. The phyletic level may be useful there as well, as has been noted by Bitterman:

> In the search both for commonalities and for differences in process, furthermore the only sensible course is to begin with markedly divergent animals. . . . Any differences in process that may exist are more likely to be discovered in comparisons of distantly related species. (1976, 219)

Although comparative psychologists have worked at both the species and phyletic levels, studies at the phyletic level have been more common.

Exceptions are such work as that of Watson (1908b) on the behavior of sooty terns and noddy terns; Schneirla (1957b) on doryline ants; Gottlieb (1963a, 1963b) on imprinting in ducks, Rosenblum (1971) on development in macaques; and Dewsbury (1975) on copulatory behavior in muroid rodents. Examples of comparisons of broad phyletic level include those of Hobhouse (1901) of dogs, cats, monkeys, otters, and elephants; Shepard (1911, 1914) of ants, rats, cats, and humans; Glickman and Sroges (1966) on over a hundred assorted zoo species; Voronin (1962) on fishes, tortoises, pigeons, rooks, hens, ducks, rabbits, rats, dogs, macaques, green monkeys, baboons, capuchins, chimpanzees, and humans; and Bitterman (1965a, 1965b) on learning in fish, turtles, pigeons, rats, and monkeys.

Because comparative psychologists ask such diverse questions, there is no simple generalization one can propose regarding the species they should study. What is important is that the species or group selected should be appropriate to the generalizations to be made. Thus, as noted by Hodos and Campbell (1969), among others, if one wishes to delineate evolutionary history, it is important that the species selected represent as close to a phylogenetic sequence as possible. Where other criteria are used in selecting species, generalizations will be limited by the criteria used in selecting species.

Domestication

Psychologists have been criticized for overuse of domesticated species from at least the time of C. O. Whitman (1898/1899) to the present (for example, Lester, 1973; Gould, 1982). The issue of domestication was raised in the controversy between Thorndike and Mills (for example, Mills, 1896b); between Hirsch and Tinbergen (for example, Tinbergen, 1957); and between Kavanau and Hawkins (for example, Hawkins, 1964). As should be apparent from the last three chapters—and as will be elaborated on in the following discussion—many important studies in comparative psychology have been done with nondomesticated animals. Nevertheless, it is true that a large number of comparative psychologists have studied laboratory rats, domestic chickens, cats, dogs, and other domesticated species. A surprising number of ethological observations have been made with domesticated animals such as pets or on animals in domestic settings (for example, aquaria, private houses, and private ponds).

Researchers do not agree on the extent of the effects of the process of domestication on animal behavior. In the view of many ethologists (for example, Eibl-Eibesfeldt, 1975), the effects of domestication are considerable and degenerative. Various behavioral differences are typically cited in support of this view. In the view of others (for example, Boice, 1973; Miller, 1977a), the behavioral effects of domestication are less substantial, nondegenerative, and often induced by the conditions of testing rather than by domestication per se.

Boice (1980) lays the "blame" for a general view that rats are degenerate on four researchers. Stone (1932) found that wild rats reacted poorly to a maze situation but learned quickly if they responded. Richter (1949) demonstrated a reduction in the size of some endocrine glands in domesticated rats. Beach (1950) pointed to limitations of research on laboratory rats. Finally, Lockard (1968) launched an all-out attack on rat research, labeling laboratory rats as "degenerate" and a "bad habit" for research. It was Lockard who went beyond implication to make such a view explicit.

There is in comparative psychology a long tradition of research on the effects of domestication on behavior. Much of this has focused on rats. Early work in the field includes the research of Small (1901), Yerkes (1913b), Stone (1932), and Richter (1954). More recently there has been a resumption of active research in the work of Robert Boice, E. O. Price, and others (for example, Boice, 1973). Accurate comparisons of the behavioral patterns and tendencies of domesticated and nondomesticated animals are difficult because they often react differently to test situations. Wild rats, for example, can be difficult subjects (see Small, 1901). Numerous differences have been documented in comparative research on domestication (see Boice, 1973, 1980). However, it seems best to view such changes as adaptations to the conditions of captivity that have made the animal better adapted to such conditions than to view the process of domestication as one promoting degeneracy (Boice, 1973; Ratner and Boice, 1975). Further, research on domesticated species may be particularly important for humans (for example, Ratner and Boice, 1975), as witnessed by the current growth of the field of "applied animal ethology."

Other confounding factors in the study of domestication are the effects of captivity and of the testing conditions themselves. Captivity itself can create changes in behavior that are different from the long-term effects of domestication (Boice, 1981). It is important that domesticated animals be tested under conditions that permit the full expression of behavior and in a manner comparable to that in which nondomesticated species are tested. When albino rats were kept in an outdoor pen throughout a cold Missouri winter, they built extensive burrows, survived, and reproduced as did wild animals (Boice, 1977b). Comparison of wild and domesticated forms of mallard ducks under appropriate testing conditions revealed few major changes in either social displays (Miller, 1977b) or production and perception of maternal alarm calls (Miller and Gottlieb, 1981).

The implication of these results is that whether one chooses to work with or to avoid domesticated animals depends on the question being asked. If asking a question of an applied nature, domesticated animals may be preferred. For questions of adaptive significance in nature, domesticated animals are generally best avoided. For other questions, domesticated or nondomesticated animals may be appropriate or inappropriate, depending on other considerations.

ANIMALS STUDIED BY COMPARATIVE PSYCHOLOGISTS

As revealed in Chapters 2, 3, and 4 comparative psychologists have studied a great variety of species. It is neither possible nor desirable to list and catalog all of these. It is instructive, however, to review some of the animals comparative psychologists have studied as this can provide some idea of the range of interests that have been displayed.

Rats

There can be no disputing the fact that rats have been the most popular subjects in comparative psychology. Although the data of Beach (1950) are open to several sources of bias (see Chapter 1), the general implication remains true that comparative psychology has been dominated by much research on rats. By 1929, Drake et al. (1930) published a bibliography of 1,353 references to papers dealing with research on rats. Not all the papers related to behavior. One wonders how many entries would appear were such a bibliography published today.

It has sometimes been stated that the choice of rats as a subject for research was accidental (for example, Beach, 1950; Lockard, 1968). However, reference to the earliest workers reveals that this was not the case (for example, Miles, 1930; Warden, 1930). Small, Kline, and others were searching for an appropriate animal with which to study learning. Again and again they emphasized the importance of selecting a task that is appropriate for the capacities and natural propensities of the animal under study. Both Small (1901) and Kline (in Miles, 1930) emphasized the importance of such appropriate testing conditions. The spread of rats as animal subjects appears to have resulted from convenience, low cost, and the bank of available knowledge. If there have been problems with this spread, they have generally stemmed from experimenters forgetting the natural capacities and limitations of their animals and generalizing in inappropriate ways from their data. Rats are neither good nor poor subjects for research; like any animal, they are appropriate for some research and inappropriate for others.

Invertebrates

In the view of John Watson, early comparative psychology was dominated by studies of invertebrates. He wrote:

> A glance at the bibliography of comparative psychology for the past two years will show that we have ten studies on the behavior of lower organisms to one on mammals. The reason is not far to seek if we consider the comparatively small amount of care and expense the lower organisms require. A jar of water and a wisp of hay suffice to give paramecium a suitable habitation. But a mammal, even so low in the scale as the rat, must have intelligent care. (1906, 151)

It is likely that Watson used the term *comparative psychology* in this passage to refer to all research on animal behavior regardless of the discipline of the researcher. Nevertheless, the perspective is interesting. Also noteworthy was the comment of Dyal and Corning (1973, 38) regarding the "dearth of research on the behavior modification in invertebrates." Particularly notable is the fact that the comment was made in the introductory chapter to a three-volume set on invertebrate learning (Corning et al., 1973).

Comparative psychologists have had a long-standing interest in acellular organisms, although clearly they have contributed less than biologists in this regard. In developing suggestions for a laboratory course in comparative psychology, Kline (1899b) suggested research on amoeba, vorticella, and paramecia. Kline (1899a) reported observations on the behavior of *Vorticella gracilis*. Comparative psychologists became involved in the considerable interest in the behavior of acellular organisms early in the century as in the studies of Day and Bentley (1911) on learning in paramecium and Mast and Lashley (1916) on ciliary currents in paramecia. With occasional exceptions (for example, French, 1940a, 1940b), interest lay dormant until Gelber (for example, 1952) stimulated renewed interest (for example, Jensen, 1957a; Katz and Deterline, 1958). Jensen (1959) developed a theory of paramecium behavior. Various studies of learning in acellular organisms have been conducted since this renewal of interest (for example, Hanzel and Rucker, 1972; Wood, 1973).

As they are the simplest organisms with a bilaterally symmetrical nervous system, it was natural that comparative psychologists would become interested in planarians. The classic study of Thompson and McConnell (1955) and the subsequent work in McConnell's laboratory (see McConnell, 1976) led to a rash of studies of instrumental and classical conditioning in planarians by professionals (see Corning and Kelly, 1973) and in hundreds or thousands of high school science-fair projects. Probably the first psychologist to study planarians, however, was E. G. Boring (1912), working in Titchener's laboratory at Cornell.

Systematic research on learning in segmented worms probably began with Yerkes's (1912) study in the *Journal of Animal Behavior.* The study of learning in earthworms has since been conducted using both classical and instrumental paradigms and in a variety of laboratories (for example, Ratner and Miller, 1959; Robinson, 1953; Wayner and Zellner, 1957; Wyers et al., 1974). Rosenkoetter and Boice (1975) suggested that some of the apparent maze learning in earthworms may in fact be behavioral change consequent upon the deposition of pheromones in the apparatus.

This is not the place for an extensive review of the diverse invertebrates that have been studied by comparative psychologists. A sample would include octopuses (for example, Schiller, 1948*b;* Sutherland, 1959); spiders (Porter, 1906*a;* Christenson et al., 1979); sea anemones (Logan and Beck, 1978); horseshoe crabs (for example, Lahue et al., 1975; Smith and Baker, 1960); and starfish (Schneirla and Maier, 1940). Students of crustaceans have included Yerkes (1902) on green crabs; Yerkes and Huggins (1903) on crayfish; Stevens (1939) on spider crabs; and Bell (1906) on crayfish. A direct line of descent can be traced among students of ants from Shepard (1911, 1914) to Schneirla (for example, 1946*c*) and Topoff (1976)—to say nothing of Barnes and Skinner (1930). Meal worms have been studied by Balfour and Carmichael (1928) and Grosslight and Ticknor (1953); *Drosophila* by Hirsch (1959) and Hirsch and Boudreau (1958); honeybees by Bermant and Gary (1966) and Couvillon and Bitterman (1980); cockroaches by Church and Lerner (1976); wasps by Kline (1899*c*); and blowflies by McGuire and Hirsch (1977).

It would be impossible in 1983 to contend that comparative psychology is dominated by the study of invertebrates. However, it is clear that comparative psychologists have turned to the study of invertebrates again and again. They have studied different species, different behaviors, and in different laboratories stemming from different traditions. Many of the studies have simply been attempts to demonstrate the presence of learning in invertebrates; this is a necessary first step. In other studies, however, analysis has moved beyond mere demonstration into systematic analyses of the processes involved in the regulation of invertebrate behavior.

Fishes

Fishes were popular subjects in research in comparative psychology around the turn of the century. Kline (1899*b*, 413) extolled the desirability of studies on fishes because "they stand at the bottom of the great back-boned series of animal life presenting in a simple and fundamental form all the essential structures characteristic of that group." Studies during this period were conducted by Thorndike (1899c), Triplett (1901), Gurley (1902), and Washburn and Bentley (1906). Interest in fishes was somewhat sporadic after this (for example, Miles, 1931; Perkins and Wheeler, 1930) but has since been revived with work in several different laboratories (for example, Schiller, 1948a; Hainsworth et al., 1967; Cole and Caldwell, 1956; Munn, 1958; Warren, 1960; Dewsbury, 1966). Bitterman's laboratory has been particularly active in the study of learning in fish (for example, Bitterman et al., 1958; Bitterman, 1965a). Particular interest was generated in the study of the role of the teleost telencephalon in learning and performance (for example, Dewsbury and Bernstein, 1969; Hainsworth et al., 1967; Warren, 1961).

Amphibians and Reptiles

The study of amphibians and reptiles has never played a major role in the development of comparative psychology. However, as with other taxa, comparative psychologists have periodically turned their attention to "herps," and some interesting studies have been conducted. Most of the research has related to learning, feeding, sensory function, and development. Salamanders were used by Carmichael (1926, 1927, 1928) and Goldstein (1960). Frogs and toads have been studies by Yerkes (1903), Carmichael (1926, 1927, 1928), Munn (1939), Miller et al. (1974), and Boice (1970). In the Boice (1970) study, ease of conditioning varied with the ecological adaptations of the species studied. Turtles have been studied by Yerkes (1901), Daniel and Smith (1947), Tinklepaugh (1932a), and Bitterman (1965a). Snake behavior has been studied by Kellogg and Pomeroy (1930), Burghardt (for example, Burghardt et al., 1973), and Chiszar (for example, Chiszar et al., 1976).

Birds

Interest in bird behavior by comparative psychologists has been both substantial and continuous. Although much of the research has been with domesticated chickens and ducks, a surprising variety of studies of bird species have found their way into the psychological literature.

Domestic chicks and ducks have been popular subjects at least from the time of Spalding (1873; 1875) and Morgan (1894). Both used them in developmental studies, and this has been their primary use ever since. Many studies throughout the century have been directed at the development of pecking and/or eating as noted in the controversy initiated by Mills (1896a) and in the work of Breed (1911), Shepard and Breed (1913), Moseley (1925), Bird (1925, 1926, 1933), Cruze (1935), Padilla (1935), and

Hogan (1973). Innate perceptual preferences were studied by Rheingold and Hess (1957) and Fantz (1957). Many researchers have studied imprinting using domestic fowl (for example, Hess, 1964; Jaynes, 1956; Moltz, 1960). Such animals also figured in the controversy over the hawk-goose phenomenon (for example, Hirsch et al., 1955) and in the developmental studies of Kuo (1932*a*, 1932*b*). Adult chickens have been studied in work on learning and social behavior as in the work of Dunlap (1933), Murchison (1935), and Smith and Hale (1959).

Pigeons have become to contemporary operant psychologists what rats were to the learning theorists of the 1940s. However, pigeons have also been used in studies of reproductive behavior (Carpenter, 1932, 1933), genetics of the tumbler mutation (Mowrer, 1940), orientation (Gundlach, 1931, 1932; Meyer, 1964*a*, 1964*b*), visual function (Towe, 1954), and maze learning (Hunter, 1911).

Although ring doves are best known to psychologists through the work of Lehrman on reproductive behavior (for example, Lehrman, 1958, 1965), they were used earlier in a variety of studies of visual function and perception (Yerkes and Eisenberg, 1915; Warden and Rowley, 1929; Warden and Baar, 1929; Siegel, 1953).

Among the other species to be found in single-species research are crows (Coburn, 1914; Coburn and Yerkes, 1915), sooty and noddy terns (Watson and Lashley, 1915), ducks (Gottlieb, 1963*a*, 1963*b;* Melzack et al., 1959), starlings (Adler and Dalland, 1959), English sparrows (Porter, 1904), mynahs (Kamil and Hunter, 1970), buzzards (Dennis, 1941), cariana (Swindle, 1919*a*), ravens and goose eagles (Swindle, 1919*b*), and parrots (Lashley, 1913).

Some psychologists have done comparative research on birds. Porter (1906*b*, 1910) studied cowbirds, pigeons, vesper sparrows, English sparrows, white-crowned sparrows, fox, song, and tree sparrows, blue jays, bluebirds, Baltimore orioles, and juncos. Sanborn (1932) studied hand-reared canaries, Baltimore orioles, cardinals, brown thrashers, robins, bluebirds, goldfinches, indigo buntings, English sparrows, red-wing blackbirds, orchard orioles, finches, larks, and nightingales. Kuo (1967) included observations on Japanese gray quail, Asian song thrushes, mynahs, South China white eyes, Peking robins, strawberry finches, masked jay thrushes, pigeons, chickens, and ducks. Gossette and Gossette (1967) compared reversal learning in crows, red-billed blue magpies, Greater Hill mynas, pigeons, ring doves, trumpeters, chukars, bob-white quail, and white leghorn chickens.

Mammals

Despite all the research just cited, it remains true that psychologists have devoted a disproportionate amount of research to mammals. There is little to be gained by listing the number of studies completed with hamsters, house mice, guinea pigs, gerbils, deer mice, and myriad other rodents and other species. A few examples of the breadth of research on mammals will suffice.

A reasonably complete comparative psychology could be written for cats. As early as 1915, Cole could write of the psychology of mammals as "a mere generalization of the psychology of cats" (1915, 159). Adams (1929) reviewed much of the early research on cats including the work of Mills, Romanes, Hobhouse, and others. It was Thorndike's dissertation (1898a) that first established the place of cats in the psychological laboratory. Other research on learning includes that of Hamilton (1911), Shepherd (1915a), Adams (1929), Carmichael and Marks (1932), Guthrie and Horton (1943), and Warren and Baron (1956). Imitation has been studied by Berry (1908), Thorndike (1898a), and Herbert and Harsh (1944). The student of cat behavior can find information on reproductive behavior (for example, Cooper, 1944; Beach and Zitrin, 1945; Whalen, 1963; Schneirla et al., 1963), social behavior (for example, Winslow, 1944a, 1944b), sensory function (for example, Swindle, 1917; Riesen and Aarons, 1959), and orientation (Gundlach, 1931; Rosenblatt et al., 1969). Cats have been popular subjects in the study of development as in the development of orientation (Rosenblatt et al., 1969), the righting reflex (Carmichael, 1934; Warkentin and Carmichael, 1939), and inter-actions with rodents (Berry, 1908; Yerkes and Bloomfield, 1919; McDougall and McDougall, 1927; Rogers, 1932; Kuo, 1938). This quick review merely touches the surface of the literature on domestic cats. Other felidae have been studied as well (for example, Cooper, 1942; Lanier and Dewsbury, 1976).

Other carnivores have served as popular subjects in psychological research. Raccoons have long been popular (for example, Cole, 1907, 1915; Davis, 1907; Hunter, 1911; Shepherd, 1911; Michels and Brown, 1959). Many workers have used dogs as subjects as in the study of learning by Shepherd (1915a), response to cues from humans (Warden and Warner, 1928), and reproductive behavior (for example, Beach and Gilmore, 1949)—to say nothng of studies in classical conditioning.

Other examples of the range of mammals studied by psychologists include bison (Lott, 1974), elephant seals (LeBoeuf, 1974), moose and elk (Altmann, 1952, 1963), sheep and goats (Liddell, 1925), dolphins (McBride and Hebb, 1948; Kellogg, 1959, 1961), squirrels (Yoakum, 1909), rabbits (for example, Stone, 1932a), coati-mundis, cacomistles, and skunks (Gossette and Gossette, 1967), and assorted zoo animals (Hobhouse, 1901; Glickman and Sroges, 1966).

Primate research in comparative-psychology laboratories began around the turn of the century with the work of Thorndike (1901a), Hobhouse

(1901), Watson (1908*a*), Kinnaman (1902*a*, 1902*b*), and Lashley (1917). Books could be written to review the subsequent literature on primate behavior generated by psychologists. Literally hundreds of publications have come from Yerkes and the Yerkes Laboratories and from Harlow's Wisconsin laboratory. Many other prominent psychologists have made considerable contributions to the literature in primatology (for example, I. S. Bernstein, C. R. Carpenter, B. T. Gardner, R. A. Gardner, R. W. Goy, W. A. Mason, E. Menzel, H. W. Nissen, A. J. Riopelle, A. H. Riesen, D. M. Rumbaugh, and J. M. Warren).

Conclusion

Comparative psychologists have been more limited in their choice of species than many observers would have them be. Nevertheles, even a superficial survey reveals that a remarkable number of species has been included in comparative-psychological research.

It should be emphasized that there is no virtue in developing a large catalog of species studied for the sake of the catalog. Diversity is valuable when it permits tests of the generality of phenomena that have been observed and when it helps in the development of principles of generality.

Schrier (1969) predicted little change in the behavior of animal psychologists following the pleas of Beach (1950) and Lockard (1968). He proposed that "the primary reason for this is that few, if any, unequivocal, consistent qualitative differences of any kind between species have been uncovered yet by comparative psychologists . . . " (1969, 682). Schrier refers primarily to the literature on learning and reinforcement. The reader is, of course, free to agree or disagree with this view; in my view, many important differences have been demonstrated.

COMPARATIVE PSYCHOLOGY IN LABORATORY AND FIELD

Only rarely has the issue of field versus laboratory research been perceived as controversial in comparative psychology. Most comparative psychologists have agreed that both field and laboratory work are necessary; both have their advantages and disadvantages. That the overwhelming majority of comparative psychologists have worked primarily in the laboratory can be attributed to both the necessity for controlled observations at the time of development of the science and logistics. Nevertheless, numerous comparative psychologists have conducted field studies and made contributions with such work. Almost all comparative psychologists are sympathetic with the field approach; many report tinges of guilt at not doing more themselves.

Sympathy Toward Field Research

A first step in developing a field approach is to generate a sympathetic attitude toward field studies. Perhaps the most grudging recognition of this came from Kuo, himself an amateur birdwatcher. "Naturalistic observations are valuable only insofar as they help the student of behavior broaden his outlook so that in devising experimental programs he will look beyond the narrow confines of the laboratory animal" (Kuo, 1967, 22). Grudging it may be, but this shows how Kuo, so often attacked by ethologists, did recognize the limitations of laboratory work.

Once they are "converted" to fieldwork, psychologists often write with more enthusiasm. Menzel wrote:

> What can a laboratory psychologist do once he has been bitten by the bug of field work(?) . . . I would say that what we are trying to discover, reconstruct, analyze and ultimately generalize to, is behavior as it occurs in nature without interference. If our present theoretical biases and methodological inhibitions are so great that they obscure this fact, let us forget theory and method, and try to approach the phenomena of behavior as if for the first time. (1967, 184)

Mason (1968a) wrote of the kinds of personal characteristics, training, and approach that characterize the field comparative psychologist. Gustavson (1982) wrote an article entitled "A Psychologist Responds to the Call of the Wild." Similar personal attributes have been noted by popular writers, as in O'Reilly's (1953) portrayal of Schneirla and Price's (1968) portrayal of Carpenter. Lott (1975) commented on the extent to which colleagues view fieldwork as a vacation.

Comparative psychologists have always been aware of the advantages of field research. In Chapter 2, I quoted Kinnanman (1902a), Davis (1907), Hall (1908), and Watson (in Cohen, 1979). This recognition has continued throughout most of the century:

> I am extremely anxious to see field studies develop. I feel that most of our problems are to be raised by field studies and that after we have turned our animals out of the lab we ought to retest our hypotheses in the field. (Watson to Yerkes in 1913, quoted by Cohen, 1979, 72)

> Field observation must always hold a place of honor in the biological sciences and particularly so in comparative psychology. (Warden et al., 1935, 30)

> Ultimately, however, the natural setting is required to test the all-round harmonious working of all action systems of the organism. (Stone, 1947, 345)

In a forceful review of the role of naturalistic observation in comparative psychology, Miller (1977a) specified five roles of naturalistic observation: (1) to study nature for its own sake, (2) to serve as a point of departure from which to develop a program of laboratory research, (3) to validate or add substance to previously obtained laboratory findings, (4) to increase the efficiency of utilization of animals in the laboratory, and (5) to use the field as a 'natural' laboratory.

Methods in Field Research

The next step in fieldwork entails developing methods for such studies. Many fieldworkers have developed methods as they conducted their work, and there is a wealth of valuable information in their studies. Carpenter, in particular, is credited with establishing standards of breadth and objectivity that have become the model in current fieldwork (see DeVore, 1965; Teleki, 1981). Nevertheless, in his concluding comments of *Naturalistic Behavior of Nonhuman Primates* (1964), Carpenter noted the limitations of his work and pointed to some methodological improvements that might be made.

A classic paper in the discussion of field methods is Schneirla's "The Relationship between Observation and Experimentation in the Field Study of Behavior" (1950). The editors of his selected works chose this paper with which to begin the volume. Schneirla viewed the laboratory and field as lying along a continuum and believed that both were important. He delineated methods whereby improved control, reliability, and validity of observations could be generated in the field situation. For Schneirla, the fieldworker was never simply an observer but was an active participant in the research process whose own behavior needed control.

Field Studies in Comparative Psychology

It takes more than attitude or methodological sophistication to make a field study; one still must go and do the work. Each decade of comparative psychology in the twentieth century has seen some development with respect to field research. These developments have been discussed in their appropriate time frames in Chapters 2, 3, and 4. I shall briefly summarize the magnitude of this work in an effort at closure. Easily the most substantial effort at early fieldwork was that of Watson with his studies of noddy and sooty terns in the Dry Tortugas (1907a, 1908b, 1910a, 1915; Watson and Lashley, 1915). Other early field observations were made by Yerkes (1903).

Although Yerkes probably did more than any other single person to facilitate field studies of nonhuman primates, he did not conduct sustained fieldwork of his own. He did make one trip to Africa, and he conducted research on primates in a great variety of settings. It was under Yerkes's guidance, however, that Nissen (1931) initiated his field study of chimpanzees, Bingham (1932) conducted his fieldwork on gorillas, and Carpenter (1934) launched his career as a field comparative psychologist. Yerkes (1932b) envisaged the program of the Yale Laboratories of Comparative Psychobiology as three-pronged, with one prong being field research in the natural setting. He planned full-scale research in Africa soon after Nissen's work, but this plan was thwarted by the Depression, World War II, and upheavals in Africa (Hahn, 1971).

The two workers with the longest and most substantial field-research programs have been Carpenter and Schneirla. Carpenter's fieldwork is best summarized in his 1964 book, and Schneirla's in the book of his selected writings (Aronson et al., 1972).

More recent field researchers have included Margaret Altmann (1952, 1963), Gilbert Gottlieb (1963a, 1963b), Eckhard Hess (1972), William Mason (1968a, 1968b), Irwin Bernstein (1967, 1968), Emil Menzel (1966, 1967, 1968), Charles Snowden (Snowden and Hodun, 1981), Lewis Petrinovich (Petrinovich et al., 1976), Howard Topoff (1976), Terry Christenson (Christenson et al., 1979), Robert Lockard (1975), Stephen Glickman (1980), Dale Lott (1974), Burney LeBoeuf (1974), and Carl Gustavson (1982; Gustavson et al., 1974).

Conditions for Laboratory Studies

Early workers in comparative psychology generally conducted laboratory studies but with an eye toward behavior in the field and for the nature of the conditions under which the animals were tested. Wesley Mills (1898, 1899) was an early champion of a naturalistic approach in comparative psychology. Linus Kline and W. S. Small, the early pioneers of research on rats in mazes and other learning problems, repeatedly emphasized the importance of natural conditions in their work (Kline, 1899a; Small, 1900, 1901; Miles, 1930; Warden, 1930). As succinctly noted by Kline, "I was impressed with the importance of working with animals in as natural moods as conditions permitted" (in Miles, 1930, 326). The early work with rats in mazes and puzzle boxes was not designed arbitrarily; it was designed originally to mimic as best as possible the behavior of rats as it was understood to occur in nature.

Many workers have adapted the animals and procedures of the early workers. Some have remained conscious of the conditions that exist in nature, and others have not. Such cognizance is clearly more important for some problems than for others. Nevertheless, a considerable number of workers have always been concerned with the extent to which their conditions mimicked those in nature. Laboratory rats are good subjects for studies in maze learning; their usefulness in studies of visual acuity is less clear. The kind of data generated in research laboratories has been, in part, a function of the closeness of the match between the demands of the task and the adaptations of the organism for life in its environment (for example, Bolles, 1970; Seligman, 1970). The extent to which testing conditions can affect behavior and even mask evolutionarily adapted behavior in domesticated species has recently been emphasizd by Miller (Miller, 1977*b;* Miller and Gottlieb, 1981). Although the match between field and laboratory conditions has not always been close, the desirability of such a match has rarely been disputed.

ANECDOTES AND EARLY OBJECTIVISM

There is nothing intrinsically wrong with an anecdote. Unique sets of conditions occurring outside the controlled laboratory situation may call forth feats of animal behavior that could not easily be elicited in the less-challenging laboratory situation. However, the difficulties with giving such occasional occurrences a proper interpretation are serious. The problems center on the lack of control and inability to repeat. Under the conditions prevailing when most anecdotes have been gathered, there has been no way to record observations properly to ensure accuracy nor to determine the aspects of the situation responsible for the behavior—thus permitting the observer to separate behavior that is truly remarkable from that which occurs by chance. One is reminded of Thorndike's quip (1898*a*) about the number of lost dogs that never return and the one that happens to find its way from Yonkers to Brooklyn. We simply have no grounds with which to determine whether the dog that found its way responded by chance (for a small proportion of wandering, lost dogs must eventually head in the correct direction) or displayed true homing.

Warden (1928) listed six objections to anecdotes as a source of scientific information: (1) the observer is likely to be untrained; (2) observation and interpretation are often mixed together; (3) phenomena are difficult to interpret without knowledge of the animal's history; (4) anecdotes are highly selected according to criteria that are unstated; (5) errors of memory often occur; and (6) it is difficult to select the reliable material from the available sources.

The anecdotal movement in comparative psychology was triggered by Darwinism and the effort to demonstrate behavioral continuity between humans and nonhuman species. This relationship was demonstrated by selecting anecdotes demonstrating reasoning, high-order social behavior, or humanlike emotions in nonhuman animals (Warden, 1928). Romanes,

Buchner, Lindsay, and Perty were among the leading anecdotalists, but Darwin himself often utilized such material; there was little else at the time. In *Animal Intelligence,* Romanes (1882) relied on numerous anecdotes from diverse taxa in demonstrating continuity. For example:

> The parrot which belonged to the Buffon family showed much sympathy with a female servant to whom it was attached when the girl had a sore finger, which it displayed by its never leaving her sick room, and groaning as if itself in pain. As soon as the girl got better the bird again became cheerful. (p 275)

Darwin (1873*b*) transmitted to *Nature* a letter from a William Huggins purporting to demonstrate a genetic basis for an aversion to butcher shops in a line of English mastiffs owned by individuals in different villages. Darwin treated the case as an instance of an instinct that "may have arisen suddenly in an individual and then been transmitted to its offspring, independently both of selection and serviceable experience ... " (1873*b*, 281).

The anecdotalists were aware of the difficulties inherent in relying on such information. In the preface to *Animal Intelligence,* for example, Romanes discussed the problem and listed the criteria that he used in sifting out the reliable observations from those of questionable value. Most contemporary readers believe that he was unsuccessful in making these discriminations. It should be remembered, however, that solid experimental data were rare in 1883.

The difficulty in securing scientific information is underscored in a note written by G. Stanley Hall and R. R. Gurley in *Science.* They request "data as to habit, instincts or intelligence in animals, above all, minor and trifling ones not in the books" (1896, 482). They asked the reader to "answer as fully as possible, always stating age, sex, place, date (or season), species, breed, and whether personally observed" (1896, 482).

The anecdotal movement was important in triggering an early objectivist movement in reaction to it. Many biologists and psychologists pointed to the various difficulties with the anecdotal method and conducted better-controlled studies. Among those opposing the anecdotal movement were Wundt (1894), Morgan (1894), Thorndike (1898*a*), Lubbock (1888), Verworn, Loeb (for example, 1900), and Washburn (1908*a*). By and large, the arguments made by these workers and others prevailed, and the experimental movement spread throughout comparative psychology and biology, whereas the use of anecdotes faded.

It should be noted that early objectivists were not unified in the approach to behavior that they advocated. Loeb's theory based on tropisms resulting from physico-chemical reactions, for example, drew heavy criticism from workers such as Angell (1939), von Buddenbrock (1916), and especially Jennings (1906). Mills (1898) wrote favorably of Romanes's contribution. Although there were differences in approach, however, the standards for scientific evidence in the first part of the twentieth century were much more rigorous than those that could be used in the heyday of the anecdotalists.

It is a mistake to view anecdotalism solely as a problem characteristic of the last century. The issue of the use of anecdotal information resurfaces again and again in the study of animal behavior. Watson criticized observations by Witmer as "a return to the worst type of anecdotalism" (1911, 445). In reviewing a book on the adaptive significance of intelligence by W. E. Ritter, Warden noted:

> One is impressed also by the fact that the method of treatment adopted by this author is quite as archaic as the problem itself. Surely this learned biologist knows that the method of anecdote has long since been discarded by all serious students of animal behavior. (1927c, 346)

The issue of anecdotalism has arisen in the interpretation of some data in the sociobiological literature. Beach (1978), for example, was critical of the way some sociobiologists interpret evidence. The primary case in point concerned infanticide in Indian langurs. There is no doubt that numerous infants died in various langur troops under study. Few of the deaths were observed, however. It is inferred that these deaths resulted from evolutionarily adapted behavior displayed by adult males taking over troops of females. However, there are so few observations of the actual events causing death that it is difficult to determine whether these deaths are in fact the result of adapted behavior or of chance events perhaps related to disturbance of the habitat (see Curtin and Dolhinow, 1978). Curtin and Dolhinow note that there were only four observed instances of males killing infants; interpretation of these occurrences is difficult.

The issue of anecdotalism was also raised in the literature on ape language. In discussing the work of Gardner and Gardner (for example, 1969) with the chimpanzee Washoe, Savage-Rumbaugh et al. wrote, "We believe that there is not evidence, other than richly-interpreted anecdote, to suggest that Washoe and other signing apes are producing anything more than short-circuited iconic sequences" (1978, 551). As might be expected, the Gardners disagree with this interpretation (for example, Gardner, 1981).

A similar discussion appears in the literature on extrasensory perception. It appears that the better controlled the testing conditions, the less extrasensory perception is apparent. This can be interpreted as meaning that the phenomenon does not exist since it breaks down under controlled conditions. As objective scientists, however, we must also recognize the possibility that the controlled conditions destroy the phenomenon. There is no obvious way in which to separate these two possible explanations. Most scientists would not accept the existence of extrasensory perception in the absence of controlled data demonstrating its reality.

In studying animal behavior, we must always be alert to the possibility that the sterile conditions of the controlled laboratory destroy the phenomenon of interest. This does not mean that we should accept anecdotes uncritically. The solution would be to work toward enriched testing environments in which the behavior can be displayed, but controlled observations are possible. This is often difficult.

LLOYD MORGAN'S CANON

Perhaps the most quoted statement in the history of comparative psychology is Lloyd Morgan's canon. It has been adopted throughout psychology and other sciences as a basis for making sound inferences concerning the determinants of behavior. Because I wish to discuss the canon in some detail, I shall add to the frequency of its quotation by repeating it once more:

> In no case may we interpret an action as the outcome of the exercise of a higher psychical faculty, if it can be interpreted as the outcome of the exercise of one which stands lower in the psychological scale. (1894, 53)

Morgan emphasized the canon by restating it six pages later. Newbury (1954) noted that Morgan's terminology changed with successive revisions of his book. In later editions Morgan referred to "higher psychological processes," "processes which stand lower in the scale of psychological evolution and development," "a lower level of emergence," and, in Morgan (1932), to "an earlier and lower stage of mental development."

In the prevailing view, Morgan's canon is essentially equivalent to the "law of parsimony" or "Occam's razor." My first teacher in the history of psychology, P. L. Harriman, termed Morgan's canon "a restatement of the principle expounded by William of Occam" (1947, 225-226; see also 255). I followed Harriman and others (Dewsbury, 1973a, 1978a). This appears generally inaccurate. Morgan's canon refers to the level of psychical faculty or mental development assumed when explaining behavior. It refers particularly to comparisons across species and was related to the theory of emergent evolution. Occam's razor and the law of parsimony relate not to psychical level but to the *number* of assumptions used in explanation. What William of Occam wrote was, "It is vain to do with more what can be done with fewer" (quoted by Gray, 1963a, 221). This is sometimes altered to read "Entities are not to be multiplied without necessity" (Gray, 1963a, 221). The *law of parsimony* refers to a looser version of Occam's razor that has a variety of meanings, some of which can be traced back as far as Aristotle (Newbury, 1954). As noted by Newbury, "It is only confusing to say, without adequate qualification, that Morgan's Canon is derived from either, and of doubtful accuracy to identify it with them" (1954, 72). In essence, Morgan's canon relates to complexity of psychological processes, whereas the law of parsimony and Occam's razor relate to the *number* of assumptions or processes inferred.

Application of Morgan's canon may often result in a reduction of the number of processes required and/or assumed to operate in the control of behavior. Newbury noted that this is the basis for their similarity. If the canon is applied in this way, "the net effect is in line with Occam's Razor, while the admonition in the canon regards the lowness of the functions, not their paucity" (1954, 72).

Morgan's canon has often been misinterpreted (see Nagge, 1932; Gray, 1963a; Newbury, 1954; Tobach, 1978). The canon was not written in an effort to eliminate the attribution of consciousness to nonhuman animals. Morgan assumed the existence of consciousness in animals. As noted by Gray (1963a, 223), "Whatever prompted the introduction of the canon, the denial of mentality to animals was not the reason." Rather, Morgan used the canon to encourage interpretation of behavioral phenomena in terms of "sound psychological principles" (Morgan, 1894, 53; Dewsbury, 1979b). Although using the canon primarily in an evolutionary context, Morgan's goal was to reduce the degree of anthropomorphism in comparative psychology (see Morgan, 1894, 50-53); he appears not to have been completely successful in this attempt (Gray, 1963a).

In practice, Morgan's canon is difficult to apply. It involves many assumptions and entails both logical and methodological difficulties. How, for example, are we to determine which is a "higher" psychical process? As noted by Adams (1928, 243), "If he knows what he needs to know in order to apply his canon, he already has the answer to his question, and consequently no need of the canon."

Several authors have noted the extent to which wholesale application of Morgan's canon can retard the progress of science (for example, Adams, 1929; Dunbar, 1980; Griffin, 1976; Mills, 1899; Nagge, 1932; Waters, 1939; Wilson, 1975a). As these authors point out, rampant application of Morgan's canon can lead to a denial of the existence of complex processes where complex processes exist.

The law of parsimony and Morgan's canon are two closely related principles. Morgan's canon is difficult to apply. Nevertheless, the general rule of assuming neither more processes nor more complex processes than necessary unless such processes are required appears sound. It has served the developing science well. What needs emphasis, however, is that the principle should not be overapplied. Where complex processes exist, the researcher should not be dissuaded from believing they exit. The law of parsimony and Morgan's canon should guide science but should not be permitted to stifle it.

THE CLEVER HANS PHENOMENON

Oskar Pfungst's *Clever Hans (The Horse of Mr. Von Osten)* appeared in English in 1911. The horse Clever Hans was reputed to be capable of performing remarkable feats of arithmetic and of expressing answers by tapping his foot the appropriate number of times. Pfungst, working in collaboration with psychologist Carl Stumpf, determined that Hans was able to ascertain when to begin and to stop tapping by responding to subtle cues provided by his questioner. Thus Hans needed visual contact with his questioner. The cue for Clever Hans to begin tapping was a slight forward leaning on the part of Von Osten or other questioners. The questioner would inadvertently straighten up when the correct number of taps had been reached. Bringing the phenomenon into the laboratory, Pfungst found that twenty-three of twenty-five individuals cued Pfungst in a manner similar to that in which Clever Hans had been cued.

Ever since the publication of Pfungst's work, psychologists have been especially aware of the potential confounding of experiments resulting from inadvertent cuing by the experimenter and have taken steps to avoid it. In his introduction to the 1965 reprinted edition of Pfungst's book, Rosenthal (1965) reviewed the history of the problem and the various instances of similar inadvertent cuing.

The most recent allegations of a Clever Hans effect have arisen in conjunction with the research on language learning in apes. It has been proposed that cuing, of the sort detected by Clever Hans, may have been important in the performance of these animals. Sebeok and Umiker-Sebeok (1980) dedicated their book, *Speaking of Apes,* to Pfungst and included his photograph as a frontispiece; Sebeok and Umiker-Sebeok (1979) featured a photograph of Herr Von Osten and Clever Hans on the front page of their article, "Performing Animals: Secrets of the Trade." In both places they proposed that cues from the experimenter may have been used in these feats of animal communication. As stated by Terrace (1979, 76) "I have reason to believe that prompting by the teacher also influenced Washoe's signing." The debate over this issue became vituperative (see

Wade, 1980). Sebeok was quoted as saying, "The alleged language experiments with apes divide into three groups: one, outright fraud; two, self-deception; three, those conducted by Terrace. The largest class by far is the middle one" (Sebeok and Umiker-Sebeok, in Wade, 1980, 1351). Although the possibility of a Clever Hans effect is a real one, there are other issues in the debate over ape language that appear more central, as noted by Menzel (1981) in his review of Sebeok and Umiker-Sebeok's book entitled "Is Clever Hans a Dead Horse?" In a critical review, Ristav and Robbins (1982) considered the effect an unlikely explanation of chimpanzee feats.

A related issue concerns the extent to which humans read their own interpretations into the behavior of animals. Johnson (1912) reported another investigation by Pfungst, this time of a "talking dog." The animal made sounds resembling eight different words, although it appeared to have no capacity to use them with any degree of flexibility as is characteristic of language. After investigating the phenomenon, Pfungst concluded that uncritical observers knowledgeable regarding the correct answer did not discriminate the actual sounds produced by the dog from those they themselves associated with the correct answer.

This phenomenon too is one that may recur in the ape studies. There is some indication that the words produced by Hayes and Hayes's chimpanzee, Viki, may have been difficult to discern by the untutored observer. Sebeok and Umiker-Sebeok (1979) note that some of Gardner and Gardner's experiments were done using a double-blind procedure. They proposed, however, that "observers experienced in the ways of Washoe could also inadvertently pick up familiar nonverbal clues given off by the chimpanzee in response to certain objects . . ." (1979, 82).

The extent to which these two sources of bias in fact produced the remarkable feats of chimpanzee performance cannot be determined by a distant reviewer. To this observer, it seems unlikely that these cues can fully explain the performance of Washoe, Sarah, and Lana. The point of this discussion is not to resolve the issue; several authorities consider that it may be unresolvable (for example, Menzel, 1981). Rather, it should be noted that the issues raised by Clever Hans, like other methodological issues in the field, tend to arise again and again and point to important methodological precautions that must be taken by investigators of complex animal behavior.

BEHAVIORISM

Few areas of psychology have led to as many confusing interpretations as has behaviorism. Although some of the issues have been discussed earlier in their chronological context, as in 1910-1919 and

1920-1929, there is value in restating and bringing together some of these matters.

What Is Behaviorism?

I would follow Hunter with a simple definition of *behaviorism.* "Behaviorism is the point of view in psychology which holds that an adequate account can be given of psychological problems without reference to the terms consciousness and introspection" (Hunter, 1952, 186). The emphasis on the study of behavior with the concomitant lack of necessity of invoking either consciousness or the introspective method provides the essence of behaviorism. The implication is that a broad program can be developed and human behavior can be included within its framework. Gray (1980) lists a set of five assumptions of behaviorism: humanism, determinism, objectivism, phyletic realism, and psychological materialism. All can be seen as relating to a consistent application of the principle that the study of *behavior* can provide a complete account for psychology. In the first paragraph of the paper credited with the founding of behaviorism, Watson wrote:

> Psychology as the behaviorist views it is a purely objective experimental branch of natural science . . . . Introspection forms no essential part of its methods . . . . The behaviorist, in his efforts to get a unitary scheme of animal response, recognizes no dividing line between man and brute. (1913, 158)

What Is the Image of Behaviorism?

In the minds of many, the image of behaviorism differs markedly from that just stated. As noted by Skinner, Watson is remembered "for a too narrow interpretation of self-observation, for an extreme environmentalism, and for a coldly detached theory of child care, no one of which was a necessary part of his original program" (1959, 198).

According to Gould (1982), there are three basic assumptions to Watsonian-Skinnerian behaviorism: (1) The elements of behavior are not prewired neural circuits but reflexes linked together through conditioning; (2) the ultimate basis of behavior is learning; and (3) events occurring within the organism are irrelevant or even dangerous to the analysis of behavior. Gould writes of "the obsession of behaviorism with controlling the only variable admitted in behavior—the animal's physical environment" (1982, 7).

Hebb (1960, 737) notes that "it has been suggested that Behaviorism was a monstrous perversion, so bad that only a very brilliant man could have thought it up." He states that others regard it to be "imperceptive instead of brilliantly perverse" (1960, 737).

In writing of the history of comparative psychology, Jaynes wrote of its flowering in the first decade of this century and "its decadence under the dry paradigms of behaviorism" (1969, 603).

According to Lorenz:

> What behaviorists exclude from the narrow circle of their interest is not only other learning processes, but simply everything that is not contained in the process of learning by reinforcement—and this neglected remainder is neither more nor less than the whole of the remaining organism. (1981, 71)

There is little point in giving more examples; it should be clear that there is a considerable divergence of viewpoint on the essential tenets of behaviorism.

Forms of Behaviorism

The images held by intelligent people such as those cited in the previous section do not appear from a vacuum; they result from real events in the real environment. In my view, the notion that it is behavior, and not consciousness, that is the target for study constitutes the essence of behaviorism. However, various forms of behaviorism have been developed by certain prominent workers at different times in their careers. Thus we can easily distinguish early-Watsonian behaviorism, later-Watsonian behaviorism, Skinnerian behaviorism, Hullian behaviorism, Tolmanian behaviorism, and the like. What appears to have happened is that various attributes of these particular forms of behaviorism have come to be identified as defining attributes of the entire behavioristic enterprise. Unfortunately, it is later-Watsonian behaviorism, the form least compatible with a comparative-psychological-ethological approach, that has provided many of these "defining" characteristics.

Early-Watsonian Behaviorism.   Watson's *Behavior: An Introduction to Comparative Psychology* (1914), was based on his historic lectures at Columbia University in 1913 and provides the clearest statement of his early behavioristic approach. The first chapter is identical with "Psychology as the Behaviorist Views It" (Watson, 1913). In it Watson delineates the major assumptions of behaviorism and his reasons for rejecting consciousness as fit for study in psychology.

The most interesting chapters to a comparative psychologist are those on instinct. Watson could not be more clear in stating the nature of instinct as he viewed it: "Instincts are thus rightly said to be phylogenetic modes of response (as contrasted with habit, which is acquired during the lifetime of the individual)" (1914, 106-107). Watson discusses the importance of field research and the value of the isolation experiment; he also discusses instinctive behavior in birds, reptiles, and fishes. In his chapter on the origin of instincts, Watson provides thirty-six pages on behavioral evolution including discussions of natural selection, mutation, and sexual selection.

Recall that the John Watson who wrote this book is the same John Watson who was studying terns on the Dry Tortugas and that this is the book that fully established the revolution that is attributed to behaviorism. Clearly, early-Watsonian behaviorism bears little resemblence to the "behaviorism" whose image appears to have been preserved in the views of many.

Late-Watsonian Behaviorism. As Watson applied his behaviorist program, the study of human behavior became focal, and he drifted away from the study of nonhuman animals. He became concerned with the application of behaviorism for the betterment of society, and with these changes, Watson moved toward environmentalism. According to Gray (1980), there were four characteristics of Watson's own brand of metaphysics that led to his particular brand of behaviorism, or what I would call "late-Watsonian behaviorism." These are peripheralism, reductionism, social control, and environmentalism. Gray regards these as "antiscientific presuppositions" and noted that they were unique to Watson.

With the ready availability of Watson's *Behaviorism*, written in 1924 and revised in 1930, late-Watsonian behaviorism came to be veiwed as the essence of behaviorism itself. Watson's position implied extreme enviornmentalism, a conditioning approach to behavior, and a peripheralist view of its control.

Skinnerian Behaviorism. B. F. Skinner is properly credited with leading the development of the methodology of operant conditioning. The topic of his analysis is learned behavior, as studied primarily with rats depressing levers and pigeons pecking keys. In his best-known work, there is little of instinct or genetics, and his model for social change incorporates little genetic manipulation.

However, Skinner never was either a late-Watsonian behaviorist or as extreme an environmentalist as is often written. Skinner (1977) noted that his first five papers were about innate behavior, and he also conducted two additional studies on ethological topics. When he began studying operant conditioning, Skinner used inbred strains of rats, planning to make genetic tests, and with W. T. Heron, he studied the rate of extinction in an operant situation of maze-bright and maze-dull rats (Heron and Skinner, 1940). He chose to emphasize learned behavior primarily because of the ease of its study and the powerful alterations of behavior he could produce. The demonstration that environmental variables were powerful in altering certain forms of behavior had implications not only for the development of the science but for social application as well. The record of the operant-conditioning approach in these spheres is impressive. It is, however, something different from comparative psychology.

In recent years Skinner has dabbled in the issues relating to comparative psychology, ethology, and instinctive behavior. In *About Behaviorism,* he (1974, 34) noted, "Courting, mating, building nests, and caring for young are things organisms *do,* and again presumably because of the way they have evolved." In "The Phylogeny and Ontogeny of Behavior," Skinner (1966) noted certain parallels between the ways in which instinctive (that is, "phylogenic") behavior and learned (that is, "ontogenic") behavior are formed. In both there is a kind of shaping by environmental factors. Skinner pointed to the various problems inherent in the study of the evolution of behavior. He speculated on the ways in which phylogenic behavior evolves (1975). He was particularly concerned with the changes in the topography of the response, the change in stimuli controlling the behavior, and the maintenance of a high rate of occurrence. He found his best example of behavioral evolution in homing. According to Skinner (1977, 1006), "Operant conditioners have not neglected relevant genetic contributions." It should be noted that Herrnstein (1977*a*, 1977*b*) disagrees with some aspects of Skinner's analysis.

In his paper "Behaviorism at Fifty," Skinner termed the debate over genetic endowment and behavior "another disturbing digression" (1963, 952). He noted, "All this made it easy to lose sight of the central argument—that behavior which seemed to be the product of mental activity could be explained in other ways" (1963, 952).

Origins of Behaviorism

There were a number of workers early in the century whose contributions were important in the establishment of a science of behavior without reference to consciousness. The older German structuralism that had been dominant in psychology was replaced with a functionalism and an emphasis on the ways in which consciousness functioned rather than how it was structured. In a sense, behaviorism is an extension of the functionalism to which Watson was exposed at Chicago.

Others played important roles in establishing the objective study of behavior, including Thorndike, Loeb, Jennings, and Dunlap. Many authors have pointed out that Watson did not single-handedly invent behaviorism. Some would go so far as to suggest that one or another of the scientists just named should be credited as the "founder" of behaviorism. This has sparked a bit of controversy in the literature. According to Hirsch, "It was Loeb . . . who established and proclaimed the importance of the objective study of behavior and who decried the futility of subjectivism and anthropomorphism, not Watson, who in 1913 merely attached the label of behaviorism to that point of view . . . " (1973, vi).

For Donald Jensen (1962), it was Watson's colleague H. S. Jennings who deserves much of the credit. Watson learned first from Loeb and then moved to Johns Hopkins where he encountered Jennings. According to Jensen, "By 1914 he had adopted a point of view which differed little in principle from that of Jennings" (1962, xix).

Joncich (1968) would credit Thorndike with the founding of behaviorism. She states that Watson termed his proposals to eliminate consciousness from psychology "crass and raw." In Joncich's view, however, "The words might better describe his effort to usurp behaviorism, particularly on this site" (1968, 414). The site referred to was Columbia University — the site of Watson's lectures and the home university of Thorndike.

Knight Dunlap, another colleague at Johns Hopkins, said of Watson that "he was interested in the iconoclastic activity I was developing, and was influenced by my views, but carried them out to extremes" (1932, 45). Watson wrote of Dunlap, "He probably stated my indebtedness to him better than I can express it myself" (1936, 277). Dunlap's (1912) "The Case Against Introspection" was an important early paper, but its argument is different from Watson's (see Cohen, 1979, 63).

A case might also be made for Kirkpatrick who regarded "physiology, biology, and psychology as all being concerned in the study of behavior, whether conscious or unconscious" (1907, 543).

True to the spirit of biographers, Cohen (1979) held out for Watson as the founder of behaviorism. Relying on the extensive correspondence between Watson and Yerkes, he proposed that Watson's ideas of behaviorism grew gradually and that he was uncertain as they began to emerge. Cohen also tried to rebut the claims of others for their candidates, writing, for example, "To argue, as had been done, that Watson filched Jennings's ideas is misguided" (1979, 54). He notes that Watson began thinking of behaviorism in 1904 and that it differed appreciably from "neuromechanism."

In a review that appears to be particularly objective, Burnham (1968) stated that Watson deserves credit not just for advocating the demise of consciousness, but for proposing a constructive program in its place.

He noted that Watson did not merely propose sets of verbal mediating responses, advocate social control, and propose the application of methods used with nonhumans to humans. Rather, "Watson combined these elements into a synthesis, the whole of which was greater than its parts" (1968, 145). Burnham differentiated Watsonian views from those of the other contributors while giving the others credit for their contributions. In Burnham's view, "Rather than founder, Watson is better viewed as the charismatic leader of behaviorism" (1968, 151).

Little Albert

It should be clear that over time the image of a field can change even as the field changes little. Scientists sometimes display selective perception and retention that can affect the way an approach is viewed. The same can happen to a simple experiment. It will be recalled that Watson and Rayner (1920) conducted an experiment in which they established a "conditioned fear" in a boy, "Albert B.," by banging a steel bar, thus creating an offensive noise, whenever Albert touched a rat. Recently several authors have summarized and traced various erroneous portrayals of these experiments in prominent sources (Harris, 1979; Prytula et al., 1977; Samelson, 1980*b;* Seligman, 1980; and the notes following Seligman's). The breadth of distortion of the original experiment and the difficulty in attributing the sources of the distortions provides an interesting study in scientific communication.

Conclusion

The adoption of a behavioristic approach, in its general sense, has been a major reason for the progress made in comparative psychology in this century. Many on both sides of the ethology-comparative psychology controversy have expressed disdain for "behaviorism" (for example, Lorenz, 1981; Lehrman, 1970). Although they may disagree on some aspects of some forms of behaviorism, attacks on behaviorism per se appear misguided. Virtually all students of animal behavior have adopted the essential characteristics of behaviorism and have profited from it.

Some have adopted late-Watsonian behaviorism. A case can be made that such an approach greatly retarded the development of a broadly based comparative psychology.

Although adoption of a general behaviorist approach was important to progress in animal psychology, the field may not need to remain inflexibly tied to it. Conscious experience is reported by most humans and remains a topic of wonder. With advances in the study of behavior made possible by a behavioristic approach, it may some day be possible to probe consciousness. It appears worthwhile to have at least a few behaviorists working at this most important task (for example, Griffin, 1976; Mason, 1976a, 1980). For the majority of animal behaviorists, however, it appears that the primary topic for study will remain the study of behavior.

THE CONCEPT OF LEVELS

The concept of levels of organization has been interpreted by Schneirla and his students and associates as a fundamental principle in the study of animal behavior. Although it has gained virtually no recognition outside of this group, the centrality that they assign to it justifies some discussion of the principle.

Schneirla's Concept of Levels

In Schneirla's view there exists a hierarchical ordering of energy from the simplest organized entities to the most complex. Humans order their knowledge in conformity with such a hierarchy from cosmology and physics to biology and sociology. When considering animals, one can see a hierarchical arrangement with respect to neural organization, social organization, type of communication or other processes. As a result of the progressive nature of evolution, animals organized at higher levels are fundamentally and qualitatively different from those at lower levels. For that reason, it is a mistake to generalize across levels. Schneirla was particularly critical of ethologists, who use terms such as *releaser* and *fixed-action pattern* across a wide range of species. To quote the exact wording:

> For the wide range of existing animals, levels of integration are conceived as a series of progressive advances from the acellular (or "single-celled") animals through the multicellular. Each of these levels refers to animal groups which have in common a set of distinctive capacities for behavior. Any one level of integration in behavior, although certain to be similar in some respects to levels judged "lower" in the scale to which it is related through evolution, differs from them sufficiently to warrant its separate categorization. For example, the analysis of the physiological and behavioral interactions that prevail among bees in a hive gives no adequate preparation for studying human societies. (Tobach and Schneirla, 1968, 68)

Schneirla applied the concept of levels to social orgnaization (Schneirla, 1951, 1953; Tobach and Schneirla, 1968) to psychological capacities (Schneirla , 1949) and in other contexts. He emphasized that if the same word were used to describe processes that seem similar in different levels, there is a danger that one will infer that underlying processes are identical. The latter need not be the case. Schneirla noted, "When terms such as 'learning' are used in sweeping fashion on widely separate levels they encourage thinking conclusively of homogeneous agencies presumably understood in the various cases, rather than processes of very different nature still requiring explanation" (1949, 248).

The Usage of Schneirla's Students and Associates

Students and associates of Schneirla have relied heavily on the concept of levels. For example, in his classical critique of Lorenz's theory, Lehrman (1953) relied heavily on it. The paper includes sections on levels of "innateness," evolutionary levels, levels of neural organization, levels of behavioral function, and the human level. In his conclusion, Lehrman criticized Lorenz's theory by noting, "It is rigidly canalized by the merging of widely different kinds of organization under inappropriate and gratuitous categories," and "it habitually depends on the transference of concepts from one level to another, solely on the basis of analogical reasoning" (1953, 358).

Tobach (1978) made similar use of the levels concept in criticizing similar generalizations across species in the sociobiological movement. The concept has also been applied to the study of the evolution and development of emotion (Tobach, 1970) and to the study of communication (Tavolga, 1970). In the latter application, Tavolga defined six levels of communication: the vegetative, tonic, phasic, signal, symbolic, and language. In the view of Greenberg, "It was Schneirla who first systematically utilized evolution in comparative psychology by adopting a phylogenetic use of the integrative levels concept" (1982, 18).

Historical Antecedents of the Levels Concept

The reader may have noted many uses of concepts related to levels throughout the chronological history of comparative psychology. The concept of a *Scala Naturae* can be found in the writings of Aristotle (see Singer, 1981; Hodos and Campbell, 1969). Warden (1928) traced the historical development of various views on the concept of psychic levels, from Loeb and Morgan through Schneider, Kirkpatrick, and Yerkes. I shall consider four uses.

Romanes (1888) used a system that included fifty levels that referred to the products of emotional development, will, and intellect. The levels varied both developmentally and phyletically. Thus, for example, level 17, which is characterized by the presence of memory, is characteristic of

Echinodermata and of the seven-week old human. Consciousness appears somewhere between levels 14 and 18.

Morgan (1894) considered three different models of evolution: the method of levels, the method of uniform reduction, and the method of variation (see Figure 4). In Morgan's view, most workers of the time would adopt the method of variation as the "most probable mode of interpretation" (1894, 58). He wrote:

> According to the method of levels the dog is just like me, without my higher faculties. According to the method of uniform reduction he is just like me, only nowise so highly developed. But according to the method of variation there are many possibilities of error in estimating the amount of such variation. Of the three methods that of variation is the least anthropomorphic, and, therefore, the most difficult. (1894, 58)

Yerkes (1905) proposed six criteria, three structural and three functional, for the attribution of consciousness to nonhuman organisms. From these criteria, he proposed three grades of consciousness—the discriminative, the intelligent, and the rational. Yerkes's main point was that we should not rely on any single criterion in attributing consciousness or ranking species.

Voronin (1962) reviewed some Russian literature on the comparative and physiological bases of higher nervous activity. He proposed the existence of four "phylogenetical levels . . . based on the quantitative growth and complication of the conditioned reflex mechanisms" (1962, 190). The four levels are shown (1) by animals with primitive nervous systems; (2) by fish, amphibians, and reptiles; (3) by modern birds and mammals; and (4) by humans.

It is apparent that many workers have proposed hierarchical notions or organization. The systems differ with respect to what is classified, the bases of the classification, and the purpose of the classification. Schneirla's concept of levels can be seen as one unique variant on the general theme.

Evaluation of the Levels Concept

The levels concept has received so little evaluation by workers outside of the Schneirla tradition that it is difficult to develop a consensus of opinion. Clearly, the notion has had little direct influence through the wide range of the study of animal behavior. Among the few to comment on the levels notion, Beer (1980) notes that the concept is at variance with evolution when viewed as a radiating pattern and difficult to apply in that context.

The basic problem that Schneirla tried to remedy with the levels

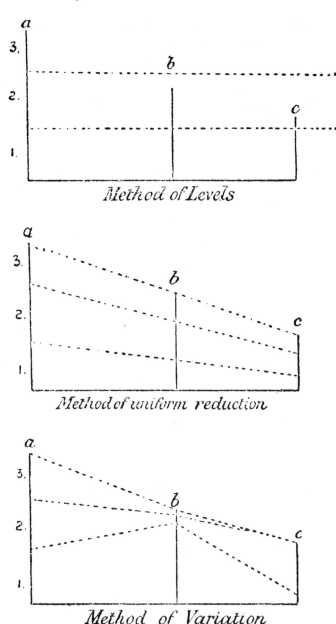

Figure 4. C. Lloyd Morgan's conceptualizations of the method of levels, the method of uniform reduction, and the method of variation (from Morgan, 1894, 56). **Letters represent the psychical statures of three different species, and the numbers represent ascending faculties.**

concept was that use of a single label to apply to analagous behavior in divergent organisms can lead to the inappropriate assumption that there is commonality of underlying processes. This is an important point and one that is often unrecognized. Used as a means of combating such erroneous assumptions, the concept of levels can serve as a useful corrective. It might be argued, however, that use of such terms of analagous processes need not lead to the assumption of similar underlying processes if the worker is careful to make it clear that classification is by function, not by process. This approach is taken by Lorenz (1981). One might counter that such use makes it easy to slip into an assumption of similar underlying processes. This in turn may be countered by noting that this is a misuse of the concept and that the individual writer cannot be responsible if someone else misuses a term. At the very least, individuals using functional categories should heed Schneirla's warning and use care against assumption of similar underlying processes.

The major difficulty that many seem to have with the concept of levels is its hierarchical nature. This appears to be a carryover from its historical antecedents and not necessary for the main point that Schneirla was trying to make. Suppose, for example, that there are six attributes that are relevant to a given process. With the hierarchical view, one would suppose that there has been a progressive evolution and that attainment of level 5 implies the presence of the characteristics of levels 1 through 4. An alternative view of evolution is that different processes have developed to different degrees in different evolutionary lines in response to recurring circumstances and pressures from natural selection. We may thus have one group with attributes 1, 2, and 4 and another with processes 1, 3, and 5. It would make no sense to attempt either to rank these species or to place them in different "levels." They are different, but they do not fall into a natural hierarchy. The point that one must use caution in generalizing across species is just as valid when one views species as organized in this way as when one adopts a hierarchical model. However, the "excess baggage" inherent in a hierarchical model is reduced. It would seem that such an approach is more in line with the opportunistic and branching nature of evolution that is a view that assumes a single, unidimensional hierarchy.

As a related problem, users of the concept of levels have rarely developed it as a positive tool for understanding evolution. To seriously apply the concept of levels in a positive way, one would need to determine how many levels there are, establish criteria, and assign animals to the appropriate levels. Once this was done, however, it is not clear what would be gained. As noted by Warden, "The point was quite generally overlooked that little or nothing would be gained by the mere classification of organisms into two or three rough groups of the types suggested, even if the validity of the criteria employed were granted" (1928, 510). Again, the point that very different processes may be operating in very different organisms can be made without the assumption that the organisms form a hierarchy. This is essentially a negative or critical point. Further, if the reason we cannot use analogies across diverse species is because they occupy different levels, does this not imply that we can generalize freely within levels? If the concept of levels is to become influential in comparative psychology, it would seem that its advocates will have to show how it can be used in a positive way to organize the data of the field and to lead to new discoveries not possible without it.

Schneirla's caution against the assumption of continuity in underlying processes is an important one. The necessity and validity of a hierarchical organization of species and/or processes remains to be established.

DESCRIPTIVE TERMS IN COMPARATIVE PSYCHOLOGY

Comparative psychologists have long grappled with the problem of the application of certain terms to the behavior of animals. With what descriptive terms shall we record animal behavior, and how may these terms be used across species? The major problem lies in the use of terms derived from human experience in the description of animal behavior. It is an issue that has been grappled with throughout the century (for example, Yerkes, 1906, 1933*b*; Bawden 1906; Kirkpatrick, 1907) and that is with us today. The topic has been touched on in several sections, especially the last, but requires further elaboration.

The most extensive use of terms drawn from human experience have been made by ethologists and sociobiologists. Some comparative psychologists have been quite critical of such usage. Konrad Lorenz (for example, Lorenz, 1981) is willing to use terms such as *falling in love, jealously,* and *marriage* when referring to animal behavior. Sociobiologists have been at least as liberal, using such terms as *rape* (for example, Barash, 1977*b*), *homosexuality* (for example, Aberle and Gilchrist, 1977), and *slavery* (for example, Wilson, 1975*b*).

Schneirla and Beach have been the primary critics of such usages. As noted above, Schneirla used the concept of levels to point out that different processes may regulate the behavior of very different organisms. He believed that use of such terms entails a risk that the reader will assume common underlying mechanisms. Further, Schneirla believed such use to be teleological. For example, he noted, "The dangers inherent in the teleological practice of naming behavior functions according to similar adaptive outcomes, such as food-getting, or protective behavior" (Schneirla, 1952, 589). Schneirla would have us drop such terms as *food getting, protective behavior, learning, dominance,* and *instinct* (Schneirla, 1949, 1952). Lehrman (1953) raised similar objections to ethological theorizing.

Beach (1978*a*) was equally critical of the sociobiological use of such terms—especially Wilson's (1975*a*) use of *homosexuality.* Beach stated that he could find in Wilson's book neither a precise definition of what the term is intended to designate nor an explicit recognition that the phenomena displayed in diverse species may have very different proximate mechanisms. Quoting from Lewis Carroll's writings, Beach (1979) introduced the term "Humpty Dumptyism" to refer to the procedure of using a single term with multiple meanings, often changing with the context. Beach was particularly critical of the use of the term *orgasm* in comparative studies.

Similar issues were raised by Estep and Bruce (1981). Their list of objectionable terms includes *incest, homosexuality, prostitution, adultery, slavery, orgasm,* and *rape.* They noted, following Beach, that application of a term from human experience to animal behavior does not make the phenomena similar even if an attempt is made to redefine the term. Estep and Bruce were particularly concerned about the social and ethical implications of words such as *rape.* They note:

> By using the term to describe non-human behavior we are forcing certain human cultural standards on non-humans. We assume that scientists who apply the term to non-human behavior do not intend these connotations, yet they cannot be avoided. (Estep and Bruce, 1981, 1273)

The issues are certainly not new ones; the discussions began before the arrival of either ethology or sociobiology on the doorstep of comparative psychology. Precisely these issues of terminology were involved in the controversy between Schnerila (1942, 1943) and L. J. Lafleur (1942, 1943, 1944) over "cruel" ants. Schneirla (1942) entitled one paper "'Cruel' Ants—and Occam's Razor" and in the other noted:

> Mr. Lafleur overlooks the fact that the implications of terms such as "cruelty" and "sadism" vary so greatly intraindividually and interindividually in man, and are so inadequately understood in their complexities on the human level that they are most unsatisfactory labels of insect behavior. (Schneirla, 1943, p. 233)

Lefleur defended the use of reasoning from analogy noting, "The possibility of abuse, however, does not mean that a method of investigation must be thrown away" (1944, 21).

Beach (1945*b*), in his paper on "'Angry' Mosquitoes," objected to these terms on grounds of (1) implicit assumptions of similar processes in diverse species, (2) substitution of a process of naming for one of analysis, and (3) applying terms to behaviors not well understood in humans.

Lorenz (1981, 90) defended his use of reasoning by analogy and wrote that "psychologists have protested that it is misleading to use terms such as falling in love, marrying, or being jealous when speaking of animals. I shall proceed to justify the use of these purely functional concepts." Lorenz noted that because similar behavioral patterns sometimes evolve in diverse taxa, it is unlikely that they result from homology or from chance. He wrote, "We know for certain that it was more or less identical survival value which caused jealousy behavior to evolve in birds as well as in man" (1981, 91). Lorenz went on to write that "this, however, is all that the analogy is able to tell us. It does not tell us wherein the survival value lies . . . " (1981, 91). Lorenz was quite clear:

> It does not tell us anything about the physiological mechanisms bringing about jealousy behavior in the two species; they may well be quite different in each case . . . . These terms refer to functionally determined concepts, just as do the terms legs, wings, eyes, and the names used for other bodily structures that have evolved independently in different phyla of animals. (1981, 91)

Thus it is quite clear that Lorenz is fully aware of the dangers inherent in using the terms he prefers but believes the advantages of their use outweigh their problems.

When one considers Schneirla's consistent opposition to the use of terms appropriate to one taxon with another, some of his applications are difficult to understand. For example, *trophallaxis* may be defined as "interchange of food between larvae and adults in certain insects, especially social insects, where it bonds insect societies together" (Holmes, 1979, 447). Schneirla noted, "A somewhat comparable process of trophallaxis is basically involved in the socialization of the human infant. From the infant the mother receives agreeable stimulation, especially tactual stimulation. . . " (1946*b*, 392).

I see no way in which this application differs from others except that it is a generalization to, rather than from, human behavior. O'Reilly noted, "Because the activities of army ants resemble closely the operations of human armies, Doctor Schneirla speaks of 'raiding parties,' 'booty,' 'bivouacs,' and 'battles' " (1953, 177). Similarly, Beach (1945*a*) used the term *play* in a manner that Schlosberg (1947) regarded as inappropriate.

As should be apparent from the long history of this debate, these issues are not easily resolved. The use of descriptive terms drawn from human behavior with diverse taxa can help uncover similar adaptions in response to similar ecological pressures. Such terms can be useful in using the method of adaptive correlation in the study of adaptive significance (Dewsbury, 1978a). Applied overzealously, furthermore, the conservative view would greatly impoverish the richness of concepts we have with which to describe and classify behavior. If we drop terms such as *learning, dominance,* and *food getting,* should we not also drop *behavior, locomotion, taxis,* and virtually all other terms in the field? What of *arms, legs,* and *eyes* — should we drop such terms because the eyes, for example, of octopuses and mammals evolved independently?

Clearly, we need to apply certain terms to the behavior of diverse taxa. Some of these terms may be drawn from human experience. We must endeavor to educate the reader and make explicit the limited functional context in which such terms are applied broadly. Further, we must guard against the tendency to slip into sloppy assumptions of similarity of mechanism such as can result from the use of such terms. The latter risk is very real and very dangerous. The question, however, as noted by Lafleur, is that of whether the potential for misuse necessitates that the entire process be discarded.

I see little danger of teleology in this process. The distinction between teleology and teleonomy is becoming well known in the scientific literature, and with the advent of the sociobiological approach, it should now be well understood.

The one legitimate issue not resolved with this approach relates to the social implication of such terminology. A paper on "rape" in a nonhuman species published in *Science* will typically be publicized in the popular press and may lead to grossly inappropriate and harmful social implications. This can be a serious problem — one for which there is no simple answer. Perhaps the socially responsible scientist must refrain from using the most emotionally charged of terms that have been applied to animals — such as *homosexuality* and *rape.* The scientist may suffer some impoverishment of terminology in the scientific process, but this would be more than offset by the avoidance of social harm. Advocacy of restraint in this issue is based on potential social harm, however, rather than necessary scientific harm. Within the science the risk of misuse calls not for elimination but for use with care.

Chapter 6

Topics of Study in Comparative Psychology

In this chapter—the second of three devoted to the analysis of comparative psychology with respect to the continuity of concerns over time—we consider the subject matter of the field. Having discussed methods in the last chapter, we shall now consider the problems to which these methods have been applied. The effort herein is to determine what comparative psychologists have studied and how these problems have changed through the century thus far.

INDIVIDUAL BEHAVIOR

General Descriptions of Behavior

Most psychologists have directed their attention toward the study of particular problems and/or particular behavioral patterns. A few, however, have concentrated on studying a broad range of behavioral patterns in a particular species. Examples of this approach include the work of Gurley (1902) on fishes; Porter (1906a) on spiders; Watson (1908) on terns; Schneirla (1938) on army ants; Richter (1927) and Munn (1950) on rats; Cooper (1942) on lions; McBride and Hebb (1948) on dolphins; and Dewsbury et al. (1982) on red-backed voles. Such an approach has also characterized much of the primate research by Yerkes and his associates (for example, Yerkes, 1943*b;* Yerkes and Yerkes, 1929) and most of the primate fieldwork (for example, Carpenter, 1964).

Orientation

Orientation has been of interest to psychologists since the last century. The topic includes taxes and kineses, short-range orientation, and long-distance orientation. With the exception of Schneirla (1954*a*, 1954*b*), few have integrated these various subproblems into a unified consideration of the problems of orientation.

The simplest orientation responses are the taxes, kineses, compass reactions, and tropisms that characterize much of the behavior of invertebrates with simple nervous systems. Such responses have been studied by workers such as Loeb (for example, 1900, 1912, 1918) and Fraenkel and Gunn (1940); psychologists have played a rather minor role in this endeavor. Kline (1899*b*) described some experiments on taxes that are appropriate for laboratory courses in comparative psychology. Warden et al. (1940) reviewed much of this material in the context of a comprehensive volume on plants and invertebrates. Schneirla (1953*b*, 1954*a*) integrated this material into his general treatment of orientation in insects. Several psychologists have studied such responses early in their careers before turning to other matters (for example, Boring, 1912; Barnes and Skinner, 1930).

Another area of research on orientation has concerned the stimulus control of movements of vertebrates over relatively short distances. Included in this topic are such responses as the direction finding toward water by newly hatched sea turtles (Daniel and Smith, 1947) and the orientation of developing kittens toward home (Rosenblatt et al., 1969; Gundlach, 1931). The most-studied topic in this subarea has been stimulus control of orientation in mazes, as illustrated in the classic study of Carr and Watson (1908), much of the research throughout the career of John F. Shepard, and in many other states.

Long-distance orientation, however, has truly captured the interest of psychologists. Such orientation has been a common topic in general reviews of progress in comparative psychology (for example, Watson, 1911, 1912*b;* Hess, 1953*a*) and has been the topic of whole review papers (Kline, 1898; Warner, 1931*a;* Adler, 1970; Meyer, 1964*b*). In his early paper Kline (1898) was frankly interested in the antecedents of migratory behavior in humans and reviewed information on crustaceans, insects, fishes, birds, and mammals. By contrast, Gurley (1902) wrote "The Habits of Fishes" and treated the topic of orientation strictly within the context of fish behavior. In more recent reviews the primary motivation for study lies in the incredible feats accomplished in long-term orientation and the need to understand the sensory and neural control of such remarkable behavior.

The work of Watson (for example, 1908*b*, 1910*a*, 1915) is the best-known empirical research on long-distance homing. The classic is the study of Watson and Lashley (1915) in which long-distance orientation over open water was demonstrated. It was calculated that the birds could not have used visual cues from landmarks over such distances. Watson and Lashley also provided a useful review of relevant literature. Although some psychologists have conducted similar homing studies (for example, Gundlach, 1932), the primary research interest has been the sensory capacities of these animals as they relate to the demands of orientation (for example, Adler and Dalland, 1959; Meyer, 1964*a*).

Psychologists have also been active in meetings arranged to consider research on orientation (for example, Carmichael, 1963; Schneirla, 1954*a*, 1954*b*).

Activity

Research on activity patterns has been somewhat sporatic. Much of the early research was reviewed by Munn (1950). There was a burst of research on the effects of various factors on running-wheel and other forms of activity in the 1920s (for example, Richter, 1927; Wang, 1923, 1924). Other studies have appeared periodically, generally in the context of motivational theory (for example, Rundquist, 1933; Finger, 1965; Campbell and Sheffield, 1953). Recent interest has centered around the study of biorhythms and their endogeneity (for example, Morin et al., 1977; Richter, 1971; Rusak and Zucker, 1975).

Locomotion

Psychologists have devoted far less study to motor function, as exemplified by the study of locomotion, than in the study of sensory function. A few representative papers include the work of Stone (1935) on horses; Schneirla and Maier (1940) on starfish; and Warner (1928) on bird flight.

Ingestive Behavior

Psychologists have long been interested in the factors that affect eating and drinking (for example, Richter, 1927; Siegel and Stuckey, 1947). The long research program of P. T. Young (for example, Young, 1932) provides an excellent example. Studies of particular species include those of Jensen (1959) on paramecia and Goldstein (1960) on salamanders. Recent emphasis has been placed on the physiological control of ingestive behavior (see Carlson, 1981) and on attempts to relate foraging and feeding to ecological considerations and theorizing regarding foraging strategies (for example, Kamil and Sargent, 1981).

Hoarding

The study of hoarding has occupied a continuous place in the literature of comparative psychology for some forty years. Hess (1953a) considered the study of hoarding to be an "isolated" instance of the study of instinctive behavior at a time he felt psychologists had abandoned such study. I have been unable to trace the study of hoarding prior to the studies of Wolfe (1939); Morgan et al., (1943); and other research in the 1940s. It appears as though interest in hoarding began soon after the Great Depression and has continued ever since (for example, Nyby et al., 1973). This literature has been reviewed by several authors (for example, Morgan, 1947; Munn, 1950; Ross et al., 1955). Among the variables listed by Ross et al. (1955) that psychologists have studied in this context are deprivation, diet, prior experience, frustration, sex and age, cortical factors, emotion, activity, social factors, material, activity, temperature, and characteristics of the apparatus. Although most of the research has been done with rats, some has been done with species such as hamsters (for example, Smith and Ross, 1950) and gerbils (Nyby et al., 1973). The study of hoarding has played a major role in research by comparative psychologists of the last forty years. What is remarkable is the apparent sudden initiation of research around 1939.

Nest Building

Comparative psychologists have conducted but a scattering of studies on nest-building behavior as in the study of Swindle (1919a) on birds and Kinder (1927) on rats. More recent interest has been focused on nest building in relation to reproductive behavior (for example, Rheingold, 1963) and behavior-genetic analysis (for example, Lee, 1973).

Exploration

The study of exploratory behavior had a rapid onset of intense research in the 1950s related to attacks on primary-drive theory. It was argued that as animals sought novel stimulation and would learn tasks in order to gain access to such stimulation, either there exists an "exploratory drive" or drive theory lacks generality. Most contemporary behaviorists seem to prefer the latter alternative. Berlyne (1960) provided a comprehensive treatment of much of the research in this area. In some studies animals would be permitted to locomote in an apparatus, and the amount of locomotion was taken to be a measure of the drive to explore (for example, Montgomery, 1958). In other research individuals had the opportunity to explore particular objects such as the wooden blocks, steel chains, wooden dowels, rubber tubing, and crumpled paper balls used by Glickman and Sroges (1966). It is particularly notable that in the latter study, three hundred animals of over one hundred species were utilized. In other research the animal had to perform an arbitrary task in order to gain access to the novel stimulus (for example, Butler and Harlow, 1954).

Play

The category of "play" has been difficult to define, and there is difference of opinion regarding its utility (for example, Beach, 1945; Schlosberg, 1947). More recently animal behaviorists from many disciplines have begun serious investigation of the nature, development, and evolution of play (see Muller-Schwarze, 1978). An early classic in the study of play was Karl Groos's *The Play of Animals,* which appeared in English in 1898. Groos treated play as the result of instinctive tendencies and as preparation for later life. Many studies of animal behavior include information on play behavior, as in Small's (1899) study of development in rats and Cole's (1912) study of raccoons. Small noted that at day 28, "The plays certainly cover a great many of the serious activities of life—including those of sex" (1899, 88). Many instances of play were recorded by Yerkes and his associates (for example, Bingham, 1927; Yerkes, 1943*b*). Beach's paper (1945) was important in focusing interest on and developing scientific legitimacy for the study of the play. Welker (1959) traced the development of play in raccoons, and Schiller (1952, 1957) stressed the role of manipulative experience gained in play on performance of chimpanzees in tests of higher processes.

Tonic Immobility

The topic of "tonic immobility" (or as it is sometimes called, "death feigning," "animal hypnosis," *"Totstellung,"* "catalepsy," or "letisimulation") has fascinated many comparative psychologists. The dramatic nature of the immobility and the nonresponsiveness of the animals make it an appealing topic for study. Such behavior was noted by early comparative psychologists; it was one of the more controversial of Mills's (1898) topics (see Whitman, 1898-1899). Kline (1899*b*) reported observations of death feigning in fishes. Interest in the characteristics, evolutionary history, adaptive significance, development, and physiological bases of tonic immobility has grown rapidly in recent years. Gallup (1974) provided a comprehensive review, and Maser and Gallup (1977) published a forty-page "tricentennial" bibliography. An entire issue of the *Psychological Record* of 1977, dedicated to the memory of Stanley Ratner, included many useful studies of tonic immobility. Although much of the research has been done with chickens and anoles, many other species have been studied (for example, Ratner, 1977; Maser and Gallup, 1977).

Miscellaneous

Comparative psychologists have turned their attentions to a wide variety of other behavioral patterns on a very scattered basis. These included handedness (Franz, 1913; Lashley, 1917), setting in dogs (Bingham, 1916), reaction to blood in cattle (Blodgett, 1924), fear (Kellog, 1931), hibernation (Mills, 1898), and grooming (Richmond and Sachs, 1980). Others have dealt with thermoregulation, predation, elimination, and tool use.

REPRODUCTIVE BEHAVIOR

It must first be recognized that, although never as difficult as work with human sexuality, the study of reproductive behavior was made more difficult by the problem of social acceptance for research on sex. The social climate has so changed that it may be difficult to appreciate the difficulties encountered by early researchers. Beach (1978*b*) noted that in 1947 an invited review paper was almost turned down by *Physiological Reviews* because certain passages were judged "indelicate." After a conference presentation, a colleague congratulated Beach and noted, "But for the life of me I cannot understand how you worked up the courage to use all those sexual words in public" (Beach, 1978*b*, 33). Such attitudes affected both professional work and personal conduct. The dismissals of Max Meyer from Missouri (Esper, 1967) and both Baldwin and Watson from Johns Hopkins (Cohen, 1979) were over sex-related indiscretions that would be treated as commonplace today.

Description

The first adequate description of copulatory behavior in rats, the most popular species for research, was by Stone (1922). Although much fine research was done with rats and other species thereafter, it was not until the papers of Beach and Jordan (1956) and Larsson (1956) that ejaculatory series were fully described and the set of measures that has become standard was defined. Research on guinea pigs began with the work of Avery (1925) and Louttit (1927). Descriptive material has been provided on many other species, including chimpanzees (Yerkes, 1939), rhesus monkeys (Carpenter, 1942a), sheep (Bermant et al., 1969), and various rodents (Dewsbury, 1975). I developed a system for classifying copulatory patterns (Dewsbury, 1972).

Descriptive studies of parturition and maternal behavior were conducted in rats by Sturman-Hulbe and Stone (1929) and Causey and Waters (1939), in primates by Hartman and Tinklepaugh (1930), Tinklepaugh and Hartman (1930), and Yerkes (1925), in cats by Cooper (1944), and in various species as reported in Rheingold (1963).

Not all animal sexual behavior entails the normative pattern of male-female heterosexual interaction. Early descriptions of variations in sexual behavior were provided by Hamilton (1914) on monkeys and baboons, Stone (1924b) on "feminine" behavior in adult male rats, Beach (1942d) on mounting in female rats, and diverse behaviors in dolphins (McBride and Hebb, 1948), and Carpenter (1942b) in rhesus macaques.

Development

The study of the genetic bases of sexual behavior was slow in developing, and little was done before the work of Goy and Jakway (1959) with guinea pigs, Whalen (1961) with rats, and McGill (1962) on house mice.

Study of the ontogeny of reproductive behavior began virtually simultaneously with the first descriptions of behavior. Developmental data on sexual development in apes were provided by Bingham (1928) and in rats by Stone (1922,1924a). Stone (1940) induced precocial sexual behavior in male rats with testosterone injections.

Particular interest has been directed at the study of the effects of early experience on reproductive behavior (for example, Beach, 1942c; Kagan and Beach, 1953). Although the early research indicated that there may be no deficits from early isolation, later results, revealed detrimental effects of early isolation, (for example, Gerall et al., 1967).

Control

The stimuli responsible for the initiation and regulation of sexual behavior derive from various modalities. Among the important papers in this regard are those of Stone (1922, 1923), Beach (1942a), and Ball (1943a).

By far the greatest attention over the last forty years has been given to the study of the physiological control of sexual behavior. Representative papers reviewing the neural and endocrine control of sexual behavior have been prepared by Beach (1942*b*, 1947*a*, 1947*b*, 1967; see also Bermant and Davidson, 1974).

Much writing and research have been devoted to motivational questions. Lashley (1924) considered Freudian theory in relation to available information on 'libido' in comparative and physiological psychology. A wave of studies in the 1920's followed introduction of the Columbia Obstruction Box (for example, Warner, 1927; Nissen, 1930; Stone et al., 1935). A number of studies were stimulated by a conceptual model of rat sexual behavior proposed by Beach (1956) (for example, Beach and Whalen, 1959; Fisher, 1962).

Lehrman's research on reproductive cycles in ring doves (for example, 1958, 1965) illustrates how different proximate factors are integrated to generate complex cycles.

Evolutionary Questions

Beach (1942*b*, 1947*a*) developed important hypotheses regarding the evolution of neural and hormonal control of sexual behavior. In the Roe and Simpson volume, Beach (1958) discussed the evolution of endocrine control of behavior.

A link between behavior and adaptive significance can be seen in the relationship between female stimulus requirements for pregnancy initiation and male copulatory behavior, as in the work of Ball (1943*b*), Wilson et al. (1965), and Dewsbury (1978*b*).

Books

A vast literature has been generated by comparative and physiological psychologists working on reproductive behavior. The reader is referred to various books for more detail. Ford and Beach (1951) reviewed *Patterns of Sexual Behavior*. Hormonal control was reviewed by Beach (1948) and Leshner (1978). Studies of maternal behavior were presented by Rheingold (1963). A general introduction to the study of reproductive behavior was written by Bermant and Davidson (1974). I have reviewed the history of these questions in greater detail and reprinted some classic papers (Dewsbury, 1981). Among the interesting symposuim volumes are those of Beach (1965) and McGill et al. (1978).

SOCIAL BEHAVIOR

Although Fremont-Smith (in Schaffner, 1955, 131) contended that a major difference between ethology and comparative psychology lies in the fact that ethologists often study interactions between conspecifics, social behavior has, in fact, always been a prominent part of comparative psychology. Material on social behavior can be found in most works in comparative psychology from the time of the anecdotalists through virtually all textbooks, and into the present. In their early studies of rat learning, for example, Kline (1899a) and Small (1900) studied two rats working at problems simultaneously and noted their interactions.

In his Lecture 28, Wundt (1894) presented a diverse mixture of facts and supposed facts. He noted, for example, that "most animals are monogamous, although polygamy is a well-known institution among birds. Polyandry does not appear to have been observed in animals; it is confined to certain savage tribes" (1894, 412). Most contemporary workers would regard monogamy as most typical of birds. Wundt noted that "male song-birds contend for females in song" (1894, 412) and that "insect-states are really extended families" (1894, 415). Like Lorenz, he showed little hesitation in writing of animal "marriages."

Among the more influential synthetic papers on animal social behavior of more recent vintage are the papers by Thompson (1958) and Carpenter (1958) in *Behavior and Evolution,* and Hebb and Thompson (1954) in the *Handbook of Social Psychology.*

Different students of animal social behavior have focused on either the overall social structure and fabric of animal societies or the details of individual social interactions. This is somewhat like analyzing either the total flow of a football play or individual blocks and tackles.

Several psychologists have made major contributions to the study of social organization. Carpenter's series of field studies on nonhuman primates (see Carpenter, 1964) provided a wealth of information on diverse primates in their natural habitats. The work of the Yerkes group (for example, Yerkes, 1943b) revealed many aspects of chimpanzee social behavior in captivity, as well as some information regarding apes in the field (Bingham, 1932; Nissen, 1931). Schneirla was a consistent contributor to literature on social organization, both by collecting original data and by attempting to integrate information (for example, Schneirla, 1946b, 1951; Schneirla and Rosenblatt, 1961; Tobach and Schneirla, 1968). Many primatologists have collected valuable information on social behavior (for example, Bernstein and Mason, 1963), as have students of other taxa (for example, LeBoeuf, 1974; Lott, 1974).

Material on individual social interactions was organized by Zajonc (1969) in his *Animal Social Psychology.* The study of social facilitation began with Triplett (1898) and includes studies such as those of Harlow (1932), Larsson (1956), and James (1953). Among studies of affiliation are those of Butler (1954) and Pratt and Sackett (1967). Students of aggressive behavior have included Hall and Klein (1942), Moyer (1968), and Ulrich and Azrin (1962). Communication was studied by Watson (1903), Church (1959), and Mason and Hollis (1962). Competition has been studied by Lepley (1937), Bayroff (1939), and Winslow (1940, 1944*a*, 1944*b*). Among the studies of cooperation are those of Crawford (1937,1941) and Daniel (1942, 1943).

Dominance has been popular with students of social behavior, with research on primates (for example, Crawford, 1942*a*,1942*b;* Maslow, 1936; Maslow and Flanzbaum, 1936; Nowlis, 1941; Yerkes, 1940, 1941), fowl (for example, Murchison, 1935; Smith and Hale, 1959), and other species (for example, Ross and Scott, 1949).

Other aspects of social behavior that have received attention have been the evolutionary importance of primate grooming (Yerkes, 1933*a*) and the origins of food sharing in primates (Nissen and Crawford, 1936).

These few pages and references provide but a smattering of the research by psychologists on social behavior. The place of social behavior in comparative psychology appears to be increasing at the time of this writing and appears likely to occupy a significant niche in the field for many years.

IMITATION

The topic of imitation has long fascinated comparative psychologists, and the phenomenon has great importance for the transmission of acquired behavioral patterns as in the classic example of the spread of potato washing in Japanese macaques (Kawamura, 1963).

Several early researchers failed to obtain any evidence of imitation—at least of any "higher-order" imitation. In his work with cats, dogs, and chicks, Thorndike (1898*a*) concluded that they do not imitate. In his work with monkeys, Thorndike noted, "Nothing in my experience with these animals, then, favors the hypothesis that they have any general ability to learn to do things from seeing others do them" (1911, 222). Other negative results in this period were obtained with raccoons (Cole, 1907; Davis, 1907; Shepherd, 1911) and primates (Watson, 1908*a*). Watson (1908*c*) reviewed the available literature and later called for more research on imitation (1904).

Early results indicative of at least some form of imitation were reported in fishes (Triplett, 1901), birds, (Porter, 1910), rats (Small, 1900; Berry, 1906), cats (Berry, 1908), monkeys (Kinnaman, 1902*a;* Haggerty, 1909), and various other species (Hobhouse, 1901).

Interest in the study of imitation has continued for many years. Miller and Dollard's study of rats entitled *Social Learning and Imitation* (1941) is a classic. Examples of other research include that on primates (Warden and Jackson, 1935; Warden et al., 1940; Crawford and Spence, 1939; Hayes and Hayes, 1952; Darby and Riopelle, 1959), rats (Bayroff and Laird, 1944), and cats (Herbert and Harsh, 1944).

One interpretation of the literature on imitation is that it lies along a continuum with other learning processes (for example, Church, 1957). It is possible that for some species stimuli from conspecifics do not differ in any fundamental way, as related to the modification of behavior, from other inanimate stimuli in the environment.

It would be interesting for a historian of comparative psychology to conduct a more detailed analysis of the literature on imitation and the different results generated. Riopelle and Hill (1973) have made a start in this endeavor. Certainly part of the reason for the discrepancies in results lies in the kind of imitation for which different investigators have searched and the criteria they pose for concluding that imitation has occurred. Beyond that it would be interesting to explore the different situations used by the early and later workers to determine why so many early workers reported negative results. It is now clear that some kinds of imitation are quite prevalent, and their continued study appears warranted.

BEHAVIOR GENETICS

According to Lockard, one of the ten premises that would have been widely accepted by psychologists of the 1950s was that "because so little is built into animals, genetics and evolution are irrelevant to psychology" (1971, 170). This appears to be an unfair statement. Although the growth of behavior genetics proceeded slowly in the century from the early work of Darbishire (1903) to the sophisticated analyses of the present, growth has been steady, and the number of workers expressing extreme environmentalism has not been great. As noted earlier, B. F. Skinner wrote: "The mere inheritance of behavioral traits is so patent that there would seem to be no necessity for an experimental demonstration of the fact" (1930, 344). In reviewing literature on the heredity of behavior traits in animals, Burlingame noted, "The inheritance of behavior traits is a subject of great interest and importance to students of animal psychology as well as geneticists" (1927, 62). Indeed, it has generally been psychologists who have taken the lead in the study of behavior genetics; many geneticists and zoologists believed behavior too ephemeral to be analyzed in a scientific manner. A call for research on behavior genetics was made by Watson (1906), and he later reviewed the little available evidence for genetic bases of behavior (1914). Yerkes (1907, 1913*b*) conducted behavior-genetic research, as did Stone (1932*b*). Stone (1947) reviewed and contrasted the different methods available in behavior genetics and pointed to the advantages of armadillos (in which quadruplets develop from a single ovum), parasitic insects, inbred strains, egg transplants, genetic crosses, and other methods. The 1946 Bar Harbor Conference on Genetics and Social Behavior provided a showcase for the development of behavior genetics at that time. Chapters on behavior genetics, or "individual differences," written by such authors as J. L. Fuller, C. S. Hall, and R. C. Tryon appeared in each version of the edited textbook of comparative psychology (Moss, 1934, 1942; Stone, 1951; Waters et al., 1960; Dewsbury and Rethlingshafer, 1973).

Several major publications played an important role in establishing behavior genetics as a viable subdiscipline. Hall (1951) published an article, "The Genetics of Behavior," in Stevens's *Handbook of Experimental Psychology* that had considerable influence in establishing the field among experimental psychologists. Hall reviewed available data and methods and made a solid case for a genetic influence on behavior and of the importance of its study. The first textbook in the area, Fuller and Thompson's *Behavior Genetics* (1960), solidly established the field. The volume provided a comprehensive review of the information available at the time. Jerry Hirsch's *Behavior-Genetic Analysis* (1967) brought together contributions from numerous researchers and played a large role in the increased methodological sophistication of the field. Other textbooks have appeared more recently as the field has shown very rapid growth in the past two decades (for example, McClearn and DeFries, 1973; Thiessen, 1972; Vale, 1980). The field has its own journal, *Behavior Genetics,* and its own society, The Behavior Genetics Association, which sponsors an annual scientific meeting.

The importance of individual differences in behavior was recognized in comparative psychology more readily than in some other fields of psychology. An early proponent was Wesley Mills, who wrote, for example, "I have all along endeavored to emphasize the importance of individual differences" (1899, 265). The point was still being made by Hirsch in "Behavior Genetics and Individuality Understood" (1963) and Vale and Vale in "Individual Differences and General Laws in Psychology" (1969).

Psychologists have used many different methods in studying genetic influences on behavior. Comparisons of animals of different strains have been used to provide presumptive evidence of genetic influences. A. W. Yerkes (1916) and N. Utsurikawa (1917), working in Yerkes's laboratories, compared inbred and outbred rats. By contrast, Small (1901), Yerkes (1913b), and Stone (1932) compared wild with domesticated rats. Different inbred strains of mice were compared by Hall (1947), Lindzey (1951), and Thompson (1953a). Inbred strains of mice have since become the most popular animals in mammalian behavior genetics. Stamm (1956) compared levels of hoarding, and Whalen (1961b) compared copulatory behavior in different inbred strains of rats. Goy and Jakway (1959) studied sexual behavior in inbred strains of guinea pigs.

The method of artificial selection, so heavily relied on in the theorizing of Darwin, has become widespread in behavior genetics. Although it may be somewhat of an exaggeration to write that "all studies conducted thus far attempting to select for any behavior trait among animals have been successful in changing the distribution of that trait in the experimental population" (Barash, 1977a,45), selection experiments have been successfully conducted with a variety of behavioral phenotypes. Early studies were done with maze learning, a trait susceptible to problems of reliability and interpretation of observed differences. Nevertheless, the genetic influence on the observed phenotype was demonstrated clearly (for example, Tolman, 1924; Tryon, 1930, 1940; Heron, 1935). Rundquist (1933) selected for activity level. Many behavioral traits have now been selected successfully. The study of Hirsch and Boudreau (1958) on phototaxis in *Drosophila* provides a useful exemplar. One advantage of the selection method is that the animals that have been selectively bred can serve as subjects in future research. Much use has been made of the S1 and S3 strain, descendents of animals from Tryon's research (for example, Bennett et al., 1964). An early example is provided by Krechevsky's use of animals from Tryon's F_7 generation in a comparison of hypothesis behavior (1933). Hall and Klein (1942) compared levels of aggressiveness in lines selected for fearfulness. W. T. Heron and B. F. Skinner (1940) compared the rate of extinction of an operant response in the maze-bright and maze-dull lines of Heron.

The advantages of mass screening and the importance of individual measurement were emphasized by Hirsch and Tryon (1956). Here, as elsewhere, psychologists were particularly influential in encouraging improvements in the methodology of behavioral study.

Among the mutant animals that have been studied have been Darbishire's Japanese waltzing mice (1903); Yerkes's classic study of dancing mice (1907); Coburn's "singing" mice (1913); and Mowrer's tumbler pigeons (1940).

It was McDougall (1927, 1938; J. B. Rhine and McDougall, 1933) who conducted the experiment suggested by Watson (1906) to test the possibility of Lamarckian inheritance of a learned trait. Although the rats descended from trained animals did learn the task of escaping from a water tank faster over successive generations, no control group was run. When Agar et al. (1954) repeated the experiment with a control group, they replicated McDougall's effects but obtained it in both the experimental and control groups. The latter result rendered invalid McDougall's interpretation relating to Lamarckian inheritance. The reason for the progressive improvement over generations in both studies has never been fully established (see Fuller and Thompson, 1960).

The method of parent-offspring correlation in behavior genetics was used by Maier and Glaser (1940a) in a study of the inheritance of a "neurotic" pattern and by Finger (1943) working with audiogenic seizures.

The availability of inbred strains renders more complex analyses of patterns of inheritance possible. In an early behavioral study using a classical Mendelian analysis, Witt and Hall (1949) studied audiogenic seizures in house mice. A design in which the F_1 lines of three or more strains are compared is the diallel cross. An argument can be made that the results of a diallel-cross study indicate the direction in which natural selection has acted in the field (for example, Bruell, 1964). Wilcock (1972) was so enamored of the method that he replied to Lockard's classic critique of comparative psychology with a paper entitled "Comparative Psychology Lives on Under an Assumed Name— Psychogenetics!" (1971). Maxson (1973) suggested that such enthusiasm should be dampened somewhat.

Behavior-genetic analyses have been a part of comparative psychology throughout the century, and the approach has become both sophisticated and widespread since the publication of Fuller and Thompson's book (1960).

DEVELOPMENT

According to Klopfer and Hailman, "The notion that nearly all behavior was learned arose from the writings of Watson and other psychologists who were preoccupied with learning phenomena. Surprisingly little experimental work on the ontogeny of behavior in animals was undertaken by psychologists" (1967,72). It is true that the later writings of Watson and others in the 1920s discouraged some kinds of investigations. Nevertheless, the study of behavioral development has been a primary focus of comparative psychology since its infancy in the early part of the century. Watson's contributions to the study of behavioral development were so great that he, together with Wesley Mills, might be regarded as a "fathers" of comparative developmental psychology. The developmental approach, together with the evolutionary emphasis, may indeed be regarded as the major emphasis in comparative psychology throughout the century (for example, Adler, 1980; Warden et al., 1935, p.162; Aronson et al., 1970). As noted by Beach and Jaynes, "Not until the emergence of comparative psychology in the closing years of the nineteenth century did the subject of behavioral development attract serious scientific interest" (1954, 239).

Early comparative psychologists were supportive of the developmental, or as it was then called, "genetic," approach (for example, Washburn,

1904). Kinnaman (1902*a*) noted the value of the method both in the study of instincts and in relation to genetic psychology and education. The tradition was continued in Stone's (1927*a*) review of the development of "congenital" behavior and was emphasized by Schneirla when he wrote, "The concept of *development*, connoting a pattern of changes occurring in a system through time, is fundamental to the psychological study of animals. This is a cardinal precept of animal psychology, stimulated by the evolutionary movement in biology . . . " (1957*a*, 78).

Wesley Mills made what appear to be the first systematic observations of behavioral development. His attitude toward such study was stated repeatedly as, "For mind and body alike the past determines the present in no small degree; hence it follows that the more perfectly the history of each step in the development of mind is traced, the better will the final product . . . be understood" (1898, 113); "The study of the development of the animal mind (genetic psychology) is of the highest importance" (1899, 273); and "The most fruitful work thus far done has been the observation of animals from birth upward . . . " (1904, 756.)

In his *The Nature and Development of Animal Intelligence* (1898), Mills provided normative data on the development of behavior in several species. His sixty-two pages on the development of dogs portrays the gradual development of their behavior from day 1 through day 61. Mills included his discussion of the various periods of development in dogs and of the development of specific systems such as fright, humor, consciousness, and will. A similar diary of cat behavior runs just thirty pages. This is followed by briefer developmental records of mongrel dogs, rabbits, guinea pigs, pigeons, and domestic fowl. Even Mills's nemesis, E. L. Thorndike (1898*c*), praised Mills's observations, noting, "Such records are of the greatest value, and to Professor Mills is due the credit for doing more of such work, I suppose, than any one else has yet done" (1898*c*, 520). Thorndike did criticize certain aspects of Mills's methods and terminology.

Watson's contribution to the study of development began with his dissertation, *Animal Education (*1903), which bore the subtitle, "An Experimental Study on the Psychical Development of the White Rat, Correlated with the Growth of its Nervous System." Watson compared the performance of rats in various labyrinths at different ages. In the last section of the monograph, Watson provided twenty-seven figures of developmental anatomy of the rat's nervous system and attempted to correlate changes in performance with medullation. Yerkes (1904*b*) reviewed the work favorably.

Watson (1908*b*) provided a detailed description of sooty and noddy terns. Representative of the detail in Watson's description of the development of instincts is one of his three paragraphs on four-day-old noddies:

Their sleeping attitudes were observed for the first time. They lie with their ventral surface of the breast down; head stretches out and turned to one side, sometimes both legs stretched out, sometimes only one. They were noticed to-day preening their feathers by movements characteristic of the adult. This was a very complete act. (1908*b*, 239)

In later writings (for example, Watson, 1910*b*, 1912), Watson continued to emphasize the importance of developmental studies. In his classic 1914 book Watson devoted a large section to the development of instincts noting, "The study of instinctive development of young animals reared in captivity has been extremely fruitful" (1914, 124). In that book, so important in the development of behaviorism, Watson provided detailed descriptions of the "serial unfolding of instincts in young captive animals" (1914, 128), including guinea pigs, rats, monkeys, and sooty terns. He also considered both the genetic bases of instincts and improvement of instinctive behavior with practice.

Lashley and Watson (1913) published "Notes on the Development of a Young Monkey." They noted, for example, "The first complex play movement appeared in the third week. Beginning as a simple thrusting out of his hands against his mother it developed rapidly into the more complex stalking of various objects in the cage" (1913, 137).

As Watson moved from comparative psychology into his studies of humans, he retained his developmental focus (for example, 1919, 1927, 1930; Watson and Rayner, 1920).

Development Over Time

As repeatedly noted by Schneirla (for example, 1957*a*), development is a very complex process with stages blending into each other and with changes in one system producing wide-ranging changes in other systems. Schneirla wished to emphasize the continuity and complex interactions in development. The difficulty is that in analyzing behavior, one has to isolate phenomena for study; few of us can focus on all aspects of development at once. Thus, whereas some authors have focused on changes in behavior over time, as did Mills and Watson, others emphasized the appearance of instinctive behavior or the role of experiences in behavioral ontogeny. Although Schneirla was critical of such a fragmented approach, it may be an experimental necessity.

The study of behavioral development begins with prenatal behavior. The continuity of pre- and postnatal development was a continuous theme in the research of Zing-Yang Kuo (for example, 1932*a*, 1932*b*, 1967). Rose (1947) analyzed the role of the thyroid in prenatal behavioral development. In both his APA presidential address and his contribution to the 1947 Symposium on Heredity and Environment, Carmichael (1941, 1947) discussed the development of sensory function in animals or "The Experimental Embryology of the Mind" (1941). Gottlieb (1970) emphasized the constancy of the order of development of sensory systems throughout the vertebrates. The prenatal behavioral patterns of birds was reviewed by Gottlieb (1968a). Interest in prenatal development and the spontaneous nature of neurogenic activity continues (for example, Provine, 1973).

The young animal sometimes displays remarkable behavioral capacities. Allen (1904) showed that guinea pigs can learn simple paths to their mothers when two days old. Tsai (1931) studied nipple preferences in young suckling rats. Munn (1939) conducted experiments on learning in larval frogs.

Small and Kline followed in the tradition of Mills in their studies of behavioral development in chicks (Kline, 1899a) and rats (Small, 1899). Small believed that young rats "find the teats largely by accident" (1899, 88) and discussed the role of huddling in thermoregulation. Yerkes (1907) studied behavioral development in dancing mice, and Thorndike (1899a) in chicks. The development of copulatory behavior was studied by such workers as Stone (1922, 1924a), Louttit (1929a), and Larsson (1956).

Primatologists have shown a special interest in behavioral development, as might be expected from the long and complex developmental periods of most primates. There were various studies of behavioral development in chimpanzees (for example, Jacobsen et al., 1932; Kellogg and Kellogg, 1933; Nissen, 1942; Tomlin and Yerkes, 1935). Schiller (1952, 1957) emphasized the role of early play in the performance of later complex tasks. The development of sexual behavior was emphasized by such workers as Bingham (1928) and Nissen (Riesen, 1971). Examples of more recent work can be found in the papers of Harlow et al. (1971) and Rosenblum (1971).

Among other behavioral patterns whose development has been studied are filial behavior (Seward, 1940), righting (Carmichael, 1934, Warkentin and Carmichael, 1939), and grooming (Richmond and Sachs, 1980).

Early Experience

Fueled by interest in Freudian and Hebbian theory and by social concerns, interest in effects of early experience mushroomed in the past thirty years (for example, Beach and Jaynes, 1954; Fiske and Maddi, 1961; Newton and Levine, 1968; Daly, 1973).

The archetype of early-experience effects was filial imprinting in precocial birds. Comparative psychologists took to laboratory and field research on imprinting like "ducks to water" and conducted extensive research programs. Representative research includes the work of Gottlieb (1963a, 1963b); Hess (1959, 1964, 1972); Hoffman (for example, Hoffman and Ratner, 1973); Jaynes (1956); and Moltz (1960; Moltz and Rosenblum, 1957). Campbell and Pickleman (1961) showed the imprinted object to be a reinforcer for the learning of an instrumental response.

Much early-experience research on mammals has utilized the method of providing stimulation beyond that normally occurring in the laboratory setting. Presumed benefits of such early stimulation are accelerated development, reduced emotionality, improved learning performance, and more adaptive psychological-stress responses (see Daly, 1973). Representative research includes the work of Denenberg (1962), Levine (1957), Hall and Whiteman (1957), and others as summarized by Fiske and Maddi (1961) and Newton and Levine (1968). Some of the early research on effects of early experience on neural development was summarized by Bennett et al. (1964).

In other paradigms the level of stimulation normally encountered is reduced through some kind of deprivation procedure. Many studies have shown impaired sensory function after various kinds of sensory deprivation during development (for example, Lashley and Russell, 1934; Hebb, 1937; Nissen et al., 1951; Melzack and Scott, 1957; Riesen and Aarons, 1959). Although early research suggested that early social deprivation has no deleterious effects on the development of rodent copulatory behavior, more recent research has generally revealed various deficits (for example, Beach, 1942c; Kagan and Beach, 1953; Gerall et al., 1967). Other effects have been observed by Melzack (1954) and Thompson and Heron (1954). The best-known deficits in behavior resulting from early experience are those observed in the long-term program conducted by Harry Harlow and his associates on rhesus monkeys (for example, 1971).

Integration

As repeatedly noted by Schneirla, behavioral development is complex, and far-reaching effects of experiential events can occur over time and in various systems. Research and theory are needed to permit an integrated approach to behavioral development. Schneirla (1939, 1959) believed that his approach-withdrawal theory could be of great importance in this regard. Most animal behaviorists accept some form of epigenetic approach, according to which genes and environment interact continuously throughout development. There are some differences of opinion, however, in respect to the ways in which behavioral epigenesis occurs (Gottlieb, 1970, 1981). No matter how they are resolved, it is clear that behavioral development will remain an important topic in comparative psychology.

At the level of empirical research, studies of the development of complex instinctive behavior such as bird song (for example, Conradi, 1905; Sanborn, 1932) should provide a focus for the study of the complex interactions of genes and various environmental factors in development.

INSTINCT AND INSTINCTIVE BEHAVIOR

The problem of instinct has been a focal one since the dawn of comparative psychology. I would concur with Hess that through much of the history of comparative psychology, "Although the term 'instinct' has certainly fallen into ill repute . . ., it yet remains as the central problem in comparative psychology" (1953*a*, 242).

Definitions

The problem of the multiple meanings of instinct has been long apparent, as, for example, in Wundt's recognition of the "museum of conflicting opinions"(1894, 389). A primary difficulty in the literature has stemmed from the confusion of *instincts* viewed as broad integrated behavioral tendencies and *instinctive behaviors* viewed as behavioral patterns developing in the absence of specific learning. The complexity of all the variations on these themes was portrayed graphically by Morgan:

> Instinctive activities are unconscious (Claus), non-mental (Calderwood), incipiently conscious (Spencer), distinguished by the presence of consciousness (Romanes), accompanied by emotions in the mind (Wundt), involve connate ideas and inherited knowledge (Spalding); synonymous with impulsive activities (James), to be distinguished from those involving impulse proper (Haffding, Marshall); not yet voluntary (Spencer), no longer voluntary (Lewes), never involuntary (Wundt); due to natural selection only (Weismann), to lapsed intelligence (Lewes, Schneider, Wundt), to both (Darwin, Romanes); to be distinguished from individually-acquired habits (Darwin, Romanes, Sully, and others), inclusive thereof (Wundt); at a minimum in man (Darwin, Romanes), at a maximum in man (James); essentially congenital (Romanes), inclusive of individually-acquired modifications through intelligence (Darwin, Romanes, Wallace). (1895, 326)

Herrnstein (1972) attempted to trace the references for each of these attributed views of instinct. It should be clear that when scientists have used the terms, *instinct* or *instinctive behavior*, they have often meant very different things.

Bernard (1924) randomly surveyed both scientific and other literature regarding the kinds of instinct proposed. He found and classified literally hundreds of hypothetical instincts such as concealment, conquest, conservative, cooperation, and criminal.

Changes over Time

With a concept as complex as instinct, it is impossible to delineate any clear-cut history; different individuals used or criticized the term in different ways at different times. A few broad trends can be isolated, but it must be remembered that there are important exceptions to such generalizations.

Early comparative psychologists generally used the term recognizing its complexity but with little apology. Thorndike, for example, defined instinct as "any reaction which an animal makes to a situation *without experience*" (1911, 37). Well aware of the problems with the term, he then noted, "Any one who objects to the word may substitute 'hocus-pocus' for it wherever it occurs" (1911, 37). Watson (1912a, 1914) also used the term readily.

There have been two major anti-instinct revolts—both coming soon after world wars. The first, described in Chapter 3, began with the papers of Dunlap (1919) and Bernard (1921) attacking broad concepts of instinct, of the type often associated with McDougall (for example, 1911) but generally accepting the existence of instinctive behavioral patterns. This was followed by Kuo's initial total rejection of instinctive behavior (1921, 1922) and later rejection of the view that genetic and environmental factors could be differentiated (1924, 1929). During the 1920s various aspects of instinct theory were defended by Geiger (1922), Tolman (1920, 1922, 1923), Dunlap (1922), and Carmichael (1925).

For the next quarter of a century or so, comparative psychologists continued to do research on instinctive behavior but generally shied away from calling it *instinctive* (see Hunter, 1947). Usage gradually crept back into the literature (for example, Stone, 1943; Lashley, 1938b, 1947). The textbooks edited by Moss (1934, 1942) and Stone (1951) each included a chapter on the development of instinctive behavior.

The second anti-instinct revolt was triggered by the arrival of European ethology. Perhaps the primary work was Lehrman's (1953) critique of Konrad Lorenz's theory. Other relevant papers were written by Hebb (1953), Schneirla (1952, 1956), Beach (1955), Verplanck (1955), Moltz (1965), and Jensen (1961). Many ethologists accepted some of the criticisms proposed by comparative psychologists (for example, Tinbergen in Schaffner, 1955).

It is unlikely that the instinct question will ever be fully settled. The term *instinctive behavior* would seem to be useful in designating a category of behavior. However, it must be remembered that instincts may have complex developmental histories. The latter position amounts to using the term in a descriptive, rather than explanatory, sense (see Hall, 1961).

There are several loose ends in the history of the instinct concept. Herrnstein (1972) has traced some of the more subtle nuances of instinctive theory as they have changed during the period discussed. Ghiselin (1973) summarized Darwin's views on instinct. The views of Hall (1908) and Morgan (1910) are worthy of attention. The paper of Breland and Breland (1961) on the "misbehavior" of organisms helped to facilitate reintroduction of the instinct concept into comparative psychology, as with their use of "instinctive drift." Finally, the models of instinct proposed by Swindle (1919a), Tolman (1920), and Lashley (1938b) anticipate developments in ethology in interesting ways. A detailed study of the latter developments would be of interest.

Conflicts

It is worth noting that some of the major conflicts in comparative psychology have centered about the concept of instinct. It is generally agreed that these battles have generated "more heat than light" and often has been counterproductive. They have, however, brought together important behaviorists and had impact on the formulation of significant problems. Thus there have been beneficial effects as well. The controversy initiated by Wesley Mills (1896a), which raged in the pages of *Science* in 1896, began over the question of instinctive eating and drinking patterns in chicks as described by Morgan. The 1910 London instinct symposium featured Morgan and McDougall (see Washburn, 1911; Chapter 2). The instinct concept was important in setting the stage for the controversy between Watson and McDougall and the "Battle of Behaviorism" (Watson and McDougall, 1929, see Chapter 3). The 1947 Symposium on Heredity and Environment was stimulated largely by considerations of the problem of instinct (see Chapter 3). the Florida Psychological Association brought together a psychologist, a sociologist, and biologist to discuss instinct at the 1953 Daytona Beach Instinct Symposium (see Chapter 4). The controversy between Skinner and his student Herrnstein centered over Skinner's use of a separate category of instinctive, or "phylogenic," behavior (Herrnstein, 1977a, 1977b; Skinner, 1977).

Empirical Research on Instinctive Behavior

For reasons that are not always apparent, a few behavioral patterns have become the focus of research and controversy regarding instinct. Perhaps the leading behavior has been the stimulus control over pecking in young chicks. Among the many workers on the problem have been Spalding (1873), Morgan (1894), Thorndike (1899d), Breed (1911), Shepard and Breed (1913), Bird (1925, 1926, 1933), Moseley (1925), Kuo (1932a, 1932b), Cruze (1935), Padilla (1935), and Hogan (1973). It generally appears that birds reared in darkness so that they do not peck are generally inferior to controls when first allowed to peck but improve rapidly when permitted practice (see Beach and Jaynes, 1954). Particularly striking was Padilla's observation (1935) that when dark-reared chicks were fed from a spoon for two weeks after hatching, then placed in light, they never developed the pecking response and "starve to death even in the midst of plenty" (1935, 442). Various aspects of innate-form preferences in chicks were studied by such workers as Fantz (1957) and Rheingold and Hess (1957).

The nature of the response of cats to rats and mice has been the topic of repeated analyses (for example, Spalding, 1875; Berry, 1908; McDougall and McDougall, 1927; Kuo, 1938, 1967; Yerkes and Bloomfield, 1910; Rogers, 1932). Different authors detect different roles of instinct, imitation, and learning in the development of these responses.

Various researchers have restricted the ability of animals to move and then looked at the development of locomotor behavior. Spalding (1875) restricted movement of birds and later tested their ability to fly; Dennis (1941) repeated the study with a different species. Carmichael (1926, 1927, 1928) found remarkably coordinated swimming in young salamanders and frogs reared in anesthetic. Although the purpose of this book is not to reprint papers in full, Morgan's paper is presented in full below:

> I have just tested the inherited powers of swimming in newly hatched pheasants. I find that when placed in tepid water, at the age of about thirty hours, they swim easily with well-coordinated leg-movements and show very little sign of distress. (1901, 208)

Would that contemporary research could be presented with such brevity!

The development of maternal behavior became a focal topic of conflict between psychologists and ethologists in the 1950s (see Birch, 1956; Riess, 1954; Eibl-Eibesfeldt, 1975; Eibl-Eibesfeldt and Kramer, 1958). Responses to the "Hawk-goose" model were equally controversial (Tinbergen, 1948; Hirsch et al., 1955; Tinbergen, 1957; Hirsch, 1957; Melzack et al., 1959; Gray, 1966; Rockett, 1955).

Various authors have been concerned with the development of fear of snakes (for example, Kellogg, 1931; Yerkes and Yerkes, 1936; Haslerud, 1938; Schiller, 1952; Mineka et al., 1980). In the Mineka et al. study, it was noted that whereas wild-born rhesus macaques showed considerable fear of snakes, laboratory-reared macaques showed only mild responses.

Other behavior patterns that authors have tried to relate directly to the matter of instinct have been sucking in cats (for example, Lashley, 1914) and killing by hawks (Haggerty, 1912).

It is apparent that a few behavioral patterns have repeatedly been targets of instinct-related research through the history of comparative psychology. In some cases, however, the development of the behavior is not yet fully understood. Although many comparative psychologists would be willing to use the instinct concept, most appear agreed that the interesting questions regarding these behavioral patterns relate to the factors affecting their development, control, evolution, and adaptive significance—not whether or not they are categorized as "instinctive."

SENSORY-PERCEPTUAL PROCESSES

As noted by Morgan, "The sense-experience . . . forms the foundation of our psychic life; and it can hardly be questioned that it forms the foundation of the psychic life of animals" (1894, 157). Morgan devoted a good bit of his *Introduction to Comparative Psychology* to discussion of sensory-perceptual processes; similarly, later authors have devoted much of their writing to the topic. The prominent role of the study of sensory function in comparative psychology can be seen in its textbooks, in reviews of the field, and in the careers of virtually all its leading figures.

In her classic *The Animal Mind*, Margaret Floy Washburn (1908a) devoted six of the thirteen chapters to sensory function. She included separate chapters on methods, chemical senses, hearing, and vision, and two chapters on spatial perception. In his 1914 *Behavior: An Introduction to Comparative Psychology*, Watson devoted four chapters to discussions of four sensory modalities. At least one chapter on sensory and/or perceptual function was included in each of the various edited texts in comparative behavior—often under the title of "Discrimination Behavior." D. M. Purdy and P. E. Fields each wrote a chapter for Moss (1934); Fields also wrote a chapter for Moss (1942); K. U. Smith prepared a chapter for Stone (1951); Water et al. (1960) included a chapter on sensory function by E. H. Hess; and Dewsbury and Rethlingshafer (1973) included a chapter on sensory function by Hess and one on perceptual processes by A. H. Riesen. Similar emphasis can be seen in virtually all textbooks of comparative psychology.

Reviews of progress have occurred at various stages of the development of comparative psychology; sensory functions are discussed prominently in virtually all of these. Representative of the series in the *Psychological Bulletin* is Watson's (1908c) treatment that includes major sections on visual, auditory, and kinesthetic function. The last issue of each volume of the *Journal of Animal Behavior* contains summaries of progress in the field; sensory processes are discussed prominently in each (for example, Watson, 1911, 1912b). It was not uncommon for half of such papers on vertebrates to deal wit sensory function. Similarly, when chapters of the *Annual Review of Psychology* have been devoted to comparative psychology, discussion of sensory function has often been prominent (for example, Russell, 1954; Meyer, 1955; Hess, 1956).

Virtually all prominent comparative psychologists have devoted at least part of their research effort either to the sensory-perceptual capacities of animals or to the role of particular sensory modalities in the control and regulation of behavior. A few examples follow. Representative of Watson's commitment to the study of sensory function were his classic on kinesthetic cues in maze learning (Carr and Watson, 1908), his study of spectral sensitivity in birds (in Watson and Lashley, 1915), and his collaborative effort with Yerkes on methodology in the study of color vision (Yerkes and Watson, 1911). Watson (1910b), like Herrick (1907), approached von Uexküll's concept of the *Umwelt*. Among Yerkes's contributions were his study of frogs (1903), devotion of substantial portion of *The Dancing Mouse* (1907) to sensory function, and the work of Yerkes and Eisenberg (1915) on color vision in ring doves. A substantial part of Kline's recommended course (1899b) in comparative psychology concerned sensory function. Lashley was a lifetime student of sensory function. The last in his numbered series of papers on "The Mechanisms of Vision" was number 18 (1948). Thirty-six years earlier Lashley began his career with a study of visual discrimination in rats (1912). Lashley noted, "An essential first step toward an understanding of the mechanism of instinct is the analysis of the properties of the stimulus situation which are really effective in arousing the behavior" (1938b, 468). Bingham (1913) studied form perception in chickens.

Later comparative psychologists were equally interested in questions of sensory control. Warden and Baar (1929) studied the Müller-Lyer illusion in ring doves; Warden and Rowley (1929) studied brightness discrimination in the same species. Warner (1931b) reviewed information on color vision in fishes. Stone (1922, 1923) was greatly interested in the nature of the stimuli important for sexual behavior, as was Beach (for example, 1942a). Carmichael (1941, 1947) was especially interested in the embryological growth of sensory function. Köhler's contributions to Gestalt psychology are well known (for example, Asch, 1968). Schneirla wrote often of perceptual function (for example, 1954a, 1954b, 1957a, 1962). Kellogg (1959, 1961) conducted classic work on sensory function in dolphins; Harlow conducted many studies of brain function and behavior in monkeys; many of which entailed sensory processes (for example, 1939). Daniel Lehrman's whole program of research on ring doves provided an excellent example of the ways in which external stimuli and internal factors interact in the regulation of behavior (for example, 1965). The nature of sensory-perceptual processes and their ontogeny was a major part of Hebb's theorizing (for example, 1937, 1949*b*). Eckhard Hess prepared chapters on sensory function for the volumes edited by Waters et al. (1960) and Dewsbury and Rethlingshafer (1973).

PHYSIOLOGICAL CORRELATES

Like the study of sensory-preceptual processes, the study of neural and endocrine correlates of behavior has long been a part of comparative psychology. Indeed, some of the individuals who made great contributions to comparative psychology made contributions as great or greater to physiological psychology and might best be treated as comparative-physiological psychologists. Beach (1981) has provided an excellent summary of the history of the study of hormone-behavior interactions, most of which has occurred in this century. Historical considerations can be found in some textbooks of physiological psychology (for example, Morgan, 1943; Groves and Schlesinger, 1982).

Certainly Lashley provides an excellent example of the way in which comparative and physiological interests can be combined in a single career. Lashley's 109 publications included many experimental studies of brain and behavior. His review papers on the physiological bases of such topic as learning and libido have become classics (for example, 1924, 1930, 1950). Similarly, Beach has made numerous important contributions to physiological psychology. His *Hormones and Behavior* (1948) brought together diverse information on behavioral endocrinology and played a role similar to Fuller and Thompson's *Behavior Genetics* in establishing a field of inquiry. Beach's numerous scholarly reviews of the physiological bases of reproductive behavior set the tone of the developing field (for example, 1942*b*, 1947*a*, 1947*b*, 1967). Stone has a long-standing interest in the role of hormones in affecting behavior (for example, 1927*b*, 1932*a*, 1940). Hebb is noted as a physiological psychologist, whose *Organization of Behavior* (1949*b*) led the way in the postwar revitalization of physiological psychology. Harlow's long career as a physiological psychologist had great influence on the development of physiological psychology, as did Hebb's (for example, 1939; Harlow and Woolsey, 1958). Morgan's *Physiological Psychology* (1943) helped bridge comparative and physiological approaches. Lehrman's manipulations of endocrine function in ring doves provided an integral part in delineating the complex interplay of internal and external factors so prominent in his work (for example, 1958, 1965).

Numerous other comparative psychologists have made contributions to physiological analysis. In *Animal Education,* Watson (1903) correlated behavioral development in rats with the development of medullation of the nervous system. Knight Dunlap (1917) considered the role of hormones in learnng. Curt Richter (1922, 1927, 1947) and Josephine Ball (1937*a*) both made contributions to physiological analysis. L. H. Warner (1927) considered the effect of estrous-cycle variations on performance in the Columbia Obstruction Box, while Nissen (1929) studied effects of physiological manipulations in the same apparatus. C. R. Carpenter (1932, 1933) studied various effects of gonadectomy on the behavior of pigeons.

Chapters on physiological bases of behavior have been characteristic of the edited textbooks in comparative psychology as well. Moss (1934) included a chapter by physiological-comparative psychologist Shepard Ivory Franz dealing with the neurology of learning; a similar chapter was prepared by D. G. Marquis for Moss's 1942 edition—a volume that also contained a chapter by Moss on the effects of drugs and hormones on behavior. Marquis again prepared a chapter on the neurology of learning for Stone's edition (1951), and W. C. Young contributed a chapter on hormones and behavior. Waters et al. (1960) included a chapter on behavior and the nervous system by J. V. Brady and B. N. Bunnell; Dewsbury and Rethlingshafer (1973) included a chapter on brain-behavior relationships by J. A. Horel and one on hormones and behavior by N. T. Adler.

Physiological analysis has probably never been quite as integral a part of comparative psychology as has the study of sensory function. Certainly it was slower in starting; one finds much less material on physiology and behavior in the early part of the century, despite the existence of the *Journal of Comparative Neurology and Psychology.* However, many later comparative psychologists have found physiological studies to be as much a part of their interest as is the comparative focus. Certainly physiological analyses are an important part in obtaining a completed understanding of behavior as with the study of its development, immediate control, evolution, and adaptive significance.

MOTIVATION

The early history of concepts of motivation and drive has been traced by Cofer (1981). One of the persistent issues related to motivation concerns the extent to which organisms require external stimulation to be active (that is, motivated) or whether such activity is an intrinsic property of living neural tissue. The latter view seems to be preferred by most workers at this time.

The primary focus of debate regarding motivation has centered on the concept of drive or "drives." Although most writers credit Woodworth (1918) with first using the term *drive* as an explanatory concept (for example, Cofer, 1981), it appears that it was in fact used a year earlier by Watson and Morgan (1917; see Remley, 1980). Although they did not use the term, the contributions of Yerkes and Dodson (1908) and the Yerkes-Dodson law should also be recognized.

Drive theory was fully developed by Curt Richter, who built on the foundation of Jennings's views (1906) on the importance of internal factors in controlling behavior and on W. B Cannon's views on homeostasis (Richter, 1922, 1927). In this approach, deprivation in a drive system produces local stimuli such as stomach contractions with food deprivation, which stimulate the animal to increased activity. A disturbance of the internal environment thus stimulates the animal to activity that is ended when the drive stimulus is removed. Much research was consistent with this view of the effect of drives on activity (for example, Richter, 1922; Wang, 1923, 1924).

It was in the 1920s that Moss, Warden, Warner, and their associates began extensive work on the assessment of drives and their relative strengths using the Columbia Obstruction Box (for example, Jenkins et al., 1926; Moss, 1924; Nissen, 1930; Stone et al., 1935; Warner, 1927). The method was criticized by Leuba (1931). According to this view, drives were thought to impel animals to action, and the overcoming of obstacles reflected this effect.

With time the "local theories" of drive came to be viewed as inadequate and yielded to "central-state theories," according to which overt behavior was the result of changes in the central nervous system rather than of peripheral and local origin.

The concept of drive that came to dominate motivation theory was developed by Mowrer, Hull, Miller, Dollard, and Spence (see Bindra, 1959). According to this theory, there were a few primary drives such as hunger, sex, thirst, and pain. Deprivation was thought of as increasing drive, and drive reduction, or later drive-stimulus reduction, was thought to be a reinforcing event. Drive theorists sought to demonstrate how the myriad behavioral patterns could flow from a few basic drives. To do this, they relied on the concepts of secondary reinforcement (for example, Cowles, 1937; Wolfe, 1939) and secondary drive.

It appears to have been no accident that drive theory became popular at the time that instinct theory went out of fashion. Indeed, as pointed out byLashley (1938b) and Herrnstein (1972), some drive theories differed little from instinct theory and could be veiwed as "instinct in disguise" (Herrnstein, 1972). The point was clearly made in a graph plotted by Herrnstein showing that the frequency of citations of "instinct" in the *Psychological Abstracts* was decreasing as the use of motivational terms was increasing. Clearly, the drive concept functioned, in part, to permit psychologists to operate in an atmosphere in which the instinct concept had been eliminated.

In the view of many, primary-drive theory generally proved inadequate as an explanation of behavior. Nissen (1953, 1954) proposed that many behavioral patterns appear to have their own regulation and control rather than being governed by the level of some central drive. He noted:

> Observation of animals and people in "free" and even in highly structured situations indicates that much time and energy is taken up by brief, self-contained, often repetitive acts which are their own reason, which are autonomously motivated, and which are not to be interpreted as being small contributions to some remote, critically important aim. (1954, 314)

> Instead of starting with a dozen or so drives, instincts, or propensities, under one or another of which all behavior is ordered, we may, instead, postulate a multiplicity of self-motivated activities (1953, 293).

The ethological influence is apparent in Nissen's writings. Hebb (1955) raised a similar objection to primary-drive theories. Both Hebb and Nissen believed that drive theory was inadequate to explain the broad range of behavioral phenomena.

The response to such criticism was to rely either on secondary drives and refinement in ways that seemed to stretch credibility or to add to the number of drives postulated. It was at this point that workers such as Berlyne (1955, 1960), Harlow (1953), and Montgomery (1955) demonstrated the role of curiosity, exploration, and similar tendencies in animal behavior. Sheffield et al. (1951) among others showed that copulation was rewarding even if a male rat did not ejaculate (that is, there was no drive reduction). Some of the research on curiosity and sexual behavior indicated that apparent increases in drive could be reinforcing. Should additional primary drives be postulated?

Like many ethologists (for example, Hinde, 1966), many comparative psychologists find that they can do well without the concept of drive or a drivelike notion. Analysis of the causes and effects of behavior can proceed in the absence of such motivational constructs. As viewed by Bunnell for example:

> If we had no genes, no anatomy, no physiology, no ecology, and no past experience, we might need to invent motivation. Since we have all these

things, together with a set of evolutionary principles, to guide us, we have all we need in terms of a framework within which to work at the problem of the *how* of behavior. (1973, 117)

EVOLUTION

Evolution has played an integral part in comparative psychology since its inception. One can hardly imagine comparative psychology without the theory of evolution; indeed, one must wonder about the impact of evolutionary theory were it not for some kind of thinking regarding comparative psychology. Darwin was well aware of the importance of his theory for psychology and believed that it would be "securely based on the foundation" of an evolutionary perspective (1859, 373). A study of Darwin and evolutionary psychology has been made by Ghiselin (1973). The period of rapid growth toward the founding of an empirically based comparative psychology was fueled by the anecdotalists bent on demonstrating mental continuity between human and nonhuman animals (for example, Romanes, 1882, 1883, 1888). What was remarkable was not resistance within psychology, but rather the extent to which evolutionary thinking spread rapidly through psychology (for example, Angell, 1909; Baldwin, 1900; Howard, 1927). As expressed by Baldwin, "This theory turns out to be not merely a law of biology as such, but a principle of the natural world, which finds appropriate application in all the sciences of life and mind" (1909, 218).

Psychologists have repeatedly brought the basic facts and theories of evolution to the attention of their colleagues. Not all students of psychology gain basic grounding in the biological sciences. Not all schools of psychology have been receptive to certain forms of evolutionary thinking. Nevertheless, it is difficult to pick up a general work in a broad range of areas of psychology without finding at least passing reference to evolution. Workers from comparative psychology have often gone beyond the surface to summarize the facts as perceived at their time. Hall (1908) summarized the basics of the "phyletic background of genetic psychology." Watson devoted a long chapter in his 1914 book to the theory of evolution, mutation, natural selection, and related topics. Writing as APA president, Stone wrote a "brief survey of a century of progress" (1943, 23) in the study of evolution. Hodos and Campbell (1969) and Hodos (1970) summarized information relevant to the study of homologies in brain and behavior. LeBoeuf (1978) interpreted the basics of sociobiology for psychologists.

In a somewhat more advanced form of activity, psychologists have played a role in the formation and testing of evolutionary theory, albeit a relatively minor role in comparison to biologists whose primary function lies in such work. Perhaps the foremost contribution in this respect is that of James Mark Baldwin (1896c), who along with Lloyd Morgan (1896b) and H. F. Osborn (1896), formulated the "Baldwin effect", an explanation for the inheritance of traits acquired in the lives of individuals without reliance on a Lamarckian model of inheritance, (see Simpson, 1953; Waddington, 1953). Baldwin engaged in other evolutionary theorizing as well (see Broughton, 1981).

The notion of tracing behavioral homologies through comparative study has long been in the psychological literature. Writing in the *American Journal of Psychology*, R. R. Gurley, an M.D. affiliated with Clark University, noted:

> In the study of animal psychology one method especially offers a chance which should not be neglected, namely the comparative method. Careful observation and comparison from species to species of a genus, from genus to genus of a family, and from area to area (geographical distribution), may be expected to give some clue to relative antiquity of instincts; the oldest instincts, like the oldest structures, being (in general and subject to more or less qualification) those in which the most species of a genus, genera of a family, etc, agree; and the most recent being those in which the species, genera, etc., differ the most. (1902, 409)

The paper virtually cries out for a Lorenzian "shaving-brush" model. Gurley was well aware of what he was writing; in a footnote he added, "No one will suppose that this is regarded as a new method. In Comparative Psychology, however, it has not been utilized to any extent" (1902, 409). We have no way of knowing if Gurley was aware of Whitman's similar proposals of 1898 (see Hess, 1962).

Psychologists also became involved in the testing of Lamarckian inheritance as related to behavior. In paper after paper and book after book early in this century, the issue of Lamarckian versus Weismannian inheritance appears. Both Thorndike and Watson (1906) proposed the experiment conducted by McDougall (for example, 1938) on such a possibility. The flaws in the design were pointed out by Agar et al. (1954), although Watson was apparently unaware of the difficulty produced by a failure to run a control group.

Another psychologist to propose a mechanism for evolution was Skinner who proposed that through evolutionary time, phylogenic behavior can be shaped in ways that are somewhat analogous to the shaping of operant behavior in the lives of individual organisms (1975). In the past fifteen years or so, Skinner has turned his attention to evolutionary questions to a greater extent than previously (for example, 1966, 1977).

With the advent of sociobiology, psychologists are again contributing to evolutionary theory as in Whitney's paper (1976) on sex chromosomes and the evolution of human sociality and my paper on the cost of ejaculates as related to sexual selection (Dewsbury, 1982).

Given their long-standing interest in evolution, it is not surprising that comparative psychologists have organized various symposia on such topics. The classic *Behavior and Evolution* (1958), edited by A. Roe and G. G. Simpson, came about as the result of cooperation between the American Psychological Association and the Society for the Study of Evolution. Chapters were contributed by F. A. Beach, R. W. Sperry, K. Pribram, H. W. Nissen, C. R. Carpenter, H. F. Harlow, and W. R. Thompson, in addition to various biologists. The subsequent Tallahassee conference on brain, behavior, and evolution (Masterton et al., 1976a, 1976b) was organized to provide an updated version of the Roe and Simpson book and was organized by psychologists R. B. Masterton, M. E. Bitterman, W. Hodos, and H. Jerison, in cooperation with various biologists. In addition to the organizers, psychologists contributing chapters included D. Tucker and J. C. Smith, K. H. Brookshire, W. Welker, J. M. Warren, W. A. Mason, W. J. Corning, J. A. Dyal and R. Lahue, and G. Whitney.

One difference between many ethological studies of behavioral evolution and many such studies by psychologists is that the former often compared relatively precisely defined motor patterns within groups of closely related species (King's [1963] "species level"). Comparative psychologists have often, though not always, sought to delineate the broad sweep of behavioral evolution by working at the phyletic level. Often the behavioral patterns studied have been less well defined. Originally, of course, the goal was the study of the evolution of mind or consciousness. This rapidly gave way to the study of learning (for example, Thorndike, 1911; Harlow, 1958; Bitterman, 1965a, 1969). Many other contributions were made in studying the broad sweep of evolutionary history. Beach, for example, wrote a series of papers on the evolution of hormones, the role of hormones in regulating reproductive behavior, and the evolution of neural mechanisms governing reproductive behavior (for example, 1942b, 1947a, 1947b, 1958, 1967). Thompson (1958) considered the evolution of social behavior; S. E. Glickman and R. W. Sroges (1966) examined the evolution of curiosity in a variety of vertebrates. One of the major recent contributors to this field has been psychologist Jerison (for example, 1970, 1973) who has worked with endocasts and other ways of estimating brain size and written extensively and penetratingly regarding the evolution of brain and behavior.

Yerkes's paper on the evolution of grooming in primates provides another example of the evolutionary influence (1933a). Yerkes wrote, "If we are to trace the evolution of primate social service the world must be our laboratory and all students of life investigators" (1933a, 23).

The distinction between *proximate* and *ultimate* causation has long been known to comparative psychologists. C. L. Morgan's paper (1905) was quoted in this regard in Chapter 2. The study of adaptive significance has been relatively slow to catch on in comparative psychology. A primary early exception was P. F. Swindle's early paper (1917) on the biological significance of eye appendages. Such approaches have appeared more recently, as in Gallup's writings on tonic immobility (for example, 1974) and my own on copulatory behavior (for example, Dewsbury, 1975).

There have been times when psychologists could have profited by devoting more attention to the study of evolution than they did and by becoming better grounded in the basic principles of evolution than they often are. Students of evolutionary psychology have never been a large group. Nevertheless, there exists a historical continuity in the study of evolution within psychology from its earliest days to the present. Although never large, this important thread should be acknowledged and its importance recognized.

LEARNING

The area of learning is one that biologists have generally left to the province of psychologists. Just as psychologists such as Skinner have recognized the importance of instinctive behavior but investigated learning almost exclusively, many biologists recognize that learning is important but shun active research in favor of investigations of instinctive behavior. Just as some psychologists actively avoid literature on instinctive behavior, some biologists shun the learning literature. Hailman (1979), for example, complimented my textbook because the material on learning was in a separate section in the book's conclusion; this apparently allows biologists not interested in the material to ignore it. Although I would not agree that the study of learning dominated comparative psychology to the extent proposed by Lockard (1971), it has been a major interest throughout the century.

Demonstrating an Ability to Learn

The first, and lowest-level, problem in the comparative psychology of learning is the mere demonstration that an animal is capable of showing the kind of behavioral modifications resulting from experience that merit the term *learning*. This became an issue early in the history of comparative psychology partially because of the lack of an adequate catalog of descriptive data on learning in various species. Interest was fueled because the ability to learn was taken by some to be one of the criteria for demonstrating consciousness in animals and hence related to the attempt to demonstrate mental continuity between human and nonhuman as implied by Darwin's theory. Many early studies, such as that of Thorndike (1899c) on fishes and Yerkes (1901) on turtles, had few goals other than to demonstrate learning and hence "measure" intelligence. Yerkes could write "On the basis of the studies of animal behavior which are now on record, we may safely say that mere ability to learn is common to all animals, and that it is indicative of low grades of consciousness" (1905, 147).

The problem of the ability to learn in various taxa has persisted, and for some taxa, it is still not clear whether the behavioral modifications observed should be labeled as "learning". Much of the work on this problem in the 1950s and 1960s concerned simply the capacity of paramecia and planarians to learn (for example, Gelber, 1952; Thompson and McConnell, 1955). Jensen (1965, 18) remained unconvinced, writing, "Some of us have quested for learning in paramecia and in planaria and we have found only pseudo-learning. . . .There appears to be little justification for the view that paramecia and planaria learn." Jensen likened the quest to demonstrate learning in these species to the quest for the Holy Grail. He suggested that time spent studying these species would be better spent "investigating taxon-specific behavioral organization than by seeking to demonstrate in them phenomena observed originally in higher animals" (1965, 18). Many have effectively heeded Jensen's advice. Nevertheless, there appears to be definitive evidence for learning in planarians (Jacobsen et al., 1967); the question of paramecia remains difficult to assess.

Process-Oriented Studies

After demonstrating the existence of an ability to learn, one of the next steps is to determine the nature of the process or processes underlying learning. This endeavor has been a major effort within animal psychology but has generally not been a part of comparative psychology as defined herein. The interested reader is referred to textbooks on animal learning (for example, Rachlin, 1976).

Quantitative Comparisons

From the time of Aristotle's *Scala Naturae,* if not before, thinkers have wished to be able to compare and to rank species with respect to their levels of intelligence. Often this has been stimulated by the view that evolution has produced progressive improvements in traits such as learning ability or anagenesis (Yarczower and Hazlett, 1977). There are at least two ways in which such comparisons can be made—qualitative and quantitative. If one believes in a continuity of process among living species, one would generally make quantitative comparisons to compare the level of learning ability among species. If, on the other hand, one believes that the processes are fundamentally different in different taxa so that they might form different grades or levels, one might make qualitative comparisons.

The view that there is only one process involved in learning and common to all species was developed most fully by Thorndike:

> Experiments have been made on fishes, reptiles, birds and various mammals, notably dogs, cats, mice, and monkeys, to see how they learned to do certain simple things in order to get food. All these animals manifest fundamentally the same sort of intellectual life. Their learning is after the same general type. (1910*b*, 58)

As such a view became dominant, psychologists attempted to compare the learning ability of different animals—often with the implicit assumption that there was such a thing as "intelligence" as a unidimensional trait. The comparative psychologist's task was considered to be assessing how much of it each species possessed. The obvious first way to try was with relatively simple learning tasks—classical conditioning, simple instrumental learning, and the like. Students of learning appear generally agreed that there is little evidence of consistent, meaningful species differences in the rate of learning different problems. Often, for example, the rates at which animals of a given species learn two different problems produce far greater differences than the rates at which different species learn the same problem (see Brookshire, 1970; Warren, 1965*a*). As Gardner and Nissen noted,"There is no regular increase in the rate of simple habit formation at progressively 'higher' levels of the mammalian series" (1948, 163).

Because relatively simple problems yielded few meaningful differences, psychologists turned to more complex tasks. These generally involved more complex stimuli, responses, or information processing for their solution. Such tasks as imitation and tool use were among the first used in such comparisons. Hunter (1913) introduced the delayed response method, believing it superior because the nature of the stimuli controlling the behavior could be delineated more clearly than with other procedures. The method became widely used (for example, Harlow et al., 1932).

Other tasks became widely used in species comparisons. These included oddity learning (see Robinson, 1933), and alternation learning, and double-alternation learning (see Warren, 1965*a*). A task that became especially popular was reversal learning. The rate of learning successive reversals in a relatively simple discrimination-learning problem has been much studied and often proposed as providing meaningful differentiations among species (for example, Gossette and Gosette, 1967; Hodos and Campbell, 1969).

Even more popular has been the study of *learning sets*, and *learning to learn*. The notion proposed by Watson was that "In our own experience with the behavior of rats we have the feeling that they work more quickly and more intelligently upon complex problems if they have had experience with simpler problems" (1906, 152). The method for testing ideas such as Watson's was developed and used most extensively by Harlow and his students (for example, Harlow, 1949). Numerous workers have summarized data on learning sets in various species (for example, Warren, 1965*b*, 1973; Hodos, 1970). Warren concluded that "the data indicate an orderly quantitative improvement in capacity for learning-set formation" (1965*a*, 110). By 1973, however, Warren's view changed, and he noted that his earlier conclusions regarding learning sets "can no longer be defended" (1973, 484).

Various authors have been highly critical of these attempts at quantitative comparisons among species (for example, Harlow, 1958; Warren, 1973; Bitterman, 1965*a*). In general, it has proven difficult, if not impossible, to account for individual difference within species, equate across species for differences in motivational level, equate reinforcements, equate sensory demands, allow for differences in motor capacities, and eliminate effects of species-typical preparedness. The more recent comparisons have not produced data that correlated with brain development as well as had earlier results (for example, Kamil and Hunter, 1970). Formation of learning sets within different modalities in one species can be quite different. Rats form olfactory learning sets quite readily although they have difficulty with those based on visual stimuli (Nigrosh et al., 1975).

Qualitative Comparisons

Arguing that the difficulties inherent in quantitative comparisons were irresolvable, Bitterman (1960, 1965*a*, 1965*b*) has argued that functional comparisons among species are more appropriate. Whereas we may be unable to equate testing conditions among different species, we may be able to systematically vary level of motivation, reinforcement, and so on, and examine performance under varying conditions. Bitterman believes that, counter to the view handed down from Thorndike, there may be qualitative differences in learning—as, for example, in reversal learning and probability learning. Bitterman's approach was criticized by Warren (1973) and modified by Bitterman (1975).

Surplusage

An interesting sidelight to the history of learning studies can be found in the literature on surplusage—the view that animals may have evolved a greater ability to learn than appears useful in the natural habitat. The history of the problem was reviewed by Boice (1977*a*).

Ecological Approaches

More recently comparative psychologists interested in learning have come to emphasize the study of problems of greater ecological relevance than in the somewhat arbitrarily chosen tasks used in some of its history. The influence of the ethologists, the impact of the writings of Breland and Breland (1961) on the "misbehavior" or organisms, and recent findings from the psychology laboratory sparked this change in focus (see Mason and Lott, 1976). Most influential was the finding of Garcia and his associates (for example, Garcia and Koelling, 1966; Garcia et al., 1974) that rats would form some stimulus-response associations more readily than others. Seligman (1970) popularized the notion that such "preparedness" was important in learning. Various other workers contributed to the spread of the ecological approach to learning (for example, Hinde and Stevenson-Hinde, 1973; Seligman and Hager, 1972; Kamil and Sargent, 1981).

Although much of the initial impact of this research was to stimulate rejection of older approaches to learning, it appears that various reconciliations are occurring, and modified theories are being established that relate better to the unique ecological demands faced by different species (for example, Timberlake, 1980, 1981).

It appears as though most comparative psychologists specializing in the study of learning have abandoned the notion of simple comparisons of the level of intelligence among different species and proceeded to a more ecologically based approach.

COMPLEX PROCESSES

Among the persistent problems of comparative psychology has been the issue of whether or not the feats of complex mammals such as primates can be explained using the same principles as are used in explaining other animal behavior or whether some more complex processes such as reasoning or insight must be invoked. The problems studied are more complex than other tasks by virtue of the nature of the stimuli presented, the responses required, or the information processing required for solution of the problem.

Once more the tone was set by Thorndike. Many of his test situations were established in order to permit controlled tests of the possibility of the complex feats reported by the anecdotalists (Thorndike, 1898*a*, 1911). Thorndike concluded that animals could not reason. Not only did he find no evidence of reasoning in his experimental work but he observed no such behavior in his day-to-day contact with his cats, dogs, chicks, and monkeys. He noted "in a life among these animals of six months for from four to eight hours a day I never saw any acts which even *seemed* to show reasoning powers, and did see numerous acts unmentioned here which pointed clearly to their absence" (1899*b*, 490).

Thorndike's conclusions immediately drew criticism. Mills (1899) criticized the artificiality and lack of opportunity for insight in Thorndike's test situations. Hobhouse (1901) not only devised new tests that he interpreted as demonstrating the existence of insight but interpreted Thorndike's own data as being consistent with such conclusions.

The controversy between L. W. Cole (for example, 1907, 1915) and the Chicago functionalist group (for example, Hunter, 1915) centered on the question of whether raccoons form images. Yerkes called Cole's 1907 study "the most important contribution to comparative psychology that has yet been made by a single investigator" (Yerkes, 1908, 277).

Several workers expanded on the methods of Hobhouse and others in efforts to study insight and related higher processes in primates. Köhler (1925, 236) concluded that chimpanzees "can *possibly* show insight," and Yerkes (1916*a*, 131) termed the performance of the primates he observed in California "indicative of ideation of a high order, and possibly of reasoning." Some facts of the Köhler-Yerkes interaction were summarized by Haslerud (1979). In follow-up research various authors considered the role of motivation and experience in producing the kind of tool use in problem solving observed by Hobhouse, Yerkes, and Köhler (for example, Bingham, 1929*a*, 1929*b*; Schiller, 1952, 1957; Birch, 1945; Yerkes, 1943*b*). The thrust of Schiller's argument was that the use of sticks and boxes in problem solving is based on reinforcement of the use of species-typical behavioral patterns that occur in the absence of particular test situations. Warren, by contrast, believes that "tool using in primates depends more importantly on such cognitive processes as insight and imitation than is suggested by several influential treatments of the subject" (1976, 407). The debate continues.

During his career, N. R. F. Maier, Schneirla's collaborator on the 1935 textbook and later an outstanding industrial psychologist, functioned as a bit of an intellectual gadfly in animal psychology. In one line of endeavor Maier devised a number of problems that he proposed indicated the presence of reasoning in rats (for example, Maier, 1929, 1938). In a typical problem, the three-table problem, a rat would be given experience on three tables connected by narrow runways, fed on one of the three and then placed on another of the three tables. The task was to go to the correct table and could not be solved by any motor form of learning. Rats solved the problem. Psychology in general was not receptive to many of Maier's ideas. This led him to formulate "Maier's law," which reads, *"If facts do not conform to the theory, they must be disposed of"* (Maier, 1960, 208). Maier considered several means by which contradictory data are swept away in the interest of protecting psychologists' pet theories. Maier reviewed the reaction to Köhler's result on insight learning within such a paradigm.

Recent years have seen a resurgence of interest in cognitive explanations of primate performance. Whatever else they may or may not show, observations on chimpanzee "language" learning do show problem solving and performance of a degree of complexity unmatched in other species (for example, Gardner and Gardner, 1969; Premack, 1970; Rumbaugh and Gill, 1976). Following this research, other tests of reasoning have been used with chimpanzees (for example, Gillan et al., 1981; Premack and Woodruff, 1978). Herrnstein (1979) reported evidence of an ability of pigeons to extract a "natural concept" from photographs.

CONSCIOUSNESS AND MIND

Comparative psychology started out as the study of the evolution of consciousness and the mind. The objectives were to compare human and animal minds and to determine how and when consciousness evolved. With the rise of objectivist approaches such as functionalism and behaviorism the initial objectives were by-passed. It was argued in some cases that such processes did not exist; in other cases that a complete account of behavior could be provided without consideration of such processes; and in other cases that such processes exist and affect behavior but are not accessible with the available methodology. Psychologists came to study behavior, rather than the mind, and the approach served it well. Many of the accomplishments of comparative psychology in the twentieth century have stemmed in part from the adoption of behavior as the topic of inquiry. The study of behavior presented problems that were tractable.

The fact remains, however, that virtually all humans report conscious experiences. These experiences are generally not accounted for in behavioristic interpretations of behavior. It may be argued, therefore, that comparative psychology has failed in its initial mission to uncover the nature and evolution of consciousness. We find that repreatedly throughout the history of comparative psychology, groups of psychologists return to the issues of the mind and consciousness. Wheeler (1916) noted the dilemma of comparative psychology; if it is objective, it loses its uniqueness as a separate science of the mind; if it becomes a science of the mind, it cannot be purely objective.

Adams (1928) argued that there is no logical reason why we cannot study the mind; Morgan's canon is not relevant in this respect. In his APA presidential address, Carr (1927) agreed that there were no logical errors in attempts to make inferences to the mind. However, Carr believed there were errors from which one starts in making such attempts—particularly with respect to knowledge of the human mind, which must serve as the standard for comparison when studying the minds of nonhumans.

In writing of the "American revolution" in psychology, Hebb (1960) argued that complex thought processes must be returned to animal psychology. Hebb argued that "the self is neither mythical nor mystical, but a complex mental process. It can be manipulated and analyzed . . ." (1960, 743).

Recent years have seen proposals to return to the study of animal minds recurring at an increasing pace. The most widely discussed proposals were made by biologist Donald Griffin (1976) in his book *The Question of Animal Awareness: Evolutionary Continuity of Mental Experience.* Griffin argued that studies of animal communication such as those on honeybee communication and language learning in chimpanzees may provide a "window" through which we may be able to study the animal mind.

William Mason (1976*a*) was very critical of Griffin's approach, arguing, for example, that Griffin failed to appreciate the attempts of workers such as Yerkes, Köhler, Lashley, Tolman, Hebb, Harlow, and Skinner to not lose sight of the problems of the animal mind while avoiding unbridled anthropomorphism. Mason emphasized his view of the centrality of the problem of the animal mind for comparative psychology, writing: "Comparative psychology is about the evolution of mental processes, and the various forms and aspects of minding in different animals species" (1980, 964). In Mason's view it is essential that comparative psychologists study the animal mind and its contribution to adjustments to environmental change by animals. Razran (1971) has been another advocate of the return of problems of the mind to comparative psychology.

From his experiments on the reactions of animals to mirrors, Gordon Gallup (1977, 1979) has argued that chimpanzees, but not monkeys, display self-recognition. Furthermore, he argued that such self-recognition is intimately related to the existence of consciousness and self-consciousness.

According to Gallup, "Some of the most intriguing problems in psychology involve the discovery of ways to infer and map experience in other organisms" (1977, 337). Epstein et al. (1981) demonstrated behavior in pigeons that bore certain similarities to that reported by Gallup in chimpanzees. Epstein et al. concluded that "at least one instance of behavior attributed to self-awareness can be accounted for in terms of an environmental history" (1981, 696).

Building on the kind of results suggested in the last section, Premack and Woodruff (1978a) suggested that chimpanzees may have a "theory of mind." They suggested that an individual has a theory of mind if it imputes mental states to itself and to others. The relevant research entails showing chimpanzees videotapes of humans attempting to solve certain problems, then permitting the animal to choose from among photographs that show the appropriate solution. Premack and Woodruff interpreted the fact that the chimpanzees performed consistently well in such tasks as indicating that "the animal recognized the videotape as representing a problem, understood the actor's purpose, and chose alternatives compatible with that purpose" (1978a, 515).

The current status of these issues was assessed at the Dahlem Workshop on Animal Mind-Human Mind (Griffin, 1982). The extent to which these various attempts to broach the problem of the animal mind—so long as part of comparative psychology—have been successful is difficult for me to evaluate. Like most comparative psychologists, I have my hands full with the study of *behavior*—and with the analysis of its evolution, function, control, and development. At the same time, however, it would be a mistake to lose sight totally of the problem of the nature of the animal mind. I am not convinced as to whether the problem is solvable in principle. However, it is very important that a portion of the effort of comparative psychologists be devoted to the problem and to the continued consideration of the implications of results from the rest of comparative psychology for the study of consciousness and the animal mind.

SKELETONS IN THE CLOSET?

I am making an effort to establish a positive image for comparative psychology. However, this should be done only with some consideration of its weaknesses as well. Psychologists have adopted some questionable views on occasion. William McDougall, for example, though never really a comparative psychologist, was a champion of Lamarckian inheritance (for example, McDougall, 1938). Comparative psychologists have sometimes adopted typological views (for example, Warden et al., 1935, p. 162).

A more serious concern, however, relates to questions of race. In investigating the literature of comparative psychology, one finds numerous references to questions of race in humans. I have not investigated either the reasons behind this or the motives of the workers. However, I believe it would be a mistake to attempt to sweep these under a rug.

Sociobiologists have often been accused of being susceptible to issues of racism at the hands of comparative psychologists (for example, Adler, 1980) and others (for example, International Committee Against Racism, 1977). If there is a risk of racism in comparative psychology, recognition may provide the best defense against such susceptibility.

One finds a surprising number of papers in journals of comparative psychology dealing with these topics. For example, the early issues of the *Journal of Comparative Psychology* included the papers, "The Relation of Degree of Indian Blood to Score on the Otis Intelligence Test" (Hunter and Sommermier, 1922) and "A Questionary Study of Certain National Differences in Emotional Traits" (Washburn, 1923). The annals of *Comparative Psychology Monographs* include the papers "The Comparative Abilities of White and Negro Children" (Peterson, 1923); "Racial Differences in the Mental and Physical Development of Mexican Children" (Paschal and Sullivan, 1925); and "The Mental Capacity of American-born Japanese Children" (Darsie, 1926). Gould (1981) was highly critical of Yerkes's activities in mental testing during World War I and the implications of these activities for racial and ethnic differences.

In Morgan's *An Introduction to Comparative Psychology*, one reads:

> Among civilized men of like social grade, and somewhat similarly educated, the individual differences are mainly quantitative . . . . But in the study of uncivilized men, not only of different social grade, but living under a different social system, . . . we find differences which are not merely quantitative but qualitative. (1894, 46).

Watson (1919, 260) wrote, "Psychologists persistently maintain that *cleanliness* is instinctive, in spite of the filth of the negro, of the savage, and of the child." After comparing chimpanzees, organutans, and gorillas, Yerkes (1925, 56) wrote, "Certainly these three types of ape do not differ more obviously than do such subdivisions of mankind as the American Indian, the Caucasian, and the Negro."

The fact that one notes or investigates racial differences in a scientific manner by no means makes one a racist. I shall not presume to try to judge these works—especially as I have not fully investigated the prevailing views of the times and the context within which the work was done. However, I do think that when we view the potential for racism in the houses of others, we ought to recognize the potential for it in our own.

Chapter 7

Practical Affairs of Comparative Psychology

The story of comparative psychology can be found not only in the methods used and the topic addressed but also in myriad practical affairs. These include such matters as textbooks, societies, funding, interaction with other disciplines, and related material.

TEXTBOOKS

One way to detect changes in a field is through analysis of its textbooks. In general, changes in the field affect the kinds of courses that are taught, and these both determine and are determined by the nature of the available textbooks. Indeed, Chiszar (1972) suggested that historical analysis through consideration of the textbooks of comparative psychology forces a modification of the conclusions drawn by Lockard (1971) regarding the status of comparative psychology.

I will consider some of the major books written as texts in comparative psychology. Teachers of comparative psychology have often used books written by biologists; in keeping with the general tenor of this book, these texts will not be considered here. Further, I will not consider any of the more specialized books—books dealing specifically with behavioral development, sociobiology, or learning.

Single-or-Joint-Authored Texts

Although one can find earlier texts in the field (see Jaynes, 1969), Romanes's *Animal Intelligence* (1882) was probably the first really influential book written in English as a textbook. In his preface Romanes noted that he had two objectives: "First, I have thought it desirable that there should be something resembling a text-book of the facts of Comparative Psychology, to which men of science, and also metaphysicians, may turn . . . " (1882, v). Romanes's "second, and much more important object, is that of considering the facts of animal intelligence in their relation to the theory of Descent" (1882, vi). After an introductory chapter, the book contains sixteen additional chapters—organized by taxon. There are whole chapters, for example, on spiders and scorpions, elephants, and dogs. Although the emphasis of the book is on "general intelligence," there is also material on other "habits" and "emotions."

C. Lloyd Morgan's *An Introduction to Comparative Psychology* was published in 1894. The book is anthropocentric throughout. Typically, there is a chapter or two on some human faculty followed by one in which analagous faculties are considered for nonhuman animals. For example, in Chapter 7 Morgan tells the reader that whereas humans have systematic memory, animals have only desultory memory. In Chapter 14 we learn that animals do not perceive relations and that they have some powers of indicative communication but lack descriptive communication. Morgan also anticipated many later developments in the study of animal behavior. Thus he discussed trial-and-error learning and presented early versions of the concepts of preparedness and the *Umwelt* (see Dewsbury, 1979*b*).

Margaret Floy Washburn's *The Animal Mind: A Text-book of Comparative Psychology* was published in 1908. The book included 10 pages of preface and 333 pages of text and sold for $1.60. It was written in the Wundt-Titchener tradition, with a heavy emphasis on sensory and perceptual phenomena. Washburn acknowledged that *"all psychic interpretation of animal behavior must be on the analogy of human experience"* (1908, 13). After considering the methods of comparative psychology and the kind of evidence required to infer the existence of mind, Washburn considered the minds of simplest animals, speculating, for example, on whether or not the amoeba has a mind. She noted that "it is even possible that the 'stream of consciousness' for an Amoeba may not be a continuous stream at all" (1908, 48-49). The book was revised in 1917, 1926, and 1936 and was a standard text in comparative pscyhology for twenty-five years.

The modern era of textbooks really began in the 1930s. Maier and Schneirla's *Principles of Animal Psychology* was published in 1935 and reprinted in 1964; it is still used in some courses in the field. The book was designed "to serve as a systematic textbook of animal behavior for courses in psychology and biology" (1935, ix). Maier and Schneirla were sanguine about the development of animal psychology in the 1930s, noting the increasing emphasis in both teaching and research. They were optimistic about the future as well: "It is probable that in the near future a training in psychology which does not include a study of lower animals will be regarded as inadequate" (1935, ix). Part I of the book includes eleven chapters and is organized by taxon. Tables in each chapter include information on receptor equipment, sensitivity, conduction, and the action system for a given taxon. Parts II and III deal with mammalian behavior; Part II includes just three chapters, dealing with natively determined behavior, sensory function, and neural mechanisms. The six chapters in Part III concern learning and mental processes in mammals.

Warden, Jenkins, and Warner's *Comparative Psychology: A Comprehensive Treatise* included three volumes, published in 1935, 1936, and 1940, and was intended as "a textbook for advanced courses in comparative and genetic psychology" (1935, iv). The first volume, published in 1935, dealt with principles and methods. Among other things, the book is an excellent source of diagrams and photographs of apparatus used in early comparative psychology. Volume 3 was published in 1936 and cost $4.50 for its 560 pages. Material was again organized by taxon. Volume 2, which appeared in 1940, dealt with plants and invertebrates and was also organized by taxon.

There was then a dearth of single-authored textbooks in comparative psychology for a period of three decades. Indeed, as best I can determine, no comparative psychologist authored any text in the area in that thirty-year period. The book by Maier and Schneirla was dominant during this time, just as Washburn had been during the earlier era. Books by zoologists found some favor.

Probably the next single- or joint-authored text in the field was that of Richard A. Maier and Barbara M. Maier, dedicated to N. R. F. Maier. The book is entitled *Comparative Animal Behavior* and appeared in 1970. Part 1 of the book concerns the sensory and neural bases of behavior. Part 2 included chapters on functional behavior patterns (for example, feeding and reproduction). Part 3 concerns the dynamics of behavior—behavior genetics, experience, learning, and emotion. A chapter on evolution concludes the book.

Joseph B. Cooper's *Comparative Psychology* appeared in 1972. The book includes a discussion of the methods and issues in the study of behavior, behavior genetics and development, and functional categories of behavior.

In his *Comparative Psychology: Phyletic Differences in Behavior* (1973), David Lester emphasized behavioral comparisons as the primary objective in comparative psychology. Much of the work consists of an attempt to generate tables in which different species are compared.

My *Comparative Animal Behavior* (Dewsbury, 1978a) is organized about the four questions concerning behavior proposed by Tinbergen (1963)—development, control, evolutionary history, and function. After a series of chapters dealing with these questions in relation to naturally occurring behavior, a section on learning recapitulates the system.

Several single-authored shorter books, under two hundred pages, have been prepared for use with other materials. W. N. Tavolga's *Principles of Animal Behavior* (1969) was dedicated to T. C. Schneirla and written in the Schneirla tradition. Maier and Maier's *Comparative Psychology* (1973) covers similar material to that in the longer book by the same authors. F. J. Mortenson's *Animal Behavior: Theory and Research* (1975) has a strong historical approach and attempts a unification of material from comparative psychology and ethology.

Edited Texts

The era of the edited textbook began with Moss's *Comparative Psychology* (1934). Moss edited a second edition in 1942, and Stone (1951) was the editor of the book's third edition. R. H. Waters, who had contributed chapters to each of the first three volumes, collaborated with D. A. Rethlingshafer and W. E. Caldwell on *Principles of Comparative Psychology* (1960), a book that can be treated as a fourth edition of *Comparative Psychology* in principle, if not formally a fourth edition. Dorothy Rethlingshafer had begun a fifth volume when she died in 1969; I was asked to complete the volume that became *Comparative Psychology: A Modern Survey* (Dewsbury and Rethlingshafer, 1973).

An examination of these five volumes reflects change over the four decades of their publication (with intervals of eight, nine, nine, and thirteen years separating them). The first book (Moss, 1934) was structured into fifteen chapters as follows:

I.	Why Study Animal Psychology	E. L. Thorndike
II.	The Historical Background of Comparative Psychology R. H. Waters	
III.	Maturation and "Instinctive" Functions	C. P. Stone
IV.	Motivation: Incentives and Drive	C. P. Stone
V.	The Effect of Drugs and Internal Secretions on Animal Behavior F. A. Moss	
VI.	The Functions of the Receptors	D. M. Purdy
VII.	Discrimination	P. E. Fields
VIII.	The Neurology of Learning	S. I. Franz

IX.   The Conditioned Reflex   H. S. Liddell
X.   Learning   W. T. Heron
XI.   Complex Learning Processes   W. T. Heron
XII.   Theories of Learning   E. C Tolman
XIII.   Individual Differences   R. C. Tryon
XIV.   Social Psychology of Animals   O. L. Tinklepaugh
XV.   "Gifted" Animals   O. L. Tinklepaugh

The organization originated not at the whim of one individual but at a meeting of workers in animal psychology convened at the meeting of the American Psychological Association at Cornell University. The topics were selected by a committee. Given the definitions used in this volume, the Moss book provided a good summary of animal psychology but was top heavy in its coverage of learning. The use of *comparative psychology* in its title may have helped spread confusion regarding what I believe to be the more specialized field of comparative psychology as differentiated from other fields within animal psychology. Perhaps the other most notable feature is the chapter on "gifted animals."

The second edition must have fared better than the first as copies are much easier to obtain. It is very similar in structure to the first edition. The chapters on sensory function and gifted animals were dropped, and D. G. Marquis and K. W. Spence replaced S. I. Franz and E. C. Tolman, respectively, as authors.

With a new editor, the 1951 edition saw more changes of author and topic, though retaining the same general structure. The most notable changes involved the addition of a chapter on abnormal psychology of animals and two chapters on primates—one by Harlow on primate learning and one by Nissen on primate social behavior.

Learning was greatly deemphasized in the books edited by Waters et al. (1960) and Dewsbury and Rethlingshafer (1973). Waters was the only author in common between the Stone (1951) and the Waters et al. (1960) volumes. Comparative psychologists such as V. H. Denenberg, E. H. Hess, A. H. Riesen, A. J. Riopelle, and W. R. Thompson contributed chapters. The most characteristic chapter for the first time was one entitled "Acquired Drives and Curiosity-Investigative Motives" by R. A. Butler.

The basic organization of the Dewsbury-Rethlingshafer volume resembled the earlier books in many respects. For the first time there were separate chapters on animal communication and behavioral evolution.

One method of analyzing changing content in comparative psychology over this period is to analyze the frequency of citation of various authors. I have summarized these frequencies by noting the number of pages on which a number of authors have been cited (excluding bibliographic citations) in the five basic edited volumes. Although the analysis is subject to some sources of bias, it is instructive, and is presented in Table 3. The first five authors in Table 3 are classic founders of comparative psychology. It is somewhat remarkable that neither James Mark Baldwin nor Wesley Mills was mentioned in any of the five books. Linus Kline received one citation in each of the first three volumes before disappearing. Both Hobhouse and Small decreased from four citations in 1934 to one in each of the last two books.

The second group of authors in Table 3 includes comparative psychologists showing decreasing influence over time. Watson, for example, dropped from twenty-two citations in 1934 to two in 1973; Washburn received just one mention in the last three books. The third group, composed of Beach, Carpenter, Harlow, Skinner, and Schneirla, showed sharp increases during the period of 1934 to 1973. Among ethologists, Lorenz and Tinbergen show a sharp and sudden increase in influence in the last two volumes. Much of vonFrisch's early work on sensory function was discussed in Purdy's chapter on sensory function in Moss (1934). The remaining authors show mixed patterns of citation.

Two other edited volumes are noteworthy; both were heavily influenced by programs in animal behavior at particular universities. Bermant's *Perspectives on Animal Behavior: A First Course* (1973) came from the University of California, Davis. The organization resembles that of other volumes, although there are chapters on reflexive behavior, courtship and mating, and parental behavior. M. R. Denny's *Comparative Psychology: A Evolutionary Analysis of Animal Behavior* (1980) was dedicated to Stanley Ratner and has a strong Michigan State influence. The twenty-two chapters cover such topics as human behavioral ecology, and two are entitled "An Application of the Comparative Method: Is Conditioned Avoidance a Classical or Instrumental Process in Goldfish?" and "Insect Behavior: Using the Cricket as a Comparative Baseline."

Books of Readings

There have been numerous books of readings (that is, reprinted versions of previously published papers) edited by ethologists and sociobiologists. The one volume by a comparative psychologist is that of T. E. McGill (1965) entitled *Readings in Animal Behavior*. Later editions were published in 1973 and 1977. The first edition was especially influential because it came at a time when competing volumes were becoming outdated, and it offered an attractive selection of readings. In addition, the volume influenced the structure for various later books and approaches to comparative psychology. An introductory section included works by E. H. Hess, W. H. Thorpe, R. A. Hinde and N. Tinbergen, and Beach's "The Snark

Table 3. Number of Citations of Various Authors in Edited Texts in Comparative Psychology

	Moss 1934	Moss 1942	Stone 1951	Waters et al. 1960	Dewsbury and Rethlingshafer 1973
Baldwin, J. M.	0	0	0	0	0
Mills, W.	0	0	0	0	0
Kline, L.	1	1	1	0	0
Hobhouse, L. T.	4	1	0	1	1
Small, W. S.	4	3	2	1	1
Watson, J. B.	22	7	3	1	2
Yerkes, R. M.	23	13	9	7	5
Washburn, M. F.	7	2	0	1	0
Warden, C. J.	18	9	5	4	2
Hunter, W. S.	15	9	6	0	1
Stone, C. P.	16	11+	3	4	1
Thorndike, E. L.	22	6	9	9	7
Beach, F. A.	0	1	13	22	23
Carpenter, C. R.	1	1	3	8	3
Harlow, H. F.	3	2	21	27	15
Skinner, B. F.	1	1	4	16	10
Schneirla, T. C.	0	0	3	12	9
Lorenz, K. Z.	0	0	0	21	34
Tingergen, N.	0	0	1	19	48
Frisch, K. von	11	1	1	15	12
Nissen, H. W.	6	6	7	25	8
Maier, N. R. F.	7	6	18	12	5
Darwin, C.	6	4	6	11	10
Lashley, K. S.	17	6	11	17	13
Morgan, C. L.	8	3	3	4	4

was a Boojum" and "The Descent of Instinct." The remaining sections dealt with (Part II) behavior genetics; (Part III) neural, hormonal, and chemical control of behavior; (Part IV) the development of behavior, critical periods, and imprinting; (Part V) sensory processes, communication, and orientation; (Part VI) learning and motivation; and (Part VII) social behavior, ethology, and evolution. Although the second edition contained a completely new set of readings, the third contained both new material and some from previous editions.

Hybrid Volumes

Some books consist of a mixture of original text and reprinted material. Breland and Breland's *Animal Behavior* (1966) includes five chapters on the nature of animal-behavior study followed by five readings by Fabre, Pavlov, Keller and Schoenfeld, Lorenz, and Harlow.

More substantial are the volumes put together by Ratner and Denny (1964) and Denny and Ratner (1970) entitled *Comparative Psychology: Research in Animal Behavior.* Each of the thirteen or fourteen chapters begins with about ten to fifteen pages of original text interspersed with some abstracts of particular studies. This is followed by three to five reprinted papers. The organization of chapters resembles that in other similar books, including a strong dose of material on learning.

Books not Published

One wonders how many excellent instuctors have had excellent material for textbooks in comparative psychology but never committed them to paper. J. F. Shepard, for example, was an excellent teacher of comparative psychology who inspired many to enter the field. Yet Shepard never published either his course material or much of his research (see Raphelson, 1980). Madison Bentley wrote *Manual of Comparative Psychology* in 1911 (see Dallenbach, 1956). The book was written in the tradition of Titchener and used in courses over many years. However, in his quest for perfection, Bentley delayed publication so long that other events and the appearance of Watson's behaviorism rendered it out of date. Dallenbach (1956a) speculated that the course of comparative psychology might have been different, and less behavioristic, had Bentley published his book.

In 1957 Frank Beach secured a leave of absence from Yale, one of his goals being to write a textbook of comparative psychology based on his William James lectures at Harvard (see Beach, 1974). Beach notes that he wrote and rewrote the sixteen chapters that were to form the book but became disillusioned and wondered whether there *was* a field of comparative psychology. He wrote, "At best there might be an 'animal psychology,' but that wasn't what I wanted to write about," (1974, 55). It is sad that the book has not yet appeared.

Robert Boice has written a book entitled *Ethological Psychology,* which I have not seen but which has already established a good reputation. As of this writing, publication difficulties appear to have placed the book in jeopardy.

Evaluation

It is difficult to evaluate individual books. Most have been reviewed in one or more journals shortly after publication (for example, Allee, 1936; McAllister, 1935; Waugh, 1908). A survey of textbooks in comparative psychology appeared in the 1981 *Comparative Psychology Newsletter*

(Vol. 1, No. 4). With just fourteen respondents, the survey was less than conclusive. Bermant (1965) surveyed the texts used in ten courses in comparative psychology as of that time. The most consistent conclusion from the survey was the remarkable diversity of choices made by different instructors.

One can find reasons in favor of and against each type of work. With a book of readings, students gain firsthand experience with the writings of the leaders of the field; such works lack continuity, however. Edited volumes expose students to material digested by individuals knowledgeable in the topic covered by each chapter. Such books too are subject to a lack of continuity, gaps and overlaps in coverage, and jarring alterations of style from chapter to chapter. Single-authored books have an advantage with respect to structure and continuity, but no single author can cover all fields equally well.

If comparison is the goal of comparative psychology, a text may still be organized around that theme or by taxon. If as herein, however, the objective of comparative psychology is viewed as the generation of broad principles, a book organized around problem areas is more logical. It is likely that most future books will be so organized.

JOURNALS

The fast-breaking events in the science are reported in journals long before they appear in texts and other books. Further, many findings that turn out in the long run to be important are not recognized as such by the authors of books and may languish in the journals. To know a discipline, one must know its journals.

The growth of journals in psychology in general and comparative psychology in particular has been rapid and progressive throughout the century. Boring (1943) published a photograph of the psychological journals in the Robbins Library at Harvard by quinquennia (that is, five-year periods) from 1890 to 1940. The pile increased progressively from the single journal available in 1890 to an impressive pile available in 1940. The growth of journals publishing work in comparative psychology was greater after 1940 than before that time.

The first North American journal of psychology was the *American Journal of Psychology*, founded by G. Stanley Hall in 1887. The journal was identified with the Wundt-Titchener-Hall tradition for many years. It has faced some crises in its history. In the 1890s a group of psychologists who believed that the journal was too much a house organ for Hall and Clark University proposed either to buy the journal from Hall or to at least establish a broad-based board of editors. When Hall refused, they founded the *Psychological Review* (Langfeld, 1944). Hall added Titchener as a cooperating editor in 1895, and Titchener exerted great influence on the journal. In 1925 Hall decided to sell the journal, and there was some conflict among Titchenerian psychologists Boring, Langfeld, and Dallenbach regarding its fate. Finally, Dallenbach borrowed the money to buy the *American Journal of Psychology* for Titchener. When Titchener and Dallenbach came into conflict over the journal, Dallenbach turned it over to Boring, Bentley, and Washburn, who served as a joint board of editors. Titchener collaborated with Carl Murchison to found the *Journal of General Psychology* (see Boring, 1961).

When they failed to persuade Hall to change the policies of the *American Journal of Psychology,* James McKeen Cattell and James Mark Baldwin, who had been an assistant to Hall on the journal, founded the *Psychological Review.* At the same time, 1894, they also founded the *Psychological Index,* edited by Howard C. Warren and Livingston Farrand and which published the titles of psychological publications from around the world. From the beginning, Cattell and Baldwin had difficulties, as they were very different men — Baldwin a theorist and Cattell a quantitative psychologist. They succeeded in running the journal by alternating editing in successive years. In 1903 when Baldwin moved to Johns Hopkins, Cattell suggested that one should buy out the other. Langfeld told the fascinating story of the fate of the *Psychological Review:*

> A private auction was therefore arranged in Cattell's office with the two editors as the only bidders. When the sum reached $3400, Baldwin added $5. Cattell went to $3500 and when Baldwin again added $5, Cattell gave up as he had promised himself not to go higher. So the *Review* went to Baltimore with Baldwin. (1944, 145)

The *Psychological Review* had several additional offspring. *Psychological Monographs* started as the *Psychological Review Monograph Supplement* in 1895. The *Psychological Bulletin* was founded in 1904 with Warren and Baldwin as editors. Warren bought out Baldwin in 1910, becoming the sole owner of the journals, Watson became the editor of the *Psychological Review,* with Warren going to the *Index. The Journal of Experimental Psychology* was founded with Watson as its editor in 1925.

Warren offered the Psychological Review Publication Company to the American Psychological Association in 1925. The asking price for the journals and all back stock was $5,500. When, after raising dues and electing associates, the APA could not muster more than $3,500, the rest of the debt was cancelled by Warren (see Langfeld, 1944; Kantor, 1935; Fernberger, 1943a; Hilgard, 1978). Today the APA publishes eighteen journals and a monthly newspaper.

On the occasion of the jubilee of the *Psychological Review,* Langfeld (1944) polled seventy prominent psychologists to determine the most important papers in its first fifty volumes. The overall winner was Watson's "Psychology as the Behaviorist Views It" (1913). Lashley's "Basic Neural Mechanisms in Behavior" (1930) finished sixth, and Carmichael's "The Development of Behavior in Vertebrates Experimentally Removed from the Influence of External Stimulation" tied for eighth.

The *Journal of Comparative Neurology* became the *Journal of Comparative Neurology and Psychology* from 1904 through 1910. Yerkes and Watson served on the editorial board (see Pfaffmann, 1973).

The editorial noting that the *Journal of Comparative Neurology* would return and the *Journal of Animal Behavior* would split off appeared in 1910.

The *Journal of Animal Behavior* published seven volumes between 1911 and 1917. Yerkes served as managing editor. Psychologists Madison Bentley, Harvey Carr, E. L. Thorndike, Margaret Floy Washburn, and J. B. Watson joined biologists S. J. Holmes, H. S. Jennings, and W. M. Wheeler on the initial editorial board. The journal published a lively and exciting collection of papers in its seven volumes and fulfilled in part its goal, "to bring into more sympathetic and mutually helpful relations the 'naturalists' and the 'experimentalists'" (*Journal of Comparative Neurology,* 1910, **20**:625). Publication ceased in 1917 due to the unfavorable conditions created by World War I.

Behavior Monographs was founded in 1911 and edited by Watson. Among the important papers published were those of Shepard and Breed (1911) on chicks; Hamilton (1916) on perseverence; Yerkes and Watson (1911) on methods in the study of vision; Yerkes (1916a) on the mental life of monkeys; and Hunter (1913) introducing the delayed-response method.

Psychobiology was founded with Knight Dunlap as editor in 1917. Its two volumes were heavy in rat learning and neurology and included few papers of lasting interest to comparative psychologists.

In 1921 the *Journal of Comparative Psychology* was founded as the successor to the *Journal of Animal Behavior* and *Psychobiology.* Dunlap and Yerkes coedited the journal from its inception until 1943. Dunlap (1932) regarded his editorship as temporary. He noted, "I am not a comparative psychologist, . . . but there is a distinct advantage, at times, in having an editor who does not know much about the subject and has no particular bias" (1932, 54). Roy M. Dorcus served as managing editor from 1944 through 1946. When the journal became the *Journal of Comparative and Physiological Psychology* in 1947, Stone assumed the editorship. He was succeeded by H. F. Harlow (1951), William K. Estes

(1963), Elliott Stellar (1969), Garth Thomas (1975), and Richard F. Thompson (1982). The journals were again split in 1983. This has been the primary journal for research in comparative psychology for over sixty years. During much of this period there was an editorial bias toward studies of learning to the exclusion of nonexperimental studies. As the issue of its contents was discussed in some detail in Chapter 1, it will not be repeated here. Suffice it to say that much has been written about the journal (for example, Lorenz, 1950; Beach, 1950; Demarest, 1980; Boice, 1971; Kemble, 1981). The editorials of Thomas (1975) on definitional problems and Harlow (1962) on preparation of articles (written with typical Harlow humor) are worthy of attention.

Williams & Wilkins began publishing *Comparative Psychology Monographs* with W. S. Hunter as editor in 1923. As of December, 1951, it had published 107 monographs in twenty-one volumes. Papers ranged from Richter's 1922 study of activity in rats and Nissen's 1931 field study of chimpanzees to a psychosocial analysis of Hopi life history. Noncomparative-psychologist Dunlap assumed the editorship in 1928 with Dorcus taking over in 1936.

Meanwhile the European ethologists established journals of their own. In 1937 the first volume of the *Zeitschrift für Tierpsychologie* consisted of just 289 pages; by 1973 it published over 1,000 pages in the year (Eibl-Eibesfeldt, 1975). The *British Journal of Animal Behavior* began in 1953 with Alastair Worden and B. A. Cross as editors. Thorpe (1953) wrote the initial editorial. It was preceded by a *Bulletin of Animal Behaviour*, a publication of the British Institute for the Study of Animal Behaviour, which began in 1938 and continued until 1951, by which time nine issues had been produced. In 1958 the *British Journal of Animal Behaviour* became *Animal Behaviour*. This change was the result of the interactions and cooperation between British animal behaviorists and some of the American workers influential in the founding of the Animal Behavior Society (M. W. Schein, L. R. Aronson, J. P. Scott, and D. E. Davis, see Anonymous, 1958). The international journal of animal behavior, *Behaviour*, was founded in 1948. Five of the seven editors were European; Beach and Carpenter joined them.

The origin of the more recent journals is described in Chapter 4. Briefly, there has been a proliferation of journals in which comparative psychologists publish. The *Worm Runner's Digest/Journal of Biological Psychology* lasted from 1959 to 1979. The current stable of journals of the Psychonomic Society, including the *Bulletin of the Psychonomic Society* and *Animal Learning & Behavior*, was established in 1973. The forerunner of *Behavioral and Neural Biology, Communications in Behavioral Biology*, began in 1968.

Among the specialty journals in the field are *Developmental*

Psychobiology, Hormones and Behavior, Behavior Genetics, Sleep, Behaviour Analysis Letters, and *Aggressive Behavior.*

The most recent crop of journals has a decidedly ethological flavor and includes *Applied Animal Ethology, Behavioral Ecology and Sociobiology, Behavioural Processes, Biology of Behaviour, Behavioral and Brain Sciences,* and *Ethology and Sociobiology. Animal Behaviour Abstracts* helps the interested reader keep up with so many journals.

Zoo Biology, under the editorship of comparative psychologist Terry L. Maple, began publication in 1982.

The founding in 1980 of the *Comparative Psychology Newsletter,* with Jack Demarest as editor, served to greatly improve communication among comparative psychologists and to make concerted action in behalf of comparative psychology more effective.

Comparative psychologists in 1983 have more publication outlets than ever in their history. However, they have not had a single, primary journal devoted to comparative psychology in all its aspects and as a major influence. It is hoped that the reborn *Journal of Comparative Psychology,* which just began publication under the sponsorship of the American Psychological Association, will fulfill that need.

SOCIETIES

Professional societies and related organizations provide a means for individuals with similar interests to communicate and meet with others of similar interests. They have grown in importance through the century. Their importance was emphasized by Cattell (1917) on the occasion of the twenty-fifth anniversary of the founding of the American Psychological Association:

> Groups of this character, whose individuals are bound together by common interests and objects, may become institutions more dominant over our lives, having greater claims to our loyalty and service, than the conventional family, the helpless church, or the blood-stained nation. (1917, 276)

Early Organizations

Perhaps the first professional organization in North America of interest to comparative psychologists is the Association for the Study of Comparative Psychology. The group was founded by T. Wesley Mills at McGill University and, though open to all, was composed primarily of students and faculty in veterinary medicine at McGill (see Mills, 1898).

In September, 1912, there was established at Elberfeld, Germany, the Society for Animal Psychology. The purpose was "to promote the investigation of the mental life of the mammals, and especially of dogs, apes, and elephants" (Yerkes, 1913c, 303). The proceedings of the society were published under the title *Mitteilungen der Gesellschaft für Tierpsychologie* under the editorship of H. E. Ziegler. The first number contained studies of the trained horses of Elberfeld. Yerkes noted:

> This is the first Society for the promotion of the experimental study of animals to be founded and it is greatly to be hoped that those who are interested in the subject, no matter where they happen to be located, may join the organization as fellows and thus further its work and keep in touch with the progress of investigation through the proceedings of this Society. (1913c, 304)

I have found no further mention of the organization.

American Psychological Association

The founding of the American Psychological Association (APA) in 1892 has been described by several authors (Cattell, 1917, 1943; Dennis and Boring, 1952; Fernberger, 1943a; Hilgard, 1978). This birthdate makes the APA one of the oldest professional organizations in the country. The association had twenty-six charter members including William James, G. Stanley Hall, James Mark Baldwin, and James McKeen Cattell. The meeting to organize the APA was held on July 8, 1892, at Clark University with Hall hosting. It is not fully known which of the charter members were present, although James and Baldwin both seem to have missed the meeting (see Dennis and Boring, 1952). The first formal meeting of the organization was held December 27, 1892, at the University of Pennsylvania. On that occasion five additional members, including Mills and Titchener, were added.

Growth curves of the membership of the APA were presented by Fernberger (1943a) and Hilgard (1978). The membership at the time of Hilgard's publication was approximately 45,000 having shown a rapid exponential growth.

In its early days the APA met jointly with other organizations. The December meeting time was chosen to coincide with that of the American Association for the Advancement of Science (AAAS). In 1914 the APA decided to meet with the AAAS only on alternate years and later, when hotels became too crowded, moved the meeting to late summer and began meeting independently. In his presidential address at the Chicago meetings of December, 1907, President Henry Rutgers Marshall (1908) remarked that "no little significance is to be attached to the fact that the American Psychological Association has chosen this year to meet here in affiliation with the American Association of Naturalists rather than with the American Philosophical Association at Cornell" (1908, 1-2). Attendance at the meetings grew steadily. Two exceptions occurred in 1936 and 1939, when the association met in Michigan and California, respectively. Fernberger (1943a) noted that these facts indicated wisdom of not meeting too far west. The 1972 meetings were held in Honolulu.

Fernberger (1943a) plotted the number of papers presented by year and subdiscipline. It is notable that the curve for animal psychology begins its sharp ascent in the *late* 1920s and rises sharply through the 1930s corresponding with other indices discussed in earlier chapters.

Among those to serve as APA presidents have been Hall (1892, 1924); James (1894, 1904); Baldwin (1897); Thorndike (1912); Watson (1915); Yerkes (1917); Franz (1920); Washburn (1921); Dunlap (1922); Lashley (1929); Hunter (1931); Tolman (1937); Carmichael (1940); Stone (1942); Harlow (1958); Köhler (1959); Hebb (1960); and Lindzey (1967). The APA began awards for Distinguished Scientific Contributions in 1956. Among the recipients have been Spence (1956); Köhler (1956); Richter (1957); Tolman (1957); Beach (1958); Skinner (1958); Harlow (1960); Hebb (1961); Young (1965); Krech (1970); and Garcia (1979).

In recent years comparative psychologists have often been critical of the small size of their own role in the APA. At the Detroit meeting of 1947, the Division of Physiological and Comparative Psychology was merged with the Division of Experimental Psychology. It was not until 1964 that the Division of Physiological and Comparative Psychology (Division 6) was reconstituted. Even that did not represent only comparative psychology. In the opinion of Boice, for example, "Comparative psychologists have no real organization within the American Psychological Association; Division 6 appears to be dominated by physiologists" (1971, 858). Some comparative psychologists are seeking better representation than that provided through Division 6 (see Demarest, 1980). The role of comparative psychologists in the APA has declined as the organization has grown rapidly, especially in the applied areas, while the basic areas have continued to grow more modestly. The place of comparative psychology on the program of the annual meeting has declined over recent years.

There are encouraging signs of a rejuvenation of comparative psychology within the APA. Meeting at its 1977 convention, the APA Division 6 created a Committee on the Status of Comparative Psychology. With a New York-based core committee and a National Corresponding Committee, this group improved communication among comparative psychologists. The *Comparative Psychology Newsletter* was an outgrowth of this organization. The recent commitment by the

APA to publish a separate *Journal of Comparative Psychology* provides a further indication of the improved status of comparative psychology.

Society of Experimental Psychologists

The Society of Experimental Psychologists is both an honorary and scientific organization, derived from E. B. Titchener. The first informal meeting of the group was held at Cornell in 1904, and informal meetings continued until 1928 (see Boring, 1938). Comparative psychologists such as Lashley, Watson, and Yerkes were influential members of the group. When Watson hosted the 1910 meeting, Boring noted that "Holt and Yerkes called each other by their first names, and Titchener was distressed by such unBritish conduct" (Boring, 1938, 413). The Committee of Fifteen, organized in 1928 to formalize the group, included Bentley, Hunter, Lashley, and Yerkes. The society was founded with the restriction that there should be no more than fifty members and that membership should be an honor. The next group elected included Carr, Dunlap, Stone, and Washburn, making twenty-six charter members, the same number as in the APA. The history through 1938 was described by Boring (1938).

The Psychonomic Society

As portrayed by Garner (1976), the first germ of an idea for the Psychonomic Society came at a bar in Washington, D.C. during the 1958 AAAS meetings. Times had changed. The stimulus for the founding of the society was the changed emphasis in the APA. An organizing committee was formed and met at the 1959 AAAS meeting in Chicago. Some eight hundred individuals were invited to become charter members. The first meeting of the society was held at the University of Chicago in September, 1960, just before the Chicago APA meetings. The Psychonomic Society has held annual meetings that have provided a forum for all approaches to experimental psychology.

The name was provided by W. S. Verplanck, who, together with some classicists found that there was an existing word, *psychonomy*, that meant "science of the mind" (Garner, 1976). It is notable, however, that James Mark Baldwin (1902) used the word in his *Development and Evolution*.

Animal Behavior Society

The Animal Behavior Society (ABS) was formally organized at a special meeting during the Montreal AAAS meeting on December, 17, 1964. Like other such organizations, however, the ABS had an interesting history prior to its formal organization. This is told by Guhl and Schein, (1976). The Conference on Genetics and Social Behavior held at Bar Harbor in 1946 provided the first landmark event. At this time the Committee for the Study of Animal Societies under Natural Conditions (CSASNC) was formed. Beginning in 1950 the CSASNC met regularly during the AAAS meetings. Over the next years, the fledgling group established relationships with the American Institute of Biological Sciences, the AAAS, and the Association for the Study of Animal Behavior, and it also became a section of the Ecological Society of America and a division of the American Society of Zoologists. The first independent meeting was held at Logan, Utah, in 1971.

Comparative psychologists have been active in the Animal Behavior Society, with such comparative psychologists as B. Beck, I. Bernstein, G. Burghardt, C. Carter, T. Christenson, D. Dewsbury, G. Gottlieb, R. Goy, J. Hirsch, G. Jensen, and B. Sachs serving as officers at various times.

Other Organizations

The first International Ethological Conference was held in 1947 and conferences continued to be held in alternate years. The meetings provide an opportunity for ethologists and comparative psychologists to meet and interact and have played an important role in mediating the influences that each group has had on the other.

Various organizations have served groups of comparative psychologists and others with specialized interests. The Conference on Reproductive Behavior has held annual meetings of workers in that field since the initial meeting in East Lansing, Michigan, in 1969. I have compiled an informal history (Dewsbury, 1979c). Other organizations are the Behavior Genetics Association, the International Society for Research on Aggression, the International Society for Developmental Psychobiology, and the Society for Neuroscience.

FACILITIES

The conduct of research requires facilities in which to do the work. The basic requirements are a physical plant capable of housing the animals, equipment, personnel, and support materials for research. In addition, nonacademic staff, supplies, and basic equipment are necessary. The amount required has varied over time and with the nature of the research effort. Even modest research, however, requires some investment in facilities.

There was a steady spread of laboratories in animal psychology in the United States during the first three decades of the century (Warden and Warner, 1927). The first organized laboratories were established at Clark and Harvard in 1899, with Chicago a close third (1903). Laboratories were established at Texas and Johns Hopkins in 1908 and Cornell and Michigan in 1909. Seven new laboratories were established in the next decade, and there were twenty-three established by 1926.

The typical laboratory, both in the early days of comparative psychology and at present, generally houses only one or two comparative psychologists together with their students, associates, and staff. The typical laboratory in comparative psychology, then, is organized along the lines of "small," as opposed to "big science." Early comparative psychologists felt a need for larger facilities. Watson, for example, noted the need of comparative psychology for an experimental station "for working out the larger problems of comparative psychology" (1906, 155). It will be recalled that Watson believed that "the need to the psychologist of an experimental station for the study of the evolution of the mind is as great as is the need to the biologist of an experimental station for the study of the evolution of the body and its functions" (1906, 156). In his proposed experimental station, Watson would have studied the possibility of a Lamarckian inheritance of learning, learning to learn, imitation, and related problems. He was especially concerned about facilities for mammals. He also noted that no laboratories had adequate provisions for birds and insects. "At Chicago a simple large basement room is all that can be spared for comparative purposes. Clark seems to be somewhat better prepared than this. The conditions at Cornell and Columbia are, I believe, not much better than here" (1906, 153-154). In his addendum to Watson's paper, Baldwin noted that the original Advisory Committee on Psychology of the Carnegie Institution in 1902 recommended as its first priority the establishment of a station for animal psychology in cooperation with zoology.

Yerkes (1916b) proposed an experimental station for the study of monkeys and apes. He wanted to establish the facility in a favorable climate and would use it for study of a variety of problems of primate biology in addition to behavior. At his facility Yerkes would include six professional scientists—a behaviorist, an assistant in comparative physiology, a geneticist, an assistant with training in anatomy, histology, and embryology, and expert in experimental medicine, and an assistant trained in pathology and neurology. In addition, Yerkes would employ a business manager, a clerical force of three, a mechanic, a carpenter, and at least four laborers. If built in Southern California in 1916, Yerkes estimated that the facility would require an annual budget of approximately $50,000, and thus an endowment of approximately $1 million.

Yerkes's Facilities

Yerkes described the facilities in which he worked in greater detail than any other scientists whose work I have ever read. Because Yerkes and his facilities were such an important part of the growth of comparative psychology, I have described certain aspects of their growth in the section on chronology. Therefore, I will not go into great detail regarding matters already discusseed but simply expand where appropriate.

In his first paper on facilities, Yerkes (1914) described the Harvard laboratories, giving a room-by-room description including the inevitable Yerkes floorplan. The Yerkes family farm in Franklin, New Hampshire, was described as the "Franklin field station," with six photographs included in the paper. It took some time before Yerkes got the facility he wanted. In the meantime he described the facilities at which he did work. Having failed to get to Tenerife, Yerkes spent his 1915 sabbatical at G. V. Hamilton's private primate facility in Montecito, California. In his report of the work, Yerkes (1916a) provides a complete description of the facility including floorplan and photographs. Similarly, the report of his work at Madam Abreu's facility in Havana is richly illustrated (Yerkes, 1925).

When he moved to Yale in 1924, Yerkes was given adequate space and a commitment for facilities to support primate research. The New Haven facility was described by Yerkes (1932b).

It was, of course, the facility that would be named the Yerkes Laboratries of Primate Biology in Orange Park, Florida, that was especially influential in comparative psychology. Its history has been told repeatedly (Gray,1955; Hahn, 1971; Yerkes, 1932b, 1943b). After demonstrating the feasibility of keeping chimpanzees in captivity in New Haven, Yerkes secured funds from the Laura Spelman Rockefeller Memorial Fund and purchased the two hundred acres of land in Orange Park in 1929. Construction was begun in January of 1930 and finished in June. When Madam Abreu died in November, 1930, her collection was disbanded, and Yerkes went to Havana to select fifteen assorted chimpanzees to be moved to Orange Park. By 1940, the combined facilities in New Haven and Orange Park included some forty chimpanzees.

In 1942 Lashley succeeded Yerkes and director, the facility was named for Yerkes, and Harvard joined Yale in sponsoring the operations. Nissen succeeded Lashley as director in 1955.

Hebb (1980) described life at the Orange Park laboratories and provided an interesting contrast between Yerkes and Lashley. Yerkes was concerned that things be done in a orderly manner. When he first arrived, Hebb found in his desk a book from the earlier regime that noted at one point that originality was important in research but other matters were too. Numerous rules and regulations were listed. Lashley had other priorities and fostered creativity in research, relying on Nissen to attend to "housekeeping" details.

Many of the world's outstanding comparative and physiological psychologists received part of their training at Orange Park.

NIH Primate Research Centers Program

Primate research in a variety of disciplines was greatly facilitated with the founding of the Primate Research Center program under the sponsorship of the National Institute of Health. The program was started with congressional action in 1959 and 1960 (see Bourne, 1973). Regional Primate Research Centers were established at Beaverton, Oregon; Seattle, Washington; Covington, Louisiana; Madison, Wisconsin; Southborough, Massachusetts; Davis, California; and Atlanta, Georgia. By 1975 the facilities were run with a budget of $11 million a year, operated some nine hundred different research projects, and maintained colonies with 7,800 primates representing forty-eight species. Approximately 141 scientists and 502 other investigators worked at the facilities (see Goodwin and Augustine, 1975).

With time and the gradual loss of staff from Harvard and Yale, the administration of the Orange Park facility had become burdensome. When Emory University in Atlanta offered to assume responsibility for the facility, it was turned over to Emory as a gift in 1956. With the founding of the Regional Primate Centers, funds were made available for a new facility in Atlanta, the Yerkes Regional Primate Research Center, and the Orange Park facility was moved. The move of more than one hundred great apes and nearly two hundred monkeys from Florida to Atlanta was described by Bourne (1965) and in the JAMA (Anonymous, 1965).

American Museum of Natural History

The Department of Experimental Biology of the American Museum of Natural History (AMNH) in New York, the only such museum department in the world, was the creation of G. Kingsley Noble. Beach accepted a position in the department in 1937 at a salary of $1,800 (Beach, 1974). When Noble died in 1940, there were plans to disband the department. With the aid of letters from Yerkes and Lashley, the department was saved and renamed the Department of Animal Behavior, with Beach as its chairman. Beach got Lester Aronson appointed as a curator, and Schneirla accepted a part-time appointment in the museum.

When Beach moved to Yale in 1946, Schneirla succeeded him as chairman of the Department of Animal Behavior. Schneirla (1958, 1959b) described the study of animal behavior and its relation to museum activities. Various activities and facilities at the museum were portrayed. The department became an important training ground for future leaders of comparative psychology and, with Lehrman and Schneirla showing the way, a focal point for both the battle and resolution with the European ethologists.

Sadly, the board of the trustees of the American Museum of Natural History finally decided to close the Department of Animal Behavior in 1980.

Institute of Animal Behavior

The Institute of Animal Behavior at Rutgers University in Newark was, in a sense, a propagule of the Department of Animal Behavior at the AMNH. Lehrman moved from the museum to Rutgers and became director of the fledgling institute in 1959 (*New York Times,* August 12, 1972). By 1963 the institute had developed a strong staff, and the complete autonomy of the graduate program and the institute were defined by the board of governors in 1966 (Rosenblatt, 1982). The institute grew organically from the interests of Lehrman and his colleagues and brought together a group of outstanding scientists interested in animal behavior but from a variety of disciplines. Jay Rosenblatt joined Lehrman very early, with Ernst Hansen, from Harlow's laboratory; Colin Beer, from Tinbergen's Oxford; Barry Komisaruk, Harvey Feder, and younger colleagues joining the staff. The Institute of Animal Behavior has probably been to comparative psychology in recent years what the Yerkes laboratories were in earlier years, in that many outstanding comparative psychologists were trained as either graduate students of postdoctoral fellows at the facility.

Jackson Laboratory

I have mentioned the Jackson Laboratory in Bar Harbor, Maine, repeatedly in passing. The animal-behavior program at the Jackson Laboratory was run by J. P. Scott and John L. Fuller. Both made important contributions to the study of animal behavior in general and comparative psychology in particular. However, as I have defined comparative psychology, they fall on its fringe, as they are biologists by training. Therefore, I have given them and the Jackson Laboratory less treatment that would occur were I not focusing on psychologists as defined in Chapter 1.

Scott was recruited to Bar Harbor by President C. C. Little in 1945. Fuller joined him in 1947. Psychologists have played an important role in the programs on genetics and the behavior of dogs and mice at the

Jackson Laboratory. Walter C. Stanley, a comparative-developmental psychologist, was a member of the permanent staff in the 1960s. Many other psychologists participated in the summer programs in Bar Harbor either as faculty or students. During my summer in Bar Harbor, 1961, for example, psychologists V. H. Denenberg, D. D. Thiessen, J. Church, E. Satinoff, C. Boelkins, and C. Kent were in attendance. Sherman Ross was a frequent participant. Through research and training, the Bar Harbor laboratories exerted much influence on comparative psychology.

Zing-Yang Kuo

An appreciation of the effects of political events on facilities and research can be gained from consideration of the career of Zing-Kang Kuo (Gottlieb, 1972). Kuo returned to China from Berkeley in 1923 and accepted a position as professor of psychology at Fuh Tan University. Wealthy relatives provided funds for the construction of a three-story laboratory building. Kuo rose to be president of the university. Political turmoil forced Kuo to leave Fuh Tan in 1926, before fully utilizing the facility. Kuo then began research in more modest facilities in the country. Kuo moved to a new laboratory in Hangchow in 1929, and when the government got into trouble, he moved to Nanking in 1931. In 1933 he was sent back to Hangchow. Finally, political unrest led Kuo to leave China in 1936. After finding some temporary employment in the United States, Kuo had no promise of a permanent position and returned to China, then under invasion from Japan, in 1940. With the exception of a brief period in Raleigh in 1963, Kuo never again had a laboratory in which to work (Gottlieb, 1972).

National Laboratory of Comparative Psychology

The experimental station for comparative psychology proposed by Watson (1906) was never built. Just as Watson (1906) and Yerkes (1916b) proposed research facilities for their times, we can speculate about what such a facility would do in ours. Let us call my fantasy the "National Laboratory for Comparative Psychology" (NLCP).

In order that a variety of species can be maintained, the National Laboratory of Comparative Psychology should be built in a warm-weather state of the United States. It should be near an ocean or gulf so that marine species can be maintained. In order to attract the best talent, it should be reasonably near an urban center. Ideally, it would be near at least one major university. The physical plant should be modern with full facilities for maintaining a variety of species. These would include insects, aquatic species, and other small and large vertebrates and invertebrates. Some outdoor housing should be available for larger vertebrates and social groups. It would have a variety of fully equipped shops.

The NLCP should be staffed by approximately ten comparative psychologists, including individuals of diverse backgrounds, ages, and so on. They should study a variety of taxa including invertebrates and "lower" vertebrates, as well as mammals. At least one of the ten should be studying each of the four basic questions—mechanism, development, function, and evolution. The staff would be supplemented by three individuals from related disciplines—perhaps a physiologist, an ethologist, and a sociobiologist. A full-time Ph.D. statistician should be available, as should a modern computer facility. Some twenty to thirty technicians and animal caretakers should be provided to help in the maintenance and testing of animals. Shop technicians would be available, and a staff of some seven secretaries and a business manager would be employed.

The NLCP would function in training as well as research. It would fund ten postdoctoral fellowships per year so that young workers could come and enjoy the facilities of the center. In addition, there would be funds for another ten young scientists to come to conduct dissertation research. A summer program could accommodate undergraduates and a limited number of exceptional high school students.

The NLCP would provide services internationally as well. It would maintain a fully equipped library with a full staff and be able to provide bibliographic assistance using the latest methods. An archival branch would maintain records and papers related to the history of comparative psychology. A translation branch would provide easy translation of older materials as well as current materials intended for publication.

A conference center would be made available to various scientific organizations so that meetings could be held at the NLCP. Appropriate rooms for meetings and posters would be available.

Funds would be provided for a visiting-speaker series so that visitors could come to the NLCP to present either a lecture or a week of presentations in a "minicourse" format to keep the staff current with respect to recent developments in a variety of fields.

Practically, it is unlikely that a national commitment would ever be made to permit the construction and development of the National Laboratory of Comparative Psychology. It is interesting to contemplate the progress that might be made, however, should such a facility be available, There is a very realistic need for improved bibliographic, conference, translation, and research facilities and services relating to comparative psychology.

FUNDING

The conduct of science requires funding, and although it is possible to spend great sums and accomplish little, it is difficult to accomplish much without incurring some expenses. Perhaps nowhere in the history of comparative psychology is the contrast between the early days and the present greater than in the area of funding.

Early Days

The literature on comparative psychology in the early days is full of anecdotes regarding the difficult funding situation faced by the pioneers of the fields. Cohen (1979) summarized some of John Watson's battles with university administration over funds. Watson was somewhat more emphatic in his demands than was expected of faculty of the times and repeatedly found himself apologizing to university presidents for "impertinence." He was expected to teach animal psychology with no expenditure of funds. In February, 1905, for example, Watson wrote to President Harper of the University of Chicago explaining the need for a $100 projection lantern for use in teaching material on the nervous system and sense organs and reminding him that Professor Judson had promised the funds. The exchange of letters must have been quite caustic as President Harper wrote to Angell, acting as an intermediary, that Watson's letter to him was either "an indication of insanity or intentional impertinence" (Cohen, 1979, 40). Angell eventually smoothed things over, but by May, Watson was again in trouble for making equipment requests that were regarded as excessive. Watson later encountered similar problems with the president of Johns Hopkins. Watson did eventually succeed in securing funds from the University of Chicago to buy the four monkeys used in his study of imitation (1908a). During the continued correspondence between Watson and Yerkes, "They often moaned to each other about the need for better facilities to study the higher animals" (Cohen, 1979, 44).

In 1906 Watson met Dr. Alfred Mayer who ran the Carnegie Institution's Marine Biological Station. It was Mayer who offered Watson the opportunity to work on the Dry Tortugas. Cohen notes that Watson was delighted in part because the extra $255 meant that he and his wife could hire a maid for a few months.

Animal psychology was formally begun at Harvard in the school year of 1899-1900 with two and later three rooms in Dane Hall. The facility was moved to Emerson Hall in 1906. The initial equipment in the Dane Hall laboratory included a tank for frogs, cases for birds, and a box for tortoises. As noted by Hilgard (1965), it is instructive in this day of federal funding, to examine the budget for Yerkes's laboratory during its

Table 4.   Expenditures in Support of Yerkes's Harvard Laboratory

Year	Expenses	Number of Investigators
1899-1900	$ 75.00	3
1900-1901	26.78	5
1901-1902	36.34	3
1902-1903	15.00	5
1903-1904	20.00	4
1904-1905	50.00	4
1905-1906	120.00	4
1906-1907	15.00	5
1907-1908	140.00	8
1908-1909	300.00	5

Source: From E. R. Hilgard, 1965, Robert Mearns Yerkes, *Biographical Memoirs of the National Academy of Sciences* **38**:395.

first decade of existence. It is presented in Table 4. By the 1908/1909 year the budget had reached $300 per year! Yerkes was able to raise outside funds. In 1909/1910 he raised $150 from private sources and in 1912/1913 he secured $500 from the Bache Fund of the National Academy of Sciences to work on color vision in birds. Yerkes was able to raise funds repeatedly, as in securing support from the Laura Spelman Rockefeller Memorial and the Rockefeller Foundation for his three winter trips to Sarasota, Florida, to study the gorilla, Congo (Yerkes, 1927*a*,1927*b*, 1928) and in his securing of funds from various sources to support Bingham, Nissen, and Carpenter in their early field research.

National Research Council Committee for Research on Problems of Sex

A major source of funding during a critical phase of development of comparative psychology was the National Research Council Committee for Reasearch on Problems of Sex. The history of the committee from 1922-1947 was described in detail by Aberle and Corner (1953). Preliminary events surrounding the formation of the committee revolve about one Earl F. Zinn, a graduate student in psychology who had worked under G. Stanley Hall at Clark and Max J. Exner, a physician on the staff of the YMCA. Zinn convinced Exner of the need for greater understanding of human sex and through Katharine Bement Davis went directly to John D. Rockefeller, Jr. for support. Davis was director of the Rockefeller-sponsored Bureau of Social Hygiene. The bureau and Rockefeller Foundation funded the NRC committee throughout its existence.

It is fortunate that these events occurred during the time that Robert

Yerkes was functioning as a Washington administrator, serving as chairman of the NRC Research Information Service during the interlude between his two careers as an active researcher. Yerkes was impressed with the idea of a committee to facilitate research on sex and sought an administrative home for it. The initial response from the National Research Council was negative, in part because of the risks in research in such an uncharted field and in part because the work lay outside of the traditional physical sciences in which the NRC was most active. The bureau of Social Hygiene provided $10,000 for a conference to develop the proposed program; the conference was held October 28 and 29, 1921. The result of the conference was the decision to go ahead with the project with the support of the NRC, gained in part by the efforts of Walter B. Cannon.

The first formal meeting of the committee was held on January 17, 1922, and was attended by the first four members appointed: Yerkes, Cannon, biologist E. G. Conklin, and psychiatrist T. W. Salmon. Yerkes was elected chair—a post he would hold for twenty-five years; Zinn was appointed to a salaried post as executive secretary. Biologists and endocrinologists were well represented on the committee throughout. In addition, Yerkes asked Lashley, as an outside consultant, to draw up a list of problems in the neurology and psychobiology of sex that merited attention. Yerkes was thus able to ensure that problems of reproductive behavior in animals were included in the program of the committee. Comparative psychologists indeed played an important role on the committee, with Yerkes serving as its first chairman (1921-1947), Lashley serving on the committee beginning in 1934, and Beach serving as its last chairman.

The total budget for the NRC committee was minuscule by today's standards. During the period covered by Aberle and Corner's survey, the annual budget began with expenditure of $6,096.34 in 1921/1922 and reached $44,349.53 in 1946/1947. The high point was reached in the 1931/1932 year when $74,451.15 was spent. My estimate is that comparative psychologists received a total of $104,050 in forty-six grants between 1922 and 1947. These grants are summarized in Table 5. The mean size of the forty-six grants was $2,262.

Although the sums were small, the NCR committee played a major role in the development of research in comparative psychology in this country partly because it was one of the few sources of funding at a time. The committee was a long-term supporter of Calvin Stone's studies of sexual behavior in rats, beginning in 1922/1923 with a $250 grant for the study of sexual behavior as affected by inanition. Lashley paid Beach's salary during his year at Harvard with funds from the NRC committee and during the period of 1937-1953 the NRC committee was practically the sole source of outside support for Beach's work (see Beach, 1978b, 1981).

Table 5.   Summary of Grants for Research in Comparative Psychology from the National Research Council Committee for Research in Problems of Sex, 1922-1947

Principal Investigator	Number of Grants	Total Dollar Value
Beach, F. A.	6	25,000
Carpenter, C. R.	1	500
Dunlap, K.	1	2,500
Lashley, K.	4	7,600
Liddell, H. S.	1	1,800
Slonaker, J. R.	12	18,500
Stone, C. P.	15	18,650
Yerkes, R. M.	6	29,500
Total	46	104,050

Source: Data from S. D. Aberle and G. W. Corner, 1953, *Twenty-five Years of Sex Research,* Saunders, Philadelphia, Appendix 7.

It supported Knight Dunlap for study of the effects of copulatory activity on learning, Liddell for studies of estrous cycles in old swine and dogs, and Slonaker for various studies of activity rhythms and physiology. Lashley's work was for physiological studies of sexual and maternal behavior. Yerkes's grants were all for primate work; the 1932/1933 grant for $2,500 for studies of the social life and reproductive cycle of howler monkeys launched C. R. Carpenter's career as a field psychologist. The committee later supported Carpenter's study of red spider monkeys in Panama (Carpenter, 1935) with $500.

In the late 1950s Beach became first a member and later chair of the NRC committee. At a time when federal grants were increasing, the annual operating budget of approximately $50,000 appeared insignificant. The decision was made that no new grants would be made after 1961. The committee then deliberated about its future. Beach (1965, viii) noted that "committees, being in the main reluctant to dissolve themselves, will expend vast quantities of time and energy seeking to rationalize their own continued existence." Faced with a choice between dissolving the committee or finding new problems to solve, the committee decided that the former course was the more appropriate.

As its final act, the committee decided to organize and sponsor an international conference on the status of research on sexual behavior. Ironically, the conference was held largely as a result of funding from the National Institute of Mental Health and the National Science Foundation. The meetings were held at the University of California, Berkeley, in 1961 and 1962 and resulted in the publication of Beach's (1965) *Sex and*

Behavior. At the final meeting after the 1962 session, the Committee for Research in Problems of Sex unanimously adopted the following resolution:

> It is recommendd to the Chairman of the Division of Medical Sciences that the Committee for Research in Problems in Sex should be discharged when the book resulting from the Conference on Sex and Behavior has been prepared for publication. (Beach, 1965, ix)

The notion that the job was not done until the publication was complete is a pure Frank Beach touch. An important era in the funding of research had ended. It ended, however, only because a new era had begun.

National Science Foundation

The National Science Foundation (NSF) can be said to have begun on May 10,1950, when President H. S. Truman signed a bill, S. 247, into law, Public Law 507 of the 81st Congress. Passage of the bill followed a five-year period of formation and debate following the end of World War II, at which time Vannevar Bush, director of the wartime Office of Scientific Research, had proposed a national foundation to coordinate science. Issues in the debate included ownership of patents, geographical and institutional access to funds, eligibility for funding of the social sciences, basic versus applied research, and control of the agency (see England, n.d.; Lomask, 1975). The twenty-four person National Science Board was established and met for the first time on December 12, 1950. The board functioned to oversee and control the foundation.

NSF has grown and changed throughout its thirty odd years of existence. The first operating budget, that for fiscal year 1952, was $3.5 million; the budget for fiscal year (FY) 1981 was over $1,022 million. The original law has been amended several times. The statutory authority is currently defined in the National Science Foundation Act of 1950 as amended. The various functions of NSF are laid out in this act. According to Section 3.(a)(1), NSF is authorized and directed:

> to initiate and support basic scientific research and programs to strengthen scientific research potential and science education programs at all levels in the mathematical, physical, medical, biological, engineering, social, and other sciences, by making contracts or other arrangements (including grants, loans, and other forms of assistance) to support such scientific and educational activities and to appraise the impact of research upon industrial development and upon the general welfare. . . .

As NSF has grown and changed over the years, there have been a number of interesting developments. In general, efforts to keep NSF out of politics have been successful. Whereas the initial charter restricted NSF to supporting basic research prior to 1968, applied research is now supported. The foundation has begun supporting a limited number of projects in "big science," wherein major cooperative scientific endeavors can be undertaken. These and other changes have altered the face of NSF over time but have not changed its basic function and operation (see England, n.d.; Lomask, 1975).

Funding for comparative psychology has come primarily from the Psychobiology Program, which is currently a part of the Division of Behavioral and Neural Sciences within the Directorate for Biological, Behavioral, and Social Sciences of NSF. The Psychobiology Program, like NSF itself, has grown and changed since its inception in 1952. Some of the administrative changes make it difficult to evaluate properly the growth and changes in patterns of funding for compartive psychology. In its early years, the Psychobiology Program encompassed a broad range of area in the biobehavioral field. In 1971 a separate program in neurobiology split off from psychobiology. In 1975 separate programs in sensory physiology and perception and in memory and cognitive processes were established. Changes in funding at the points of establishment of these related programs do not represent overall decreases in funding for the field of psychobiology. It should also be noted that some funding for comparative psychology comes from programs other than psychobiology.

The actual pattern of changes in the funding for the Psychobiology Program can be seen in Table 6, which shows that the budget for the program rose from $23,300 in FY 1952 to $4,250,529 in FY 1981. The peak year was in FY 1971, just before the establishment of the Neurobiology Program.

It is difficult to assess the support of comparative psychology from the Psychobiology Program. The primary problems relate to definitions of comparative psychology, as discussed in Chapter 1. I have examined the records of the Psychobiology Program in an effort to isolate that part of the effort devoted to comparative psychology. I have used the definitional structure suggested in Chapter 1, and in addition, a simple rule of thumb: Would the research be appropriate for my courses in comparative psychology? Many arbitrary decisions had to be made; in some cases the research of a given individual would be included in one year and not another—depending on the title and presumed nature of the research activity. Given that the data are the result of some arbitrary decisions, I believe them still interesting. The first NSF grant that I included was given to C. P. Stone in 1953 for his study of the behavior of hypophysectomized rats. The number of grants and dollar value awarded to comparative psychologists represented but a small part of the Psychobiology Program, generally 10 percent or less, until the last few years. Indeed, 1978 represents the first fiscal year in which more than

Table 6. Summary of National Science Foundation Grants Through the Psychobiology Panel, 1952–1981

Year	Psychobiology Program		Estimated Comparative Psychology Only	
	Number of Grants Awarded	Total Dollar Amount	Number of Grants Awarded	Total Dollar Amount
1952	2	23,300	0	0
1953	8	100,000	1	7,400
1954	26	400,000	5	52,800
1955	56	640,000	5	143,600
1956	60	700,000	3	40,500
1957	56	850,000	4	44,900
1958	62	936,300	4	84,300
1959	77	1,518,300	7	113,800
1960	83	2,150,100	4	75,900
1961	82	2,355,200	8	172,200
1962	97	2,645,600	9	154,000
1963	118	3,313,300	12	379,400
1964	121	3,519,500	16	454,100
1965	122	4,128,900	7	249,700
1966	143	4,846,200	14	538,300
1967	118	4,641,650	9	343,300
1968	115	4,363,100	12	573,200
1969	122	4,444,350	11	660,600
1970	119	4,449,370	6	129,200
1971	174	5,683,417	9	321,000
1972[a]	119	4,072,100	11	332,500
1973	125	4,083,500	11	298,600
1974	128	4,347,800	7	302,200
1975	139	5,101,350	9	211,200
1976[b]	145	5,398,000	12	486,500
1977[c]	83	3,135,950	12	694,700
1978	93	3,654,400	25	1,171,300
1979	95	3,940,395	21	1,166,500
1980	106	4,267,785	24	1,031,300
1981	94	4,250,529	22	1,340,600

[a]Neurobiology split from psychobiology in 1972.
[b]Includes transition quarter (July–September, 1976) when the timing of the fiscal year was changed.
[c]Sensory physiology and perception and memory and cognitive processes split from psychobiology in 1976.

sixteen grants were awarded in comparative psychology. With the current structuring, comparative psychology represents approximately one-quarter of the activity of the Psychobiology Program. There are some other sources of bias in these data in Table 6 that require comment. At various times there have been shifts concerning whether single- or multiple-year grants are awarded and listed as funded. Some changes in the relative number of grants are affected by these procedures. Further, NSF has given major support to a few large programs such as Gardner and Gardner's studies of language in chimpanzees and to Nissen to support research at the Yerkes Laboratories. Some of the year-to-year variability is due to changes in a few such large programs rather than to changes in overall policy.

By my estimate, the Psychobiology Program awarded some three hundred grants in comparative psychology from FY 1953 through FY 1981. The mean size of the award rose from $10,560 in 1953 to $61,00 in 1981. The three hundred grants were awarded to a total of some 104 comparative psychologists or other psychologists doing research that may be treated as comparative psychology. These individuals are listed in Table 7.

In addition to funding research grants, NSF has had other functions as well—particularly in funding pre- and post-doctoral fellowships, some of which have been in comparative psychology. NSF has funded travel and scientific conferences, as in its support for the 1961 and 1962 Berkeley conferences on Sex and Behavior, William Verplanck's conference on the problems of comparative behavior, and Anne Roe's efforts on Behavior and Evolution (see Roe and Simpson, 1958).

Recommendations regarding the awarding of grants are made by a panel of scientists from around the nation. In the early years of the Psychobiology Program, comparative psychology was not well represented on this panel. Beach was an early member who finished his service in 1956. D. R. Meyer, a physiological-comparative psychologist, served from 1966 through 1968. In recent years, however, representation on the panel has been more appreciable. Most individuals have served three-year terms. Some of the psychologists with a comparative orientation (as defined in Chapter 1) serving on the panel and the year of their appointment have been: B. T. Gardner (1972); N. E. Spear (1972); J. E. R. Staddon (1974); N. D. Henderson (1975); T. E. McGill (1978); E. K. Adkins (1979); E. M. Blass (1979); G. M. Burghardt (1979); G. P. Sackett (1979); F. R. Brush, (1979); J. R. Alberts (1980); D. A. Goldfoot (1981); G. N. Wade (1981); and D. A. Dewsbury (1983). Clearly, the vast majority of the comparative psychologists serving as panel members in the thirty-odd year history of the program have been appointed in recent years. This period corresponds with the period of growth in support for comparative psychology. It is difficult to separate cause and effect.

National Institutes of Health

The National Institutes of Health (NIH) began as the one-room Laboratory of Hygiene in 1887. It was given bureau status in the Public Health

Table 7. Comparative Psychologists Receiving National Science Foundation Grants from the Psychobiology Program, 1953–1981

Adkins, E.	Gandleman, R.
Adler, H.	Gardner, B.
Adler, N.	Gardner, R.
Alberts, J.	Gibson, E.
Altmann, M.	Glickman, S.
Beauchamp, G.	Goldfoot, D.
Beecher, M.	Gordon, T.
Bermant, G.	Gossette, R.
Bernstein, I.	Gottlieb, G.
Bitterman, M.	Grosslight, J.
Blass, E.	Hall, W. G.
Block, M.	Hein, A.
Bunnell, B.	Held, R.
Burghardt, G.	Henderson, N.
Campbell, B.	Herman, L.
Candland, D.	Hill, W.
Carpenter, C. R.	Hutchinson, R.
Carter, C. S.	Ireland, L.
Daly, M.	Jaynes, J.
Denenberg, V.	Jensen, D.
Dewsbury, D.	Johnston, R.
Domjan, M.	Kamil, A.
Erickson, C.	Kellogg, W.
Estep, D.	Krech, D.
Fatnz, R.	Kristal, M.
Finger, F.	LeBoeuf, B.
Fouts, R.	Lehrman, D.

Service in 1943, and the Public Health Service Act, approved on July 1, 1944, gave NIH the legislative basis for a postwar program of conducting research. The Research Grants Office of NIH was created in 1946. The National Institute of Mental Health was created as a part of NIH on April 15, 1949. In the time since their initial founding, the National Institutes have expanded, proliferated, and undergone repeated reorganization. The National Institute of Mental Health (NIMH), for example, was separated from NIH in 1967, rejoined NIH on July 1, 1973, and became a part of the Alcohol, Drug Abuse and Mental Health Administration (ADAMHA) on September 15, 1973. Other institutes were established as the NIH organism grew. The National Institute of Child Health and Human Development (NICHD) began in 1962. The National Institute of Neurological Diseases and Blindness began in 1950; in 1965 this became the National Institute of Neurological and Communicative Disorders and Stroke (NINCDS).

Table 7. *(continued)*

Leon, M.	Rosenzweig, M.
Leshner, A.	Rozin, P.
Levine, S.	Rumbaugh, D.
Lockard, R.	Schneirla, T.
McClintock, M.	Schrier, A.
McGill, T.	Schusterman, R.
McReynolds, P.	Seay, B.
Marx, M.	Silver, R.
Mason, W.	Staddon, J.
Menzel, E.	Stern, J. M.
Meyer, D.	Stettner, L.
Mineka, S.	Stone, C.
Moltz, H.	Suomi, S.
Montgomery, K.	Svare, B.
Moore, C.	Tavolga, W.
Moyer, K.	Thompson, T.
Nadler, R.	Thompson, W.
Nagy, Z.	Tobach, E.
Nissen, H.	Topoff, H.
Nyby, J.	Walk, R.
Olton, D.	Ward, I.
Petrinovitch, L.	Warren, J.
Premack, D.	West, M.
Ratner, S.	Whitney, G.
Richter, C.	Winston, H.

Note: Other individuals received support from other programs.

According to the 1981 *NIH Almanac* (NIH, 1981) the total appropriation for NIH rose from $464,000 in 1938 to $3,425,685,000 in 1980. Because support for research in comparative psychology is scattered throughout the various institutes it is more difficult to determine the level of funding for comparative psychology at NIH than at NSF. The expenditure of grants at NIMH rose from $4,344,000 to $130,662,000 between 1950 and 1967 while it was part of NIH. The budget allowance for grants at NICHD rose from $26,294,000 in 1964 to $139,232,000 in 1980. Some funds for comparative psychology are included in those sums; they are a relatively small part, however.

Scientific review of grant applications at NIH is provided by the Division of Research Grants. Comparative psychological applications would typically be referred to the Behavior and Neurosciences Review Section, established in 1978. Their review groups include one on Bio-psychology (1959); Neurology A (1953); Neurology B (1962); Neurological Sciences (1977); and Social Sciences and Population (1971).

APPLIED COMPARATIVE PSYCHOLOGY

Although comparative psychology is a basic science not always oriented toward human applications, it is natural and important that psychologists, like other scientists, consider the application of their results for the immediate as well as the long-term good of society. Indeed, one could argue that such activity is a responsibility of a socially concerned scientist. In a model paper, Hebb and Thompson (1954) considered "The Social Significance of Animal Studies."

Animal Training

Perhaps the broadest application of principles from animal psychology has been in the practical training of animals. Often this has been done by individuals trained in the Skinnerian-operant tradition, rather than by comparative psychologists per se. Nevertheless, this has been a major part of applied animal psychology with implications for comparative psychology. The best-known program is that of Breland and Breland (for example, 1951, 1961). The Brelands made a successful commercial venture out of training animals for zoos, circuses, and other applications.

Among the most dramatic applications was the use of animals in the space program. Prior to manned space missions, the National Aeronautics and Space Administration (NASA) conducted two flights in which trained chimpanzees were launched in rockets as part of the Mercury-Redstone series (Rohles, et al., 1963). The chimpanzees were trained on complex operant tasks that they performed during the flights. It was concluded that performance was relatively little affected by weightlessness, that eating and drinking could be accomplished without difficulty, and that behavioral measures could be useful in assessing effects of space flight.

The research of Pryor, et al. (1969) is of interest to comparative psychologists. Working at the Makapuu Oceanic Center in Hawaii, Pryor et al. trained rough-toothed porpoises to emit novel responses. In each series of training sessions, the animal had to emit a behavioral pattern not reinforced in previous sessions. Pryor et al. concluded that the animals were capable of emitting quite "creative" responses, including some that were species-typical in other species of porpoises but not their own.

Abnormal Behavior

Many psychologists have been interested in using nonhuman animals to provide a "model" for abnormal behavior in humans. The legitimacy of this approach was recognized by early comparative psychologists. Yerkes (1908, 279) wrote that "if we approach the study of abnormal mental states in man by way of the study of the mental life and types of reaction in other animals we may escape many errors of interpretation and inference and save ourselves innumerable mistakes of action." Hamilton (1927, 221) proposed that "teachers and investigators in the field of comparative psychology must take greater pains to acquaint themselves with the currently arising problems, methods, concepts, research activities and finding of psychopathology." Lashley (1914) studied abnormal "pleasure sucking" in cats.

The study of abnormal behavior in animals, though one aspect of comparative psychology, is a departure from the major themes of this book. Therefore, I will refer the interested reader to relevant sources but provide no detailed account of this research area. Reviews of research on the abnormal behavior of animals can be found in Munn's *Handbook of Psychological Research on the Rat* (1950) and in the chapters by Patton (1951) and Dinsmoor (1960) in the edited textbooks of comparative psychology published by Stone and Waters et al., respectively. Fox (1968) edited a collection of papers on the abnormal behavior of animals, and Keehn (1979) collected some of the major works in the field into a book of readings. The area remains an active research area in animal psychology.

One of the major research areas centers about "experimental neuroses." Experimental neuroses were formed and studied in Pavlov's conditioning laboratory in Russia in situations involving the administration of powerful stimuli, requiring very fine discriminations or with abrupt changes in task requirements. The reaction varied with different individual dogs (see Dinsmoor, 1960). The most extensive work in this country on experimental neuroses was conducted at the Cornell Behavior Farm under the direction of H. S. Liddell (for example, Liddell, 1953; Altmann, 1941).

A controversial series of experiments was conducted by N. R. F. Maier and his associates (for example, Maier, 1961; Maier and Glasser, 1940*a*, 1940*b*). In his basic situation Maier used a Lashley Jumping Stand, and apparatus that required a rat to jump across a gap and strike a card blocking a door. A correct choice would permit the animal to enter the compartment behind the card; and incorrect choice would cause the animal to fall down into a net. An air puff was used to coax animals that were slow to jump. Maier found that animals faced with insoluble problems sometimes developed strong fixations for one response that persisted even when the problem was later made soluble. Others showed a variety of neurotic symptoms including rapid running, tics, and seizures. The controversy centered about the effective stimulus for the behavior, as some authors (for example, C. T. Morgan) believed the seizures to be triggered by the air blast itself (see Munn, 1950).

The topic of audiogenic seizures has received much study—particularly in relation to genetic and developmental effects on seizure susceptibility (for example, Finger, 1943; Hall, 1947; Witt and Hall, 1949).

Other abnormal behavioral patterns studied by comparative psychologists have included regression (for example, O'Kelly, 1940); addiction (for example, Spragg, 1940); and tumbler pigeons (Mowrer, 1940).

Conservation

Although they have not played a major role in conservation efforts, comparative psychologists have made some contributions. Watson (1907*a*) reported on the condition of the colonies of noddy and sooty terns on Bird Key in the Dry Tortugas. Miles (1931) proposed that his studies of fish in elevated water bridges may help in guiding fish across polluted water courses. Carpenter (1940*b*) considered problems of conservation and supply of rhesus monkeys. Studies of orientation and imprinting in birds have had impact on conservation efforts with these animals.

Humane Human-Nonhuman Interactions

Psychologists have long been concerned about the ethics of human-nonhuman interactions in research and other situations. A code of ethics for animal experimentation in psychology was drawn up in 1925 (Young, 1928, 1930) and has been revised frequently since.

The image of animal psychology as projected by those most active in the current controversy over animal experimentation is not favorable (for example, Rollin, 1981). Research is perceived as pointless and cruel. Only positive action will change the image of animal psychology in this respect.

As psychologists have expertise in the behavior of both human and nonhuman animals, they should take the lead in the study of interactions between humans and nonhumans. Research and integrative writing may help solve the problem of developing standards whereby humans can interact with nonhumans in research and other settings in ways that are regarded as humane on the one hand and minimally intrusive on the progress of science on the other. Psychologists should be in the lead in this endeavor.

Training of Psychologists

In one of the offbeat replies to Lockard's critique of comparative psychology, Ardilla (1971) argued that one important, but overlooked, function of comparative psychology is to train students of other fields of psychology in the rigor of experimental methods that are applicable to a wide range of problems. Although this is not a powerful justification for the research efforts of comparative psychology, it is a valuable by-product of teaching and research in the area. Among the research in comparative psychology that has been done by psychologists who later make substantial contributions elsewhere in psychology, one could cite the work of O. H. Mowrer (1940); A. H. Maslow (1936); J. S. Bruner and Cunningham (1939); G. A. Miller (1945); Kellogg and W. B. Pomeroy (1936); Boring (1912); and J. Kagan and Beach (1953).

INTERACTIONS OUTSIDE
OF PSYCHOLOGY

Although some would have comparative psychology as a discipline unto itself, most comparative psychologists have welcomed interactions outside their discipline. These have been deemphasized thus far in an effort to delineate clearly the nature of comparative psychology itself. It is time now to consider a few of these interactions.

Interactions with Zoologists

From the very beginning, comparative psychologists interacted with zoologists in the study of behavior. The dividing line between behavior as studied by psychologists and that studied by biologists was as difficult to draw in the first decade of the century as it has been in the present decade. Zoologists such as Loeb, Jennings, Whitman, Craig, Wheeler, Herrick, Mast, Donaldson, and others interacted intensively and continuously in the formation of the field of animal behavior. Comparative psychologists, for their part, welcomed such interaction. Hall (1900, 276) noted, "Psychologists never had so warm a welcome for biologists who enter this field as now." Watson (1910b, 346) presented his views, saying, "The subject is large enough, however, for both the psychologist and the biologist. The goal of both is the same—the right understanding of all the factors which enter into the development of human life." In his paper "The Perpetuation and Evolution of Biological Science," Beach (1966) emphasized the degree to which disciplines can gain vigor as the result of outbreeding with other disciplines.

Psychologists and biologists collaborated in editing the early journals in the field, including the *Journal of Comparative Neurology and Psychology,* the *Journal of Animal Behavior, Psychobiology,* and the *Journal of Comparative Psychology.*

Psychologists have often been active in and have collaborated with biological societies. The Roe and Simpson volume on *Behavior and*

Evolution (1958) was the result of collaboration between the American Psychological Association and the Society for the Study of Evolution. Many comparative psychologists have joined the Society for the Study of Evolution, the American Society of Mammologists, the American Society of Zoologists, or other groups. A particularly close relationship has existed with one of the foremost organizations of biologists—the American Society of Naturalists. On at least one occasion, the Chicago meeting of 1907, the APA met jointly with the American Society of Naturalists. Two comparative psychologists have served as president of the American Society of Naturalists—Yerkes in 1938 and Lashley in 1947. Comparative psychologists have published papers in the *American Naturalist* throughout our history. Examples are the papers of Baldwin (1896c) on the Baldwin effect; Thorndike (1899c) on learning in fishes; Wang (1924) on activity; Beach (1945a) on play; Dewsbury (1982) on ejaculate cost and male choice.

Interaction with Ethologists

Interaction with ethologists have been especially close over many years. This began well before the advent of ethology per se with interaction between comparative psychologists and both Charles Otis Whitman and Wallace Craig, two of the major pioneers of early ethology (see Thorpe, 1979). Schneirla (in Schaffner, 1955, 86-87), for example, wrote of a "Whitman-Wheeler-Craig-Carr school" in animal psychology.

Whitman was a long-time faculty member of the University of Chicago—the birthplace of the functionalist school in psychology and the school from which Watson received the Ph.D. It is clear that there was substantial interaction between Whitman and comparative psychology. Walter Hunter (1920) cited Whitman's work in his discussion on the ontogeny of instinctive behavior. In his classical *Animal Intelligence,* Thorndike noted that "Professor Whitman a decade ago showed the possibility of phylogenetic investigation of instinctive connections in a study which should be a stimulus and a model for many others" (1911, 275). Thorndike (1915) criticized Watson's book (1914) for not including more cases where the phylogeny of behavior was studied in a concrete way—as in Whitman's research. Hall (1900) wrote a favorable review of Whitman's 1898 volume based on lectures at Woods Hole. The work of Whitman was also cited by Yerkes (1906) and Kuo (1920). When the *Posthumous Works of Charles Otis Whitman* was published by the Carnegie Institution, it was functionalist psychologist Harvey Carr who edited the third volume (Carr, 1919). Whitman, for his part, was well aware of comparative psychology and sometimes quite critical of it (for example, 1898/1899).

Interaction with Craig was just as close. Craig is best known for his work on appetites and aversions. His paper "Attitudes of Appetion and Aversion in Doves" was presented at the twenty-second annual meeting of the American Psychological Association, with an abstract published in the *Psychological Bulletin* (Craig, 1914). In the *Psychological Bulletin* volumes of 1919 and 1920, Craig contributed papers reviewing recent progress in the study of tropisms and instinctive activities (1919, 1920). Watson (1912*b*) cited Craig's work and Tolman (1923) discussed Craig's theory noting its affinity to that of Woodworth. Craig's *curriculum vitae* was published in the 1932 *Psychological Register* (Murchison, 1932).

Various comparative psychologists proposed ideas and concepts that had much in common with ethological ideas. I do not wish to pretend that psychologists somehow deserve credit for the discoveries of ethologists. Ethologists developed a coherent approach and system for the study of animal behavior for which they deserve full credit. I do wish to suggest, however, that some thinking in comparative psychology was much closer to ethological theory than is often recognized. The research of Watson on the behavior of terns (1908*b*) deserves to be recognized as a classic early study in the ethological tradition. It was a field study of instinctive behavior with some very fine descriptions of instinctive motor patterns. Watson (1912*a*) recommended the deprivation experiment as a means to study the ontogeny of instinctive behavior. Tolman (1920) developed a primitive hierarchical model for the control of instinctive behavior and empasized the role of feedback in the termination of behavior. In the paper of Lashley (1938*b*) one can find the antecedents of the *Sollwert* ("should-be-value") and sign stimulus in addition to descriptions of behavioral patterns such as those of terns and the web building of spiders. This is the paper so highly commended by Thorpe (1979). Nissen (1953, 292) suggested "that reflexes, instincts, and the inherited capacity to learn may be distributed on a continuum. What is inherited may be *a more or less specific readiness to learn.*" The resemblence to Lorenz's "innate school marm" is clear.

It is not clear when comparative psychologists began to interact with the ethologists of the Lorenz-Tinbergen generation. VonFrisch's work on sensory function was cited often in the 1930s (for example, Moss, 1934). Maier and Schneirla (1935) cited Tinbergen's papers. Comparative psychologists such as Beach, Carpenter, Lehrman, and Schneirla led the way toward the interaction with ethologists that led to the comtemporary interdisciplinary field of animal behavior. Beach's role was emphasized by Hinde (1978). William Verplanck's glossary of terms (1957) used in behavior was designed to aid in communication between the disciplines.

Led by the comparative psychologists just mentioned and ethologists such as Tinbergen, Lorenz, and Baerends, comparative psychologists have interacted continuously with ethologists resulting in changes in both fields. There remain a few differences in emphasis. However, it becomes increasingly difficult to tell an ethologist from a comparative psychologist.

Interaction with Sociobiology

The field of sociobiology represents an attempt to apply some principles of the theory of evolution to the study of social behavior. It is part of the area of behavioral ecology in which the role of behavior in ecological adaptation is the target of study. The sociobiology-behavioral ecology area has come into vogue in biology and psychology in the 1970s and 1980s and, indeed, seems to be driving out, or at least causing a de-emphasis of some other fields of inquiry. To the reader of Calvin Stone the advent of behavioral ecology comes as no surprise; he clearly and unequivocally forecast its development (1943, 24).

Many of the basic concepts of sociobiology are not new to psychology. Morgan was well aware of the distinction between proximate and ultimate causation and provided an example in his discussion of the causes of play (1905, 87). Watson (1914) provided a discussion of the nature of sexual selection and related matters. Swindle (1917) provided a discussion of the evolution of eye appendages using the method of adaptive correlation comparing the lifestyles of animals with and without markings and appendages of various sorts. Kuo's discussion (1921) of the adaptationist paradigm resembles some of the points emphasized by Gould and Lewontin (1979), among others. The musings of Kline (1898) regarding the differences between migrating and nonmigrating species ring true in a discussion of r- and K-selection. Wundt (1894, 412) considered the occurrence of polygamy and polyandry in different taxa and of the role of song in male-male competition for females. The issue of whether animals display altruistic behavior was dealt with in an experimental context by Church (1959), Rice and Gainer (1962), and Lavery and Foley (1963). Baldwin (1897a) used his concept of "social heredity" in a manner that resembles Richard Dawkins's "mene" (1976).

One current issue in sociobiology is the extent to which terms drawn from human behavior should be applied to that of nonhumans (see Estep and Bruce, 1981). That issue was dealt with in the conflict between Schneirla (1942, 1943) and Lafleur (1942, 1943, 1944) and further discussed by Schneirla (1953a) and Beach (1945b).

Psychologists have differed in their reactions to sociobiology. Some of the negative reaction was provoked by Wilson's unfortunate diagram (1975a) portraying sociobiology as not only opposing comparative psychology but eventually cannibalizing it. Some comparative psychologists have been quite negative about sociobiology (for example, Beach, 1978a;

Greenberg, 1982; Tobach, 1978). Others have either wholeheartedly endorsed the approach (for example, Daly and Wilson, 1978; LeBoeuf, 1978) or recognized the strengths and weaknesses and attempted a reconciliation similar to that achieved with ethology (for example, Dewsbury 1978*a;* Glickman, 1980; Mason and Lott, 1976).

Wilson's proposed cannibalism of comparative psychology triggered a symposium on "The Sociobiological Challenge to Psychology" at the 1978 APA meetings. Different authors reacted in different ways to the "sociobiological challenge." Wyers and Menzel (1980), for example, tried to differentiate comparative psychology from sociobiology using four criteria. Unfortunately, the criteria do not really differentiate sociobiology from comparative psychology. For example, Wyers and Menzel p... psed that psychologists, not sociobiologists, are interested in the behavior of individuals. In fact, most comparative psychologists publish group means, and the current emphasis in sociobiology appears to be on frequency-dependent selection and "evolutionarily stable strategies"—topics very much characteristic of the behavior of different individuals in a population, Indeed, it is the recognition that selection works at the level of the individual or gene that has triggered much of the work in this field. Flanagan (1980) cautioned against "biologizing" comparative psychology. As should be apparent throughout the current work, this is impossible; comparative psychology has been "biologized" since its inception. A balanced presentation was provided by Glickman (1980, 962) who discouraged "the glib uses of analogy and terminology found in much sociobiological writing" but refused to throw out the baby with the bathwater.

It is unfortunate that Wilson's advocacy resulted in the perception of comparative psychology and sociobiology as representing "challenges" that must be countered. However, that appears to be the way in which progress is effected. In fact, I believe that the sociobiological approach lies within the long tradition of comparative psychology, and the new approaches and ideas can greatly enrich our field. On the other hand, the firm grasp of knowledge and methodology that has been developed in the history of comparative psychology can be of great value in guarding against the excesses of some sociobiological writing.

International Interaction

In an effort to emphasize the continuity of the development of comparative psychology, developments in North America have been emphasized throughout this book. It must be stressed, however, that important advances were also made in other countries. Comparative psychologists have generally been open to information regarding such advances and sought close contact with scientists from other nations. However, the language barriers that impede communication among nations have had an important retarding effect in this regard; Amerians are not noted for fluency in other tongues.

The ties have been closest with Great Britain—perhaps for reasons of common language. The early scientists such as McDougall, Morgan, Spalding, and Hobhouse had profound influence on the development of comparative psychology in its formative years. Washburn (1911) reported on the Symposium on Instinct in London in 1910. In more recent years as well, English animal psychologists have made important contributions (for example, Sutherland, 1954).

Influences from Germany have been profound as well. Some of the founding fathers of American psychology were products of Wundt's laboratory, and through them, German psychology had a strong influence on early-American comparative psychology. Loeb and Münsterberg moved to the United States and had especially strong influence. Yerkes (1913c) sought support for the German Society of Animal Psychology.

Washburn (1908c) summarized progress in comparative psychology in France in an effort to secure interest and interaction with that country.

The interaction with Russian psychology has been especially important, although greatly retarded by problems of language. Yerkes and Morgulis (1909) first described Pavlovian psychology in a manner that communicated to a wide psychological audience. Hahn (1971) relates an interesting story about the interaction of Pavlov and Yerkes. In the early days of Yerkes's Yale primate laboratory, Pavlov attended a world zoological congress in New Haven and was taken on a tour of the facilities. As Pavlov spoke no English, a Yale professor, Alexander Petrunkevich, served as interpreter. Pavlov entered the room housing chimpanzees as the workers from the laboratory remained outside. As relayed by Hahn (1971) from an associate of Yerkes:

> Suddenly there was a sort of shout inside there, and the two Russians came out with the laboratory assistant, all talking at once," he said. "Pavlov was furious. Petrunkevich called out to us, 'Oh, the apes bespat him! The apes bespat him!' Pavlov seemed to want Petrunkevich to say something else, but Petrunkevich obviously didn't want to, and protested. Finally, Pavlov had his way, and Petrunkevich said to us, "He says this is not science—it is *nonsense.*" (Hahn, 1971, 60).

Fortunately, American-Russian scientific relationships endured the incident. The early translation by G. V. Anrep of Pavlov's *Conditioned Reflexes* (Pavlov, 1927) was very important in bringing knowledge of Russian psychology to the United States. In later years Voronin (1962) from Russia attempted to bring results of Russian comparative studies to the comparative psychologists in the United States. Razran (1961,

1971), from the United States, tried to bring some of the results from Pavlovian psychology to the attention of American psychologists, and Kovach (1971, 1973) popularized results from Russian ethology. For their part, Russians have been receptive to information from the United States, as in the recent translation into Russian of my *Comparative Animal Behavior* (Dewsbury, 1978a).

Other countries have produced important comparative psychologists. The contributions of the Chinese psychologist Zing-Yang Kuo have been repeatedly discussed throughout the book. Knut Larsson of Sweden has had important impact on the study of sexual behavior in rats (for example, 1956). Ryo Kuroda (for example, 1926) made repeated contributions to the study of animal sensory function. Comparative psychology is an international endeavor, and communication among comparative psychologists and others from different nations requires fostering.

ARCHIVES

The bulk of this volume, and of most similar volumes, is based on the published record as is appears primarily in books and journals. However, fresh perspectives on specific incidents and events can be gained from examination of the unpublished record. Such information can be of great values in filling in the gaps and unresolved issues inherent in the published record. Such materials are preserved in various archival services around the country. The correspondence, papers, photographs, films, and other artifacts of comparative psychologists and others can be found in such locations. For example, I was able to locate some reprints of Linus Kline, previously unknown to me, by searching the archives of the University of Minnesota, Duluth, a school on whose faculty Kline served from 1902-1918.

The primary repository of documents and other materials relating to American psychology is the Archives of the History of American Psychology (AHAP) at the University of Akron, in Ohio. The AHAP was founded in 1965 to serve the needs of scholars by collecting, cataloging, preserving, and in other ways maintaining the materials that provide the sources for the history of psychology. It is administered by John A. Popplestone, its director, and Marion White McPherson, its associate director.

I have conducted a search at AHAP in an effort to locate materials relating specifically to comparative psychology. This is somewhat difficult because materials that have a bearing on comparative psychology or comparative psychologists may properly be inventoried under some other heading.

Archival holdings are cataloged only by the names of individual psychologists, organizations, and journals. That is, material relevant to the history of comparative psychology is not identified, but holdings relevant to comparative psychologists are controlled.

The corpus of the papers of an individual is referred to as a *manuscript collection* and those of an organization and publication as *archives.* There is an individual name card for each psychologist, organization, and journal that is referred to in any of the archives's holdings ($n = 70,000$). Each card indicates the presence in the archives of a manuscript collection or archives, and for each of these an inventory or table of contents has been compiled. This furnishes details about the papers as well as the dates when they were generated ($n = 600$).

The name card also specifies the location of additional items relevant to the individual or group named on the card. In these references the content of the holdings is merely categorized as: "Or" (items written by), that is, originated by the person or organization named on the card; "Re" (materials received); and "Di" (discussions, which may consist merely of a routine bibliographic citation or may designate an extensive commentary as, for example, materials gathered for the writing of a necrology. The number of Or's, Re's, and Di's is not specified within any one storage unit, and each box may contain only one or several. The inventories inform researchers about the contents of the documents and are completed as soon as a total collection is accessed and processed. The card references cue the historian only to the structure of the content and are incomplete in that additions are made on a card each time the principal's name appears in deposits being processed and in the future accessions.

The ways in which these findings direct researchers to relevant documents can be illustrated by excerpts from the card entries for three individuals, as follows: D. K. Adams—the archives preserves his manuscript collection, and additional references to him exist in thirty-eight other collections and archives. These contain Or's in eight storage boxes. Re's in seven boxes, and Di's in fifty-four. Robert Yerkes's manuscript collection is at Yale University, but the AHAP contains materials relevant to him in 96 different collections. John Watson's papers, as he collected them, have been dispersed, but there is relevant material in 104 collections in the psychology archives. These include only thirteen Or's, a reflection of the scarcity of his papers. The Di's include an APA invited address by his son, 1981.

A few of the comparative psychologists and workers related to comparative psychology whose manuscript collections are housed in AHAP, include:

1. *D. K. Adams* (30 boxes: M362-M375; M375.1-M375.6; M750-M759). Class notes taken by Adams at Harvard during 1924/1925 and material related to Adams's associations with Gestalt psychologists and to his

career at Duke. Among the many letters is correspondence with such workers as Yerkes, Schneirla, Lorenz, Tinbergen, Gottlieb, Köhler, and Krech. Other materials relate to the growth of comparative psychology at Duke and to related interactions with McDougall, Klopfer, and others.

2. *D. Krech* (23 boxes: M540-M554; M554.1-M554.8). Extensive correspondence (primarily from Krech's years at Berkeley) and manuscripts. Also included are some photographs and transcriptions of Krech's lectures in introductory psychology.

3. *A. H. Maslow* (90 boxes: M393-M399; M399.1-M399.4; M400-M449; M449.1-M449.30). Assorted materials relating primarily to Maslow's career in humanistic psychology rather than to his early work on non-human primates.

4. *S. C. Ratner* (29 boxes). Sealed until the year 2028.

5. *D. A. Rethlingshafer* (9 boxes: M300-M307; M307.1-M307.2). Correspondence, class and reading notes, and materials relating to the publication of books such as the comparative test of Waters, Rethlingshafer, and Caldwell (1960). *Note:* I retain some of Dr. Rethlingshafer's correspondence regarding early stages of preparation for the book that would become Dewsbury and Rethlingshafer (1973).

6. *T. C. Schneirla* (15 boxes: M577-M585; M585.1-M585.6). Extensive collection of correspondence regarding various professional, funding, and evaluational matters. Includes some field notes from ant research, manuscripts of published papers, and notes relating to conferences Schneirla attended.

7. *K. W. Spence* (12 boxes: M936-M943; M943.1-M943.4). Relates mainly to learning theory and includes long correspondence dating back as far as the 1930s.

8. *E. C. Tolman* (9 boxes: M128-M136). Correspondence, manuscripts of writings, research designs, lecture notes, and related material. Includes correspondence with Kuo, Bitterman, and Tinbergen.

9. *P. T. Young* (6 boxes: M98-M100; M387; M612-M613). Miscellaneous correspondence and photographs.

Various other documents relating to comparative psychologists are noteworthy. Inventoried under Beach's name are materials donated by Beach but that are the work of Yerkes (three boxes: M270-M272). Included are handwritten and typed lecture notes from courses in comparative psychology, animal behavior, and genetic psychology taught by Yerkes from approximately 1902 to 1918.

The main document relating to H. A. Carr is a bound volume of letters sent to Carr on the occasion of his retirement from the University of Chicago (one box: M694). Included are letters from such writers as Watson, Yoakum, Hunter, and Warden.

There are nine boxes relating to Knight Dunlap (M565-M570;

M570.1-M570.3). Included are correspondence with such individuals as Watson and Jennings, notes and manuscripts relating to various papers, and even a collection of wine and whiskey labels.

J. L. Fuller's material (three boxes: M741, M742, M745) includes correspondence with such workers as Ginsburg, Broadhurst, and Beach, and it also includes miscellaneous notes and preparations for lectures and meetings. Also included is a folder regarding the Behavior Genetics Association and the issue of racism.

Although the corpus of the work of G. Stanley Hall is at Clark University, there are nine boxes at AHAP (M62-M70). This collection primarily includes notes from Hall's readings of the professional literature, some correspondence, numerous manuscripts, and drafts of publications, as well as collected material on such topics as fear, play, and various emotions.

The six boxes relating to J. F. Dashiell (M571-M576) contain various lecture notes, manuscripts, and correspondence. One box from D. O. Hebb (M91) contains miscellaneous correspondence. A box from N. R. F. Maier (M49) contains various correspondence and bibliographical material. Oral historical materials and tapes are also preserved. Miscellaneous correspondence and drafts of papers from Gregory Razran are preserved in four boxes (M561-M564). Material from R. C. Tryon (boxes M226, M688, M1229) deals mainly with cluster analysis.

AHAP also has a locator file to aid scholars in locating the papers of psychologists that are deposited in other locations. The resources of AHAP and other archival services should receive greater use from historians of comparative psychology than they do now.

Leading workers in comparative psychology and individuals with access to the papers of workers in the field should consider the possibility of donating relevant papers to AHAP or other archival services. Sensitive documents can be either sealed or limited with regard to usage. Archivists work to strike a balance between proper use of the unpublished record and restriction of sensitive material. Continued deposition of documents in archival services will make the task of future historians of comparative psychology much easier.

Chapter 8

Biographical Sketches of Comparative Psychologists

In the preceding chapters, the nature of comparative psychology and its history have been delineated chronologically and with respect to its methods, problems of study, and practical affairs. A third perspective can be derived by considering the lives of the individuals who have made comparative psychology the exciting discipline that it is. In these brief sketches I portray a few of the aspects of the lives of some important comparative psychologists. I list some sources for those who wish to learn more about these workers or for those who wish to conduct historical research on some of them. With one exception, I have limited the sketches to those who are deceased; I believe that Frank Beach's contributions have been so substantial that this section would not be complete without him.

Many different sources were used. Three of them are especially useful. In the *Psychological Register,* Murchison (1932) included what amounted to brief curriculum vitae of virtually all psychologists (and some other scientists) active in 1932. Complete publication lists are included. Zusne (1975) provided brief sketches of the 538 individuals whose contributions were regarded as most important by the panel of nine judges rating important psychologists for Annin et al. (1968). Hilgard (1978) provided biographical sketches for each of the presidents of the American Psychological Association through 1977. Various necrologies and other biographies and autobiographies are also extremely useful. The psychological necrologies of Boring (1928*a*, 1928*b*) and Bennett and Boring (1954) are also helpful. Another source of the *National Cyclopaedia of American Biography* (NCAB).

JAMES MARK BALDWIN
Born: Columbia, South Carolina, January 12, 1861
Died: Paris, France, November 8, 1934

Baldwin received an A.B. degree from Princeton in 1884 and then spent a year at Leipzig and Berlin. After terms as an instructor in modern languages at Princeton and on the faculty at Lake Forest University, he received a Ph.D. degree from Princeton in 1889. Baldwin then served on the faculties of the University of Toronto (1890-1893), Princeton (1893-1903), and John Hopkins (1903-1909).

Baldwin was a theorist, editor, and organizer who did little empirical work. He is best known in comparative psychology for his work on the evolution of behavior and other characters as in the "effect" that bears his name (Baldwin, 1896*c*). Baldwin also made contributions to social and developmental psychology, and he has an optical illusion named after him.

Baldwin was in the original group that founded the American Psychological Association in 1894. He served as its sixth president at the age of thirty-six. He was cofounder of the *Psychological Review* and became its editor after the famous auction with Cattell. Baldwin later helped found the *Psychological Index, Psychological Monographs,* and the *Psychological Bulletin.* His *Dictionary of Psychology and Philosophy* was also influential. Although not an empiricist himself, Baldwin founded psychological laboratories at Toronto in 1889 and Princeton in 1893; later he reestablished Hall's laboratory at Johns Hopkins.

The 1909 *Psychological Bulletin* carried a notice that "Professor Baldwin has resigned his position in the Johns Hopkins University. He is advised to give his voice a prolonged rest from continuous lecturing" (1909, 256). According to Cohen (1979, 53), however, "The lively philosopher committed a heinous academic crime; he was caught in a negro brothel in a position that could not be described as philosophical." Baldwin was forced to resign and walked to Watson's office to inform him that he was now editor of the *Psychological Review.* Baldwin then moved to the National University of Mexico and then to Paris.

According to Kantor (1935, 3), "James Mark Baldwin was one of those rare individuals whose record of work and achievements stands so clear as to make it unnecessary to embroider upon his strength as psychologist or scholar. Although Baldwin published 20 books and 150 articles, he is virtually forgotten in American psychology.

Sources: Baldwin, 1930; Broughton, 1981; Gottlieb, 1979; Hilgard, 1978; Jastrow, 1934; Kantor, 1935; Urban, 1935; Washburn, 1935; Zusne, 1975.

FRANK AMBROSE BEACH
Born: Emporia, Kansas, April 13, 1911

Frank Beach completed undergraduate work with a major in English in 1932 at the Kansas State Teachers College at Emporia, where his father was professor and head of the Department of Music. He completed an M.S. degree in psychology at the same school. After a year of graduate school at the University of Chicago where he felt the influences of Carr, Thurstone, and Lashley, Beach took a year off to teach high school English in Kansas. He finished his dissertation research at Chicago in 1936 and moved for a year to Lashley's laboratory at Harvard. This was followed by positions at the American Museum of Natural History (1937-1946); Yale (1946-1957); and Berkeley (1958 to the present). He received the Ph.D. degree from Chicago in 1940.

Beach has been a mainstay of comparative psychology since his first publication in 1937. He is best known for his research on the neural and endocrine bases of reproductive behavior and especially for his lead in the establishment of behavioral endocrinology as a major field of inquiry. His early books *Hormones and Behavior* (1948) and *Patterns of Sexual Behavior* (Ford and Beach, 1951) were influential in shaping the field. The proceedings of the Berkeley conferences, *Sex and Behavior,* contain excellent papers by workers from many disciplines and an important synthetic last chapter by the editor—rare in such volumes. He has been called the "conscience of comparative psychology," and his "The Snark was a Boojum" (1950), "Descent of Instinct" (1955), and "Experimental Investigations of Species-Specific Behavior" (1960) were among the most influential of the 147 papers he had published by 1977. His 11 papers on the control and evolution of reproductive behavior published in 1942 alone would ensure his place in the history of the field.

Beach received the Warren Medal of the Society of Experimental Psychologists in 1953 and the APA Distinguished Scientific Contribution Award in 1958. He has held various lectureships, served on many administrative boards, and is a member of the National Academy of Sciences. The appreciation of his former students and colleagues was expressed in McGill et al. (1978).

Sources: Beach, 1974, 1978*b*; Fleming and Maxey, 1975; McGill et al., 1978.

(ISAAC) MADISON BENTLEY
Born: Clinton, Iowa, June 18, 1870
Died: Palo Alto, California, May 29,1955

Madison Bentley's father, Charles E. Bentley, was a Baptist clergyman and the Liberty Party's candidate for the office of president of the United States in 1896. Madison Bentley received a B.S. degree from the University of Nebraska in 1895 and a Ph.D. degree from Cornell under Titchener in 1898. He was identified with the Titchenerian school throughout much of his career. Bentley remained on the faculty in psychology at Cornell until 1912, when he accepted a position as department head at the University of Illinois. On Titchener's death, Bentley returned to Cornell succeeding Titchener as Sage Professor of Psychology and chairman of the department.

"Bentley's genuis lay in his erudition and his critical acumen" (Dallenbach, 1956, 179). He served as editor of the *Psychological Index* from 1916 to 1925; editor of the *Journal of Experimental Psychology* from 1926 to 1929; and cooperating and coeditor of the *American Journal of Psychology* from 1903 to 1950. During his career as a book reviewer, Bentley reviewed over 250 books. He was elected president of the American Psychological Association in 1925.

Other than his editorial work, Bentley's most notable contributions to comparative psychology were his study of color discrimination in fishes (Washburn and Bentley, 1906) and his controversial study of "learning" in paramecia (Day and Bentley, 1911). He also had an interest in phrenology and was an excellent teacher.

"He was bold to criticize wherever criticism was pertinent; he let the chips fall where they would" (Dallenbach, 1956, 186).

Sources: Bentley, 1936; Dallenbach, 1956; Hilgard, 1978; NCAB, 1962; Zusne, 1975.

HAROLD CLYDE BINGHAM
Born: Rowan, Iowa, January 21, 1888
Died: Laconia, New Hampshire, August 26, 1964

Harold C. Bingham received a B.A. degree from Ellsworth College in 1910 and an M.A. degree from Harvard in 1912. After teaching and coaching at Ellsworth Junior College and serving in World War I, Bingham received the Ph.D. degree from Johns Hopkins in 1923. He taught at Wesleyan University from 1923 to 1925 and served on the faculty at Yale beginning in 1924.

Bingham was best known in comparative psychology for his work with primate behavior, largely in association with Yerkes. Bingham's classic on the behavior of gorillas in the natural habitat in the Belgian Congo

(1932) was a major pioneering effort among field studies of primate behavior. Among other things, he noted that gorillas sleep but one night in each sleeping nest, and he tracked their wanderings over days. Bingham's first publication was on size and form perception in chickens (1913), and he later worked with dogs (1916). He is best known for his work on problem solving (1929*a*, 1929*b*) and sexual development in apes (1928). Bingham accompanied Yerkes to Cuba to work with Madam Abreu's chimpanzees.

Bingham is much respected for his public service. He rose from first lieutenant to major in World War I and from major to lieutenant colonel in World War II. He was in charge of personnel consultants to the U. S. Army in World War II and worked closely with such agencies as the Emergency Relief Administration, the Works Progress Administration, and The Veterans Administration. He was active in community affairs after his retirement to New Hampshire.

Sources: Murchison, 1932; NCAB, 1969; *New York Times,* August 27, 1964.

LEONARD CARMICHAEL
Born: Philadelphia, Pennsylvania, November 9, 1898
Died: Washington, D.C., September 16, 1973.

Leonard Carmichael was graduated with a B.S. degree from Tufts College in 1921. He received the Ph.D. degree from Harvard in 1924 and then studied in Berlin on a Sheldon traveling fellowship. Carmichael was on the faculty at Princeton 1924-1927 and Brown University 1927-1936. During 1936-1938 he was dean of the faculty of arts and sciences at the University of Rochester. He served as the president of Tufts during 1938-1952 and as secretary of the Smithsonian Institution 1953-1964. Later he became an officer of the National Geographic Society.

Carmichael's major contributions to comparative psychology per se were made relatively early in his career and concern the study of behavioral development. His classic work on the ontogeny of behavior in frogs and salamanders showed a greater role of heredity than had been anticipated (1926, 1927, 1928). He also participated in the debate over instinct in the 1920s (1925). In his other relevant research Carmichael was interested in such problems as the development of the righting response and the embryology of behavior and sensory function. His APA presidential address of 1940 was entitled "The Experimental Embryology of the Mind" (1941).

Much of Carmichael's career was spent as an administrator in various posts. In such capacities he often spoke for and facilitated the development of psychology. During World War II, he was director of the National Roster of Scientific and Specialized Personnel (1946) and aided in mobilizing effective use of scientific talent. He was much honored, receiving twenty-three honorary degrees and many other awards. As noted by Pfaffmann (1980, 37), the citation on his honorary degree from Harvard notes that he was "a psychologist who combines distinction in his science and success in administration."

Sources: Murchison, 1932; NCAB, 1942; Pfaffmann, 1980; Zusne, 1975.

CLARENCE RAY CARPENTER
Born: Lincoln County, North Carolina, November 28, 1905
Died: Athens, Georgia, March 1, 1975

Clarence Ray Carpenter attended Duke University, receiving an A.B. degree in 1928 and an M.A. degree in 1929. His doctoral degree was earned at Stanford University under Calvin Stone in 1932. Carpenter was associated with Columbia University between 1934 and 1940 and joined the faculty at Pennsylvania State University in 1940. After retiring from Penn State in 1970, he became a research professor at the University of Georgia. Carpenter's tenure as a National Research Council Fellow at Yale brought him into contact with Yerkes and launched his career as a field primatologist.

Carpenter's early work was on the endocrine control of reproductive behavior in pigeons (1932, 1933). He is best known, however, for his field studies of primate behavior. In dedicating his 1965 *Primate Behavior* volume to Carpenter, Irven DeVore noted, "Virtually nothing systematic was known about the natural behavior of a single monkey or ape until Clarence Ray Carpenter began his study of the howler monkeys of Panama in 1931" (1965, vii). Carpenter's study of howler monkeys (1934) can be regarded as the beginning of modern field studies of primate behavior. In 1937 he went to Southeast Asia to study orangutans and gibbons (for example, 1940a). In 1938 he traveled to India to collect a hundred rhesus macaques for transportation to Cayo Santiago, an island near Puerto Rico. The colony still thrives and has provided a location for numerous studies of primate behavior. Carpenter regarded the rhesus project as his most productive effort and his work with gibbons as his most fascinating experience (Price, 1968).

Carpenter's long-term interest in field research departed from the norm in the discipline at his time. However, he was the product of the tradition of comparative psychology, being influenced by McDougall at Duke (see Carpenter, 1933), completing his degree with Calvin Stone, and being assigned to do his first primate field study by Robert Yerkes.

Another important contribution of Carpenter centered on his work in educational technology. He contributed importantly to the areas of film production and editing, curriculum design, closed-circuit television, and other modern methods. He was a past-president of the Joint Council on Educational Telecommunications and the Association for Higher Education.

"By the time of his death in 1975, Ray Carpenter was a renowned scientist and scholar, an educator and author of international reputation, and electric professional whose vita included at least seven areas of acknowledged expertise" (Teleki, 1981, 384).

Sources: Carpenter, 1964; *Leaders in American Science,* Vol. VII, 1966-1967; *New York Times,* March 4, 1975; Price, 1968; Teleki, 1981.

KNIGHT DUNLAP
Born: Diamond Spring, California, November 21, 1875
Died: Columbia, South Carolina, August 14, 1949

Knight Dunlap attended the University of California, Berkeley, receiving the degrees of Ph.B. in 1899 and L.M. in 1900. He then went to Harvard where he completed the Ph.D. degree in 1903. Among his major influences were George M. Stratton at Berkeley and Münsterberg, Royce, Dewey, and James at Harvard. After serving on the faculty at Berkeley during 1904-1906, Dunlap joined Stratton at Johns Hopkins, where he remained until 1936. Dunlap then moved to the University of California, Los Angeles, in order to develop a graduate program and laboratory.

Among his major contributions to psychology, Dunlap (1932) listed the attack on introspection, the insistence on responses as the basis of mental processes, the elimination of "instincts," and the reformation of prevailing views on heredity. It was Dunlap's 1919 paper "Are there any Instincts?" that can be considered as starting the major anti-instinct revolt of the 1920s.

Although not a comparative psychologist, Dunlap exerted great influence on comparative psychology through his editorial work. He founded the journal *Psychobiology* in 1917 and edited its two volumes. When the *Journal of Comparative Psychology* was founded, Dunlap and Yerkes served as editors from its inception in 1921 until 1943. In addition, he was the editor of *Comparative Psychology Monographs* from 1928 until 1936.

Dunlap is remembered as an iconoclast and for his "vehement attacks on many psychological doctrines and theories" (Dorcus, 1950, 114). In his other activities, Dunlap exerted influence on anthropology and sociology, wrote on the psychology of religion, served in the Medical Research Laboratory during World War I, and interacted with John Watson during the early development of behaviorism.

Sources: Dorcus, 1950; Dunlap, 1932; Moore, 1949; Zusne, 1975.

HARRY F. HARLOW
Born: October 31, 1905
Died: Tucson, Arizona, December 6, 1981

Harry F. Harlow received the B.A. degree in 1927 and the Ph.D. degree in 1930—both from Stanford University. At Stanford he completed his graduate work under Calvin Stone and was also influenced by L. M. Terman and W. R. Miles. He joined the faculty of the University of Wisconsin in 1930 and retired as George Cary Comstock Research Professor of Psychology in 1974. He then served as a visiting scholar at the University of Arizona. In two leaves of absence from Wisconsin, Harlow served as a Carnegie Fellow in Anthropology at Columbia and headed the Human Resources Research Branch of the Department of the Army from 1950 until 1952.

Harlow's bibliography of 1978 includes some 323 entries. He is best known throughout psychology as well as outside of it for his work on the development of affectional systems in rhesus macaques. This work included the development of "surrogate mothers," and studies of mother-infant relationships, sibling relationships, abnormal behavior, and therapy. This work was originally designed as part of this long-term effort at discrediting primary-drive theory. Many comparative and physiological psychologists respect Harlow as much for his efforts in the study of the evolution of learning, the neural control of learning, and the capacities for learning—as in his studies of learning sets. Earlier he worked with both rats and goldfish.

Harry Harlow was the editor of the *Journal of Comparative and Physiological Psychology* from 1951 to 1963. He was president of the American Psychological Association in 1958 and was a member of the National Academy of Sciences. He also received the Warren Medal in 1956 and the Distinguished Psychologist Award in 1960.

Perhaps the best ways in which to convey Harlow's writing style is with a sample. Harlow, as retiring editor of the comparative journal, prepared a satirical paper that included incisive comments on much journal writing. He noted:

> Although some psychologists write simple, straightforward introductions, this is commonly considered to be *declassé*. In the sophisticated or "strip-tease" technique you keep the problem a secret from the reader until the very last paragraph. Indeed, some very sophisticated authors keep the problem a secret forever. (1962, 893)

Sources: Evans, 1976; Hilgard, 1978; Sears, 1982; Suomi and Leroy, 1982; Unpublished biographical sketch.

LEONARD TRELAWNEY HOBHOUSE
Born: Saint Ives near Liskeard, Cornwall, England, September 8, 1864
Died: Alencon, Normandy, France, June 21, 1929

Leonard Hobhouse was educated at the Marlborough School and at Oxford University. At Oxford he was appointed a fellow of Merton College in 1887 and of Corpus Christi in 1894. He is best known as a sociologist and philosopher and was appointed the first Martin White Professor in Sociology at the University of London in 1907. Early in his career, Hobhouse was active in the social liberalism and labor movements in England. From 1897 to 1902 he served on the staff of the *Manchester Guardian.* During the later part of his career, however, he concentrated on academic pursuits in philosophy and sociology as well as comparative and social psychology.

Hobhouse's major contribution to comparative psychology lies in his *Mind in Evolution,* first published in 1901 and revised in 1915. In that book Hobhouse proposed that apes and monkeys have a near-human capacity for mastering concrete perceptual relationships; he called it "practical judgment." Hobhouse proposed that the capacity for reasoning can be seen even in Thorndike's own data—as in the sudden improvements that can be seen in the learning curves of individual animals. He also conducted his own studies and was the first to use box stacking and tasks that entailed the raking in of food and other objects with sticks and ropes. Yerkes confessed that in his more behavioristic days, he was unable to read the first edition of Hobhouse's book. However, he praised the second edition noting that it "fires one with enthusiasm for experimental inquiry" (1917*b*,160). Yerkes noted, however, that Hobhouse's experimental techniques were crude. Nevertheless, Yerkes added, "Hobhouse has imagination and insight. He formulates clearly many problems . . . I believe that *Mind in Evolution* has done much and will continue to aid greatly to advance a profitable genetic psychology" (1917*b*, 160).

Zusne (1975, 282) credits Hobhouse with founding *"the science of phylogenetic psychology,"* contending that, in *Mind in Evolution,* Hobhouse was the first to present a comprehensive treatment of the psychological development of animals by examining the evolution of instinct, habits, and complex processes in a wide range of species.

Sources: Ginsberg, 1968; Gottlieb, 1979; Razran, 1971; Stout, 1967; Warden, 1930; Zusne, 1975.

WALTER SAMUEL HUNTER
Born: Decatur, Illinois, March 29, 1889
Died: Providence, Rhode Island, August 3, 1954

Walter Hunter studied at the Polytechnic College in Fort Worth, Texas, and then at the University of Texas, where he completed his undergraduate work in 1910. He became interested in psychology through exploration and reading on his own, with the works of Charles Darwin exerting great influence on him. Hunter carried out graduate study at the University of Chicago, where he was strongly influenced by Angell and Carr. He received his doctorate in 1912. His dissertation entailed the development of the delayed-response method of comparative investigation and gave him immediate status in the field. Hunter served on the faculty of the University of Texas from 1912 until 1916. In 1916, at the age of twenty-seven, he became professor and head of the department at the University of Kansas. He spent sixteen months during World War I as a psychological examiner. Hunter moved to Clark University as the first G. Stanley Hall Professor of Genetic Psychology in 1925. In 1936 he became professor and chairman at Brown University, where he closed his career. The psychology building at Brown is named in his honor.

Hunter is known for his pioneering experiments, his orienting papers, and his administrative activities. His work on the delayed response (1913) and the temporal maze (1918) were important in establishing those methods. He also worked on the development of T-mazes and alternation learning tasks. Hunter (1920) discussed the modification of instinctive behavior; his summary on the 1947 heredity-environment symposium put psychological research on instinctive behavior into clear perspective. In his APA presidential address, Hunter (1932) attempted to distinguish psychology from related sciences. He was the first editor of *Comparative Psychology Monographs,* serving from 1922 until 1927. He also edited *Psychological Abstracts* during 1926-1946 and served on various other editorial boards.

Hunter received many honors for his work in research and administration, including election to the National Academy of Sciences. The esteem of his students and colleagues is conveyed by Graham (1958) and Hunt (1956). As noted by Hunt, "On the shoulders of such giants do we build the future" (1956, 216).

Sources: Graham, 1958; Hilgard, 1957: Hunt, 1956; Hunter, 1952; NCAB, 1958; Zusne, 1975.

WINTHROP NILES KELLOGG
Born: Mount Vernon, New York, April 13, 1898
Died: Fort Lauderdale, Florida, June 22, 1972

After attending Cornell University in 1916/1917, Winthrop Kellogg served in the air service during World War I. After the war he enrolled at Indiana University, majoring in philosophy and psychology; he was graduated in 1922. He then went to Columbia University, where he received an M.A. degree in psychology in 1927 and the Ph.D. in 1929. His dissertation, directed by Robert S. Woodworth, compared psychophysical methods. Many of his early publications dealt with apparatus for psychophysical research. Kellogg joined the faculty at Indiana in 1929 and became director of the Indiana Conditioning Laboratory. He served as a captain and major in the U. S. Army Air Corps in World War II and joined the faculty of Florida State University in 1950.

Kellogg is best known for the project in which he raised a young chimpanzee, Gua, at home along with his son, Donald, for a period of nine months. Donald was born on August 31, 1930; Gua was obtained June 26, 1931; the experiment lasted until March 28, 1932. The human and the chimpanzee each excelled at some tasks; Gua never learned effective vocalization.

Kellogg also conducted a long series of distinguished studies of learning. His work at Florida State consisted of pioneering research on echolocation in bottle-nosed dolphins. Kellogg conducted well-controlled research on the capacity of dolphins to localize objects using their sonar system.

The psychology building at Florida State was recently named in honor of Kellogg.

Sources: Benjamin and Bruce, 1982; *Current Biography Yearbook,* 1963; Hahn, 1971; Murchison, 1932.

LINUS WARD KLINE
Born: Benton, Pennsylvania, October 16, 1866
Details on death not available

Linus Kline received a Licentiate of Instruction at George Peabody College for Teachers and an S.B. degree from Harvard in 1896. He wrote, "I entered Clark in 1896 with the intention of studying 'zoological psychology'" (in Miles, 1930, 325). It was at Clark that Kline made his contributions to comparative psychology. Later he served at the State Teachers College, Farmville, Virginia from 1900 to 1902 and at the State

Teacher's College, Duluth, Minnesota, 1902-1918. He assumed a position as professor of psychology and director of the Teachers' Training School of Skidmore College in 1920.

Kline's major contributions to comparative psychology were three papers in the *American Journal of Psychology:* one on migration (1898); one on methods in animal psychology (1899*a*); and one on suggestions for a laboratory course (1899*b*). The paper on migration provides a broad comparative survey of migratory behavior. That on methods includes description of research on vorticella, wasps, chicks, and rats. Kline's laboratory course in comparative psychology would include research on amoeba, vorticella, paramecia, hydra, earthworms, slugs, fish, chicks, rats, and cats. His study begun on December 3, 1898, appears to have been the first experiment on learning in rats.

Kline was an experimentalist but used relatively simple quantitative measures. He was always concerned with the naturally occurring behavior of the animal and designed his apparatus to be congruent with such behavior. He noted, "I was impressed with the importance of working with animals in as natural moods as conditions permitted" (in Miles, 1930, 326).

Kline's twentieth-century publications are reports of studies on humans concerning issues such as ownership, juvenile ethics, sermons, humor, spelling, discipline, and drawing.

In describing the nature of Kline's research Robinson wrote:

> Measurement, by and large, is ignored, or is restricted to rudimentary tabulations. The emphasis is still upon observation, reporting, careful note-taking, and, of course, theory. What the student is asked to assess is the relationship between this or that activity on one hand, and the adaptive advantage conferred by such activity on the other . . . .
>
> Might not today's student in experimental psychology benefit from demonstrations of this sort? (1977, xxiv)

Much of the contemporary study of animal behavior reflects a return to the kind of approaches used by Kline.

Sources: Miles, 1930; Murchison, 1932; Robinson, 1977; Warden, 1930.

WOLFGANG KÖHLER
Born: Revel, Estonia, January 21, 1887
Died: Enfield, New Hampshire, June 11, 1967

After attending the Universities of Tubingen and Bonn, Wolfgang Köhler completed the Ph.D. degree at the University of Berlin under Carl

Stumpf in 1909. He served at the Psychological Institute in Frankfurt in 1910 and in 1913 was appointed director of the anthropoid research station of the Prussian Academy of Sciences on the island of Tenerife, where he was stranded during World War I. Köhler became director of the psychological laboratory at the University of Berlin in 1921 and professor of psychology and philosophy a year later. On April 28, 1933, Köhler wrote for the *Deutsche Allegemeine Zeitung,* the last anti-Nazi article to be published in Germany under the Nazi regime. Köhler's struggle to save the Psychological Institute of the University of Berlin from the Nazis is graphically portrayed by Henle (1978). In 1935 Köhler resigned his position in protest and moved to the United States, where he joined the faculty at Swarthmore. He retired in 1958, settling in New Hampshire and becoming affiliated with Dartmouth College.

Köhler is known in comparative psychology primarily for his work on Tenerife, which was published in German in 1917 and in English translation as *The Mentality of Apes* in 1925. Köhler used various problems entailing the use of simple tools in his studies with chimpanzees. They had to put two small sticks together to make a longer one, stack boxes, and use other tools in securing objects. Like Hobhouse, Köhler rejected Thorndike's interpretation of the course of learning, preferring an interpretation in which insight played a role in performance. Köhler was also interested, however, in the role of imitation, chance, and play in the development of solutions to problems.

While on Tenerife, Köhler also demonstrated size constancy in the perception of objects in both chimpanzees and chickens. A 1925 lecture tour of the United State was curtailed when cancellation of his lecture at one southern university convinced Köhler that his views on intelligence in apes were not welcome in the climate of opinion on evolution prevailing at that time in parts of the country.

Köhler is known throughout psychology because at Frankfurt he was a cofounder of the Gestalt school of psychology with Koffka and Wertheimer. Asch (1968, 119) wrote of Köhler, "A bold and incisive mind that helped bring psychology into the twentieth century, he retained a serene confidence in the validity of human striving and values. There are few in any generation of his stature." He was an APA president and a recipient of both the Warren Medal and the Distinguished Scientific Contribution Award of the APA.

Sources: Asch, 1968; Cummings, 1967; Henle, 1978; NCAB, 1974; Zuckerman and Wallach, 1968; Zusne, 1975.

ZING-YANG KUO
Born: Swatow, Kwangtun, China, 1898
Died: August 14, 1970

In 1918 Zing-Yang Kuo sailed from China to California to enroll in the University of California, Berkeley. There, he was graduated magna cum laude with a major in psychology in 1921 and completed a Ph.D. degree in 1923. Kuo returned to China in 1923, accepting a position at Fuh Tan University in Shanghai. Before he could effectively use his new laboratory, political turmoil forced him to move. Turmoil interrupted his scientific career repeatedly. Finally, in 1936 he decided to return to the United States. Unable to secure permanent employment, he returned to China in 1940. In 1946 Kuo moved to Hong Kong, where he again lacked formal employment. There he conducted social-psychological analyses of the Chinese character.

Kuo was a major figure in the anti-instinct revolt of the 1920s. His first paper, "Giving Up Instincts in Psychology" (1921) was written during his senior year of college. Although in his first paper he denied a role of inheritance in behavior, he later held that the learned and the innate were so intertwined in behavioral ontogeny that they were inseparable.

Kuo's primary research dealt with the development of behavior in the chick embryo. He advocated the view that prenatal development exerts a strong influence on postnatal behavior and set about to demonstrate this experimentally. In other developmental research, Kuo studied the ontogeny of the responses of cats to rats and of fighting behavior.

Kuo's views were summarized in his book, *The Dynamics of Behavior Development: An Epigenetic View* (1967).

Sources: Gottlieb, 1972; Murchison, 1932; Kantor, 1971.

KARL SPENCER LASHLEY
Born: Davis, West Virginia, June 7, 1890
Died: Poitiers, France, August 7, 1958

Lashley grew up in West Virginia as a nature lover, keeping various collections of butterflies, snakes, frogs, and snails, as well as pet mice and raccoons. He attended West Virginia University, graduating with an A.B. degree in 1910. Lashley received an M.S. degree in bacteriology from the University of Pittsburgh in 1911. He then went to Johns Hopkins, completing his doctorate in 1914. During his graduate training, Lashley was strongly influenced by Watson, spending the summer of 1913 with him studying terns on the Dry Tortugas. In 1915 Lashley did postdoctoral work with Shepherd Ivory Franz at St. Elizabeth's Hospital in Washington, D.C. He joined the faculty of the University of Minnesota in 1917, the University of Chicago in 1929, and Harvard University in

1942. He retired from Harvard as an emeritus professor in 1955. Lashley also worked with the U.S. Interdepartmental Social Hygiene Board and the Behavior Research Fund. During 1942-1955 he was director of the Yerkes Laboratories of Primate Biology in Orange Park.

Lashley made many contributions to comparative psychology beginning with his early work on visual discrimination in rats, the behavior of paramecia, development in monkeys, sound acquisition in parrots, and the behavior of terns. He is well known for his work on the neural bases of sensory function, learning, and instinctive behavior. Included in his 109-item publication list are not only an impressive list of empirical studies but also integrative papers summarizing material and theorizing regarding the status of the major problems of the field. Beach et al. (1960) published a selection of his major papers.

Lashley's presidential address to the Eastern Psychological Association, "Experimental Analysis of Instinctive Behavior," (1938) and his APA presidential address, "Basic Neural Mechanisms in Behavior," (1930) and "The Problem of Serial Order in Behavior" (1951) are all classics. In one of his last contributions, the same Karl Lashley who had been with Watson on the Dry Tortugas wrote a scholarly introduction for a book of translations, *Instinctive Behavior* (1957) edited by his wife, C. H. Schiller. The book was important in introducing ethological thought to the United States.

Lashley was president not only of the American Psychological Association but of the American Society of Naturalists as well. He received many other awards. Hebb (1959, 142) noted that Lashley's death brought "to an end a brilliant career, perhaps the most brilliant in the psychology of this century." Beach (1961) called him "one of the great psychologists of our time" and began his paper with the following passage:

Eminent psychologist with no earned degree in psychology
Famous theorist who specialized in disproving theories, including his own
Inspiring teacher who described all teaching as useless

Sources: Anonymous, 1955; Beach, 1961; Carmichael, 1959; Hebb, 1959; Hilgard, 1978; NCAB, 1962; Zusne, 1975.

DANIEL S. LEHRMAN
Born: New York City, June 1, 1919
Died: Sante Fe, New Mexico, August 30, 1972

Daniel Lehrman attended the public schools of New York City and became interested in bird behavior during a bird walk with the Boy Scouts when he was about thirteen years old. He attended the City

College of New York, receiving the B.S. degree in 1947. As a freshman at CCNY, he worked as a volunteer assistant for G. K. Noble at the American Museum of Natural History. Lehrman listed Libby Hyman, Ernst Mayr, and Frank Beach, all of whom he met at the museum, as early influences in directing him toward the study of animal behavior. Other influences included William Vogt and Joseph Nickey, whom he met at ornithological clubs, and Max Hertzman, Joseph Barmack, and William Etkin, who were his teachers at CCNY. Lehrman first met Schneirla when he returned from the army to the museum in 1946, and he completed his doctoral work with Schneirla in 1954. He joined the faculty of the Newark branch of Rutgers University in 1950 and became professor and director of the Institute of Animal Behavior in 1958.

Lehrman's research was centered on the problems of the reproductive and social behavior of birds and its analysis via observational, endocrinological, and experimental psychological techniques. He began work on ring doves as a graduate student as a natural outgrowth of his interest in birds. Lehrman excelled in delineating the complex interrelationships among internal and external variables in the control of behavior (for example, Lehrman, 1965). His critique of Konrad Lorenz's theory of instinctive behavior (Lehrman, 1953) was a classic that triggered initial conflict and eventual resolution in the interaction between comparative psychologists and ethologists in the 1950s.

Lehrman was a member of the National Academy of Sciences and the recipient of a lifetime-career research grant from the National Institute of Mental Health. With grants from the Public Health Service and the Rockefeller Foundation, he founded the Institute for Animal Behavior; this was to serve as a major training ground for comparative psychologists. He influenced many students and colleagues in diverse ways. From 1963 until 1972, Lehrman served as associate editor of the *Journal of Comparative and Physiological Psychology* and had primary responsibility for material in comparative psychology. Lehrman wrote of the scientist:

> The scientist can also serve a function like that of an artist, of a painter, or poet—that is, he sees things in a way that no one else has seen them before and finds a way to describe what he has seen so that other people can see it in the same way. This function is that of widening and enriching the content of human consciousness, and of increasing the depth of contact that human beings, scientists and nonscientists as well, can have with the world around them. (1971, 471)

Sources: American Psychological Association 1973 Directory; Beach, 1973, 1981; Beer, 1973*b*, 1975; Klopfer and Hailman, 1972; *New York Times*, August 31, 1972; Schaffner, 1955.

HOWARD SCOTT LIDDELL
Born: Cleveland, Ohio, November 9, 1895
Died: Ithaca, New York, October, 1962

Howard S. Liddell received an A.B. degree from the University of Michigan, where he was influenced by John F. Shepard in the Department of Psychology. He received a master's degree in psychology in 1918. Liddell's Ph.D. degree, completed in 1923, was from the Department of Physiology at Cornell. Liddell joined the faculty at Cornell in 1919. When the Cornell Medical Faculty moved from Ithaca, Liddell remained as professor of psychobiology and director of the Cornell behavior farm laboratory. In 1926 he returned from post doctoral work with Pavlov in Leningrad to establish a conditioning laboratory at Cornell (Liddell, 1926).

Liddell is best known for his extensive research program relating to conditioning in sheep and goats. He was especially interested in "experimental neuroses" and conducted a variety of studies regarding the determinants of their occurrence. Liddell also was a pioneer in the investigation of hormones on behavior. Although Liddell's experiences studying with Titchener turned him away from animal research, instructors in animal physiology directed him to the study of hypothyroidism in sheep and goats and its effect on behavior.

In 1952 Liddell was cited by the Eighth Army for his consultation in Korea on stress and fatigue. He was president of the American Psychopathological Association in 1957. Liddell wrote:

> I have a feeling of guilt at being interested in so many converging sciences which meet in the study of behavior. I think many of us have this common interest in the persistent and systematic observations of the behavior of animals which we come to know as individuals. (in Schaffner, 1955, 313).

Sources: Beach, 1981; Murchison, 1932; *New York Times,* November 1, 1962; Schaffner, 1955.

WILLIAM McDOUGALL
Born: Oldham, Lancashire, England, June 22, 1872
Died: Durham, North Carolina, November 18, 1938

William McDougall entered the University of Manchester to study biology and geology at the age of fifteen. After four years at Manchester, he received a scholarship and studied for four additional years at St. John's College, Cambridge. This was followed by four years of medical study at St. Thomas's Hospital in London. At the conclusion of his medical studies, McDougall joined the Cambridge Anthropological

Expedition to the Torres Straits and then proceeded with Dr. Charles Hose to conduct studies on the indigenous tribes of Borneo. Another year of preparation was spent in Gottingen studying psychophysics under G. E. Müller.

In 1900 McDougall became a lecturer in psychology at the University College, London, and in 1904 he became Wilde Reader in Mental Philosophy at Oxford. He left England to join the faculty at Harvard in 1920 and moved to Duke University in 1927.

McDougall was a general psychologist, not a comparative psychologist per se. Nevertheless, his ideas and activities had great impact on comparative psychology, as on other fields. Most relevant were his theories of hormic psychology and instincts. McDougall viewed purposive striving as a fundamental category of psychology and believed that the energy for such striving springs from the instincts. The instincts, in McDougall's view, cannot be defined in terms of stimuli and responses but are intimately related to emotions. With his theories of purpose and instinct and his active opposition to behaviorism, McDougall's views found little favor in the United States. The famous "Battle of Behaviorism" between Watson and McDougall was a major event in this debate.

McDougall completed little empirical research in comparative psychology. His major effort was an attempt to prove Lamarckian inheritance of learned traits (McDougall 1938; Agar et al., 1954). He conducted some other research on rats, monkeys, raccoons, wasps, and cats (for example, McDougall and McDougall, 1927; 1931).

The most characteristic feature of McDougall's work is it breadth. He influenced experimental and physiological psychology, social psychology, conceptions of the mind-body problem, abnormal psychology, and related areas in addition to his influence on comparative psychology. Pattie (1939, 303) wrote, "The scope of McDougall's writings and his intellectual interests is comparable only to that of Wundt and James. He employed almost all methods of psychological investigation and he made contributions to almost all of the principal fields of the subject."

In addition to his views on purpose and instinct, there were other of McDougall's beliefs that led to disfavor in the United States. These included his belief in the soul, interest in psychic research, advocacy of Lamarckian inheritance, and beliefs in the superiority of the Nordic race. In his autobiography, he reflected this overall rejection:

> In America I was known as a writer who had flourished in the later middle ages and had written out a list of alleged instincts of the human species (1930, 216).

> Do I regret the choice of my line of work? Sometimes I do. Similar abilities, energy, and sustained effort, applied in any other line of work, might well

have brought considerable reward. . . . The more I write, the more antagonism I seem to provoke. . . . I suppose it is that my uncompromising arrogance shows through, in spite of the taming it has undergone. (1930, 223)

Sources: Adams, 1939; Drever, 1968; Flugel, 1939; McCurdy, 1968; McDougall, 1930; Pattie, 1939; Uytman, 1967; Zusne, 1975.

NORMAN RAYMOND FREDERICK MAIER
Born: Sebewaing, Michigan, November 27, 1900
Died: Ann Arbor, Michigan; September 24, 1977

Norman Maier was educated in Michigan and received a B.A. degree from the University of Michigan in 1923. In 1925 and 1926, he did a year of graduate work at the University of Berlin, where he was influenced by Köhler, Wertheimer, and Lewin. He returned to complete his doctorate at Michigan under John Shepard. He served on the faculty of Long Island University during 1928/1929; then was a National Research Council Fellow at the University of Chicago. At Chicago during 1929-1931, Maier worked with Lashley and was also influenced by Klüver. He joined the faculty of the University of Michigan in 1931.

The central theme behind Maier's research was the nature of the problem-solving processes and the factors that both facilitate and interfere with them. Maier believed there was a clear distinction between learning and reasoning and designed tests that he believed demonstrated reasoning in rats. He was especially interested in the rats that failed in discrimination-learning problems, many of which developed abnormal symptoms. This led to the formulation of his frustration theory (1961).

With Schneirla, Maier coauthored *Principles of Animal Psychology* (1935), a text of overwhelming importance in the development of comparative psychology.

In his later years, Maier turned to the study of problem solving in humans, often in consultation with business, industry, and government.

Maier's career has been characterized as "professional, lonely, always controversial, and sometimes difficult" (Solem and McKeachie, 1979, 267). His theories were not widely accepted as they ran counter to the behavioristic trends of the times. He responded by formulating "Maier's law," which he felt characterized much of science: "If the facts do not conform to the theory, they must be disposed of" (1960, 208).

Sources: Murchison, 1932; *New York Times,* September 12, 1977; Solem and McKeachie, 1979.

T(HOMAS) WESLEY MILLS
Born: Brockville, Ontario, Canada, February 22, 1847
Died: Oxford, England, February 15, 1915

T. Wesley Mills received a B.A. degree from Toronto University in 1871. He received an M.A. degree there one year later. Mills received an M.D. degree and a master of surgery degree from McGill University in 1878. He then completed medical studies in Germany and Great Britain. Returning to McGill, Mills was sequentially demonstrator of physiology, lecturer in physiology, and professor of physiology. In 1910 he was made emeritus professor and moved to Oxford. He was a fellow of the Royal Society of Canada and a vice-president of the Society of American Naturalists.

Mills is best known for his book *The Nature and Development of Animal Intelligence* (1898). He also provoked a complicated exchange of papers with his criticism of Morgan's views on the ontogeny of eating and drinking in chicks (Mills, 1896a). He was a critic of Thorndike and his methods (Mills, 1899, 1904).

If there are two characteristics that pervade Mills's writing, they are a concern for the use of natural conditions when testing animals and an emphasis on behavioral development. It was Mills who criticized Thorndike's use of puzzle boxes noting, "As well enclose a living man in a coffin, lower him, against his will, into the earth, and attempt to deduce normal psychology from his conduct" (1899, 266). Mills emphasized the need for observational studies, reference to the theory of evolution in studies of comparative psychology, opposition to Morgan's canon, and the importance of individual differences. Both Thorndike (1898c, 1899d) and Whitman (1898/1899) in turn were critical of the lack of precision in Mills's methods. Mills can be considered as a "father" of the study of behavioral development, as his book includes many detailed studies of development, and he influenced workers such as Small and Watson who conducted similar studies.

In 1886 Mills organized the Association for the Study of Comparative Psychology at McGill University. When the twenty-six charter members of the American Psychological Association held their first formal meeting in Philadelphia in December of 1892, Mills, along with Titchener, Münsterberg, and two others, was elected one of the first additional members.

Sources: Boring, 1928b; Cattell, 1917; Gottlieb, 1979; Mills, 1899; Warden et al., 1935; *Montreal Star*, February 15, 1915.

CONWY LLOYD MORGAN
Born: London, England, February 6, 1852
Died: Hastings, Sussex, England, March 6, 1936

After attending the Royal Grammar School in Guildford near London, Lloyd Morgan prepared for a career by attending the Royal School of Mines in London, intending to become a mining engineer. One night at a dinner at the school, Morgan was seated next to Thomas H. Huxley, who suggested that after finishing his present training, Morgan might switch to work with him. He did study at the Royal College of Science and became a disciple of Huxley. After graduating and serving as a tutor in North America and Brazil, Morgan obtained a post as a lecturer at the Diocesan College at Rondebosch in South Africa. He taught a variety of subjects from 1878 until 1883. In 1883 he was appointed lecturer at University College, Bristol, the institution where he remained for the rest of his professional life. Although he was initially appointed to a chair in geology and zoology, it was later changed, and he was a professor of psychology and ethics. In 1899 Morgan became the first scientist elected to the Royal Society for work in psychology.

Morgan is best known throughout psychology for the canon that bears his name. However, there are other features to his many papers and various books. He was a strong advocate of an evolutionary approach in comparative psychology and supported a doctrine of emergent evolution. Morgan conducted numerous experiments—generally relatively informal studies of animals outside a laboratory in more natural surroundings. While recognizing the limitations of anecdotes, he did use them on occasion. He wrote about instinct, learning, association, imitation, intelligence, and the perception of relations. He was an early trial-and-error learning theorist.

Morgan was a true pioneer of comparative psychology and an individual who did much to put the field on a scientific footing.

Sources: Adler, 1973; Boring, 1968; Goudge, 1967; Grindley, 1936; Morgan, 1932; Murchison, 1932; Zusne, 1975.

CLIFFORD THOMAS MORGAN
Born: Mintola, New Jersey, July 21, 1915
Died: Austin, Texas, February 12, 1976

Clifford T. Morgan did undergraduate work at Tennessee's Maryville College with Paul Fields. His graduate study was at the University of Rochester, beginning with Leonard Carmichael, but finishing with Elmer Culler when Carmichael left for Tufts. Morgan served as an instructor at Harvard during 1939-1943, first working in Lashley's laboratory. He accepted an appointment at Johns Hopkins in 1943, but the war delayed his move to Baltimore until 1946. The Psychology Department of Baldwin, Dunlap, and Watson had been abolished at Hopkins, but Morgan became the first chair of the reestablished Psychology Department and built it into a strong department. Morgan's phenomenal success as a textbook writer made him independently wealthy, and he thus chose to move frequently—to Wisconsin in 1959; to Santa Barbara in 1962; and to the University of Texas, Austin, in 1968.

Morgan is known in comparative psychology primarily for his work on hoarding behavior and audiogenic seizures. Morgan's research on food hoarding in rats consisted of a series of well-designed studies of the determinants of hoarding. He participated in the 1947 Symposium on Heredity and Environment (Morgan, 1947). It was Morgan who challenged the results of Maier on "neurotic" seizures, contending that the air puff used would have been sufficient in itself to produce the seizures (Morgan and Morgan, 1939).

Morgan was also involved in the founding of the Psychonomic Society, which he served as its first chairman. It was Morgan who was responsible, more than any other person, for establishing the stable of journals published by the Psychonomic Society.

Morgan's careers as a comparative-physiological psychologist, departmental administrator, founder of the Psychonomic Society, publisher, and textbook writer earned him his reputation as a Renaissance man.

Sources: Garner, 1976; Stellar and Lindzey, 1978.

FRED AUGUST MOSS
Born: Hayesville, North Carolina, August 31, 1893
Died: Alexandria, Virginia, July 27, 1966

Fred Moss received an A.B. degree from Mercer University in 1913 and an M.A. degree from Columbia in 1920. He received both an M.D. degree (1927) and a Ph.D. degree (1923) from George Washington University in Washington, D.C. Moss joined the faculty at George Washington in 1921 and was chairman of the department from 1924 to 1936. From 1927 until near the close of his life, he practiced medicine in Washington.

Moss is credited with devising the Columbia Obstruction Box as a means of measuring drives in animals (1924). His other major contribution lay in his editorship of the first edited textbooks in comparative psychology (1934, 1942). Most of Moss's other contributions to psychology fell outside the comparative area.

Sources: Murchison, 1932: NCAB, 1970.

HENRY WIEGHORST NISSEN
Born: Chicago, Illinois, February 5, 1901
Died: Orange Park, Florida, April 27, 1958

Henry Nissen received a B.A. degree from the University of Illinois in 1923. After working in business for three years, he attended Columbia University, where he received an M.A. degree in 1927. He turned to comparative psychology as the result of his experiences with Carl J. Warden, completing his doctorate under Warden at Columbia in 1929. On completing his work at Columbia, Nissen was picked by Yerkes to join his staff in comparative psychobiology. Nissen remained based in New Haven until 1939, when he moved to Orange Park, Florida, as assistant director of the Yerkes Laboratories. In 1955 Nissen succeeded Lashley as director.

In his early work, Nissen studied drives in rats using the Columbia Obstruction Box technique. Among his most notable early contributions was his field study of chimpanzee behavior in French Guinea. This effort at field research was pioneering not only in psychology but in the biological sciences in general. During most of his career Nissen concentrated on the study of chimpanzee behavior and was interested in a broad range of problems. He never lost his interest in motivation and made both empirical and theoretical contributions to its study. He worked in the areas of learning theory, intelligence, and social behavior. Nissen was especially interested in development and conducted some important early studies of behavioral development in general (for example, Nissen, 1942) and perceptual development in particular (for example, Nissen et al., 1951).

As noted by Carmichael (1965, 205), "Nissen was at the time of his death almost certainly the Western world's leading authority on the biology and psychology of the chimpanzee." He contributed to Stevens's *Handbook of Experimental Psychology* (1951), the *Nebraska Symposium on Motivation,* Roe and Simpson's *Behavior and Evolution* (1958), and the Daytona Beach Instinct Symposium. Nissen was elected to the National Academy of Sciences in 1953.

Nissen devoted much effort to the every-day care and maintenance of the chimpanzee colony at Orange Park, in the self-sacrificing work necessary for the success of the colony. He was familiar with the procedures for medical, dental, and surgical care, reproductive cycles, diet, and other aspects of the general biology of chimpanzees. "His extreme personal modesty and his almost deferential approach to some of his colleagues at times masked the originality of his mind and the sharp, rapier-like power by means of which he could get to the bottom of important controversies in scientific psychology" (Carmichael, 1965, 214). His writings reflect the breadth of interest of the naturalist and the careful attention to detailed accuracy and measurement of the experimental scientist" (Riesen, 1958*b*, 795).

Sources: Carmichael, 1965; Murchison, 1932; Riesen, 1958*b*; Zusne, 1975.

STANLEY CHARLES RATNER
Born: Pittsburgh, Pennsylvania, August 13, 1925
Died: December 21, 1975

Stanley C. Ratner attended Marion Military Institute in Alabama and then spent three years in the infantry in World War II. He received a B.A. degree from the University of Pittsburgh in 1948 and an M.A. degree in psychology at Kent State University in 1950. Ratner received a Ph.D. degree from Indiana University in 1954, where he was strongly influenced by J. R. Kantor and W. K. Estes. He joined the faculty of Michigan State University in 1955 and spent most of the rest of his career there, except for intervals at Florida State University, the University of Miami, and Beloit College. During 1959/1960 Ratner studied with the ethologists at Cambridge University on National Science Foundation faculty fellowship.

Ratner's research lay in the areas of conditioning and learning in earthworms (for example, Ratner and Miller, 1959), habituation, and tonic immobility (for example, Ratner, 1977). With M. R. Denny, Ratner prepared two editions of a textbook in comparative psychology (Denny and Ratner, 1970; Ratner and Denny, 1965). He also developed his own version of the comparative method (Ratner, 1972). He was a distinguished teacher.

Sources: APA Biographical Directory, 1973; Denny, 1976.

PAUL HARKAI SCHILLER
Born: Hungary, November 4, 1908
Died: New Hampshire, May 1, 1949

Paul H. Schiller was a Hungarian-born psychologist who migrated to the United States to work at the Yerkes Laboratories in Orange Park. He died, in 1949, at the young age of forty-one. Schiller planned a book of translations of work from European ethologists that was eventually completed by his wife, Claire H. Schiller (Claire later married Karl Lashley) (1957). The book brought some of the classical papers in European ethology to the attention of American comparative psychologists. Schiller believed in the importance of innate behavioral patterns as providing the basis for many of the learned behaviors studied by psychologists. Thus the course of learning was determined in part by the innate organization of the organism. Had he lived longer, Schiller and his work might have served as a bridge between European ethology and American comparative psychology.

Much of Schiller's research was on the problem-solving behavior of chimpanzees in the tradition of Hobhouse, Köhler, Yerkes, and Bingham. He noted that "since learning is a modification of the original behavior repertoire, this original inventory of available movement patterns, which becomes modified in consequence of learning, should be analyzed with some care" (P. H. Schiller, 1957, 265). While working at Orange Park, Schiller also studied learning in fishes and octopuses (1948a, 1948b).

As noted by Carmichael (1968, 60), "He made especially important contributions to what may be called quantitative psychobiology because he combined the modern ethological point of view with a clear understanding of the more quantitative American approach to animal psychology."

Sources: Bennett and Boring, 1954; Lashley, 1957; Carmichael, 1968.

THEODORE CHRISTIAN SCHNEIRLA
Born: Bay City, Michigan, July 23, 1902
Died: New York, N. Y., August 20, 1968

After attending schools in Michigan, Theodore Christian Schneirla went to the University of Michigan where he received a B.S. degree in 1924. He continued study at Michigan, receiving an M.S. degree in psychology in 1925 and an Sc.D. degree in 1928. He was strongly influenced by John F. Shepard and followed in Shepard's footsteps in studying learning and orientation in ants for his doctoral research. Schneirla joined the faculty of New York University in 1928 and spent 1930/1931 as a National Research Council Fellow in Lashley's laboratory at Chicago. Schneirla then returned to NYU and also joined the staff of the American Museum of Natural History in 1943. Later he became a curator of animal behavior at the museum and an adjunct professor at both NYU and the City College of New York.

Schneirla's contributions related to general writing, theory, and empirical research. Zusne called him "the foremost representative of comparative psychology in American between 1930 and 1968" (1975, 457). His text, *Principles of Animal Psychology* (1935), written with Maier, remains a classic in the field. His descriptions of comparative psychology in the *Encyclopaedia Britannica* introduced many to the field. Schneirla wrote numerous other papers summarizing and evaluating comparative psychology and relating it to European ethology.

In the realm of theory, Schneirla developed his concept of levels, according to which there are such major differences among animals at different levels that generalizations across them and use of common terms in describing their behavior can be greatly misleading. Schneirla was a strong advocate of the study of behavioral development with an epigenetic approach. He proposed an approach-withdrawal theory, according to which young organisms approach mild stimuli and withdraw from intense ones, and believed that the theory had the potential for integrating many diverse phenomena. Schneirla was a critic of the concept of instinct and repeatedly emphasized the complexity of the determination of behavior and of the interaction of the many factors that affect it.

He made repeated trips to Barro Colorado Island, to Mexico, and to locations in the United States to conduct field studies of ant behavior. His field research is probably the most ambitious yet undertaken by a comparative psychologist. He delineated the complex nature of the recurring cycles in the behavior of tropical army ants. Schneirla was the first to bring army ants back to New York from Central America. Among his other research, that on the development of behavior in cats is particularly notable.

Schneirla guided many outstanding students through their graduate careers, and they, in turn became some of the leaders of American comparative psychology, express their gratitude profusely. As noted by Tobach and Aronson:

> He united in his person and in his behavior a profound comprehension of the interrelatedness of phenomena together with an appreciation for precision and regard for the uniqueness of any one phenomenon; an integration of theory and activity which was constantly being developed in the course of new experience; and a concern not only for man's progress as a controller of his environment, but for his welfare and for the preservation of his human quality. (1970, xviii)

Sources: Aronson and Tobach, 1972; *Current Biography,* 1955; Gottlieb, 1968*b; New York Times,* August 21, 1968; O'Reilly, 1953; Piel, 1970; Tobach and Aronson, 1970; Zusne, 1975.

JOHN FREDERICK SHEPARD
Born: Greenfield, Illinois, January 30, 1881
Died: November 2, 1965

John F. Shepard received an S.B. degree from Lawrence University in 1901 and attended graduate school at the University of Chicago during 1902/1903. Hearing that Walter Pillsbury was searching for a student assistant at the University of Michigan, he transferred to Ann Arbor and received the Ph.D. degree from St. Lawrence University in 1925.

Shepard was a skilled researcher and for many years conducted research on the comparative abilities of organisms in maze learning. He was especially interested in the cues used and gathered evidence that rats obtained cues from the characteristics of the floor over which they walked. He pioneered the use of ants in the psychology laboratory and did comparative research on rats, cats, and humans. The tragedy of

Shepard's career is that he published little of his research and much is lost to posterity.

Perhaps the most lasting effect of Shepard's long efforts is in his students. Among the alumni of Shepard's teachings were Maier and Schneirla, in addition to Clark Hull, Howard Liddell, and M. Ray Denny—all as either undergraduates or graduate students. Shepard required students to maintain detailed notebooks, and the four-hundred page notebook kept by Schneirla appears to have provided the basis for the Maier and Schneirla text.

I was privileged to attend the first John Shepard lecture, presented by E. G. Boring in Ann Arbor. Would that a tape were available of the reminiscences of Boring and Shepard that night and the tales of the history of psychology that were told!

Sources: Murchison, 1932; Raphelson, 1980; Tobach and Aronson, 1970.

WILLARD STANTON SMALL
Born: North Truro, Massachusetts, August 24, 1870
Died: South Weymouth, Massachusetts, January 31, 1943

Willard Small attended Tufts College, receiving an A.B. degree in 1894 and an A.M. degree in 1897. He then moved on to Hall's Clark University, where he completed his doctorate under E.C. Sanford in 1900. It is Small's work at Clark that is of interest to comparative psychologists. After leaving Clark, Small served on the faculties of Michigan State Normal College and Los Angeles State Normal School. He worked in educational administration in the public schools of San Diego, California; Patterson, New Jersey; and Washington, D.C. In 1923 he became Dean of the College of Education of the University of Maryland.

As of 1932 Small's entire publication list included just the three papers in *American Journal of Psychology* for which he is known (1899, 1900, 1901). In the first, he provided a record of the behavioral (or "psychic") development of rats, doing for rats what T. Wesley Mills had done for other species. He worked toward "*a comparative embryology* of the soul" (1899, 80). In the second he studied albino rats as they obtained food from puzzle boxes. Rats had to dig and gnaw as part of the study because Small believed that such behavioral patterns were "characteristic instinctive activity in the free life of the rat" (1900, 135). In this second paper Small discovered what would later be called "instinctive drift." Rats had to remove strips of paper to reach food; however, as Small noted, on occasion "the nest-building instinct is so strong, that the mere sight of a bit of available material serves to distract the unstable attention of the rat from her quest for food" (1900, 152). The third paper was the first use of rats in mazes in a psychology laboratory. Small worked with a replica of the

322 / *Biographical Sketches*

Hampton Court maze and with both albino and wild Norway rats. Small noted that Hall provided little encouragement for these studies at first because he was not convinced of the utility of laboratory methods. However, the research was stimulated in part by "Hall's insistent interest in evolutionary psychology" (Small in Miles, 1930, 333).

It is notable that Small, like Linus Kline with whom he worked, was greatly concerned that his tasks be compatible with the instinctive behavior of the animal. After discussing rat behavior, Small noted when designing the mazes, "Conforming with such considerations, appeal was made to the rat's propensity for winding passages" (1901, 208). Small quoted Ernest Ingersoll in noting that "an animal should be made to do difficult things only in the line of its inherent abilities" (1900, 133). Thus the initial workers with rats and mazes did not select their tasks and animals arbitrarily and without considerations of the natural lives of their subjects; rather, they were intimately concerned with such matters in planning their research.

Sources: Murchison, 1932; Miles, 1930; Robinson, 1977; Zusne, 1975.

CALVIN PERRY STONE
Born: Portland, Indiana, February 28, 1892
Died: Palo Alto, California, December 28, 1954

Calvin Stone's struggle in life began when he was five years old and his home burned down on the day of his father's funeral. He attended Valparaiso University, receiving a B.S. degree in 1910 and a B.A. degree in classics in 1913. After a year of teaching high school, he went to Indiana University and there received an M.A. degree in 1916 with a thesis on light discrimination in dogs, completed under Melvin E. Haggerty. Stone followed Haggerty to Minnesota and also worked as director of research in psychology at the Indiana State Reformatory at Jeffersonville. Stone's graduate career was interrupted by World War I, during which he served in the U.S. Army Medical Corps, finishing as a captain. He then returned to Minnesota, completing a Ph.D. under Karl Lashley with a thesis on the sexual behavior of male rats. Stone went to Stanford in 1922 and remained on the faculty for the rest of his life.

Stone contributed to a number of areas. In his early research he emphasized instinctive behavior, pioneering the study of sexual behavior in rats. Stone was interested in all aspects of behavior including its genetic bases, development, endocrine control, and related matters. In addition, he studied maternal behavior and other instinctive behavioral patterns. Later in his career Stone devoted more effort to the study of learning and effects of electroconvulsive shock, in addition to physiological psychology.

Stone edited the *Journal of Comparative and Physiological Psychology* from its inception in 1947 until 1950. He also edited the *Annual Review of Psychology* from its inception in 1950. Stone was the editor of the third edition of the general textbook in the field, *Comparative Psychology* (1951). He was elected to the National Academy of Sciences and served as APA president in 1942. In his APA presidential address, Stone reviewed some major factors and theories of evolution and forecast the development of behavioral ecology in a manner that must be regarded as prescient. He was also interested in abnormal psychology and offered the first course in Freudian psychology to be given as a part of the regular university curriculum at an American University.

Stone is remembered by students and associates for his rigor, persistence, industry, high standards, and integrity. He was not swayed from his general research program by the fads and trends that swept through the discipline. "Stone was uncompromising in his insistence that a psychologist must be well-grounded in fundamentals" (Rosvold, 1955, 328). "Regularly year after year he published sound and solid reports of meticulously conducted research. . . . Furthermore, few scholars in modern psychology have pursued research so consistently, determinately, and productively as did Calvin Perry Stone" (Carpenter, 1955, 659).

Sources: Carpenter, 1955; Hilgard, 1978; Murchison, 1932; NCAB, 1970; Rosvold, 1955; Zusne, 1975.

WILLIAM ROBERT THOMPSON
Born: Toulon, France, July 10, 1924
Died: 1979

William Robert Thompson attended the University of Toronto, receiving a B.A. degree in 1945 and an M.A. degree in 1947. He then attended the University of Chicago, completing the Ph.D. degree in 1951. Thompson was on the faculty of McGill University 1951-1954; Wesleyan University, 1956-1966; and Queen's University 1954-1956 and from 1966 until his death. He received an honorary M.A. degree from Wesleyan in 1961. Thompson was a Guggenheim fellow during 1959/1960 and a fellow of the Center of Advanced Study in the Behavioral Sciences during 1963/1964.

Thompson's best-known research was in the fields of behavior genetics and early experience. Together with John Fuller, he authored the textbook that ushered in the modern era of behavior genetics (Fuller and Thompson, 1960). He served as president of the Behavior Genetics Association during 1976-1978.

Among his other notable contributions, Thompson wrote a chapter on social behavior for Roe and Simpson's *Behavior and Evolution* (1958); a chapter called "Research Trends in Comparative Psychology" for Waters et al.'s *Principles of Comparative Psychology* (1960); and, with D. O.

Hebb, a chapter called "The Social Significance of Animal Studies" for the *Handbook of Social Psychology* (1954).

Sources: American Men and Women of Science, 1978.

EDWARD LEE THORNDIKE
Born: Williamsburg, Massachusetts, August 31, 1874
Died: Montrose, New York, August 9, 1949

Edward Lee Thorndike received an A.B. degree from Wesleyan University in 1895. He then transferred to Harvard to study with William James and received a second A.B. degree in 1896 and an A.M. in 1897. Thorndike then moved to Columbia to study under Cattell, where he completed the Ph.D. degree in 1898. In 1898 Thorndike went to Western Reserve University to teach for a year and then returned to Columbia, where he remained until he became an emeritus professor in 1941. During World War I he was chairman of the committee on classification of personnel in the U.S. Army.

Thorndike's contributions to comparative psychology were made early in his career. He wrote, "I certainly had no special interest in animals and had never taken a course in biology until my last year of graduate work . . . ." (1936, 265). Thorndike's major contribution to the field was in the establishment of relatively precise experimental methods in the study of behavior. Thorndike set specific tasks for animals to learn and made precise measurements of their progress. His dissertation on the learning of cats to escape from puzzle boxes is a true classic. Thorndike developed the "law of exercise" and the "law of effect" as the basis of learning. He believed that a single process underlies learning and that species differences in learning lie in the facility with which each species forms such connections—a quantitative theory of intelligence. After World War I Thorndike confined his efforts almost exclusively to the psychology of humans.

Thorndike has been called "the most productive psychologist our country has produced" (Woodworth, 1952, 209). His full bibliography contains over five hundred titles including some fifty books; fifty of the titles were published after his retirement. His honors were legion, including membership in the National Academy of Sciences, three honorary LL.D. degrees, and four honorary Sc.D. degrees. He was president of the American Psychological Association in 1912 and of the American Association for the Advancement of Science in 1934. Zusne (1975, 315) called Thorndike "the first psychologist to study animal behavior experimentally in a laboratory."

Sources: Bitterman, 1969; Gates, 1949; Goodenough, 1950; Gottlieb, 1979; Hilgard, 1978; Humphrey, 1949; Joncich, 1968; Murchison, 1932; NCAB, 1969; Thorndike, 1936; Woodworth, 1952; Zusne, 1975.

OTTO LEIF TINKLEPAUGH
Born: Kalkaska, Michigan, August 18, 1894
Died: Details on death not available.

Tinklepaugh attended the University of California, Berkeley, receiving an A.B. degree in 1923, an A.M. degree in 1924, and the Ph.D. degree in 1927. He then went to Yale University where he began a long association with Yerkes and the Yale primate laboratories.

Tinklepaugh was interested in a variety of problems in comparative psychology. His doctoral dissertation, directed by E. C. Tolman and Warner Brown and with the aid of early suggestions from Köhler, was an attempt to demonstrate ideational representative factors in problem solving by monkeys. He continued his work on complex processes at the Yale laboratories (for example, Tinklepaugh 1932b). He was also interested in reproductive behavior and published research on the behavioral aspects of parturition in rhesus macaques (Tinklepaugh and Hartman, 1930). He also published work on maze learning in turtles, a vaginal plug in chimpanzees, the fetal heart rate of monkeys, and self-mutilation in monkeys.

Tinklepaugh contributed chapters on the social psychology of animals to the 1934 and 1942 editions of Moss's *Comparative Psychology;* he also wrote the chapter "Gifted Animals" for the 1934 edition.

Source: Murchison, 1932.

CARL JOHN WARDEN
Born: Hamilton, Missouri, March 18, 1890
Died: Deland, Florida, February 18, 1961

Carl J. Warden received an A.B. degree from Cotner College in 1915 and an M.A. degree from the University of Nebraska in 1916. He then attended Columbia University, where he completed his doctorate in 1922. After spending a year at the University of Wisconsin in 1923/1924, he returned to Columbia, where he served on the faculty until his retirement in 1955.

Warden's primary contributions to comparative psychology relate to his research, historical writings, and textbook preparation. He is best known for his work with the Columbia Obstruction Box in an effort to quantify drives and their relative strengths. He was also interested in perception, as in his study of illusions in ring doves, imitation, and comparative intelligence. Schneck and Warden (1929) reviewed available data on retention in animals. Warden was the first comparative psychologist (excluding S. J. Holmes) to write extensively on the history of comparative psychology — thus making much easier the job of later students of history. His journal papers on history (for example, 1927a, 1928) tended to be reprinted in books (for example, Warden, 1927b; Warden et al., 1935).

The three-volume *Comparative Psychology: A Comprehensive Treatise,* coauthored with L.H. Warner and T. N. Jenkins, was a major effort at coordinating the facts and theories of comparative psychology available at that time. W. C. Allee (1936, 295) wrote, "There is, however, nothing in print known to me which so completely and fairly appraises the historical combined with the general biological background of behavior."

Warden was a strong devotee of the experimental method and a skeptic of the anecdote, as he made clear in a sharply worded review in the *New Republic* (1927c). He wrote, "The attitude of the modern comparative psychologist is one of healthy skepticism toward supposed cases of animal genius and human-like levels of animal intelligence" (Warden and Warner, 1928, 1).

Sources: Murchison, 1932; *New York Times,* March 1, 1961; Zusne, 1975.

LUCIEN HAYES WARNER
Born: Irvington, New York, September 9, 1900
Died: Las Vegas, Nevada, 1963

Lucien H. Warner received an A.B. degree from Oberlin College in 1921 and attended Peking University during 1922/1923. He attended graduate school at Columbia University, completing the Ph.D. in 1926. Between 1926 and 1941, Warner served on the faculty of New York University, was a National Research Council Fellow, did research in Switzerland, and served on the faculty of Duke University. Subsequently, he worked mainly in business — with the Opinion Research Corporation, the Office of War Information, *Life* magazine, and the Claremont Graduate School.

Warner's primary contributions to comparative psychology relate to his days at Columbia and shortly thereafter. He was a coauthor of the monumental *Comparative Psychology: A Comprehensive Treatise* — a three-volume survey of comparative psychology. His research centered on studies with the Columbia Obstruction Box and animal sensory function. Warner had diverse interests, writing integrative review papers on bird orientation, facts and theories of bird flight, and color vision in fishes. He also contributed to the development of methods for training seeing-eye dogs.

Sources: Murchison, 1932; Zusne, 1975.

MARGARET FLOY WASHBURN
Born: New York, New York, July 25, 1871
Died: Poughkeepsie, New York, October 29, 1939

Margaret Floy Washburn was graduated with an A.B. from Vassar College in 1891. She then went to Columbia to work with Cattell but, despite

Cattell's efforts, was unable to enroll because of her gender. By special dispensation, she was permitted to enroll as a "hearer" and thus was a pioneer in efforts to secure educational opportunities for women. Washburn then went to Cornell and was awarded an A.M. degree in absentia by Vassar for her work at Cornell. She completed her doctorate under E. B. Titchener in 1894—the first Ph.D. candidate that Titchener recommended. She then spent six years at Wells College, two years as Warden of Sage College at Cornell, and a year at the University of Cincinnati. She then returned to Vassar in 1903 as an associate professor of philosophy and later as Vassar's first psychology professor and head of the department of psychology. She became emeritus professor of psychology in 1937.

Washburn is best known in comparative psychology for her textbook, *The Animal Mind,* which was first published in 1908 and revised in 1917, 1926, and 1936. It was the standard textbook in comparative psychology for twenty-five years. She felt a great sense of love for animals but did relatively little empirical research in animal behavior (for example, Washburn and Bentley, 1906). Washburn published more than two hundred articles. One of her most important contributions was a book, *Movement and Mental Imagery* (1916), in which she broke away from the Titchenerian tradition and proposed a motor theory of consciousness.

She was active in the editing of journals and in professional organizations. Washburn was elected to the National Academy of Sciences in 1931—the second woman to be so honored. In 1927 the *American Journal of Psychology* issued a "Washburn Commemorative Volume" containing articles by thirty-one psychologists. She served as president of the American Psychological Association in 1921.

Sources: Dallenbach, 1940; Hilgard, 1978; Martin, 1940; Murchison, 1932; NCAB, 1943; Pillsbury, 1940: Washburn, 1932; Zusne, 1975.

JOHN BROADUS WATSON
Born: Greenville, South Carolina, January 9, 1878
**Died: New York, New York (NCAB 1965; Zusne 1975) or Woodbury,
    Connecticut (Woodworth, 1959), September 25, 1958**

After growing up in Greenville, South Carolina, John Watson remained there to go to school, graduating from Furman University with an A.M. degree in 1900. He then went to graduate school at the University of Chicago, where he completed the Ph.D. degree in 1903. His dissertation, *Animal Education* (1903), was perceived immediately as an important piece of research. Watson remained on the faculty at Chicago until 1908, when he moved to Johns Hopkins. Upon revelation of his extramarital affair with Rosalie Raynor and his subsequent divorce, Watson was forced to resign from Johns Hopkins in 1920. He spent most of the rest of his career as a very successful advertising executive.

Watson's contributions to comparative psychology were early and substantial. His dissertation was a developmental study that mixed physiological techniques and analysis of sensory function. His field-work on the behavior of noddy and sooty terns on the Dry Tortugas represents excellence in careful observation and description of behavior under natural condition. His experiments on homing were classics. Watson's text *Behavior: An Introduction to Comparative Psychology* (1914) should be read by all students of comparative psychology; it cries for a reprinted edition. Watson studied imitation in monkeys, completed an early study of pheromones in rats, worked with Yerkes on methodology for the study of color vision, and considered kinesthetic cues in learning.

Watson is best known as the "founder" of behaviorism. During the later part of his academic career, Watson emphasized the study of human behavior, became an extreme environmentalist, and stressed peripheral control of behavior. It is the early Watson with whom the comparative psychologist will feel comfortable.

Watson edited the *Journal of Animal Behavior* and *Behavior Monographs* (1911-1917); the *Psychological Review* (1911-1915); and the *Journal of Experimental Psychology* (1916-1926). He served as president of the American Psychological Association in 1915 and received an honorary LL.D. degree from Furman in 1919.

Sources: Bergmann, 1956; Broadhurst, 1968; Buckley, 1982; Cohen, 1979*; Herrnstein, 1973; Hilgard, 1978; Larson and Sullivan, 1965; Murchison, 1932; NCAB, 1926, 1965; Skinner, 1959; Watson, 1936; Woodworth, 1959; Zusne, 1975.

ROBERT MEARNS YERKES
Born: Breadysville, Pennsylvania, May 26, 1876
Died: New Haven, Connecticut, February 3, 1956

Robert Mearns Yerkes received an A.B. degree from Ursinus College in 1897 and proceeded to Harvard, where he received an A.B. degree in 1898, and an A.M. degree in 1899, and a Ph.D. degree in 1902. He remained on the faculty at Harvard, where he founded the laboratory in comparative psychology. Yerkes played a major role in mobilizing psychologists for service in World War I and remained in Washington, D.C. after the war for continued administrative service. Although he accepted a position at the University of Minnesota as the war broke out, he never worked there. Yerkes moved to Yale in 1924. He remained affiliated with Yale, becoming an emeritus professor in 1944.

---

*It should be noted that the Cohen biography of Watson is controversial among historians of psychology. Several scholars have criticized the book for a variety of errors and misrepresentations (see Henderson, 1981; Harris, 1981; Levy, 1981; Larson, 1981; Samelson, 1981).

Yerkes contributed to comparative psychology in many ways over his long career in the field. His original research was pioneering and influential Yerkes's *The Dancing Mouse* (1907) was a classic and one of the earliest studies in behavior genetics and related matters. He studied a wide range of species including earthworms, crabs, frogs, turtles, mice, rats and many species of primates. Hilgard (1965) lists three major areas in which Yerkes made research contributions: sensory receptibility, habit formation, and problem solving. Yerkes studied sensory function in various species, and his work with frogs (1903) and in developing methods for the study of color vision (Yerkes and Watson, 1911) were particularly important. His studies of learning in diverse species came at a time when pioneering efforts were especially important (for example, Yerkes, 1901, 1902, 1903). Yerkes studied problem solving throughout his life and in places as diverse as Franklin, New Hampshire, New Haven, Orange Park, Havana, Sarasota, Florida, and Montecito, California. A fourth area should be added to Hilgard's list: Yerkes's contributions to the study of instinctive behavior equaled his other efforts. Particularly important were his studies of sexual behavior in primates (for example, Yerkes, 1939; Yerkes and Elder, 1936) but his studies of social behavior, maternal behavior, and related behavioral patterns in primates (for example, 1943*b*) and his study of "savageness" in rats (1913*b*) also merit recognition.

Yerkes excelled as an administrator and facilitator of the research of others. It was he who stimulated Bingham, Carpenter, and Nissen to conduct the first systematic field studies of primate behavior. He managed to build laboratories at Harvard, Franklin, New Hampshire, Yale, and Orange Park and to use other facilities effectively. He always had first-rate scientists working with him and facilitated their efforts. He was important in the war efforts associated with both world wars, and his service on the National Research Council Committee for Research in Problems of Sex was of considerable service to comparative psychology and other disciplines. Yerkes wrote several books and edited the *Journal of Animal Behavior* (1911-1917) and the *Journal of Comparative Psychology* (1921-1943).

Robert Yerkes was elected president of the American Psychological Association in 1917 and of the American Society of Naturalists in 1938. He was elected to the National Academy of Sciences in 1923. Yerkes received honorary degrees from Ursinus and Wesleyan. According to Hilgard (1965), Russian scientists honored him by placing his bust in the Darwinian Museum in Moscow.

No one made a more substantial and more sustained contribution to comparative psychology than Robert Mearns Yerkes.

Sources: Carmichael, 1957; Elliott, 1956; Evans, 1975; Hahn, 1971; Hilgard, 1965, 1978; Murchison, 1932; Yerkes, 1932*a;* Zusne, 1975.

OTHERS

There are many other excellent scientists whose contributions touched on comparative psychology but were judged less appropriate than others for inclusion in the biographical sketches just presented. Generally, they were excluded because their primary contributions lay elsewhere. In keeping with the attempt to make this book, in part, a sourcebook, some relevant references are listed below:

Allee, Warder Clyde (Schmidt, 1957)
Berlyne, Daniel E. (Furedy and Furedy, 1979; Konecni, 1978)
Bindra, Dalbir (Ferguson, 1981)
Birch, Herbert G. (Irvine, 1973)
Carr, Harvey A. (Carr, 1936; Koch, 1955; Pillsbury, 1955)
Craig, Wallace (Schorger, 1954)
Crozier, William John (Hoagland and Mitchell, 1956)
Donaldson, Henry Herbert (Dallenbach, 1938; McMurrich and Jackson, 1938)
Franz, Shepherd Ivory (Franz, 1932)
Groos, K. (Groos, 1932)
Hebb, Donald Olding (Hebb, 1980)
Herrick, Charles Judson (Bartelmez, 1960)
Jennings, Herbert Spencer (Schneirla, 1947)
Krech, David (Ghiselli, 1978)
Louttit, Chauncy McKinley (Dallenbach, 1956b; Carter, 1956)
Loeb, Jacques (Palmer, 1929)
Muenzinger, Karl F. (Krech, 1959)
Pavlov, Ivan P. (Babkin, 1949; Gantt, 1973; Konorski, 1949; Liddell, 1936)
Tolman, Edward C. (Crutchfield, 1961)
Twitmyer, Edwin Burket (Fernberger, 1943; Irwin, 1943; NCAB, 1947)
Werner, Heinz (Wapner and Kaplan, 1965; Witkin, 1965)
Yoakum, Clarence S. (Bingham, 1946; Pillsbury, 1946)
Young, Paul Thomas (O'Kelly, 1979)

Chapter 9
_____

Conclusion

I began by delineating the widely held image of comparative psychology as a human-oriented, laboratory-based, nonevolutionary study of trivial behavioral patterns in a few domesticated species. In the most common portrayal of its history, comparative psychology is perceived as originating with the efforts of some outstanding pioneers in the nineteenth and early twentieth centuries and beginning a period of decline somewhere in the 1920s, only to be rescued by the development of core ethology.

I have attempted to replace this picture with one that I believe more closely matches reality. Comparative psychologists have not always looked to human behavior for their justification, have not confined themselves to the laboratory, have often considered evolutionary questions, and have studied a wide variety of species. There is a strong continuity in the history of comparative psychology from its early pioneers (for example, Morgan, Baldwin, Mills, Small, Kline, and Thorndike) to its early developers (for example, Watson, Yerkes, and Washburn) through its mainstays during much of the century (for example, Lashley, Stone, Schneirla, Nissen, Warden, Carpenter, Beach, Harlow, and Lehrman) and into the current group of younger comparative psychologists. The period from the late 1920s through the 1940s was a time of great activity in comparative psychology with some excellent research being completed and published. In essence, comparative psychology, viewed as a broad, biologically based study of behavior as conducted by psychologists, has a history in the twentieth century that is long, continuous, and worthy of pride.

These conclusions follow in part form the definition of comparative psychology adopted here in Chapter 1. Accordingly comparative psychology was differentiated from the broader "animal psychology" by the exclusion of process-oriented learning studies and much physiological psychology. The prevalent image of comparative psychology stems in part from the lumping together of these diverse enterprises. It is true that through much of the period of 1930 through 1955 animal psychology was dominated by the study of rat learning. However, it is also true that along with that highly visible development, the comparative tradition lived on and thrived, although on a somewhat more modest scale. It is that continuous thread of the comparative tradition that provides the historical continuity for comparative psychology. If this phase of our history did not involve a large number of scientists, neither did early ethology.

Are we justified in excluding process-oriented learning studies for the corpus of comparative psychology? Many workers, including the editors of some standard works in the field (for example, Moss, 1934, 1942; Stone, 1951) did not make that differentiation. Some individuals worked in both traditions (for example, Tolman and Spence). Nevertheless, the comparative psychology of Lashley, Stone, Schneirla, Nissen, Warden, Carpenter, Beach, Harlow, and Lehrman is clearly distinct from process-oriented studies of learning. The enterprises differ with respect to their historical roots, the goals of the research, the methods and animals used and the kind of generalizations drawn form the data. The American Psychological Association has now recognized the existence of three different areas and will be publishing three different journals: one for physiological psychology, one for process-oriented learning studies, and one for comparative psychology. In differentiating comparative psychology from these approaches, it should not be inferred that the other approaches are not scientifically valid but, instead, that they are different and should be evaluated using criteria that are different and appropriate to their methods and aims. Comparative psychology is one intact area with a rich and distinctive tradition of its own.

THE TEN MYTHS REVISITED

I can now return to the ten myths about comparative psychology that were discussed in Chapter 1. It is argeud that the portrayal of comparative psychology summarized in these myths results in part from confusing the comparative tradition in Psychology with other related traditions and in part because material regarding the history on comparative psychology has been so scattered that its essential unity has not been apparent. The ten myths may appear to be but a straw man. However, I have endeavored to show in Chapter 1 that they summarize aspects of the perception of comparative psychology that are, in fact, widely held.

Myth 1. The Rationale for Comparative Psychology Stems Directly from a Human Orientation.

The difference between a comparative psychology whose justification is derived from its relevance to human problems versus one designed to work toward a broad understanding of behavior without special reference to humans was clearly elaborated by Wundt (1894). Some comparative psychology, such as the study of abnormal behavior in animals, is oriented toward human application. However, the vast majority of comparative psychologists study animals without direct application to problems of human behavior as their primary concern. Extrapolations to human behavior are relatively rare in papers in comparative psychology.

Warden et al. (1935, 26) noted that C. L. Morgan "maintained the right of the investigator to study the activities of animals for their own sake." Later they repeated the point, noting that it was recognized by "even so conservative a writer as Wundt" (1935, 54). Maier and Schneirla (1935, 6) noted that "the emphasis of practical application . . . is the long route to scientific progress." Lehrman (1971, 465) noted that "the animal itself poses problems to the investigator independent of their usefulness in understanding human life." Beach (1950, 115) noted the legitimacy of comparisons between humans and other species but proposed that "comparisons between two or more non-human species are equally admissible." According to Beach (1960, 2), "animals are not to be used as substitutes for people, and the kinds of problems investigated are not to be exclusively or even principally derived from human behavior or psychology."

Myth 2. Psychologists Lack the Aesthetic Sense and Love for Animals that Characterize Ethology.

It is certainly true that many psychologists study animals for intellectual reasons rather than for the love of animals or because of an appreciation for the aesthetic aspect of animals' behavior (for example, Thorndike, 1936). However, there are many comparative psychologists who have expressed these aspects of their approach too.

Margaret Floy Washburn (1932, 347) noted that she possessed "an almost morbidly intense love for animals." Bingham (1932, 58) quoted William Cullen Bryant's *Thanatopis*, "To him who in the love of nature holds communion with her visible forms, she speaks a various language." Thorpe (1979, 46) noted that Lashley "had in fact been an enthusiastic naturalist and pet-keeper as a boy and this attitude had animated his work on terns." Lashley (1947) waxed poetic regarding the beauty of the webs of orb-weaving spiders. Kuo (1967, 14) noted, "I have been a bird-watcher since childhood." Beach (in Fleming and Maxey, 1975, 72) noted that he had "sat up all night with more than one operated dog. You are a human being before you are a scientist, and human beings are empathetic by nature."

Lott (in Klopfer and Hailman, 1972, 274) speculated on the role that his birth and early rearing on the National Bison Range "where buffalo really roam and deer and antelope really play" might have had on his later research interests. In the same volume Klopfer and Hailman noted that Gilbert Gottlieb and his wife raise various species of waterfowl at their country home by way of combining work with pleasure. Carpenter's work was accomplished with an aesthetic appreciation of his animals. He called gibbons "beautiful animals" and noted that "their movements through the trees are awe-inspiring" (in Price, 1968, 92). Menzel (1967, 170) noted that he "would *like* to be called a naturalist first and an experimentalist second" and noted that he had "been bitten by the bug of field work" (1967, 184).

An appreciation for animals and an aesthetic sense were part of the "natural history orientation" that characterized the work of Schneirla and Lehrman (Beer, 1975; Lehrman, 1971). This is especially apparent in Lehrman's paper "Behavior Science, Engineering, and Poetry" (1971). According to Lehrman, "It is absolutely commonplace . . . among natural-history-oriented students of animal behavior that they entered the scientific profession as the continuing expression of a boyhood or girlhood fascination with the behavior of particular kinds of animals" (1971, 464). Lehrman noted the "emotional charge" that can be derived from the appreciation of the animal and the existence of its own. He noted:

> Feelings of this kind have, for the observer, more in common with the feelings involved in watching a sunset or reading a poem than they do with those involved in solving engineering problems, or in abstracting formalized general relationships from narrowly defined operations of experimenter and subject. (1971, 64)

Myth 3. Comparative Psychologists Are Not Concerned with the Study of Evolution.

The importance of the study of evolution in comparative psychology has been emphasized so repeatedly in this book that no detailed repetition is required here. It will be recalled that the very origins of comparative psychology were based on the work of Darwin (for example 1859, 1871, 1873*a*) and the attempts of the early anecdotalists (for example, Romanes, 1882, 1883) to demonstrate mental continuity between humans and nonhumans. The theory of evolution, far from being resisted in psychology, swept through it (Angell, 1909; Baldwin, 1909; Howard, 1927). The facts and theories of evolution have repeatedly been summarized by psychologists (for example, Hall, 1908; Watson, 1914; Stone, 1943; Hodos and Campbell, 1969; LeBoeuf, 1978). Psychologists have repeatedly organized and participated in symposia on the evolution of behavior (for example, Roe and Simpson, 1958; Masterton et al., 1976*a*, 1976*b*). Contributions to evolutionary thinking were made by Baldwin (1896*c*), Gurley (1902), Skinner (1966), and others. The study of evolution and particular classes of behavior has been advanced by such workers as Bitterman (1965*a* 1965*b*), Harlow (1958*b*), Beach (1942*b*, 1947*a*, 1958, 1967), Thompson (1958), Jerison (1970, 1973), Yerkes (1933*a*), among others.

Myth 4. Comparative Psychologists Confine Themselves to Artificial Laboratory Situations Rather Than the Field.

As with the study of evolution, the role of psychologists in field research has been emphasized repeatedly throughout this book. Author after author has emphasized the importance of field research (for example, Kuo, 1967; Menzel, 1967; Mason, 1968*a*; Carpenter, 1964; Kinnaman, 1902*a*; Davis, 1907; Hall, 1908; Watson in Cohen, 1979; Warden et al., 1935; Stone, 1947; Miller, 1977*a*).

The field research of Watson was a deserved classic in the comparative psychology/ethology field (Watson, 1907*a*, 1908*b*, 1910*a*, 1915; Watson and Lashley, 1915). Under Yerkes's guidance, Nissen (1931), Bingham (1932), and Carpenter (1934) launched the modern study of primates in the field. Schneirla made some fifteen trips for field research on the behavior of ants (see Aronson et al., 1972). Recent fieldworkers have included Altmann (1952), Gottlieb, (1963*a*), Hess (1972), Mason (1968*b*), Bernstein (1967), Menzel (1966), Snowden (Snowden and Hodun, 1981), Petrinovitch (Petrinovitch et al., 1979), Lockard (1975), Glickman (1980), Lott (1974), LeBoeuf (1974), Gustavson (1982), and others.

Myth 5. Comparative Psychologists Study a Limited Range of Species.

The range of species studies by comparative psychologists was explored in Chapter 5. Many studies in comparative psychology have been conducted using laboratory rats as subjects. However, as revealed in Chapter 5, a wide range of invertebrate and vertebrate species drawn from diverse taxa have also been used. Yerkes alone worked on earthworms, crayfish, crabs, frogs, turtles, crows, mice, pigs, monkeys, gorillas, chimpanzees, and orangutans. Glickman and Sroges (1966) studied over a hundred species in their research on curiosity. Some forty-three species of muroid rodents have been studied in my laboratory alone (for example, Dewsbury, 1975). A review of material on just learning in only invertebrates required three volumes (Corning et al., 1973). The role of paramecia, planarians, earthworms, octopuses, fishes, frogs, many species of birds, cats, raccoons, and may species of primates has surfaced repeatedly throughout this book. Comparative psychologists have truly studied a wide range of species.

Myth 6. Comparative Psychologists Study Only Domesticated Species.

As should be apparent from both Chapter 5 and the discussion of myth 5, comparative psychologists have not confined themselves to studying only domesticated species. It is also worth noting, however, that comparative psychologists have been leaders in studying the effects of domestication on behavior (for example, Small, 1901; Yerkes, 1913b; Stone, 1932b; Richter, 1954; Boice, 1973, 1980; Miller, 1977a 1977b). Many studies in comparative psychology have been done on laboratory rats, chickens, cats, and dogs. These convenient species that are quite appropriate for certain kinds of research. However, comparative psychologists have also studied an impressive menagerie of nondomesticated species as well.

Myth 7. Comparative Psychologists Fail to Compare Closely Related Species.

It is true that comparative psychologists have been more likely to make comparisons at what King (1963) calls the "phyletic" level than at what he terms the "species level" (that is, comparisons among closely related species). It is not true, however, that *all* comparative psychologists have confined their efforts to the phyletic level. Among the exceptions are the work of Watson on noddy and sooty terns (Watson, 1908b; Watson and Lashley, 1915); Schneirla on doryline ants (Schneirla, 1957b); Gottlieb on imprinting in ducks (Gottlieb, 1963a, 1963b); Dewsbury on copulatory behavior of muroid rodents (Dewsbury, 1975); Mason on social behavior in New-World primates (Mason, 1976b); and Rosenblum (1971) on behavioral development in macaques.

Myth 8. Comparative Psychologists Are Preoccupied with Instrumentation.

Instrumentation can be both a great labor saver and a method of ensuring objectivity in the conduct of experiments and recording data. In some learning problems (for example, Bitterman, 1960), in the study of complex tasks (for example, Rumbaugh and Gill, 1976), and in other situations, computers and complex apparatus can be invaluable. The student of color vision, for example, needs to exercise great care in choosing stimuli (for example, Yerkes and Watson, 1911). In an era in which computers can be a great labor-saving aid, it is inappropriate to disparage the use of complex equipment where available and applicable.

The fact is, however, that most significant research in the history of comparative psychology has been conducted with relatively little equipment. In virtually all the field studies, observational techniques with relatively little equipment have proved the method. Schneirla, Carpenter, Watson and others worked with relatively little equipment. Laboratory researchers such as Beach, Stone, Lehrman, Yerkes, Nissen, and Lashley generally confined their animals in relatively simple enclosures and made their primary contributions through careful description and reporting of their behavior. Complex equipment has been used to a far greater extent in physiological psychology and in process-oriented-learning research than in comparative psychology.

The avoidance of complex equipment, when applicable, is not a virtue. In my opinion, comparative psychologists should strive to combine the advantages of manipulations and observations by skilled, sensitive observers with the advantages of objectivity and efficiency can be gained with complex equipment.

Myth 9. Psychologists Rarely Begin Their Studies with Description.

Comparative psychologists have long recognized the need for descriptive studies. Kline (1899b, 399) noted that "a careful study of the instincts, dominant traits and habits of an animal as expressed in its free life—in brief its natural history—should precede as far as possible any experimental study." Mills (1899, 267) noted that "at the present stage of comparative psychology we are in need of observations down to the minutest details." Warden et al. (1935, 154) noted that "observations and experiment must go hand in hand." Watson (1910b, 348) noted that as a first step in the study of behavior, we should take our animals into the laboratory and "watch the gradual way in which their instinctive life develops." Yerkes (1908, 274) praised Jennings's work because "he is able to describe their movements accurately and in considerable detail." Topoff (1976, 65) stressed that it is important that we "observe the behavior of the species under study in the field environment." For Harlow (1953, 29) "A key to the real learning theory of any animal species is knowledge of the nature and organization of the unlearned patterns of response."

Again and again these attitudes have been translated into action. The importance of description in the study of behavior can be seen in the observations of Yerkes, Nissen, and their associates on primate social and reproductive behavior; Schneirla in his studies of ants; Lashley, Stone, Beach and Schneirla in their studies of reproductive behavior in mammals; Carpenter and others in their field studies of primates; and Mills, Small, and Watson in their studies of behavioral development. The descriptions of Watson (1908b) of the behavior of terns provides as fine an example of the role of description in the study of behavior as can be found anywhere in the literature on animal behavior.

Myth 10. Psychologists Confine Their Studies to Learning Rather Than to a Wide Range of Ecologically Relevant Behavior.

Repeatedly throughout this book, and particularly in Chapter 6, I have discussed the wide range of behavioral patterns studied by comparative psychologists. Among the patterns of individual behavior that have been studied are orientation, activity, locomotion, ingestive behavior, hoarding, nest building, exploration, play, tonic immobility, handedness, the setting reaction, hibernation, thermoregulation, predation, elimination, and tool use. In the study of reproductive behavior, comparative psychologists have worked with courtship, mating, and parental behavior in a wide range of species (for example, Dewsbury, 1972, 1981; Bermant and Davidson, 1974). Students of social behavior have analyzed grooming, dominance, communication, social organization, social facilitation, affiliation, aggression, cooperation, and competition.

Among the many comparative psychologists who have emphasized the importance of breadth in the study of behavior, Yerkes, Lashley, and Schneirla provide outstanding examples. In outlining the kind of study Yerkes wanted at his proposed primate center, Yerkes included:

(1) systematic and continuous studies of important forms of behavior, of mind, and of social relations; (2) similar studies of physiological activities, normal and pathological, with adequate provision for medical research; (3) studies of heredity (genetics), life history, embryology; (4) research in comparative anatomy, including gross anatomy, histology, neurology and pathology. (1916b, 232)

This kind of breadth was brought to reality when Yerkes finally got his experimental station (for example, 1943*b*).

In his letter to Calvin Stone of March 21, 1920, Lashley suggested possible dissertation topics to the returning graduate student. These included the comparative anatomy and physiology of the sense organs; effects of drugs, diet and so on on learning; experimental control of instinctive behavior; physiology of the nervous system in relation to learning; and general functional anatomy of the brain. Within each of these catagories Lashley had more detailed suggestions for possible lines of research (Beach, 1961).

In writing of Schneirla's approach to the study of army ants, Lehrman noted that Schneirla considered

> the widest possible range of aspects of the army ant's nature and existence; its external morphology, its use of individual experience, its sensory capacities, its learning abilities, its modes of neural integration, its behavioral ontogeny, its reproductive physiology, its ecological relationships to the environment, the functional accomplishments of its behavior, its evolutionary relationships to other kinds of ants and other families and phyla of animals. He integrated all these considerations into a marvelously detailed, richly articulated, deeply explanatory picture of the behavioral events in the life of this creature. (1971, 469)

The ten myths about comparative psychology did not develop in a vacuum. They are representative of the work of some animal psychologists in some areas at some times. However, they provide an inaccurate picture of comparative psychology throughout its history. Comparative psychology has been and is a broadly based approach to the study of animal behavior in broad biological context.

References

Aberle, S. D., and G. W. Corner, 1953, *Twenty-Five Years of Sex Research,* Saunders, Philadelphia.

Adams, D. K., 1928, The Inference of Mind, *Psychological Review* **35**:235-252.

Adams, D. K., 1929, Experimental Studies of Adaptive Behavior in Cats, *Comparative Psychology Monographs* **6**(27), 166p.

Adams, D. K., 1939, William McDougall, *Psychological Review* **46**:1-8.

Adler, H. E., 1970, Ontogeny and Phylogeny of Orientation, *in Development and Evolution of Behavior,* L. R. Aronson, E. Tobach, D. S. Lehrman, and J. S. Rosenblatt, eds., Freeman, San Francisco, pp. 303-336.

Adler, H. E., 1980, Historical Dialectics, *American Psychologist,* **35**:956-958.

Adler, H. E. and J. I. Dalland, 1959, Spectral Thresholds in the Starling *(Sturnus vulgaris), Journal of Comparative and Physiological Psychology* **52**:438-445.

Adler, H. E., and E. Tobach, 1971, Comparative Psychology Is Not Dead, *American Psychologist* **26**:857-858.

Adler, L. L., 1973, Contributions of C. Lloyd Morgan to Comparative Psychology, *Annals of the New York Academy of Sciences* **223**:41-48.

Adler, N. T., 1981, *Neuroendocrinology of Reproduction: Physiology and Behavior,* Plenum, New York.

Agar, W. E., F. H. Drummond, O. W. Tiegs, and M. M. Gunson, 1954, Fourth (final) Report on a Test of McDougall's Lamarckian Experiment on the Training of Rats, *Journal of Experimental Biology* **31**:308-321.

Allee, W. C., 1933, Gorillas in a Native Habitat, Ecology **14**:319-320.

Allee, W. C., 1936, A Background for Studies of Behavior, *Ecology* 17:295-298.

Allee, W. C., 1948, Hormones and Behavior: A Survey of Interrelationships between Endocrine Secretions and Patterns of Overt Response by Frank A. Beach, *Physiological Zoology* 21:186-188.

Allee, W. C., 1953, Instinct from the Zoologist's Standpoint, *Psychological Review* 60:287-290.

Allen, J., 1904, The Associative Processes of the Guinea Pig. A Study of the Physical Development of an Animal with a Nervous System Well Medullated at Birth, *Journal of Comparative Neurology and Psychology* 14:294-359.

Altmann, M., 1941a, Interrelations of the Sex Cycle and the Behavior of the Sow, *Journal of Comparative Psychology* 31:481-498.

Altmann, M., 1941b, A study of Patterns of Activity and Neighborly Relations in Swine, *Journal of Comparative Psychology* 31:473-479.

Altmann, M., 1952, Social Behavior of Elk, *Cervus canadensis* Nelsoni, in the Jackson Hole Area of Wyoming, *Behaviour* 4:116-143.

Altmann, M., 1963, Naturalistic Studies of Maternal Care in Moose and Elk, in *Maternal Behavior in Mammals,* H. L. Rheingold, ed., Wiley, New York, pp. 233-253.

American Psychological Association, 1973, *Biographical Directory of the American Psychological Association,* American Psychological Association, Washington, D. C.

Amsel, A., 1982, Behaviorism Then and Now, *Contemporary Psychology* 27:343-346.

Anderson, E. E., 1936, Consistency of Tests of Copulatory Frequency in the Male Albino Rat, *Journal of Comparative Psychology* 21:447-459.

Anderson, E. E., 1937, The Interrelationship of Drives in the Male Albino Rat. II. Intercorrelations between 47 Measures of Drives and of Learning, *Comparative Psychology Monographs* 14(72), 119p.

Andrew, G., and H. F. Harlow, 1948, Performance of Macaque Monkeys on a Test of the Concept of Generalized Triangularity, *Comparative Psychology Monographs* 19(100), 20p.

Angell, J. R., 1909, The Influence of Darwin on Psychology, *Psychological Review* 16:152-169.

Angell, J. R., 1913, Loeb's "The Mechanistic Conception of Life," *Journal of Animal Behavior* 3:464-468.

Angermeier, W. F., L. T. Schaul, and W. T. James, 1959, Social Conditioning in Rats, *Journal of Comparative and Physiological Psychology* 52:370-372.

Annin, E. L., E. G. Boring, and R. I. Watson, 1968, Important Psychologists, 1600-1967, *Journal of the History of the Behavioral Sciences* 4:303-315.

Anonymous, 1910, The Journal of Animal Behavior and the Animal Behavior Monograph Series, *Journal of Comparative Neurology and Psychology,* 20:625-626.

Anonymous, 1915, Dr. Wesley Mills of McGill Staff Dies at Oxford, *Montreal Star,* February 15.

Anonymous, 1916, Announcement of Change in Subscription Price, *Journal of Animal Behavior* 6:374.

Anonymous, 1917, Announcement to Subscribers, *Journal of Animal Behavior,* 7:385.

Anonymous, 1926, Watson, John Broadus, *National Cyclopaedia of American Biography* A:86-87.

Anonymous, 1933, Babe & ape, *Time* 21(25):44.

Anonymous, 1942, Carmichael, Leonard, *National Cyclopaedia of American Biography* F:200-201.

Anonymous, 1943, Washburn, Margaret Floy, *National Cyclopaedia of American Biography* 30:248.

Anonymous, 1947, Twitmyer, Edwin Burket, *National Cyclopaedia of American Biography* 33:193-194.

Anonymous, 1955, Schneirla, T(heodore) C(hristian), *Current Biography Yearbook* pp. 534-535.

Anonymous, 1955, Karl Spencer Lashley, *Science* 121:691-692.

Anonymous, 1958, Editorial, *Animal Behaviour* 6:1-2.

Anonymous, 1958, Hunter, Walter Samuel, *National Cyclopaedia of American Biography* 42:84-85.

Anonymous, 1962, Bentley, (Isaac) Madison, *National Cyclopaedia of American Biography* 45:406-407.

Anonymous, 1962, Lashley, Karl Spencer, *National Cyclopaedia of American Biography* 44:198-199.

Anonymous, 1962, Howard Liddell, 66, Taught Psychology, *New York Times,* November 1, p. 31.

Anonymous, 1963, Kellogg, Winthrop N(iles), *Current Biography Yearbook,* pp. 214-215.

Anonymous, 1964, Dr. Harold Bingham, 76, Dies; Psychologists and V. A. Advisor, *New York Times,* April 27, p. 33.

Anonymous, 1965, Watson, John Broadus, *National Cyclopaedia of American Biography* 48:548-549.

Anonymous, 1965, Major Primate Center Moves to Modern Research Quarters, *JAMA* 193(7):30-31.

Anonymous, 1966/67, Carpenter, Clarence Ray, *Leaders in American Science,* 7:93.

Anonymous, 1968, Dr. Theodore C. Schneirla Dies; Aids in Natural History Unit, *New York Times,* August 21.

Anonymous, 1961, Prof. Carl Warden Dies at 70. Retired Columbia Psychologist, *New York Times,* March 1, p. 33.

Anonymous, 1969, Thorndike, Edward Lee, *National Cyclopaedia of American Biography* 51:209-210.

Anonymous, 1970, Moss, Fred August, *National Cyclopaedia of American Biography* 52:53-54.

Anonymous, 1970, Stone, Calvin Perry, *National Cyclopaedia of American Biography* 52:426-427.

Anonymous, 1972, Daniel Lehrman, Led Rutgers Unit, *New York Times,* August 31.

Anonymous, 1974, Köhler, Wolfgang, *National Cyclopaedia of American Biography* 55:151-152.

Anonymous, 1975, C. R. Carpenter, Psychologist, Monkey-Behavior Expert, Dies, *New York Times,* March 4.

Anonymous, 1977, Norman Maier, 76; Noted Psychologist at University of Michigan, *New York Times,* September 12.

Anonymous, 1978, Thompson, William Robert, *American Men and Women of Science,* 13th ed., Bowker, New York, p. 1197.

Ardilla, R. 1971, The Great Importance of Comparative Psychology in the Training of Psychologists, *American Psychologist* 26:1035-1036.

Aronson, L. R., and E. Tobach, 1972, Preface, In *Selected Writings of T. C. Schneirla,* L. R. Aronson, E. Tobach, J. S. Rosenblatt, and D. S. Lehrman, eds., Freeman, San Francisco, pp. ix-xiv.

Aronson, L. R., E. Tobach, D. S. Lehrman, and J. S. Rosenblatt, eds., 1970, *Development and Evolution of Behavior: Essays in Memory of T. C. Schneirla,* Freeman, San Francisco.

Aronson, L. R., E. Tobach, J. S. Rosenblatt, and D. S. Lehrman, 1972, *Selected Writings of T. C. Schneirla.* Freeman, San Francisco.

Asch, S. E., 1968, Wolfgang, Köhler: 1887-1967, *American Journal of Psychology* 81:110-119.

Avery, G. T., 1925, Notes on Reproduction of Guinea Pigs, *Journal of Comparative Psychology,* 5:373-396.

Bailey, T. P., 1899, Ethological Psychology, Psychological Review 6:649-651.

Baldwin, J. M., 1896*a,* Heredity and Instinct, *Science* 3:438-441.

Baldwin, J. M., 1896*b,* Instinct, *Science* 3:669.

Baldwin, J. M., 1896*c,* A New Factor in Evolution. *American Naturalist* 30:441-451, 536-553.

Baldwin, J. M., 1902, *Development and Evolution,* MacMillan, New York.

Baldwin, J. M., 1906, Addendum to Dr. Watson's Paper, *Psychological Bulletin* 3:149-156.

Baldwin, J. M., 1909, The Influence of Darwin on Theory of Knowledge and Philosophy, *Psychological Review* 16:207-218.

Baldwin, J. M., 1930, James Mark Baldwin, in *A History of Psychology in Autobiography,* vol. 1, Clark University Press, C. Murchison, ed., Worcester, Mass., pp. 1-30.

Balfour, C. E., and L. Carmichael, 1928, The Light Reactions of the Meal Worm (*Tenebrio molitor* Linn), American Journal of Psychology 40:576-584.

Ball, J., 1934*a,* Sex Behavior of the Rat after Removal of the Uterus and Vagina, *Journal of Comparative Psychology* 18:419-422.

Ball, J., 1934*b,* Demonstration of a Quantitative Relation between Stimulus and Response in Pseudopregnancy in the Rat, *American Journal of Physiology* 107:698-703.

Ball, J., 1937*a,* Sex Activity of Castrated Male Rats Increased by Estrin Administration, *Journal of Comparative Psychology* 24:135-144.

Ball, J., 1937*b,* A Test for Measuring Sexual Excitability in the Female Rat, *Comparative Psychology Monographs* 14(67):1-37.

Barash, D. P., 1977*a, Sociobiology and Behavior.* Elsevier, New York.

Barash, D. P., 1977*b,* Sociobiology of Rape in Mallards *(Anas platyrhnchos):* Responses of the Mated Male, *Science* 197:788-789.

Barnes, T. C., and B. F. Skinner, 1930, The Progressive Increase in the Geotropic

Response of the Ant *Aphaenogaster, Journal of General Psychology* 4:102-112.

Bartelmez, G. W., 1960, Charles Judson Herrick, Neurologist, *Science* 131:1654-1655.

Bates, R. L., 1922, The Effects of Cigar and Cigarette Smoking on Certain Psychological and Physiological Functions, *Journal of Comparative Psychology* 2:371-423.

Bawden, H. H., 1906, A Comment on "Objective Nomenclature," *Journal of Comparative Neurology and Psychology* 16:389-390.

Bayroff, A. G., 1939, The Experimental Social Behavior of Animals. II. The Effects of Early Isolation of White Rats on Their Competition in Swimming, *Journal of Comparative Psychology* 29:293-306.

Bayroff, A. G., and K. E. Laird, 1944, Experimental Social Behavior of Animals III. Imitational Learning of White Rats, *Journal of Comparative Psychology* 37:165-171.

Beach, F. A., 1939, Maternal Behavior of the Pouchless Marsupial *Marmosa cinera, Journal of Mammalogy* 20:315-322.

Beach, F. A. 1942a, Analysis of the Stimuli Adequate to Elicit Mating Behavior in the Sexually Inexperienced Male Rat, *Journal of Comparative Psychology* 33:163-207.

Beach, F. A., 1942b, Central Nervous Mechanisms Involved in the Reproductive Behavior of Vertebrates, *Psychological Bulletin* 39:200-226.

Beach, F. A., 1942c, Comparison of Copulatory Behavior of Male Rats Raised in Isolation, Cohabitation, and Segregation, *Journal of Genetic Psychology* 60:121-136.

Beach, F. A., 1942d, Execution of the Complete Masculine Copulatory Pattern by Sexually Receptive Female Rats, *Journal of Genetic Psychology* 60:137-142.

Beach, F. A., 1945a, Current Concepts of Play in Animals, *American Naturalist* 79:523-541.

Beach F. A., 1945b, "Angry" Mosquitoes, *Science* 101:610-611.

Beach, F. A., 1947a, Evolutionary Changes in the Physiological Control of Mating Behavior in Mammals, *Psychological Review* 54:297-315.

Beach, F. A., 1947b, A Review of Physiological and Psychological Studies of Sexual Behavior in Mammals, *Physiological Reviews* 27:240-307.

Beach, F. A., 1948, *Hormones and Behavior,* Harper, New York.

Beach, F. A., 1950, The Snark Was a Boojum, *American Psychologist* 5:115-124.

Beach, F. A.,1955, The Descent of Instinct, *Psychological Review* 62:401-410.

Beach, F. A., 1956, Characteristics of Masculine "Sex Drive," *Nebraska Symposium on Motivation* 4:1-32.

Beach, F. A., 1958, Evolutionary Aspects of Psychoendocrinology, in *Behavior and Evolution,* A. Roe and G. G. Simpson, eds., Yale University Press, New Haven, Conn., pp. 81-102.

Beach, F. A., 1960, Experimental Investigations of Species-Specific Behavior, *American Psychologist* 15:1-18.

Beach, F. A., 1961, Karl Spencer Lashley: 1890-1958, *Biographical Memoirs of the National Academy of Sciences* 35:162-204.

Beach, F. A., ed., 1965, *Sex and Behavior,* Wiley, New York.

Beach, F. A., 1966, The Perpetuation and Evolution of Biological Science, *American Psychologist* 21:943-949.

Beach, F. A., 1967, Cerebral and Hormonal Control of Reflexive Mechanisms Involved in Copulatory Behavior, *Physiological Reviews* 47:289-316.

Beach, F. A., 1973, Daniel S. Lehrman: 1919-1972, *American Journal of Psychology* 86:201-202.

Beach, F. A., 1974, Frank A. Beach, in *A History of Psychology in Autobiography,* vol. 6, G. Lindzey, ed., Prentice-Hall, Englewood Cliffs, N.J., pp. 31-58.

Beach, F. A., 1975, Behavioral Endocrinology: An Emerging Discipline, *American Scientist* 63:178-187.

Beach, F. A., 1978a, Sociobiology and Interspecific Comparisons of Behavior, in *Sociobiology and Human Nature,* M. S. Gregory, A. Silvers, and D. Sutch, eds., Jossey-Bass, San Francisco, pp. 116-135.

Beach, F. A., 1978b, Confessions of an Imposter, in *Pioneers in Neuroendocrinology II,* J. Meites, B. T. Donovan, and S. M. McCann, eds., Plenum, New York, pp. 19-35.

Beach, F. A., 1979, Animal Models and Psychological Inference, in *Human Sexuality: A Comparative and Developmental Perspective,* H. A. Katchadourian, ed., University of California Press, Berkeley, pp. 98-112.

Beach, F. A., 1981, Historical Origins of Modern Research in Hormones and Behavior, *Hormones and Behavior,* 15:325-376.

Beach, F. A., and R. W. Gilmore, 1949, Response of Male Dogs to Urine from Females in Heat, *Journal of Mammalogy* 30:391-392.

Beach, F. A., and J. Jaynes, 1954, Effects of Early Experience upon the Behavior of Animals, *Psychological Bulletin* 51:239-263.

Beach, F. A., and L. Jordan, 1956, Sexual Exhaustion and Recovery in the Male Rat, *Quarterly Review of Biology* 8:121-133.

Beach, F. A., and R. E. Whalen, 1959, Effects of Ejaculation on Sexual Behavior in the Male Rat, *Journal of Comparative and Physiological Psychology* 52:249-254.

Beach, F. A., and A. Zitrin, 1945, Induction of Mating Activity in Male Cats, *Annals of the New York Academy of Science* 46:42-44.

Beach, F. A., D. O. Hebb, C. T. Morgan, and H. W. Nissen, eds., 1960, *The Neuropsychology of Lashley: Selected Papers of K. S. Lashley,* McGraw-Hill, New York.

Beer, C. G., 1963, Ethology—The Zoologists's Approach to Behavior, *Tuatara* 11:170-177.

Beer, C. G., 1973a, Species-Typical Behavior and Ethology, in *Comparative Psychology: A Modern Survey,* D. A. Dewsbury and D. A. Rethlingshafer, eds., McGraw-Hill, New York, pp. 21-77.

Beer, C. G., 1973b, *Daniel Sanford Lehrman, Auk* 90:485-486.

Beer, C. G., 1975, Was Professor Lehrman an Ethologist? *Animal Behaviour* 23:957-964.

Beer, C. G., 1980, Perspectives on Animal Behavior Comparisons, in *Comparative Methods in Psychology,* M. H. Bornstein, ed., Erlbaum, Hillsdale, N.J., pp. 17-64.

Bell, J. C., 1906, The Reactions of Crayfish to Chemical Stimuli, *Journal of Comparative Neurology and Psychology* 16:323-326.

Benjamin, L. T., Jr., and D. Bruce, 1982, From Bottle-Fed Chimp to Bottlenose

Dolphin: A Contemporary Appraisal of Winthrop Kellogg, *Psychological Record* 32:461-482.

Bennett, E. L., M. C. Diamond, D. Krech, and M. R. Rosenzweig, 1964, Chemical and Anatomical Plasticity of Brain, *Science* 146:610-619.

Bennett, S., and E. G. Boring, 1954, Psychological Necrology (1928-1952), *Psychological Bulletin* 51:75-81.

Bentley, M., 1936, Madison Bentley, in *A History of Psychology in Autobiography,* vol. 3, C. Murchison, ed., Clark University Press, Worcester, Mass., pp. 53-67.

Bergmann, G., 1956, The Contribution of John B. Watson, *Psychological Review* 63:265-276.

Berlyne, D. E., 1955, The Arousal and Satiation of Perceptual Curiosity in the Rat, *Journal of Comparative and Physiological Psychology* 48:238-246.

Berlyne, D. E., 1960, *Conflict, Arousal and Curiosity,* McGraw-Hill, New York.

Bermant, G., 1965, Modern Courses in Comparative Psychology, Paper presented at meetings of the American Association for the Advancement of Science, Berkeley, Calif., December.

Bermant G., ed., 1973, *Perspectives on Animal Behavior,* Scott, Foresman, Glenview, Ill.

Bermant, G., and J. M. Davidson, 1974, *Biological Bases of Sexual Behavior,* Harper & Row, New York.

Bermant, G., and N. E. Gary, 1966, Discrimination Training and Reversal in Groups of Honey Bees, *Psychonomic Science* 5:179-180.

Bermant, G., M. T. Clegg, and W. Beamer, 1969, Copulatory Behavior of the Ram, *Ovis aries,* I: A Normative Study, *Animal Behaviour* 17:700-705.

Bernard, L. L., 1921, The Misuse of Instinct in the Social Sciences, *Psychological Review* 28:96-119.

Bernard, L. L., 1924, *Instinct: A Study in Social Psychology,* Holt, New York.

Bernstein, I. S., 1967, A Field Study of Pigtail Monkey *(Macaca nemestrina),* Primates 8:217-228.

Bernstein, I. S., 1968, The Lutong of Kuala Selangor, *Behaviour* 32:1-16.

Bernstein, I. S., and W. A. Mason, 1963, Group Formation by Rhesus Monkeys, *Animal Behaviour* 11:28-31.

Berry, C. S., 1906, The Imitative Tendency of White Rats, *Journal of Comparative Neurology and Psychology* 16:333-361.

Berry, C. S., 1908, An Experimental Study of Imitation in Cats, *Journal of Comparative Neurology and Psychology* 18:1-25.

Bindra, D., 1948, What Makes Rats Hoard? *Journal of Comparative and Physiological Psychology* 41:397-402.

Bindra, D., 1957, Comparative Psychology, *Annual Review of Psychology* 8:399-414.

Bindra, D., 1959, *Motivation: A Systematic Reinterpretation,* Ronald, New York.

Bingham, H. C., 1913, Size and Form Perception in *Gallus domesticus, Journal of Animal Behavior* 3:65-113.

Bingham, H. C., 1916, Setting Reactions of Bird Dogs to Turtles, *Journal of Animal Behavior* 6:371-373.

Bingham, H. C., 1927, Parental Play of Chimpanzees, *Journal of Mammalogy,* 8:77-89.

Bingham, H. D., 1928, Sex Development in Apes, *Comparative Psychology Monographs* 5(23):1-166.

Bingham, H. C., 1929a, Chimpanzee Translocation by Means of Boxes, *Comparative Psychology Monographs* 5(25):1-92.

Bingham, H. C., 1929b, Selective Transportation by Chimpanzees, *Comparative Psychology Monographs* 5(26):1-45.

Bingham, H. C., 1932, Gorillas in a Native Habitat, *Publications of the Carnegie Institution,* Washington, D.C., No. 426, p. 65.

Bingham, W. V., 1946, Clarence Stone Yoakum (1879-1945), *American Psychologist* 1:26-28.

Birch, H. G., 1945, The Role of Motivational Factors in Insightful Problem-Solving, *Journal of Comparative Psychology* 38:295-317.

Birch, H. G., 1956, Sources of Order in the Maternal Behavior of Animals, *American Journal of Orthopsychiatry* 26:279-284.

Bird, C., 1925, The Relative Importance of Maturation and Habit in the Development of an Instinct, *Journal of Genetic Psychology* 32:68-91.

Bird, C., 1926, The Effect of Maturation upon the Pecking Instinct of Chicks, *Journal of Genetic Psychology* 33:212-234.

Bird, C.,1933, Maturation and Practice; Their Effects upon the Feeding Reactions of Chicks, *Journal of Comparative Psychology* 16:343-366.

Birney, R. C., and R. C. Teevan, 1961, *Instinct: An Enduring Problem in Psychology,* D. Van Nostrand, Princeton, N.J.

Bitterman, M. E., 1960, Toward a Comparative Psychology of Learning, *American Psychologist* 15:704-712.

Bitterman, M. E., 1965a, Phyletic Differences in Learning, *American Psychologist* 20:396-410.

Bitterman, M. E., 1965b, The Evolution of Intelligence, *Scientific American* 212(1):92-100.

Bitterman, M. E., 1969, Thorndike, and the Problem of Animal Intelligence, *American Psychologist* 24:444-453.

Bitterman, M. E., 1975, The Comparative Analysis of Learning, *Science* 188:699-709.

Bitterman, M. E., 1976, Issues in the Comparative Psychology of Learning, in *Evolution of Brain and Behavior in Vertebrates,* R. B. Masterton, C. B. G. Campbell, M. E. Bitterman, and N. Hotton, eds., Erlbaum, Hillsdale, N.J., pp. 217-225.

Bitterman, M. E., J. Wodinsky, and D. K. Candland, 1958, Some Comparative Psychology, *American Journal of Psychology* 71:94-110.

Bliss, C. B., 1899, Ethology, *Psychological Review* 6:563-564.

Bliss, E. L., ed., 1962, *Roots of Behavior,* Harper, New York.

Blodgett, H. C., 1924, A Further Observation on Cattle and Excitement from Blood, *Psychological Review* 31:336-339.

Boice, R., 1970, Avoidance Learning in Active and Passive Frogs and Toads, *Journal of Comparative and Physiological Psychology* 70:154-156.

Boice, R., 1971, On the Fall of Comparative Psychology, *American Psychologist* 26:858-859.

Boice, R., 1973, Domestication, *Psychological Bulletin* **80**:215-230.

Boice, R., 1977*a*, Surplusage, *Bulletin of the Psychonomic Society* **9**:452-454.

Boice, R., 1977*b*, Burrows of Wild and Albino Rats: Effects of Domestication, Outdoor Raising, Age, Experience, and Maternal State, *Journal of Comparative and Physiological Psychology* **91**:649-661.

Boice, R., 1980, Domestication and Degeneracy, in *Comparative Psychology: An Evolutionary Analysis of Animal Behavior,* M. R. Denny, ed., Wiley, New York, pp. 84-99.

Boice, R., 1981, Captivity and Feralization, *Psychological Bulletin* **89**: 407-421.

Bolles, R. C., 1970, Species-Specific Defense Reactions and Avoidance Learning, *Psychological Review* **77**:32-48.

Boring, E. G., 1912, Note on the Negative Reaction under Light-Adaptation in the Planarian, *Jouranl of Animal Behavior* **2**:229-248.

Boring, E. G., 1928*a*, Psychological Necrology (1903-1927), *Psychological Bulletin* **25**:302-305.

Boring, E. G., 1928*b*, Psychological Necrology (1903-1927), *Psychological Bulletin* **25**:621-625.

Boring, E. G., 1938, The Society of Experimental Psychologists: 1904-1938, *American Journal of Psychology* **51**:410-423.

Boring, E. G., 1943, The Growth of Psychological Journals in America, *Psychological Review,* **50**:80.

Boring E. G., 1957, A History of Experimental Psychology, Appleton-Century-Crofts, New York.

Boring, E. G., 1961, *Psychologists at Large,* Basic Books, New York.

Boring, E. G., 1968, Morgan, Conwy Lloyd, in *International Encyclopedia of the Social Sciences,* D. L. Sills, ed., Macmillan, New York, pp. 495-496.

Bourne, G. H., 1965, The Move to Atlanta, *Yerkes Newsletter* **2**(1):3-5.

Bourne, G. H., 1973, The Primate Research Center Program of the National Institute of Health, in *Nonhuman Primates and Medical Research,* G. H. Bourne, ed., Academic Press, New York, pp. 487-513.

Breed, F. S., 1911, The Development of Certain Instincts and Habits in Chicks, *Behavior Monographs* **1**(1):1-78.

Breed, F. S., 1912, Reactions of Chicks to Optical Stimuli, *Journal of Animal Behavior* **2**:280-295.

Breland, K., and M. Breland, 1951, A Field of Applied Animal Psychology, *American Psychologist* **6**:202-204.

Breland, K., and M. Breland, 1961, The Misbehavior of Organisms, *American Psychologist* **16**:681-684.

Breland, K., and M. Breland, 1966, *Animal Behavior,* Macmillan, New York.

Broadhurst, P. L., 1968, Watson, John B., in *International Encyclopedia of the Social Sciences,* D. L. Sills, ed., Macmillan, New York, pp. 484-487.

Brookshire, K. H., 1970, Comparative Psychology of Learning, in *Learning: Interactions,* M. H. Marx, ed., Macmillan, New York, pp. 291-364.

Broughton, J. M., 1981, The Genetic Psychology of James Mark Baldwin, *American Psychologist* **36**:396-407.

Brown, R. E., 1979, Mammalian Social Odors: A Critical Review, *Advances in the Study of Behavior* **10**:103-162.

Bruell, J. H., 1964, Inheritance of Behavioral and Physiological Characters of Mice and the Problem of Heterosis, *American Zoologist* 4:125-138.

Bruner, J. S., and G. W. Allport, 1940, Fifty Years of Change in American Psychology, *Psychological Bulletin* 37:757-776.

Bruner, J. S., and B. Cunningham, 1939, The Effect of Thymus Extract in the Sexual Behavior of the Female Rat, *Journal of Comparative Psychology* 27:69-77.

Buchanan, G. C., 1896, The Instincts of Birds, *Science* 4:728.

Buckley, K. W., 1982, The Selling of a Psychologist: John Broadus Watson and the Application of Behavioral Techniques to Advertising, *Journal of the History of the Behavioral Sciences* 18:207-221.

Buddenbrock, W. von, 1916, A Criticism of the Tropism Theory of Jacques Loeb, *Journal of Animal Behavior* 6:341-366.

Bunnell, B. N., 1973, Mammalian Behavior Patterns, in *Comparative Psychology: A Modern Survey,* D. A. Dewsbury and D. A. Rethlingshafer, eds., McGraw-Hill, New York, pp. 78-123.

Burghardt, G. M., 1973, Instinct and Innate Behavior: Toward an Ethological Psychology, in *The Study of Behavior,* J. A. Nevin, ed., Scott, Foresman, Glenview, Ill., pp. 321-400.

Burghardt, G. M., 1980, The Ethological Trip: Heresy to Acceptance, *Contemporary Psychology* 25:22-23.

Burghardt, G. M., and M. Bekoff, 1978, *The Development of Behavior: Comparative and Evolutionary Aspects,* Garland, New York.

Burghardt, G. M., H. C. Wilcoxon, and J. A. Czaplicki, 1973, Conditioning in Garter Snakes: Aversion to Palatable Prey Induced by Delayed Illness, *Animal Learning & Behavior* 1:317-320.

Burlingame, M., 1927, Literature on the Heredity of Behavior Traits in Animals, *Psychological Bulletin* 24:62-68.

Burnham, J. C., 1968, On the Origins of Behaviorism, *Journal of the History of the Behavioral Sciences* 4:143-151.

Butler, R. A., 1954, Incentive Conditions Which Influence Visual Exploration, *Journal of Experimental Psychology* 48:19-23.

Butler, R. A., and H. F. Harlow, 1954, Persistence of Visual Exploration in Monkey, *Journal of Comparative and Physiological Psychology* 47:258-263.

Campbell, B. A., and J. R. Pickleman, 1961, The Imprinting of Object as a Reinforcing Stimulus, *Journal of Comparative and Physiological Psychology* 54:592-596.

Campbell, B. A., and F. D. Sheffield, 1953, Relation of Random Activity to Food Deprivation, *Journal of Comparative and Physiological Psychology* 46:320-322.

Campbell, D. T., 1975, On the Conflicts between Biological and Social Evolution and between Psychology and Moral Tradition, *American Psychologist* 30:1103-1126.

Candland, D. K., 1981, On Scott and Erwin: Rumblings on the Status of CP, *Comparative Psychology Newsletter* 1(4):1-3.

Carlson, N. R., 1981, *Physiology of Behavior,* 2nd ed., Allyn and Bacon, Boston.

Carmichael, L., 1925, Heredity and Environment: Are they Antithetical? *Journal of Abnormal and Social Psychology* **20**:245-260.

Carmichael, L., 1926, The Development of Behavior in Vertebrates Experimentally Removed from the Influence of External Stimulation, *Psychological Review* **33**:51-58.

Carmichael, L., 1927, A Further Study of the Development of Behavior in Vertebrates Experimentally Removed from the Influence of External Stimulation, *Psychological Review* **34**:34-47.

Carmichael, L., 1928, A Further Experimental Study of the Development of Behavior, *Psychological Review* **35**:253-260.

Carmichael, L., 1934, The Genetic Development of the Kitten's Capacity to Right Itself in the Air when Falling, *Journal of Genetic Psychology* **44**:453-458.

Carmichael, L., 1941, The Experimental Embryology of Mind, *Psychological Bulletin* **38**:1-28.

Carmichael, L., 1946, The National Roster and the Science Foundation, *American Scientist* **34**:100-105.

Carmichael, L., 1947, The growth of the Sensory Control of Behavior before Birth, *Psychological Review* **54**:316-324.

Carmichael, L., 1957, Robert Mearns Yerkes 1876-1956, *Psychological Review* **64**:1-7.

Carmichael, L., 1959, Karl Spencer Lashley, Experimental Psychologist, *Science* **129**:1410-1412.

Carmichael, L., 1963, Psychology of Animal Behavior, *American Psychologist* **18**:112-113.

Carmichael, L., 1965, Henry Wieghorst Nissen, February 5, 1901-April 27, 1958, *Biographical Memoirs of the National Academy of Sciences* **38**:204-222.

Carmichael, L., 1967, Leonard Carmichael, in *A History of Psychology in Autobiography,* vol. 5, E. G. Boring and G. Lindzey, eds., Appleton-Century-Crofts, New York, pp. 25-47.

Carmichael, L., 1968, Some Historical Roots of Present-day Animal Psychology, in *Historical Roots of Contemporary Psychology,* B. B. Wolman, ed., Harper & Row, New York, pp. 47-76.

Carmichael, L., and L. D. Marks, 1932, A Study of the Learning Process in the Cat in a Maze Constructed to Require Delayed Response, *Journal of Genetic Psychology* **40**:207-209.

Carpenter, C. R., 1932, Psychobiological Studies in Aves. II. The Effect of Complete and Incomplete Gonadectomy on Secondary Sexual Activity with Histological Studies, *Journal of Comparative Psychology* **14**:59-98.

Carpenter, C. R., 1933, Psychobiological Studies of Social Behavior in Aves. I. The Effect of Complete and Incomplete Gonadectomy on the Primary Sexual Activity of the Male Pigeon, *Journal of Comparative Psychology* **16**:25-57.

Carpenter, C. R., 1934, A Field Study of the Behavioral and Social Relations of Howling Monkeys *(Alouatta palliata), Comparative Psychology Monographs* **10**(48):1-168.

Carpenter, C. R., 1935, Behavior of Red Spider Monkeys in Panama, *Journal of Mammalogy* **16**:171-180.

Carpenter, C. R., 1940a, A Field Study in Siam of the Behavior and Social Relations of the Gibbon *(Hylobates lar)*, *Comparative Psychology Monographs* **116**(84):1-205.

Carpenter, C. R., 1940b, Rhesus Monkeys for American Laboratories, *Science* **92**:284-286.

Carpenter, C. R., 1942a, Sexual Behavior of Free Ranging Rhesus Monkeys *(Macaca mulatta)*. I. Specimens, Procedures and Behavioral Characteristics of Estrus, *Journal of Comparative Psychology* **33**:113-142.

Carpenter, C. R., 1942b, Sexual Behavior of Free Ranging Rhesus Monkeys. *(Macaca mulatta)*. II. Periodicity of Estrus, Homosexual, Autoerotic and Non-conformist Behavior, *Journal of Comparative Psychology* **33**:143-162.

Carpenter, C. R., 1955, Calvin Perry Stone, Investigator and Teacher, *Science* **121**:658-659.

Carpenter, C. R., 1958, Territoriality: A Review of Concepts and Problems, in *Behavior and Evolution*, A. Roe and G. G. Simpson, eds., Yale, New Haven, Conn., pp. 224-250.

Carpenter, C. R., 1962, Field Studies of A Primate Population, in *Roots of Behavior*, E. L. Bliss, ed., Harper, New York, pp. 286-294.

Carpenter, C. R., 1964, *Naturalistic Behavior of Nonhuman Primates*, Pennsylvania State University Press, University Park.

Carr, H., 1912, Thorndike's "Animal Intelligence" *Journal aof Animal Behavior* **2**:441-446.

Carr, H. A., ed., 1919, *Posthumous Works of Charles Otis Whitman, vol. 3, The Behavior of Pigeons*, Carnegie Institution, Washington, D.C.

Carr, H., 1927, The Interpretation of the Animal Mind, *Psychological Review* **34**:87-106.

Carr, H. A., 1936, Harvey A. Carr, In *A History of Psychology in Autobiography*, C. Murchison, ed., Clark University Press, Worcester, Mass., pp. 69-82.

Carr, H., and J. B. Watson, 1908, Orientation in the White Rat, *Journal of Comparative Neurology* **18**:27-44.

Carter, J. W., Jr., 1956, C. M. Louttit, Psychologist, *Science* **124**; 526-527.

Carter, M. H., 1898, Darwin's Idea of Mental Development, *American Journal of Psychology* **9**:534-559.

Carter, M. H., 1899, Romanes' Ideas of Mental Development, *American Journal of Psychology*, **11**:166-180.

Cassel, C. A., 1971, The Snark: Twenty Years Later, Paper presented at meetings of the American Psychological Association, Washington, D.C.

Cattell, J. McK., 1917, Our Psychological Association and Research, *Science* **45**:275-284.

Cattell, J. McK.,1943, The Founding of the Association and of the Hopkins and Clark Laboratories, *Psychological Review*, **50**:61-64.

Causey, D., and R. H. Waters, 1936, Parental Care in Mammals with Especial Reference to the Carrying of Young by the Albino Rat, *Journal of Comparative Psychology* **22**:241-254.

Chiszar, D., 1972, Historical Continuity in the Development of Comparative Psychology: Comment on Lockard's Reflections, *American Psychologist*, **27**:665-667.

Chiszar, D., and K. Carpen, 1980, Origin and Synthesis, *American Psychologist* 35:958-962.

Chiszar, D., T. Carter, L. Knight, L. Simonsen, and S. Taylor, 1976, Investigatory Behavior in the Plains Garter Snake *(Thamnophis radix)* and Several Additional Species, *Animal Learning and Behavior* 4:273-278.

Christenson, T. E., P. A. Wenzl, and P. Legum, 1979, Seasonal Variation in Egg Hatching and Certain Egg Parameters of the Golden Silk Spider *Nephila clavipes* (Araneidae), *Psyche* 86:137-147.

Church, R. M., 1957, Transmission of Learned Behavior between Rats, *Journal of Abnormal and Social Psychology* 54:163-165.

Church, R. M., 1959, Emotional Reactions of Rats to the Pain of Others, *Journal of Comparative and Physiological Psychology* 52:132-133.

Church, R. M., and N. D. Lerner, 1976, Does the Headless Roach Learn to Avoid? *Physiological Psychology* 4:439-442.

Coburn, C. A., 1912, Singing Mice, *Journal of Animal Behavior* 2:364-366.

Coburn, C. A., 1913, Singing Mice, *Journal of Animal Behavior* 3:388.

Coburn, C. A., 1914, The Behavior of the Crow, *Corvus americanus,* Aud. *Journal of Animal Behavior* 4:185-201.

Coburn, C.A., and R. M. Yerkes, 1915, A Study of the Behavior of the Crow *Corvus americanus* Aud. by the Multiple Choice Method. *Journal of Animal Behavior* 5:75-114.

Cofer, C. N., 1981, The History of the Concept of Motivation, *Journal of the History of the Behavioral Sciences* 17:48-53.

Cohen, D., 1979, *J. B. Watson: The Founder of Behaviorism,* Routledge & Kegan Paul, London.

Cole, L. W., 1907, Concerning the Intelligence of Raccoons, *Journal of Comparative Neurology and Psychology* 17:211-261.

Cole, L. W., 1911, The Relation of Strength of Stimulus to Rate of Learning in the Chick, *Journal of Animal Behavior* 1:111-124.

Cole, L. W., 1912, Observations of the Senses and Instincts of the Raccoon, *Journal of Animal Behavior* 2:299-309.

Cole, L. W., 1915, The Chicago Experiments with Raccoons, *Journal of Animal Behavior,* 5:158-173.

Cole, M. B., and W. E. Caldwell, 1956, The Utilization of Light as Exteroceptive Motivation in the Comet Goldfish *(Carassius auratus), Journal of Comparative and Physiological Psychology* 49:71-76.

Conradi, E., 1905, Song and Call-Notes of English Sparrows When Reared by Canaries, *American Journal of Psychology* 16:190-198.

Coon, D. J., 1982, Eponymy, Obscurity, Twitmyer, and Pavlov, *Journal of the History of the Behavioral Sciences* 18:255-262.

Coonen, L. P., 1977, Aristotles's Biology, *Bioscience* 27:733-738.

Cooper, J. B., 1942, An Exploratory Study on African Lions, *Comparative Psychology Monographs* 17(91):1-48.

Cooper, J. B., 1944, A Description of Parturition in the Domestic Cat, *Journal of Comparative Psychology.* 37:71-79.

Cooper, J. B., 1972, Comparative Psychology, Ronald, New York.

Corning, W. C., and S. Kelly, 1973, Platyhelminthes: The Turbellarians, in *Inver-*

*tebrate Learning,*vol. 1, W. C. Corning, J.A. Dyal, and A.O. D. Willows, eds., Plenum, New York, pp. 171-224.

Corning, W. C., J. A. Dyal, and A. O. D. Willows, 1973, *Invertebrate Learning,* 3 volumes, Plenum, New York.

Couvillon, P. A., and M. E. Bitterman, 1980, Some Phenomena of Associative Learning in Honeybees, *Journal of Comparative and Physiological Psychology* **94:**878-885.

Cowles, J. T., 1937, Food Tokens as Incentives for Learning by Chimpanzees, *Comparative Psychology Monographs,* **14**(71):1-96.

Craig, W., 1914, Attitudes of Appetition and of Aversion in Doves, *Psychological Bulletin* **11:**56-57.

Craig, W., 1919, Tropisms and Instinctive Activities, *Psychological Bulletin,* **16:**151-159.

Craig, W., 1920, Tropisms and Instinctive Activities, *Psychological Bulletin* **17:**169-178.

Crawford, M. P., 1937, The Cooperative Solving of Problems by Young Chimpanzees, *Comparative Psychology Monographs* **14**(68):1-88.

Crawford, M. P., 1941, The Cooperative Solving by Chimpanzees of Problems Requiring Serial Responses by Color Cues, *Journal of Social Psychology* **13:**259-280.

Crawford, M. P., 1942*a,* Dominance and the Behavior of Pairs of Female Chimpanzees When They Meet after Varying Intervals of Separation, *Journal of Comparative Psychology* **33:**259-265.

Crawford, M. P., 1942*b,* Dominance and Social Behavior, for Chimpanzees, in a Non-competitive Situation, *Journal of Comparative Psychology* **33:**267-277.

Crawford, M. P., and K. W. Spence, 1939, Observational Learning of Discrimination Problems by Chimpanzees, *Journal of Comparative Psychology* **27:**133-147.

Crook, J. H., and J. D. Goss-Custard, 1972, Social Ethology, *Annual Review of Psychology* **23:**277-312.

Crutchfield, R. S., 1961, Edward Chace Tolman: 1886-1959, *American Journal of Psychology* **74:**135-141.

Cruze, W. W., 1935, Maturation and Learning in Chicks, *Journal of Comparative Psychology* **19:**371-409.

Cummings, P. W., 1967, Köhler, Wolfgang, In *The Encyclopedia of Philosophy,* P. Edwards, ed., Macmillan, New York, pp. 354-360.

Curtin, R., and P. Dolhinow, 1978, Primate Social Behavior in a Changing World, *American Scientist* **66:**468-475.

Dallenbach, K. M., 1938, Henry Herbert Donaldson: 1857-1938, *American Journal of Psychology* **51:**434-435.

Dallenbach, K. M., 1940, Margaret Floy Washburn: 1871-1939, *American Journal of Psychology* **53:**1-5.

Dallenbach, K. M., 1956*a,* Madison Bentley: 1870-1955, *American Journal of Psychology* **69:**169-187.

Dallenbach, K. M., 1956*b,* Chauncey McKinley Louttit: 1901-1956, *American Journal of Psychology* **69:**682-685.

Daly, M., 1973, Early Stimulation of Rodents: A Critical Review of Present

Interpretations, *British Journal of Psychology,* **64**:435-460.

Daly, M., and M. Wilson, 1978, *Sex, Evolution, and Behavior,* Duxbury, North Scituate, Mass.

Daniel, R. S., and K. U. Smith, 1947, The Sea-Approach Behavior of the Neonate Loggerhead Turtle, *Journal of Comparative and Physiological Psychology* **40**:413-420.

Daniel, W. J., 1942, Cooperative Problem Solving in Rats, *Journal of Comparative Psychology* **34**:361-368.

Daniel, W. J., 1943, Higher Order Cooperative Problem Solving in Rats, *Journal of Comparative Psychology,* **35**:297-305.

Danielli, J. F., and R. Brown, 1950, Physiological Mechanisms in Animal Behavior, *Symposium of the Society for Experimental Biology,* Academic Press, New York.

Darbishire, A. D., 1903, Miscellanea: I. Note on the Results of Crossing Japanese Waltzing Mice with European Albino Races, *Biometrika* **2**:101-104.

Darby, C. L., and A. J. Riopelle, 1959, Observational Learning in the Rhesus Monkey, *Journal of Comparative and Physiological Psychology* **52**:94-98.

Darsie, M. L., 1926, The Mental Capacity of American-Born Japanese Children, *Comparative Psychology Monographs* **3**(15):1-89.

Darwin, C., 1859, On the Origin of Species by Means of Natural Selection, or the Preservation of Favoured Races in the Struggle for Life, John Murray, London. (Modern Library Edition, n.d.)

Darwin, C., 1871, The Descent of Man and Selection in Relation to Sex, (Modern Library Edition, n.d.) John Murray, London.

Darwin, C., 1872, The Expression of the Emotions in Man and Animals, Appleton, London.

Darwin, C., 1873, Inherited Instinct, Nature, **7**:281-282.

Davis, H. B., 1907, The Racoon: A Study in Animal Intelligence, *American Journal of Psychology* **18**:447-489.

Dawkins, R., 1976, *The Selfish Gene,* Oxford University Press, Oxford.

Day, L., and M. Bentley, 1911, A Note on Learning in Paramecium, *Journal of Animal Behavior* **1**:67-73.

Deese, J., and C. T. Morgan, 1951, Comparative and Physiological Psychology, *Annual Review of Psychology* **2**:193-216.

Demarest, J., 1980, The Current Status of Comparative Psychology in the American Psychological Association, *American Psychologist* **35**:980-990.

Denenberg, V. H., 1962, An Attempt to Isolate Critical Periods of Development, *Journal of Comparative and Physiological Psychology* **55**:813-815.

Dennis, W., 1941, Spalding's Experiment on the Flight of Birds Repeated with Another Species, *Journal of Comparative Psychology* **31**:337-348.

Dennis, W., and E. G. Boring, 1952, The Founding of the American Psychological Association, *American Psychologist* **7**:95-97.

Denny, M. R., 1976, Stanley Charles Ratner, 1925-1975, *Psychological Record* **26**:145-146.

Denny, M. R., ed., 1980, Comparative Psychology: An Evolutionary Analysis of Animal Behavior, Wiley, New York.

Denny, M. R., and S. C. Ratner, 1970, *Comparative Psychology: Research in Animal Behavior,* 2nd ed., Dorsey, Homewood, Ill.

DeVore, I., 1965, Preface, In *Primate Behavior,* I. DeVore, ed., Holt, New York, pp. vii-ix.

Dewsbury, D. A., 1966, Stimulus-produced Changes in the Discharge Rate of an Electric Fish and Their Relation to Arousal, *Psychological Record* **16**:495-504.

Dewsbury, D. A., 1968, Comparative Psychology and Comparative Psychologists: An Assessment, *Journal of Biological Psychology* **10**:35-38.

Dewsbury, D. A., 1972, Patterns of Copulatory Behavior in Male Mammals, *Quarterly Review of Biology* **47**:1-33.

Dewsbury, D. A., 1973a, Introduction, in *Comparative Psychology: A Modern Survey,* D. A. Dewsbury and D. A. Rethlingshafer, eds., McGraw-Hill, New York, pp. 1-20.

Dewsbury, D. A., 1973b, Comparative Psychologists and Their Quest for Uniformity, *Annals of the New York Academy of Sciences* **223**:147-167.

Dewsbury, D. A., 1975, Diversity and Adaptation in Rodent Copulatory Behavior, *Science,* **190**:947-954.

Dewsbury, D. A., 1978a, Comparative Animal Behavior, McGraw-Hill, New York.

Dewsbury, D. A., 1978b, The Comparative Method in Studies of Reproductive Behavior, in *Sex and Behavior: Status and Prospectus,* T. E. McGill, D. A. Dewsbury, and B. D. Sachs, eds., Plenum, New York, pp. 83-112.

Dewsbury, D. A., 1979a, Animal Behavior, in *Foundations of Contemporary Psychology,* M. E. Meyer, ed., Oxford, New York, pp. 199-226.

Dewsbury, D. A., 1979b, C. Lloyd Morgan: Something Old That's Often New, *Contemporary Psychology* **24**:677-680.

Dewsbury, D. A., 1979c, An Informal History of the Eastern Conference on Reproductive Behavior or My Eleven Year Itch, University of Florida, Gainesville, Fla.

Dewsbury, D. A., ed., 1981, *Mammalian Sexual Behavior: Foundations for Contemporary Research,* Hutchinson Ross, Stroudsburg, Pa.

Dewsbury, D. A., 1982, Ejaculate Cost and Male Choice, *American Naturalist,* **119**:601-610.

Dewsbury, D. A., and J. J. Bernstein, 1969, Role of the Telencephalon in Performance of Conditioned Avoidance Responses by Goldfish, *Experimental Neurology* **23**:445-456.

Dewsbury, D. A., and D. A. Rethlingshafer, eds., 1973, *Comparative Psychology: A Modern Survey,* McGraw-Hill, New York.

Dewsbury, D. A., D. J. Baumgardner, D. K. Sawrey, and D. G. Webster, 1982, The Adaptive Profile: Comparative Psychology of Red-Backed Voles *(Clethrionomys gapperi), Journal of Comparative and Physiological Psychology* **96**:649-660.

Dinsmoor, J. A., 1960, Abnormal Behavior in Animals, in *Principles of Comparative Psychology,* R. H. Waters, D. A. Rethlingshafer, and W. E. Caldwell, eds., pp. 289-324.

Donaldson, H. H., and M. M. Canavan, A Study of the Brains of Three Eminent Scholars: Granville Stanely Hall, Sir William Osler, and Edward Sylvester Morse, *Journal of Comparative Neurology* **46**:1-95.

Donaldson, H. H., and S. Hatai, 1911, A Comparison of the Norway Rat with the Albino Rat in Respect to Body Length, Brain Weight, Spinal Cord Weight and the Percentage of Water in Both the Brain and the Spinal Cord, *Journal of Comparative Neurology* **21**:417-458.

Dorcus, R. M., 1950, Knight Dunlap: 1875-1949. *American Journal of Psychology* **63**:114-119.

Doty, R. L., ed., 1976, *Mammalian Olfaction, Reproductive Processes, and Behavior,* Academic Press, New York.

Drake, L. E., W. T. Heron, M. Burlingame, L. E. Ballachey, and G. Paulsen, 1930, The Rat: A Bibliography, *Psychological Bulletin* **27**:141-239.

Drever, J., 1968, McDougall, W., in *International Encyclopedia of the Social Sciences,* D. L. Sills, ed., Macmillan, New York, pp. 502-505.

Dukes, W. F., 1960, The Snark Revisited, *American Psychologist,* **15**:157.

Dunbar, M. J., 1980, The Blunting of Occam's Razor, or to Hell with Parsimony, *Canadian Journal of Zoology* **58**:123-128.

Dunlap, J. W., 1933, The Organization of Learning and Other Traits in Chickens, *Comparative Psychology Monographs* **9**(44):1-55.

Dunlap, K., 1912, The Case Against Introspection, *Psychological Review* **19**:404-413.

Dunlap, K., 1917, Internal Secretions in Learning, *Psychobiology* **1**:61-65.

Dunlap, K., 1919, Are There Any Instincts? *Journal of Abnormal Psychology* **14**:307-311.

Dunlap, K., 1922, The Identity of Instinct and Habit, *Journal of Philosophy* **19**:85-94.

Dunlap, K., 1932, Knight Dunlap, in *A History of Psychology In Autobiography,* vol. 2, C. Murchison, ed., University Press, Worcester, Mass., pp. 35-61.

Dyal, J. A., and W. C. Corning, 1973, Invertebrate Learning and Behavior Taxonomies, in *Invertebrate Learning,* vol. 1, W. C. Corning, J. A. Dyal, and A. O. D. Willows, eds., Plenum, New York, pp. 1-48.

Eaton, R. L., 1970, An Historical Look at Ethology: A Shot in the Arm for Comparative Psychology, *Journal of the History of the Behavioral Sciences* **6**:176-187.

Eibl-Eibesfeldt, I., 1975, *Ethology: The Biology of Behavior,* 2nd ed., Holt, New York.

Eibl-Eibesfeldt, I., and S. Kramer, Ethology, the Comparative Study of Animal Behavior, *Quarterly Review of Biology* **33**:181-211.

Elliott, H. W., 1896, Newly Hatched Chickens Instinctively Drink, *Science* **3**:482.

Elliott, R. M., 1956, Robert Mearns Yerkes 1876-1956, *American Journal of Psychology* **69**:487-494.

England, J. M., n.d., *National Science Foundation,* unpublished manuscript.

Epstein, R., R. P. Lanza and B. F. Skinner, 1981, "Self-awareness" in the pigeon, *Science* **212**:695-696.

Erwin, J., 1982, Who Do Comparative Psychologists Think They Are? *Comparative Psychology Newsletter* **2**(1):8-12.

Esper, E. A., 1967, Max Meyer in America, *Journal of the History of the Behavioral Sciences* **3**:107-131.

Estep, D. Q., and K. E. M. Bruce, 1981, The Concept of Rape in Non-humans: A Critique, *Animal Behaviour* **29**:1272-1273.

Evans, R. B., 1975, *Robert Mearns Yerkes, 1876-1956,* American Psychological Association, Washington, D. C.

Evans, R. I., 1976, Harry F. Harlow, in *The Making of Psychology: Discussions with Creative Contributors,* R. I. Evans, ed., Knopf, New York, pp. 30-40.

Ewer, R. F., 1971, Book Review, *Animal Behaviour* **19**:802-807.

Fantz, R. L., 1957, Form Preferences in Newly Hatched Chicks, *Journal of Comparative and Physiological Psychology* **50**:422-430.

Ferguson, G. A., 1981, Dalbir Bindra (1922-1980), *American Psychologist* **36**:1190-1191.

Fernberger, S. W., 1943*a*, The American Psychological Association, 1892-1942, *Psychological Review* **50**:33-60.

Fernberger, S. W., 1943*b*, Edwin Burket Twitmyer 1873-1943, *Psychological Review* **50**:345-349.

Finger, F. W., 1943, Factors Influencing Audiogenic Seizures in the Rat. II. Heredity and Age, *Journal of Comparative and Physiological Psychology* **35**:227-232.

Finger, F. W., 1965, Effect of Food Deprivation on Running-Wheel Activity in Naive Rats, *Psychological Reports* **16**:753-757.

Fisher, A. E., 1962, Effects of Stimulus Variation on Sexual Satiation in the Male Rat, *Journal of Comparative and Physiological Psychology* **55**:614-620.

Fiske, D. W., and S. R. Maddi, 1961, Functions of Varied Experience, Dorsey, Homewood, Ill.

Flanagan, O. J., 1980, Explanation and Reduction, *American Psychologist* **35**:974-975.

Fleming, J. D., and D. Maxey, 1975, Pursuit of Intellectual Orgasm, *Psychology Today* **8**(10):68-77.

Fletcher, J. M., E. A. Cowan, and A. H. Arlitt, 1916, Experiments on the Behavior of Chicks Hatched from Alcoholized Eggs, *Journal of Animal Behavior* **6**:103-137.

Flugel, J. C., 1939, Professor William McDougall, 1871-1938, *British Journal of Psychology* **29**:320-328.

Ford, C. S. and F. A. Beach, 1951, *Patterns of Sexual Behavior,* Harper, New York.

Fox, M. W., 1968, *Abnormal Behavior in Animals,* Saunders, Philadelphia.

Fraenkel, G. S., and D. L. Gunn, 1940, *The Orientation of Animals,* Oxford University Press, Oxford.

Franz, S. I., 1913, Observations on the Preferential Use of the Right and Left Hands by Monkeys, *Journal of Animal Behavior* **3**:140-144.

Franz, S. I., 1932, Sherherd Ivory Franz, in *A History of Psychology in Autobiography,* C. Murchison, ed., Clark University Press, Worcester, Mass., pp. 89-113.

French, J. W., 1940*a*, Individual Differences in *Paramecium, Journal of Comparative Psychology* **3**:451-456.

French, J. W., 1940*b*, Trial and Error Learning in *Paramecium, Journal of Experimental Psychology* **26**:609-613.

Fuller, J. L., and W. R. Thompson, 1960, *Behavior Genetics,* Wiley, New York.

Furedy, J. J., and C. P. Furedy, 1979, Daniel Berlyne and Psychonomy: The Beat of a Different Drum, *Bulletin of the Psychonomic Society* **13**:203-205.

Gallup, G. G., 1974, Animal Hypnosis: Factual Status of a Fictional Concept, *Psychological Bulletin* **81**:836-853.

Gallup, G. G., 1977, Self-recognition in Primates: A Comparative Approach to the Bidirectional Properties of Consciousness, *American Psychologist* **32**:329-338.

Gallup, G. G., 1979, Self-Awareness in Primates, *American Scientist* **67**:417-421.

Gantt, W. H., 1973, Reminscences of Pavlov. *Journal of the Experimental Analysis of Behavior* **20**:131-136.

Garcia, J., W. G. Hankins, K. W. Rusiniak, 1974, Behavior Regulation of the Milieu Interne in Man and Rats, *Science* **185**:824-831.

Garcia, J., W. G. Hankins, and K. W. Rusiniak, 1974, Behavioral Regulation of the Milieu Interne in Man and Rats, *Science* **185**:824-831.

Garcia, J., and R. A. Koelling, 1966, Relation of Cue to Consequence in Avoidance Learning, *Psychonomic Science* **4**:123-124.

Gardner, B. T., 1964, Hunger and Sequential Response in the Hunting Behavior of Salticid Spiders, *Journal of Comparative and Physiological Psychology* **58**:167-173.

Gardner, B. T., 1981, Project Nim: Who Taught Whom? *Contemporary Psychology* **26**:425-426.

Gardner, R. A., and B. T. Gardner, 1969, Teaching Sign Language to a Chimpanzee, *Science* **165**:664-672.

Gardner, L. P., and H. W. Nissen, 1948, Simple Discrimination Behavior of Young Chimpanzees: Comparisons with Human Aments and Domestic Animals, *Journal of Genetic Psychology* **72**:145-164.

Garner, W. R., 1976, Clifford Thomas Morgan: Psychonomic Society's First Chairman, *Bulletin of the Psychonomic Society* **8**:409-415.

Gates, Arthur I., 1949, Edward L. Thorndike (1874-1949), *Psychological Review* **56**:241-243.

Geiger, J. R., 1922, Must We Give up Instincts in Psychology? *Journal of Philosophy* **19**:94-98.

Gelber, B., 1952, Investigations of the Behavior of *Paramecium aurelia:* I. Modification of Behavior After Training with Reinforcement, *Journal of Comparative and Phsiological Psychology* **45**:58-65.

Gelber, B., 1957, Food or Training in *Paramecium? Science* **126**:1340-1341.

Gerall, H. D., I. L. Ward, and A. A. Gerall, 1967, Disruption of the Male Rat's Sexual Behavior Induced by Social Isolation, *Animal Behaviour* **15**:54-58.

Ghiselin, M. T., 1973, Darwin and Evolutionary Psychology, *Science* **179**:964-968.

Ghiselli, E. E., 1978, David Krech: 1909-1977, *American Journal of Psychology* **91**:731-734.

Gillan, D. J., D. Premack, and G. Woodruff, 1981, Reasoning in the Chimpanzee: I. Analogical Reasoning, *Journal of Experimental Psychology: Animal Behavior Processes* **7**:1-17.

Gilman, E., 1921, A Dog's Diary, *Journal of Comparative Psychology* **1**:309-315.

Ginsberg, M., 1968, Hobhouse, L. T., in *International Encyclopedia of the Social Sciences,* D. L. Sills, ed., Macmillan, New York, pp. 487-489.

Glickman, S. E., 1980, Notes on Survival, *American Psychologist* **35**:962-964.

Glickman, S. E., and B. B. Schiff, 1967, A Biological Theory of Reinforcement, *Psychological Review* **74**:81-109.

Glickman, S. E., and R. W. Sroges, 1966, Curiosity in Zoo Animals, *Behaviour* **24**:151-188.

Goldstein, A. C., 1960, Starvation and Food-Related Behavior in a Poikilotherm, the Salamander of *Triturus viridescens, Journal of Comparative and Physiological Psychology* **53**:144-150.

Goodenough, F. D., 1950, Edward Lee Thorndike: 1874-1949, *American Journal of Psychology* **63**:291-301.

Goodwin, W. J., and J. Augustine, 1975, The Primate Research Centers Program of the National Institutes of Health, *Federation Proceedings* **34**:1641-1642.

Gossette, R. L., and M. F. Gossette, 1967, Examination of the Reversal Index (RI) across Fifteen Different Mammalian and Avian Species, *Perceptual and Motor Skills* **24**:987-990.

Gottlieb, G., 1963a, "Imprinting" in Nature, *Science* **139**:497-498.

Gottlieb, G., 1963b, A Naturalistic Study of Imprinting in Wood Ducklings *(Aix sponsa), Journal of Comparative and Physiological Psychology* **56**:86-91.

Gottlieb, G., 1968a, Prenatal Behavior of Birds, *Quarterly Review of Biology* **43**:148-174.

Gottlieb, G., 1968b, T. C. Schneirla (1902-1968), *Developmental Psychobiology,* **1**:159-160.

Gottlieb, G., 1970, Conceptions of Prenatal Development, in *Development and Evolution of Behavior,* L. R. Aronson, E. Tobach, D. S. Lehrman, and J. S. Rosenblatt, eds., Freeman, San Francisco, pp. 111-137.

Gottlieb, G., 1972, Zing-Yang Kuo: Radical Scientific Philosopher and Innovative Experimentalist (1898-1970), *Journal of Comparative and Physiological Psychology* **80**:1-10.

Gottlieb, G., ed., 1973, 1974, and 1976, *Studies on the Development of Behavior and the Nervous System,* Academic Press, New York.

Gottlieb, G., 1976, *Comparative Psychology* **31**:295-297.

Gottlieb, G., 1978, Untitled. *Behavioral and Brain Sciences* **1**:446-447.

Gottlieb, G., 1979, Comparative Psychology and Ethology, in *The First Century of Experimental Psychology,* E. Hearst, ed., Lawrence Erlbaum, Hillsdale, N.J., pp. 147-173.

Gottlieb, G., and Z.-Y. Kuo, 1965, Development of Behavior in the Duck Embryo, *Journal of Comparative and Physiological Psychology* **59**:183-188.

Goudge, T. A., 1967, C. Lloyd Morgan, in *The Encyclopedia of Philosophy,* P. Edwards, ed., Macmillan, New York, pp. 392-393.

Gould, J. L., 1982, *Ethology: The Mechanisms and Evolution of Behavior,* Norton, New York.

Gould, S. J., 1981, *The Mismeasure of Man,* Norton, New York.

Gould, S. J., and R. C. Lewontin, 1979, The Spandrels of San Marco and the Panglossian Paradigm: A Critique of the Adaptationist Programme, *Proceedings of the Royal Society of London* **205B**:581-598.

Goy, R. W., and J. S. Jakway, 1959, The Inheritance of Patterns of Sexual Behavior in Female Guinea Pigs, *Animal Behaviour* **7**:142-149.

Graham, C. H., 1958, Walter Samuel Hunter: March 22, 1889-August 3, 1954, *Biographical Memoirs of the National Academy of Sciences* **31**:126-155.

Gray, G. W., 1955, The Yerkes Laboratories, *Scientific American* **192(2)**:67-77.

Gray P. H., 1962, Douglas Alexander Spalding: The First Experimental Behaviorist, *Journal of General Psychology* **67**:299-307.

Gray, P. H., 1963a, Morgan's Canon: A Myth in the History of Comparative Psychology, *Proceedings of the Montana Academy of Sciences* 23:219-224.

Gray, P. H., 1936b, The Morgan-Romanes Controversy: A Contradiction in the History of Comparative Psychology, *Proceedings of the Montana Academy of Sciences* 23:225-230.

Gray, P. H., 1966, Historical Notes on the Aerial Predation Reaction and the Tinbergen Hypothesis, *Journal of the History of the Behavioral Sciences* 2:330-334.

Gray, P. H., 1967a, Spalding and His Influence on Research in Developmental Behavior, *Journal of the History of the Behavioral Sciences* 3:168-179.

Gray, P. H., 1967b, The Behaviorist that Psychology Forgot, Paper presented at meetings of the American Psychological Association, Washington, D. C.

Gray, P. H., 1968/1969, The Early Animal Behaviorists: Prolegomenon to Ethology, *Isis* 59:372-383.

Gray, P. H., 1973, Comparative Psychology and Ethology: A Saga of Twins Reared Apart, *Annals of the New York Academy of Sciences* 223:49-53.

Gray, P. H., 1980, Behaviorism: Some Truths that Need Telling, Some Errors that Need Correcting, *Bulletin of the Psychonomic Society* 15:357-360.

Greenberg, G., 1982, Ethology without Instinct, *Contemporary Psychology* 27:18-19.

Gregg, F. M., and C. A. McPheeters, 1913, Behavior of Raccoons to a Temporal Series of Stimuli, *Journal of Animal Behavior* 3:241-259.

Grether, W. F., 1939a, Chimpanzee Color Vision. I. Hue Discrimination at Three Spectral Points, *Journal of Comparative Psychology* 28:167-177.

Grether, W. F., 1939b, Color Vision and Color Blindness in Monkeys, *Comparative Psychology Monographs* 15(76):1-38.

Griffin, D. R., 1976, *The Question of Animal Awareness*, Rockefeller University Press, New York.

Griffith, C. R., 1920, The Behavior of White Rats in the Presence of Cats, *Psychobiology* 2:19-28.

Grindley, G. C., 1936, Prof. C. Lloyd Morgan, 1852-1936, *British Journal of Psychology* 27:1-3.

Groos, K., 1898, *The Play of Animals*, E. L. Baldwin, trans., D. Appleton, New York.

Groos, K., 1932, Karl Groos, in *A History of Psychology in Autobiography*, vol. 2, C. Murchison, ed., Clark University Press, Worcester, Mass., pp. 115-152.

Grosslight, J. H., and W. Ticknor, 1953, Variability and Reactive Inhibition in the Mean Worm as a Function of Determined Turn Sequences, *Journal of Comparative and Physiological Psychology* 46:35-38.

Groves, P. M., and K. Schlesinger, 1982, *Introduction to Biological Psychology*, 2nd ed., W. C. Brown, Dubuque, Iowa.

Guhl, A. M., and M. W. Schein, 1976, *The Animal Behavior Society*, Animal Behavior Society, Morgantown, W. Va.

Gundlach, R. H., 1931, A Test of "Direction Sense" in Cats and Pigeons, *Journal of Comparative Psychology* 12:347-356.

Gundlach, R. H., 1932, A Field Study of Homing in Pigeons, *Journal of Comparative Psychology* 13:397-402.

Gurley, R. R., 1902, The Habits of Fishes, *American Journal of Psychology* **13**:408-425.

Gustavson, C., 1982, A Psychologist Responds to the Call of the Wild, *Comparative Psychology Newsletter* **2**(1):1-2.

Gustavson, C. R., J. Garcia, W. G. Hankins, and K. W. Rusiniak, 1974, Coyote Predation Control by Aversive Conditioning, *Science* **184**:581-583.

Guthrie, E. R., and G. P. Horton, 1946, *Cats in a Puzzle Box,* Rinehart, New York.

Haggerty, M. E., 1909, Imitation in Monkeys, *Journal of Comparative Neurology and Psychology* **19**:431-441.

Haggerty, M. E., 1912, A Case of Instinct, *Journal of Animal Behavior* **2**:79-80.

Hahn, E., 1971, On the Side of the Apes, *New Yorker* **47**:(April 17): 46-97 and (April 24):46-91.

Hailman, J. P., 1979, Book Review, *Animal Behaviour* **27**:633-634.

Hainsworth, F. R., J. B. Overmier, and C. T. Snowdon, 1967, Specific and Permanent Deficits in Instrumental Avoidance Responding following Forebrain Ablation in the Goldfish, *Journal of Comparative and Physiological Psychology* **63**:111-116.

Hale, E. B., 1969, Domestication and the Evolution of Behavior, in *The Behavior of Domestic Animals,* 2nd ed., E. S. E. Hafez, ed., Williams & Wilkins, Baltimore, pp. 22-42.

Hall, C. S., 1934, Emotional Behavior in the Rat: I. Defecation and Urination as Measures of Individual Differences in Emotionality, *Journal of Comparative Psychology* **18**:385-403.

Hall, C. S., 1947, Genetic Differences in Fatal Audiogenic Seizures, *Journal of Heredity* **38**:2-6.

Hall, C. S., 1951, The Genetics of Behavior, in *Handbook of Experimental Psychology,* S. S. Stevens, ed., Wiley, New York, pp. 304-329.

Hall, C. S., and S. J. Klein, 1942, Individual Differences in Aggressiveness in Rats, *Journal of Comparative Psychology* **33**:371-383.

Hall, C. S., and P. H. Whiteman, 1951, The Effects of Infantile Stimulation upon Later Emotional Stability in the Mouse, *Journal of Comparative and Physiological Psychology* **44**:61-66.

Hall, G. S., 1900, Review of Whitman's "Animal Behavior", *American Journal of Psychology* **11**:275-276.

Hall, G. S., 1908, A Glance at the Phyletic Background of Genetic Psychology, *American Journal of Psychology* **19**:149-212.

Hall, G. S., 1909, Evolution and Psychology, in *Fifty Years of Darwinism: Modern Aspects of Evolution,* Holt, New York, pp. 251-267.

Hall, G. S., and R. R. Gurley, 1896, Questions Regarding Habits and Instinct, *Science* **3**:482.

Hall, J. F., 1961, *Psychology of Motivation,* Lippincott, Philadelphia.

Hamilton, G. V., 1911, A Study of Trial and Error Reactions in Mammals, *Journal of Animal Behavior* **1**:33-66.

Hamilton, G. V., 1914, A Study of Sexual Tendencies in Monkeys and Baboons, *Journal of Animal Behavior* **4**:295-318.

Hamilton, G. V., 1916, A Study of Perseverence Reactions in Primates and

Rodents, *Behavior Monographs* 3(13):1-65.

Hamilton, G. V., 1927, Comparative Psychology and Psychopathology, *American Journal of Psychology* **39**:200-211.

Hanzel, T. E., and W. B. Rucker, 1972, Trial and Error Learning in Paramecium: A Replication, *Behavioral Biology* **7**:873-880.

Haraway, M., 1981, Letter, *Comparative Psychology Newsletter,* 1(5):3-4.

Harlow, H. F., 1932, Social Facilitation of Feeding in the Albino Rat, *Journal of Genetic Psychology* **43**:211-221.

Harlow, H. F., 1939, Recovery of Pattern Discrimination in Monkeys following Unilateral Occipital Lobectomy, *Journal of Comparative Psychology* **27**:467-489.

Harlow, H. F., 1949, The Formation of Learning Sets, *Psychological Review* **56**:51-65.

Harlow, H. F., 1953, Mice, Monkeys, Men and Motives, *Psychological Review* **60**:23-32.

Harlow, H. F., 1958a, The Nature of Love, *American Psychologist* **13**:673-685.

Harlow, H. F., 1958b, The Evolution of Learning, in *Behavior and Evolution,* A Roe and G. G. Simpson, eds., Yale University Press, New Haven, pp. 269-290.

Harlow, H. F., 1959, Love in Infant Monkeys, *Scientific American* **200**(6):68-74.

Harlow, H. F., 1962, Fundamental Principles for Preparing Psychology Journal Articles, *Journal of Comparative and Physiological Psychology* **55**:893-896.

Harlow, H. F., and M. Kuenne, 1949, Learning to Think, *Scientific American* **181**(2):36-39.

Harlow, H. F., and C. N. Woolsey, 1958, *Biological and Biochemical Bases of Behavior,* University of Wisconsin Press, Madison.

Harlow H. F., H. Uehling, and A. H. Maslow, 1932, Comparative Behavior of Primates: I. Delayed Reaction Test on Primates from the Lemur to the Orangutan, *Journal of Comparative Psychology* **13**:313-343.

Harlow, H. F., M. K. Harlow, and S. J. Suomi, 1971, From Thought to Therapy: Lessons from a Primate Laboratory, *American Scientist* **59**:538-549.

Harriman, P. L., 1947, *Dictionary of Psychology,* Philosophical Library, New York.

Harris, B., 1979, Whatever Happened to Little Albert? *American Psychologist* **34**:151-160.

Harris, B., 1981, A Non-historical Biography of John B. Watson, *Contemporary Psychology* **26**:62-63.

Hartman, C. G., and O. L. Tinklepaugh, 1930, Parturition in the Monkey *(Macaca rhesus), Anatomical Record* **45**:218-219.

Haslerud, G. M., 1938, The Effect of Movement of Stimulus Objects upon Avoidance Reactions in Chimpanzees, *Journal of Comparative Psychology* **25**:507-528.

Haslerud, G. M., 1979, Introduction to R. M. Yerkes's *The Mental Life of Monkeys and Apes,* Scholars Fascimiles and Reprints, Delmar, N.Y.

Hawkins, J. D., 1964, Wild and Domestic Animals as Subjects in Behavior Experiments, *Science* **145**:1460-1461.

Hayes, C. H., 1951, *The Ape in Our House,* Harper & Row, New York.

Hayes, K. J., 1950, Vocalization and Speech in Chimpanzees, *American Psychologist* 5:275-276.

Hayes, K. J., and C. Hayes, 1952, Imitation in a Home-Reared Chimpanzee, *Journal of Comparative and Physiological Psychology* 45:450-459.

Hebb, D. O., 1937, The Innate Organization of Visual Activity. II. Transfer of Response in the Discrimination of Brightness and Size by Rats Reared in Total Darkness, *Journal of Comparative Psychology* 24:277-299.

Hebb, D. O., 1949a Temperament in Chimpanzees. I. Method of Analysis, *Journal of Comparative and Physiological Psychology* 42:192-206.

Hebb, D. O., 1949b *The Organization of Behavior*, Wiley, New York.

Hebb, D. O., 1950, Animal and Physiological Psychology, *Annual Review of Psychology* 1:173-188.

Hebb, D. O., 1953, Heredity and Environment in Mammalian Behavior, *British Journal of Animal Behaviour* 1:43-47.

Hebb, D. O., 1955, Drives and the C.N.S. (Conceptual Nervous System), *Psychological Review* 62:243-254.

Hebb, D. O., 1959, Karl Spencer Lashley 1890-1958, *American Journal of Psychology* 72:142-150.

Hebb, D. O., 1960, The American Revolution, *American Psychologist* 15:735-745.

Hebb, D. O., 1980, D. O. Hebb, in *A History of Psychology in Autobiography*, G. Lindzey, ed., Freeman, San Francisco, pp. 273-303.

Hebb, D. O., and W. R. Thompson, 1954, The Social Significance of Animal Studies, in *Handbook of Social Psychology*, G. Lindzey, ed., Addison-Wesley, Cambridge, Mass., pp. 532-561.

Heffner, H. E., R. J. Ravizza, and B. Masterton, 1979, Hearing in Primitive Mammals: IV. Bushbaby *(Galago senegalensis)*, *Journal of Auditory Research* 9:19-23.

Henderson, B., 1981, Disappointing Watson, *Contemporary Psychology* 26:64.

Henle, M., 1978, One Man against the Nazis—Wolfgang Köhler, *American Psychologist* 33:939-944.

Herbert, M. J., and C. M. Harsh, 1944, Observational Learning by Cats, *Journal of Comparative Psychology* 37:81-95.

Heron, W. T., 1935, The Inheritance of Maze Learning Ability in Rats, *Journal of Comparative Psychology* 19:77-89.

Heron, W. T., and B. F. Skinner, 1940, The Rate of Extinction in Maze-Bright and Maze-Dull Rats, *Psychological Record* 4:11-18.

Herrick, C. J., 1907, Comparative Psychology, *Popular Science Monthly* 70:76-78.

Herrick, C. J., 1920, Book Review, *Psychobiology* 2:449-453.

Herrnstein, R. J., 1972, Nature as Nurture: Behaviorism and the Instinct Doctrine, *Behaviorism* 1:23-52.

Herrnstein, R. J., 1973, Introduction to John B. Watson's Comparative Psychology, in *Historical Conceptions of Psychology*, M. Henle, J. Jaynes, and J. J. Sullivan, eds., Springer, New York, pp. 98-115.

Herrnstein, R. J., 1977a, The Evolution of Behaviorism, *American Psychologist* 32:593-603.

Herrnstein, R. J., 1977b, Doing What Comes Naturally: A Reply to Professor Skinner, *American Psychologist* 32:1013-1016.

Herrnstein, R. J., 1979, Acquisition, Generalization, and Discrimination Reversal of a Natural Concept, *Journal of Experimental Psychology: Animal Behavior Processes* 5:116-129.

Hess, E. H., 1953*a*, Comparative Psychology, *Annual Review of Psychology* 4:239-254.

Hess, E. H., 1953*b*, Shyness as a Factor Influencing Hoarding in Rats, *Journal of Comparative and Physiological Psychology* 46:46-48.

Hess, E. H., 1956, Comparative Psychology, *Annual Review of Psychology* 7:305-322.

Hess, E. H., 1959, Two Conditions Limiting Critical Age for Imprinting, *Journal of Comparative and Physiological Psychology* 52:515-518.

Hess, E. H., 1962, Ethology: An Approach Toward the Complete Analysis of Behavior, in *New Directions in Psychology*, R. Brown, E. Galanter, E. H. Hess, and G. Mandler, eds., Holt, New York, pp. 157-266.

Hess, E. H., 1964, Imprinting in Birds, *Science* 146:1128-1139.

Hess, E. H., 1972, The Natural History of Imprinting, *Annals of the New York Academy of Sciences* 193:124-136.

Hilgard, E. R., 1965, Robert Mearns Yerkes, *Biographical Memoirs of the National Academy of Sciences* 38:384-425.

Hilgard, E. R., 1978, *American Psychology in Historical Perspective*, American Psychological Association, Washington, D.C.

Hinde, R. A., 1966, *Animal Behaviour: A Synthesis of Ethology and Comparative Psychology*, McGraw-Hill, New York.

Hinde, R. A., 1978, Foreward, in *Sex and Behavior: Status and Prospectus*, T. E. McGill, D. A. Dewsbury, and B. D. Sachs, ed., Plenum, New York, pp. vii-x.

Hinde, R. A., 1982, *Ethology: Its Nature and Relations with Other Sciences*, Fontana, Oxford.

Hinde, R. A., and J. A. Stevenson-Hinde, 1973, *Constraints on Learning: Limitations and Predispositions*, Academic Press, New York.

Hirsch, J., 1957, Careful Reporting and Experimental Analysis—A Comment, *Journal of Comparative and Physiological Psychology* 50:415.

Hirsch, J., 1959, Studies in Experimental Behavior Genetics: II. Individual Differences in Geotaxis as a Function of Chromosome Variations in Synthesized *Drosophila* Populations, *Journal of Comparative and Physiological Psychology* 52:304-308.

Hirsch, J., 1963, Behavior Genetics and Individuality Understood, *Science* 142:1436-1442.

Hirsch, J., ed., 1967, *Behavior-Genetic Analysis*, McGraw-Hill, New York.

Hirsch, J., 1973, Introduction to the Dover Edition of J. Loeb's *Forced Movements, Tropisms, and Animal Conduct*, Dover, New York.

Hirsch, J. and J. C. Boudreau, 1958, Studies in Experimental Behavior Genetics: I. The Heritability of Phototaxis in a Population of *Drosophila melanogaster*, *Journal of Comparative and Physiological Psychology* 51:647-651.

Hirsch, J., and R. C. Tryon, 1956, Mass Screening and Reliable Individual Measurement in the Experimental Behavior Genetics of Lower Organisms, *Psychological Bulletin* 53:402-410.

Hirsch, J., R. H. Lindley, and E. C. Tolman, 1955, An Experimental Test of an Alleged Innate Sign Stimulus, *Journal of Comparative and Physiological Psychology* **48**:278-280.

Hoagland, H., and R. Mitchell, 1956, T. William John Crozier: 1892-1953, *American Journal of Psychology* **69**:135-138.

Hobhouse, L. T., 1901, *Mind in Evolution*, MacMillan, London.

Hodon, A., C. T. Snowden, and P. Soini, 1981, Subspecific Variation in the Long Calls of the Tamarin, *Saginus fuscicollis, Zeitschrift für Tierspsychologie* **57**:97-110.

Hodos, W., 1970, Evolutionary Interpretation of Neural and Behavioral Studies of Living Vertebrates, in *The Neurosciences Second Study Program*, F. O. Schmitt, ed., Rockefeller University Press, New York, pp. 26-39.

Hodos, W., and C. B. G. Campbell, 1969, *Scala Naturae:* Why There Is No Theory in Comparative Psychology, *Psychological Review* **76**:337-350.

Hoffman, H. S., and A. M. Ratner, 1973, A Reinforcement Model of Imprinting: Implications for Socialization in Monkeys and Men, *Psychological Review* **80**:527-544.

Hogan, J. A., 1973, How Young Chicks Learn to Recognize Food, in *Constraints on Learning*, R. A. Hinde and J. Stevenson-Hinde, eds., Academic Press, London, pp. 119-139.

Holmes, S., 1979, *Henderson's Dictionary of Biological Terms*, Van Nostrand Reinhold, New York.

Holmes, S. J., 1916, *Studies in Animal Behavior*, Richard G. Badger, Boston.

Holmes, S. J., 1922, A Tentative Clasification of the Forms of Animal Behavior, *Journal of Comparative Psychology* **2**:173-186.

Howard, D. T., 1927, The Influence of Evolutionary Doctrine on Psychology, *Psychological Review*, **34**:305-312.

Hubbert, H. B., and H. M. Johnson, 1916, Habit-Formation and Higher Capacities in Animals, *Psychological Bulletin* **13**:316-323.

Humphrey, George, 1949, Edward Lee Thorndike, 1874-1949, *British Journal of Psychology* **40**:55-56.

Hunt, J.McV., 1956, Walter Samuel Hunter 1889-1954, *Psychological Review* **63**:213-217.

Hunter, W. S., 1911, Some Labyrinth Habits of the Domestic Pigeon, *Journal of Animal Behavior* **1**:278-304.

Hunter, W. S., 1913, The Delayed Reaction in Animals and Children, *Behavior Monographs* **2**(6), 86p.

Hunter, W. S., 1915, A Reply to Professor Cole, *Journal of Animal Behavior*, **5**:406.

Hunter, W. S., 1916, Titles of Behavior Papers, *Journal of Animal Behavior*, **6**:266.

Hunter, W. S., 1918, The Temporal Maze and Kinaesthetic Sensory Processes in the White Rat, *Psychobiology* **2**:339-351.

Hunter, W. S., 1920, The Modification of Instinct from the Standpoint of Social Psychology, *Psychological Review* **27**:247-269.

Hunter, W. S., 1932, The Psychological Study of Behavior, *Psychological Review* **39**:1-24.

Hunter, W. S., 1947, Summary Comments on the Heredity-Environment Symposium, *Psychological Review* 54:348-352.

Hunter, W. S., 1952, Walter S. Hunter, in *A History of Psychology in Autobiography,* vol. 4, E. G. Boring, H. S. Langfeld, H. Werner, and R. M. Yerkes, eds., Clark University Press, Worcester, Mass., pp. 163-187.

Hunter, W. S., and E. Sommerhier, 1922, The Relation of Degree of Indian Blood to Score on the Otis Intelligence Test, *Journal of Comparative Psychology* 2:257-277.

Immelmann, K., 1980, *Introduction to Ethology,* Plenum, New York.

International Committee Against Racism, 1977, Sociobiology: Laying the Foundation for a Racist Synthesis, *Harvard Crimson,* February 8.

Irvine, P., 1973, Herbert G. Birch (1918-1973): A Biographical Sketch, *Journal of Special Education* 7:340-341.

Irwin, F. W., 1943, Edwin Burket Twitmyer: 1873-1943, *American Journal of Psychology* 56:451-453.

Jacobsen, C. F., M. M. Jacobsen, and J. G. Yoshioka, 1932, Development of an Infant Chimpanzee during Her First Year, *Comparative Psychology Monographs* 9(41):1-88.

Jacobson, A. L., S. D. Horowitz, and C. Fried, 1967, Classical Conditioning, Psuedoconditioning, or Sensitization in the Planarian, *Journal of Comparative and Physiological Psychology* 64:73-79.

James, W., 1890, *The Principles of Psychology,* vol. 2, Holt, New York.

James, W. T., 1953, Social Facilitation of Eating Behavior in Puppies after Satiation, *Journal of Comparative and Physiological Psychology* 46:427-428.

Jastrow, J., 1934, James Mark Baldwin: 1861-1934, *Science* 80:497-498.

Jaynes, J., 1956, Imprinting: The Interaction of Learned and Innate Behavior. I. Development and Generalization, *Journal of Comparative and Physiological Psychology* 49:201-206.

Jaynes, J., 1969, The Historical Origins of "Ethology" and "Comparative Psychology," *Animal Behaviour* 17:601-606.

Jenkins, T. N., L. H. Warner, and C. J. Warden, 1926, Standard Apparatus for the Study of Animal Motivation, *Journal of Comparative Psychology* 6:361-382.

Jennings, H. S., 1904, Contributions to the Study of the Behavior of Lower Organisms, *Publications of the Carnegie Institution,* No. 16, 256p.

Jennings, H. S., 1906, *Behavior of the Lower Organisms,* Columbia University Press, New York.

Jensen, D. D., 1957a, Experiments on "Learning" in Paramecia, *Science* 125:191-192.

Jensen, D. D., 1957b, More on "Learning" in Paramecia, *Science* 126:1341-1342.

Jensen, D. D., 1959, A Theory of the Behavior of *Paramecium aurelia* and Behavioral Effects of Feeding, Fission, and Ultraviolet Microbeam Irradiation, *Behaviour* 15:82-122.

Jensen, D. D., 1961, Operationism and the Question "Is this Behavior Learned or Innate?" *Behaviour* 17:1-8.

Jensen, D. D., 1962, Foreword to the 1962 Edition of H. S. Jennings's *Behavior of the Lower Organisms,* University of Indiana Press, Bloomington, Ind., pp. xiii-xxi.

Jensen, D. D., 1965, Paramecia, Planaria, and Pseudo-learning, *Animal Behaviour,* Suppl. 1, pp. 9-20.

Jerison, H. J., 1970, Brain Evolution: New Light on Old Principles, *Science* **170**:1224-1225.

Jerison, H. J., 1973, *Evolution of Brain and Intelligence,* Academic Press, New York.

Johnson, H. M., 1912, The Talking Dog, *Science* **35**:749-751.

Joncich, G., 1968, *The Sane Positivist: A Biography of Edward L. Thorndike,* Wesleyan University Press, Middletown, Conn.

Kagan, J., and F. A. Beach, 1953, Effects of Early Experience on Mating Behavior in Male Rats, *Journal of Comparative and Physiological Psychology* **46**:204-208.

Kamil, A. C., and M. W. Hunter, 1970, Performance on Object-Discrimination Learning Set by the Greater Hill Myna *(Gracula religiosa), Journal of Comparative and Physiological Psychology* **73**:68-73.

Kamil, A. C., and T. D. Sargent, eds., 1981, *Foraging Behavior: Ecological, Ethological, and Psychological Approaches,* Garland, New York.

Kantor, J. R., 1935, James Mark Baldwin (Columbia, S. C., 1861-Paris, France, 1934), *Psychological Bulletin* **32**:1-3.

Kantor, J. R., 1971, In Memoriam Zing-Yang Kuo 1898-1970, *Psychological Record* **21**:381-383.

Katz, M. S., and W. A. Deterline, 1958, Apparent Learning in the *Paramecium, Journal of Comparative and Physiological Psychology* **51**:243-247.

Kawamura, S., 1963, The Process of Sub-culture Propagation among Japanese Macaques, in *Primate Social Behavior: An Enduring Problem,* C. H. Southwick, ed., Van Nostrand, Princeton, N.Y., pp. 82-90.

Keehn, J. D., ed., 1979, *Origins of Madness: Psychopathology in Animal Life,* Pergamon, Oxford.

Kellogg, W. N., 1931, A Note on Fear Behavior in Young Rats, Mice, and Birds, *Journal of Comparative Psychology* **12**:117-121.

Kellogg, W. N., 1959, Size Discrimination by Reflected Sound in a Bottle-nose Porpoise, *Journal of Comparative and Physiological Psychology* **52**:509-514.

Kellogg, W. N., 1961, *Porpoises and Sonar,* University of Chicago Press, Chicago.

Kellogg, W. N., 1968, Communication and Language in the Home-Raised Chimpanzee, *Science* **162**:423-428.

Kellogg, W. N., and L. A. Kellogg, 1933, *The Ape and the Child,* McGraw-Hill, New York.

Kellogg, W. N., and W. B. Pomeroy, 1936, Maze Learning in Water Snakes, *Journal of Comparative Psychology* **21**:275-295.

Kemble, E. D., 1981, On the Mitosis of JCPP, *American Psychologist* **36**:1462.

Kinder, E. F., 1927, A Study of the Nest-Building Activity of the Albino Rat, *Journal of Experimental Zoology* **47**:117-161.

King, J. A., 1963, Maternal Behavior in *Peromyscus,* in *Maternal Behavior in Mammals,* H. L. Rheingold, ed., Wiley, New York, pp. 58-93.

Kinnaman, A. J., 1902a, Mental Life of Two *Macacus rhesus* Monkeys in Captivity, I, *American Journal of Psychology* **13**:98-172.

Kinnaman, A. J., 1902b, Mental Life of Two *Macacus rhesus* Monkeys in Captivity, II, *American Journal of Psychology* **13**:209-218.

Kirkpatrick, E. A., 1907, A Broader Basis for Psychology Necessary, *Journal of Philosophy, Psychology, and Scientific Method* 4:542-546.

Kline, L. W., 1898a, The Migratory Impulse vs. Love of Home, *Amerian Journal of Psychology* 10:1-81.

Kline, L. W., 1898b, Review of "Animal Intelligence: An Experimental Study of the Associative Processes in Animals" by E. L. Thorndike, *American Journal of Psychology* 10:149-150.

Kline, L. W., 1899a, Methods in Animal Psychology, *American Journal of Psychology* 19:256-279.

Kline, L. W., 1899b, Suggestions toward a Laboratory Course in Comparative Psychology, *American Journal of Psychology* 10:399-430.

Kline, L. W., 1904, Contributions of Zoological Psychology to Child Study, in *Proceedings and Addresses of the National Educational Assᴜ ᵗion*, University of Chicago Press, Chicago, pp. 776-782.

Klopfer, P. H., and J. P. Hailman, 1967, *An Introduction to Animal Behavior*, Prentice-Hall, Englewood Cliffs, N.J.

Klopfer, P. H., and J. P. Hailman, eds., 1972, *Control and Development of the Behavior: An Historical Sample from the Pens of Ethologists*, Addison-Wesley, Reading, Mass.

Koch, H. L., 1955, Harvey A. Carr 1873-1954, *Psychological Review* 62:81-82.

Köhler, W., 1925, *The Mentality of Apes*, Routledge & Kegan Paul, London.

Konecni, V. J., 1978, Daniel E. Berlyne: 1924-1976, *American Journal of Psychology* 71:133-137.

Konorski, J., 1949, Pavlov, *Scientific American* 18(3):44-47.

Kovach, J. E., 1971, Ethology in the Soviet Union, *Behaviour* 39:237-265.

Kovach, J. K., 1973, Soviet Ethology: The First All-Union Conference on Ecological and Evolutionary Aspects of Animal Behavior, *Behaviour* 44:203-211.

Krech, D., 1959, Karl Friedrich Muenzinger: 1885-1958, *American Journal of Psychology* 72:477-479.

Krechevsky, I., 1933, Hereditary Nature of "Hypotheses," *Journal of Comparative Psychology* 16:99-116.

Kuo, Z.-Y., 1921, Giving Up Instincts in Psychology, *Journal of Philosophy, Psychology, and Scientific Methods* 18:645-664.

Kuo, Z.-Y., 1922, How Are Our Instincts Acquired? *Psychological Review* 29:344-365.

Kuo, Z.-Y., 1924, A Psychology without Heredity, *Psychological Review* 31:427-448.

Kuo, Z.-Y., 1929, The Net Result of the Anti-heredity Movement in Psychology, *Psychological Review* 36:181-199.

Kuo, Z.-Y., 1930, The Genesis of the Cat's Response to the Rat, *Journal of Comparative Psychology* 11:1-35.

Kuo, Z.-Y., 1932a, Ontogeny of Embryonic Behavior in Aves. III. The Structural and Environmental Factors in Embryonic Behavior, *Journal of Comparative Psychology* 13:245-271.

Kuo, Z.-Y., 1932b, Ontogeny of Embryonic Behavior in Aves. IV. The Influence of Embryonic Movements upon the Behavior after Hatching, *Journal of Comparative Psychology* 14:109-122.

Kuo, Z.-Y., 1938, Further Study of the Behavior of a Cat toward the Rat, *Journal of Comparative Psychology* 25:1-8.

Kuo, Z.- Y., 1967, The Dynamics of Behavior Development, Random House, New York.

Kuroda, R., 1926, Experimental Researches upon the Sense of Hearing in Lower Vertebrates, including Reptiles, Amphibians and Fishes, *Comparative Psychology Monographs* **3**(16):1-50.

LaFleur, L. J., 1942, Anti-Social Behavior Among Ants, *Journal of Comparative Psychology* **33**:33-39.

LaFleur, L. J., 1943, A Reply, *Journal of Comparative Psychology* **35**:97-99.

LaFleur, L. J., 1944, Ants and Hypotheses, *Journal of Comparative Psychology* **37**:17-22.

Lahue, R., L. Kokkinidis, and W. Corning, 1975, Telson Reflex Habituation in *Limulus polyphemus, Journal of Comparative and Physiological Psychology* **89**:1061-1069.

Langfeld, H. S., 1944, Jubilee of the Psychological Review, *Psychological Review* **51**:143-155.

Lanier, D. L., and D. A. Dewsbury, 1976, A Quantitative Study of Copulatory Behavior of Large Felidae, *Behavioural Processes* **1**:327-333.

Larson, C., 1979, The Watson-McDougall Debate: "The Debate of the Century," *A. P. A. Monitor* **10**(11):3, 12.

Larson, C. A., 1981, Epilogue to the Review of John B. Watson's Biography, *Contemporary Psychology* **26**:62.

Larson, C. A., and J. J. Sullivan, 1965, Watson's Relation to Titchener, *Journal of the History of the Behavioral Sciences,* **1**:338-354

Larsson, K., 1956, *Conditioning and Sexual Behavior in the Male Albino Rat,* Almquist & Wiksell, Stockholm.

Lashley, K. S., 1912, Visual Discrimination of Size and Form in the Albino Rat, *Journal of Animal Behavior* **2**:310-331.

Lashley, K. S., 1913, Reproduction of the Inarticulate Sounds in the Parrot, *Journal of Animal Behavior* **3**:361-366.

Lashley, K. S., 1914, A Note on the Persistence of an Instinct, *Journal of Animal Behavior* **4**:293-294.

Lashley, K. S., 1916, The Color Vision of Birds. I. The Spectrum of the Domestic Fowl, *Journal of Animal Behavior* **6**:1-26.

Lashley, K. S., 1917, Modifiability of the Preferential Use of the Hands in the Rhesus Monkey, *Journal of Animal Behavior* **7**:178-186.

Lashley, K. S., 1924, Physiological Analysis of the Libido, *Psychological Review* **31**:192-204.

Lashley, K. S., 1930, Basic Neural Mechanisms in Behavior, *Psychological Review* **37**:1-24.

Lashley, K. S., 1938*a*, The Mechanism of Vision. XV. Preliminary Studies of the Rat's Capacity for Detail Vision, *Journal of General Psychology* **18**:123-193.

Lashley, K. S., 1938*b*, Experimental Analysis of Instinctive Behavior, *Psychological Review* **45**:445-471.

Lashley, K. S., 1947, Structural Variation in the Nervous System in Relation to Behavior, *Psychological Review* **54**:325-334.

Lashley, K. S., 1948, The Mechanism of Vision. XVIII. Effects of Destroying the Visual "Associative Areas" of the Monkey, *Genetic Psychology Monographs* **37**:107-166.

Lashley, K. S., 1949, Persistent Problems in the Evolution of Mind, *Quarterly Review of Biology* **24**:28-42.

Lashley, K. S., 1950, In Search of the Engram, in *Physiological Mechanisms in Animal Behavior*, J. F. Danielli and R. Brown, eds., Academic Press, New York, pp. 454-482.

Lashley, K. S., 1951, The Problem of Serial Order in Behavior, in *Cerebral Mechanisms in Behavior*, L. A. Jeffress, ed., Wiley, New York, pp. 112-136.

Lashley, K. S., 1957, Introduction, in *Instinctive Behavior: The Development of a Modern Concept*, C. H. Schiller, ed., International Universities Press, New York, pp. ix-xii.

Lashley, K. S., and J. T. Russell, 1934, The Mechanism of Vision, XI. A Preliminary Test of Innate Organization, *Journal of Genetic Psychology* **45**:136-144.

Lashley, K. S. and J. B. Watson, 1913, Notes on the Development of a Young Monkey, *Journal of Animal Behavior* **3**:114-139.

Lavery, J. J., and P. J. Foley, 1963, Altruism or Arousal in the Rat? *Science* **140**:172-173.

LeBoeuf, B. J., 1974, Male-Male Competition and Reproductive Success in Elephant Seals, *American Zoologist* **14**:163-176.

LeBouef, B. J., 1978, Sex and Evolution, in *Sex and Behavior: Status and Prospectus*, T. E. McGill, D. A. Dewsbury, and B. D. Sachs, eds., Plenum, New York, pp. 3-33.

Lee, C. T., 1973, Genetic Analyses of Nest Building Behavior in Laboratory Mice *(Mus musculus)*, *Behavior Genetics* **3**:247-256.

Lehrman, D. S., 1953, A Critique of Konrad Lorenz's Theory of Instinctive Behavior, *Quarterly Review of Biology* **28**:337-363.

Lehrman, D. S., 1958, Effect of Female Sex Hormones on Incubation Behavior in Ring Dove *(Streptopelia risoria)*, *Journal of Comparative and Physiological Psychology* **51**:142-145.

Lehrman, D. S., 1962, Ethology and Psychology, *Recent Advances in Biological Psychiatry* **4**:86-94.

Lehrman, D. S., 1965, Interaction Between Internal and External Environments in the Regulation of the Reproductive Cycle of the Ring Dove, in *Sex and Behavior*, F. A. Beach, ed., Wiley, New York, pp. 355-380.

Lehrman, D. S., 1970, Sematic and Conceptual Issues in the Nature-nuture problem, in *Development and Evolution of Behavior*, L. R. Aronson, E. Tobach, D. S. Lehrman, and J. S. Rosenblatt, eds., Freeman, San Francisco, pp. 17-52.

Lehrman, D. S., 1971, Behavioral Science, Engineering, and Poetry, in *The Biopsychology of Development*, E. Tobach, L. R. Aronson, and E. Shaw, eds., Academic Press, New York, pp. 459-471.

Lepley, W. M., 1937, Competitive Behavior in the Albino Rat, *Journal of Experimental Psychology* **21**:194-201.

Lepley, W. M., and G. E. Rice, 1952, Behavioral Variability in *Paramecia* as a Function of Guided Act Sequences, *Journal of Comparative and Physiological Psychology* **45**:283-286.

Leshner, A. I., 1978, *An Introduction to Behavioral Endocrinology*, Oxford, New York.

Lester, D., 1973, *Comparative Psychology: Phyletic Differences in Behavior,* Alfred, Port Washington, N.Y.

Leuba, C. J., 1931, Some Comments on the First Reports of the Columbia Study of Animal Drives, *Journal of Comparative Psychology,* **11:**275-279.

Levine, S., 1957, Infantile Experience and Consummatory Behavior in Adulthood, *Journal of Comparative and Physiological Psychology* **50:**609-612.

Levy, F. J., 1981, Watsonian Professional Linen, *Contemporary Psychology* **26:**64.

Licklider, L. C., and J. C. R. Licklider, 1950, Observations on the Hoarding Behavior of Rats, *Journal of Comparative and Physiological Psychology* **43:**129-134.

Liddell, H. S., 1925, The Behavior of Sheep and Goats in Learning a Simple Maze, *American Journal of Psychology* **36:**544-552.

Liddell, H. S., 1926, A Laboratory for the Study of Conditioned Motor Reflexes, *American Journal of Psychology* **37:**418-419.

Liddell, H. S., 1936, Pavlov's Contribution to Psychology, *Psychological Bulletin* **33:**583-590.

Liddell, H. S., 1953, A Comparative Approach to the Dynamics of Experimental Neuroses, *Annals of the New York Academy of Sciences* **56:**164-170.

Liddell, H. S., W. T. James, and O. D. Anderson, 1934, The Comparative Physiology of the Conditioned Motor Reflex, *Comparative Psychology Monographs* **9**(15):1-89.

Limber, J., 1977, Language in Child and Chimp? *American Psychologist* **32:**280-295.

Lindzey, G., 1951, Emotionality and Audiogenic Seizure Susceptibility in Five Inbred Strains of Mice, *Journal of Comparative and Physiological Psychology* **44:**389-393.

Lockard, R. B., 1968, The Albino Rat: A Defensible Choice or a Bad Habit, *American Psychologist* **23:**734-742.

Lockard, R. B., 1971, Reflections on the Fall of Comparative Psychology: Is There a Message for Us All? *American Psychologist* **26:**168-179.

Lockard, R. B., 1975, Experimental Inhibition of Activity of Kangaroo Rats in the Natural Habitat by an Artificial Moon, *Journal of Comparative and Physiological Psychology* **89:**263-266.

Loeb, J., 1900, *Comparative Physiology of the Brain and Comparative Psychology,* John Murray, (Reprinted: London. Arno, New York, 1973.)

Loeb, J., 1912, The *Mechanistic Conception of Life,* University of Chicago Press, Chicago.

Loeb, J., 1918, *Forced Movements, Tropisms, and Animal Conduct,* Lippincott, Philadelphia.

Logan, C. A., and H. P. Beck, 1978, Long-term Retention of Habituation in the Sea Anemone *(Anthopleura elegantissima), Journal of Comparative and Physiological Psychology* **92:**928-936.

Lomask, M., 1975, *A Minor Miracle: An Informal History of the National Science Foundation,* National Science Foundation, Washington, D.C.

Lorenz, K. Z., 1950, The Comparative Method in Studying Innate Behavior Patterns, in *Physiological Mechanisms in Animal Behavior,* J. F. Danielli and R. Brown, eds., Academic Press, New York, pp. 221-268.

Lorenz, K. Z., 1952, *King Solomon's Ring,* Thomas Y. Crowell, New York.

Lorenz, K. Z., 1965, *Evolution and the Modification of Behavior,* University of Chicago Press, Chicago.

Lorenz, K. Z., 1981, *The Foundations of Ethology,* Springer-Verlag, New York.

Lott, D. F., 1974, Sexual and Aggressive Behavior of Adult Male American Bison *(Bison bison),* in *The Behavior of Ungulates and Its Relation to Management,* vol. 1, V. Geist and F. Walther, eds., International Union for Conservation of Nature and Natural Resources, Morges, Switzerland, pp. 382-394.

Lott, D. F., 1975, Protestations of a Field Person, *Bioscience* 25:328.

Louttit, C. M., 1927, Reproductive Behavior of the Guinea Pig. I. The Normal Mating Behavior, *Journal of Comparative Psychology* 7:247-263.

Louttit, C. M., 1929a, Reproductive Behavior of the Guinea Pig. II. The Ontogenesis of the Reproductive Behavior Pattern, *Journal of Comparative Psychology* 9:293-304.

Louttit, C. M., 1929b, Reproductive Behavior of the Guinea Pig. III. Modification of the Behavior Pattern, *Journal of Comparative Psychology* 9:305-315.

Lown, B. A., 1975, Comparative Psychology 25 Years After, *American Psychologist* 30:858-859.

Lubbock, J., 1888, *Ants, Bees, and Wasps,* Appleton, New York.

Lubbock, J., 1904, *Intelligence of Animals,* Hill, New York.

Lucas, F. A., 1896, The Instinct of Pecking, *Science* 3:409-410.

McAllister, W. G., 1935, Book Review, *Psychological Bulletin* 32:614-619.

McBride, A. F. and D. O. Hebb, 1948, Behavior of the Captive Bottle-nose Dolphin, *Tursiops truncatus, Journal of Comparative and Physiological Psychology* 41:111-123.

McClearn, G. E., and J. C. DeFries, 1973, *Introduction to Behavioral Genetics,* Freeman, San Francisco.

McConnell, J. V., 1974, *Understanding Human Behavior,* Holt, New York.

McConnell, J. V., 1976, Psycho-technology and Personal Change, in *Psychological Research: The Inside Story,* M. H. Siegel and H. P. Zeigler, eds., Harper & Row, New York, pp. 327-354.

McConnell, J. V., 1981, Letter, *Comparative Psychology Newsletter* l(4):3-5.

McConnell, J. V., A. L. Jacobson, and D. P. Kimble, 1959, The Effects of Regeneration Upon Retention of a Conditioned Response in the Planarian, *Journal of Comparative and Physiological Psychology* 52:1-5.

McCurdy, H. G., 1968, Willilam McDougall, in *Historical Roots of Contemporary Psychology,* B. B. Wolman, ed., Harper & Row, New York, pp. 111-130.

McDougall, K. D., and W. McDougall, 1931, Insight and Foresight in Various Animals—Monkey, Raccoon, Rat, and Wasp, *Journal of Comparative Psychology* 11:237-273.

McDougall, W., 1910, Instinct and Intelligence, *British Journal of Psychology* 3:250-266.

McDougall, W., 1911, *An Introduction to Social Psychology,* 4th ed., Luce, Boston.

McDougall, W., 1921/1922, The Use and Abuse of Instinct in Social Psychology, *Journal of Abnormal and Social Psychology* 16:285-333.

McDougall, W., 1923, *Outline of Psychology,* Scribner's, New York.

McDougall, W., 1927, An Experiment for the Testing of the Hypothesis of Lamarck, *British Journal of Psychology* **17**:267-304.

McDougall, W., 1930, William McDougall, in *A History of Psychology in Autobiography,* vol. 1, C. Murchison, ed., Clark University Press, Worcester, Mass., pp. 191-223.

McDougall, W., 1938, Fourth Report on a Lamarckian Experiment, *British Journal of Psychology* **28**:321-345.

McDougall, W., and K. D. McDougall, 1927, Notes on Instinct and Intelligence in Rats and Cats, *Journal of Comparative Psychology* **7**:145-176.

McFarland, D., ed., 1981, *The Oxford Companion to Animal Behaviour,* Oxford University Press, Oxford.

McGill, T. E., 1962, Sexual Behavior in Three Inbred Strains of Mice, *Behaviour* **19**:341-350.

McGill, T. E., 1965, *Readings in Animal Behavior,* Holt, New York.

McGill, T. E., D. A. Dewsbury, and B. D. Sachs, eds., 1978, *Sex and Behavior: Status and Prospectus,* Plenum, New York.

McGuire, T. R., and J. Hirsch, 1977, Behavior-Genetic Analysis of *Phormia regina:* Conditioning, Reliable Individual Differences, and Selection, *Proceedings of the National Academy of Sciences, USA* **74**:5193-5197.

McMurrich, J. P., and C. M. Jackson, 1938, Henry Herbert Donaldson, *Journal of Comparative Neurology* **69**:172-179.

Magoun, H. W., 1981, John B. Watson and the Study of Human Sexual Behavior, *Journal of Sex Research* **17**:368-378.

Maier, N. R. F., 1929, Reasoning in White Rats, *Comparative Psychology Monographs* **6**(29):1-93.

Maier, N. R. F., 1938, A Further Analysis of Reasoning in Rats. II. The Integration of Four Separate Experiences in Problem Solving, *Comparative Psychology Monographs* **15**(73):1-85.

Maier, N. R. F., 1960, Maier's law. *American Psychologist,* **15**:208-212.

Maier, N. R. F., 1961, *Frustration: The Study of Behavior Without a Goal,* University of Michigan Press, Ann Arbor.

Maier, N. R. F., and N. M. Glaser, 1940a, Studies of Abnormal Behavior in the Rat. II. A Comparison of Some Convulsion-Producing Situations, *Comparative Psychology Monographs* **16**(80):1-30.

Maier, N. R. F., and N. M. Glaser, 1940b, Studies of Abnormal Behavior in the Rat. V. The Inheritance of the "Neurotic Pattern," *Journal of Comparative Psychology.* **30**:413-418.

Maier, N. R. F., and T. C. Schneirla, 1935, *Principles of Animal Psychology,* McGraw-Hill, New York.

Maier, R. A., and B. M. Maier, 1970, *Comparative Animal Behavior,* Brooks/Cole, Belmont, Calif.

Maier, R. A., and B. M. Maier, 1973, *Comparative Psychology,* Brooks/Cole, Monterey, Calif.

Manning, A., 1979, *An Introduction to Animal Behavior,* 3rd ed., Addison-Wesley, Reading, Mass.

Marshall, H. R., 1908, The Methods of the Naturalist and Psychologist, *Psychological Review* **15**:1-24.

Marshall, L. H., 1982, Early Studies of Primate Behavior in the U.S.A., *Trends in Neurosciences* 5:377-380.

Martin, M. F., 1940, The Psychological Contributions of Margaret Floy Washburn, *American Journal of Psychology,* 53:7-20.

Marx, J. L., 1980, Ape-Language Controversy Flares Up, *Science* 207:1330-1333.

Maser, J. D., and G. G. Gallup, 1977, Tonic Immobility and Related Phenomena: A Partially Annotated Tricentennial Bibliography, 1636-1976, *Psychological Record* 27:177-217.

Maslow, A. H., 1936, The Role of Dominance in the Social and Sexual Behavior of Infrahuman primates: I. Observations at the Vilas Park Zoo, *Journal of Genetic Psychology* 48:261-277.

Maslow, A. H., and S. Flanzbaum, 1936, The Role of Dominance in the Social and Sexual Behavior of Infra-Human Primates: II. An Experimental Determination of the Behavior Syndrome of Dominance, *Journal of Genetic Psychology* 48:278-309.

Maslow, A. H., and H. F. Harlow, 1932, Comparative Behavior of Primates. II. Delayed Reaction Tests on Primates at the Bronx Zoo Park, *Journal of Comparative Psychology* 14:97-107.

Mason, W. A., 1968a, Naturalistic and Experimental Investigations of the Social Behavior of Monkeys and Apes, in *Primates: Studies in Adaptation and Variability,* P. C. Jay, ed., Holt, New York, pp. 398-419.

Mason, W. A., 1968b, Use of Space by *Callicebus* Monkeys, in *Primates: Studies in Adaptation and Variability,* P. C. Jay, ed., Holt, New York, pp. 200-216.

Mason, W. A., 1976a, Windows on Other Minds, *Science* 194:930-931.

Mason, W. A., 1976b, Primate Social Behavior: Pattern and Process, in *Evolution of Brain and Behavior in Vertebrates,* R. B. Masterton, M. E. Bitterman, C. B. G. Campbell, and N. Hotton, eds., Erlbaum, New York, pp. 425-455.

Mason, W. A., 1980, Minding Our Business, *American Psychologist* 35:964-967.

Mason, W. A., and J. H. Hollis, 1962, Communication between Young Rhesus Monkeys, *Animal Behaviour* 10:211-221.

Mason, W. A., and D. F. Lott, 1976, Ethology and Comparative Psychology. *Annual Review of Psychology* 27:129-154.

Mason, W. A., and A. J. Riopelle, 1964, Comparative Psychology, *Annual Review of Psychology* 15:143-180.

Mast, S. O., 1913, A Review of Yerkes' and Watson's "Methods of Studying Vision in Animals," *Journal of Animal Behavior* 3:147-148.

Mast, S. O., and K. S. Lashley, 1916, Observations on Ciliary Current in Free-swimming Paramecia, *Journal of Experimental Zoology* 21:281-293.

Masterton, R. B., and L. C. Skeen, 1972, Origins of Anthropoid Intelligence: Prefrontal System and Delayed Alternation in Hedgehog, Tree Shrew, and Bush Baby, *Journal of Comparative and Physiological Psychology* 81:423-433.

Masterton, R. B., M. E. Bitterman, C. B. G. Campbell, and N. Hotton, 1976a, *Evolution of Brain and Behavior in Vertebrates,* Lawrence Erlbaum, Hillsdale, N.J.

Masterton, R. B., W. Hodos, and H. Jerison, 1976b, *Evolution, Brain, and Behavior: Persistent Problems,* Lawrence Erlbaum, Hillsdale, N.J.

Maxson, S. C., 1973, Behavioral Adaptations and Biometrical Genetics, *American Psychologist* **28**:268-269.

Melzack, R., 1954, The Genesis of Emotional Behavior: An Experimental Study of the Dog, *Journal of Comparative and Physiological Psychology* **47**:166-168.

Melzack, R., and T. H. Scott, 1957, The Effects of Early Experience on the Response to Pain, *Journal of Comparative and Physiological Psychology* **50**:155-161.

Melzack, R., E. Penick, and A. Beckett, 1959, The Problem of "Innate Fear" of the Hawk Shape: An Experimental Study with Mallard Ducks, *Journal of Comparative and Physiological Psychology* **52**:694-698.

Menzel, E. W., 1966, Responsiveness to Objects in Free-ranging Japanese Monkeys, *Behaviour* **26**:130-150.

Menzel, E. W., 1967, Naturalistic and Experimental Research on Primates, *Human Development* **10**:170-186.

Menzel., E. W., 1968, Primate Naturalistic Research and Problems of Early Experience, *Developmental Psychobiology* **1**:175-184.

Menzel, E. W., 1981, Is Clever Hans a Dead Horse? *Contemporary Psychology* **26**:908-909.

Meyer, D. R., 1955, Comparative Psychology, *Annual Review of Psychology* **6**:251-266.

Meyer, M. E., 1964*a* Discriminative Basis for Astronavigation in Birds, *Journal of Comparative and Physiological Psychology* **58**:403-406.

Meyer, M. E., 1964*b*, Stimulus Control for Bird Orientation, *Psychological Bulletin* **62**:165-179.

Michels, K. M., and D. R. Brown, 1959, The Delayed-Response Performance of Raccoons, *Journal of Comparative and Physiological Psychology* **52**:737-740.

Miles, W. R., 1930, On the History of Research with Rats and Mazes: A Collection of Notes, *Journal of General Psychology* **3**:324-337.

Miles, W. R., 1931, Behavior of Fish in Elevated Water-Bridges Connecting Adjoining Aquaria, *Journal of Comparative Psychology* **12**:123-131.

Millard, W. J., 1976, Species Preferences of Experimenters, *American Psychologist* **31**:894-896.

Miller, D. B., 1977*a*, Roles of Naturalistic Observation in Comparative Psychology, *American Psychologist* **32**:211-219.

Miller, D. B., 1977*b*, Social Displays of Mallard Ducks *(Anas platyrhynchos)*: Effects of Domestication, *Journal of Comparative and Physiological Psychology* **91**:221-232.

Miller, D. B., and G. Gottlieb, 1981, Effects of Domestication on Production and Perception of Mallard Maternal Alarm Calls: Developmental Lag in Behavioral Arousal, *Journal of Comparative and Physiological Psychology* **95**:205-219.

Miller, G. A., 1945, Concerning the Goal of Hoarding Behavior, *Journal of Comparative Psychology* **38**:209-212.

Miller, N. E., and J. Dollard, 1941, *Social Learning and Imitation,* Yale University Press, New Haven.

Miller, R. R., and A. M. Berk, and A. D. Springer, 1974, Acquisition and Retention of Active Avoidance in *Xenopus laevis, Bulletin of the Psychonomic Society* **3**:139-141.

Mills, W., 1896a, Prof. C. Lloyd Morgan on Instinct, *Science* 3:355-356.

Mills, W., 1896b, Instinct, *Science* 3:441-442.

Mills, W., 1896c, Instinct, *Science* 3:597-598.

Mills, W., 1896d, Instinct, *Science* 3:780-781.

Mills, W., 1898, *The Nature and Development of Animal Intelligence*, MacMillan, New York.

Mills, W., 1899, The Nature of Animal Intelligence and the Methods of Investigating It, *Psychological Review* 6:262-274.

Mills, W., 1904. Some Aspects of the Development of Comparative Psychology, *Science* 19:745-757.

Mineka, S., R. Keir, and V. Price, 1980, Fear of Snakes in Wild and Laboratory-reared Rhesus Monkeys *(Macaca mulatta)*, *Animal Learning and Behavior* 8:653-663.

Misiak, H., and V. S. Sexton, 1966, *History of Psychology: An Overview*, Grune and Stratton, New York.

Moltz, H., 1960, Imprinting: Empirical Basis and Theoretical Significance, *Psychological Bulletin* 57:291-314.

Moltz, H., 1965, Contemporary Instinct Theory and the Fixed Action Pattern, *Psychological Review* 72:33-53.

Moltz, H., 1971, *The Ontogeny of Vertebrate Behavior*, Academic Press, New York.

Moltz, H., and L. A. Rosenblum, 1957, Imprinting and Associative Learning: The Stability of the Following Response in Peking Ducks *(Anas platyrhynchous)*, *Journal of Comparative and Physiological Psychology* 50:580-583.

Montgomery, K. C., 1955, The Relation between Fear Induced by Novel Stimulation and Exploratory Behavior, *Journal of Comparative and Physiological Psychology* 48:254-260.

Moore, B. R., and S. Stuttard, 1979, Dr. Guthrie and *Felis domesticus* or: Tripping over the Cat, *Science* 205:1031-1033.

Moore, K. G., 1949, Knight Dunlap 1875-1949, *Psychological Review* 56:309-310.

Morgan, C. L., 1894, *An Introduction to Comparative Psychology*, Walter Scott, London.

Morgan, C. L., 1985, Some Definitions of Instinct, *Natural Sciences* 7:321-329.

Morgan, C. L., 1896a, The Habit of Drinking in Young Birds, *Science* 3:900.

Morgan, C. L., 1896b, *Habit and Instinct*, Arnold, London.

Morgan, C. L., 1901, The Swimming Instinct, *Nature* 64:208.

Morgan, C. L., 1905, Comparative and Genetic Psychology, *Psychological Review* 12:78-97.

Morgan, C. L., 1910, II, Instinct and Intelligence, *British Journal of Psychology* 3:219-229.

Morgan, C. L., 1932, C. Lloyd Morgan, in *A History of Psychology in Autobiography*, vol. 2, C. Murchison, ed., Clark University Press, Worcester, Mass., pp. 237-264.

Morgan, C. T., and H. Waldman, 1940, "Conflict" and Audiogenic Seizures, *Journal of Comparative Psychology* 31:1-11.

Morgan, C. T., 1943, *Physiological Psychology*, McGraw-Hill, New York.

Morgan, C. T., 1947, The Hoarding Instinct, *Psychological Review* 54:335-341.

Morgan, C. T., and J. D. Morgan, 1939, Auditory Induction of an Abnormal Pattern of Behavior in Rats, *Journal of Comparative Psychology* 27:505-508.

Morgan, C. T., E. Stellar, and O. Johnson, 1943, Food Deprivation and Hoarding in Rats, *Journal of Comparative and Physiological Psychology* 35:275-295.

Morgan, L. H., 1868, *The American Beaver and His Works,* Lippincott, Philadelphia.

Morin, L. P., K. M. Fitzgerald, B. Rusak, and I. Zucker, 1977, Circadian Organization and Neural Mediation of Hamster Reproductive Rhythms, *Psychoneuroendocrinology* 2:73-98.

Mortenson, F. J., 1975, *Animal Behavior: Theory and Research,* Brooks/Cole, Monterey, Calif.

Moseley D., 1925, The Accuracy of the Pecking Response in Chicks, *Journal of Comparative Psychology* 5:75-97.

Moss, F. A., 1924, Study of Animal Drives, *Journal of Experimental Psychology* 7:165-185.

Moss, F. A., ed., 1934, *Comparative Psychology,* Prentice-Hall, New York.

Moss, F. A., ed., 1942, *Comparative Psychology,* 2nd ed., Prentice-Hall, New York.

Mountjoy, P. T., 1980, An Historical Approach to Comparative Psychology, in *Comparative Psychology: An Evolutionary Analysis of Behavior,* M. R. Denny, ed., Wiley, New York, pp. 128-152.

Mountjoy, P. T., J. H. Bos, M. O. Duncan, and R. B. Verplank, 1969, Falconry: Neglected Aspect of the History of Psychology, *Journal of the History of the Behavioral Sciences* 5:59-67.

Mowrer, O. H., 1940, The Tumbler Pigeon, *Journal of Comparative Psychology* 30:515-533.

Moyer, K. E., 1968, Kinds of Aggression and Their Physiological Bases, *Communications in Behavioral Biology* 2A:65-87.

Müller-Schwarze, D., 1978, *Evolution of Play Behavior,* Dowden, Hutchinson & Ross, Stroudsburg, Pa.

Munn, N. L., 1933, *An Introduction to Animal Psychology,* Houghton Mifflin, Boston.

Munn, N. L., 1939, Learning Experiments with Larval Frogs, *Journal of Comparative Psychology* 28:97-108.

Munn, N. L., 1950, *Handbook of Psychological Research on the Rat,* Houghton Mifflin, Boston.

Munn, N. L., 1958, The Question of Insight and Delayed Reaction in Fish, *Journal of Comparative and Physiological Psychology* 51:92-97.

Murchison, C., ed., 1932, *The Psychological Register,* vol. 3, Clark University Press, Worcester, Mass.

Murchison, C., 1935, The Experimental Measurement of a Social Hierarchy in *Gallus domesticus:* IV. Loss of Body Weight under Conditions of Mild Starvation as a Function of Social Dominance, *Journal of General Psychology* 12:296-312.

Nagge, J. W., 1932, Regarding the Law of Parsimony, *Journal of Genetic Psychology* 41:492-494.

National Institute of Health, 1981, *1981 NIH Almanac,* U.S. Department of Health and Human Services, Bethesda, Md.

Newbury, E., 1954, Current Interpretation and Significance of Lloyd Morgan's Canon, *Psychological Bulletin* 51:70-74.

Newton, G., and S. Levine, 1968, *Early Experience and Behavior: The Psychobiology of Development*, C. C. Thomas, Springfield, Ill.

Nigrosh, B. J., J. A. Nevin, and B. M. Slotnick, 1975, Olfactory Discrimination, Reversal Learning, and Stimulus Control in Rats, *Journal of Comparative and Physiological Psychology* 89:285-294.

Nimkoff, M. F., 1953, A Sociologists's View of Instinct, *Psychological Review* 60:287-290.

Nissen, H. W., 1929, The Effects of Gonadectomy, Vasotomy, and Injections of Placental and Orchic Extracts on the Sex Behavior of the White Rat, *Genetic Psychology Monographs* 5:449-550.

Nissen, H. W., 1930, A Study of Maternal Behavior in the White Rat by Means of the Obstruction Method, *Journal of Genetic Psychology* 37:377-398.

Nissen, H. W., 1931, A Field Study of the Chimpanzee: Observations of Chimpanzee Behavior and Environment in Western French Guinea, *Comparative Psychology Monographs* 8(36):1-122.

Nissen, H. W., 1942, Studies of Infant Chimpanzees, *Science* 95:159-161.

Nissen, H. W., 1953, Instinct as Seen by a Psychologist, *Psychological Review* 60:287-290.

Nissen, H. W., 1954, The Nature of the Drive as Innate Determinant of Behavioral Organization, in *Nebraska Symposium in Motivation*, vol. 2, M. R. Jones, ed., University of Nebraska Press, Lincoln, pp. 281-321.

Nissen, H. W., and M. P. Crawford, 1936, A Preliminary Study of Food-Sharing in Young Chimpanzees, *Journal of Comparative Psychology* 22:383-419.

Nissen, H. W., and J. Semmes, 1952, Comparative and Physiological Psychology, *Annual Review of Psychology* 3:233-260.

Nissen, H. W., K. L. Chow, and J. Semmes, 1951, Effects of Restricted Opportunity for Tactual, Kinesthetic, and Manipulative Experience on the Behavior of a Chimpanzee, *American Journal of Psychology* 64:485-507.

Nowlis, V., 1941, Companionship Preference and Dominance in the Social Interaction of Young Chimpanzees, *Comparative Psychology Monographs* 17(85):1-57.

Nyby, J., and G. Whitney, 1978, Ultrasonic Communication of Adult Myomorph Rodents, *Neuroscience and Biobehavioral Reviews* 2:1-14.

Nyby, J., P. Wallace, K. Owen, and D. D. Thiessen, 1973, An Influence of Hormones on Hoarding Behavior in the Mongolian Gerbil *(Meriones unguiculatus)*, *Hormones and Behavior* 4:283-288.

O'Donnell, J. M., 1979, The Crisis of Experimentalism in the 1920s: E. G. Boring and His Uses of History, *American Psychologist* 34:289-295.

O'Kelly, L. I., 1940, An Experimental Study of Regression. I. Behavioral Characteristics of the Regressive Response, *Journal of Comparative Psychology* 30:41-54.

O'Kelly, L. I., 1979, Paul Thomas Young: 1892-1978, *American Journal of Psychology* 92:551-553.

O'Reilly, J., 1953, The Swarming Killers of the Jungle, *Saturday Evening Post* 225(46):36, 177, 179-182.

Osborn, H. F., 1896, A Mode of Evolution Requiring neither Natural Selection nor the Inheritance of Acquired Characteristics, *Transactions of the New York Academy of Sciences* 15:141-142, 148.

Padilla, S. G., 1935, Further Studies on the Delayed Pecking of Chicks, *Journal of Comparative Psychology* 20:413-443.

Palmer, D. E., 1929, Jacques Loeb: A Contribution to the History of Psychology, *Journal of General Psychology* 2:97-114.

Paschal, F. C., and L. R. Sullivan, 1925, Racial Differences in the Mental and Physical Development of Mexican Children, *Comparative Psychology Monographs,* 3(14):1-76.

Pattie, F. A., Jr., 1939, William McDougall: 1871-1938, *American Journal of Psychology* 52:303-307.

Patton, R. A., 1951, Abnormal Behavior in Animals, in *Comparative Psychology,* 3rd ed., C. P. Stone, ed., Prentice-Hall, Englewood Cliffs, N.J., pp. 458-513.

Pauly, P. J., 1981, The Loeb-Jennings Debate and the Science of Animal Behavior, *Journal of the History of the Behavioral Sciences* 17:504-515.

Pavlov, I. P., 1927, *Conditioned Reflexes,* G. V. Anrep, trans., Oxford University Press, Oxford.

Perkins, F. T., and R. H. Wheeler, 1930, Configurational Learning in the Goldfish, *Comparative Psychology Monographs* 7(31):1-50.

Peterson, J., 1923, The Comparative Abilities of White and Negro Children, *Comparative Psychology Monographs* 1(5):1-141.

Petrinovich, L., T. Patterson, and H. V. S. Peeke, 1976, Reproductive Condition and the Response of White-crowned Sparrows *(Zonotrichia leucophrys nuttalli)* to Song, *Science* 191:206-207.

Pfaffmann, C., 1973, The Comparative Approach to Physiological Psychology, *Annals of the New York Academy of Sciences* 223:57-64.

Pfaffmann, C., 1980, Leonard Carmichael: November 9, 1898-September 16, 1973, *Biographical Memoirs of the National Academy of Sciences* 51:24-47.

Pfungst, O., 1911, *Clever Hans (The Horse of Mr. von Osten),* C. L. Rahn, trans., Henry Holt, New York.

Piel, G., 1970, The Comparative Psychology of T. C. Schneirla, in *Development and Evolution of Behavior,* L. R. Aronson, E. Tobach, D. S. Lehrman, and J. S. Rosenblatt, eds., Freeman, San Francisco, pp. 1-13.

Pillsbury, W. B., 1940, Margaret Floy Washburn (1871-1939), *Psychological Review* 47:99-109.

Pillsbury, W. B., 1946, Clarence Stone Yoakum (1879-1945), *Psychological Review* 53:195-198.

Pillsbury, W. B., 1955, Harvey A Carr: 1878-1954, *American Journal of Psychology* 68:149-151.

Pittendrigh, C. S., 1958, Adaptation, Natural Selection, and Behavior, in *Behavior and Evolution,* A. Roe and G. G. Simpson, eds., Yale University Press, New Haven, pp. 390-416.

Porter, J. H., S. B. Johnson, and R. G. Granger, 1981, The Snark is Still a Boojum, *Comparative Psychology Newsletter* 1(5):1-3.

Porter, J. P., 1904, A Preliminary Study of the Psychology of the English Sparrow, *American Journal of Psychology* 15:313-346.

Porter, J. P., 1906*a*, The Habits, Instincts, and Mental Powers of Spiders, Genera, Argiope and Eperia, *American Journal of Psychology* 17:306-357.

Porter, J. P., 1906*b*, Further Study of the English Sparrow and Other Birds, *American Journal of Psychology* 17:248-271.

Porter, J. P., 1910, Intelligence and Imitation in Birds; A Criterion of Imitation, *American Journal of Psychology* 21:1-17.

Pratt, C. L., and G. P. Sackett, 1967, Selection of Social Partners as a Function of Peer Contact during Rearing, *Science* 155:1333-1335.

Premack, D., 1970, A Functional Analysis of Language, *Journal of the Experimental Analysis of Behavior* 14:107-125.

Premack, D., and G. Woodruff, 1978*a*, Does the Chimpanzee Have a Theory of Mind? *Behavioral and Brain Sciences* 4:515-526.

Premack, D., and G. Woodruff, 1978*b*, Chimpanzee Problem-solving: A Test for Comprehension, *Science* 202:532-535.

Price, B., 1968, *Into the Unknown*, Platt and Munk, New York.

Provine, R. R., 1973, Neurophysiological Aspects of Behavior Development in the Chick Embryo, in G. Gottlieb, ed., *Behavioral Embryology*, Academic Press, New York, pp. 77-102.

Pryor, K. W., R. Haag, and J. O'Reilly, 1969, The Creative Porpoise: Training for Novel Behavior, *Journal of the Experimental Analysis of Behavior* 12:653-661.

Prytula, R. E., G. D. Oster, and S. F. Davis, 1977, The "Rat Rabbit" Problem: What Did John B. Watson Really Do? *Teaching of Psychology* 4:44-46.

Rachlin, H., 1976, *Behavior and Learning*, Freeman, San Francisco.

Raphelson, A. C., 1980, Psychology at Michigan: The Pillsbury Years, 1897-1947, *Journal of the History of the Behavioral Sciences* 16:301-312.

Ratner, S. C., 1972, Comparative Psychology: Some Distinctions from Animal Behavior, *Psychological Record* 22:433-440.

Ratner, S. C., 1977, Immobility of Invertebrates: What Can We Learn? *Psychological Record* 27:1-13.

Ratner, S. C., 1980, The Comparative Method, in *Comparative Psychology: An Evolutionary Analysis of Behavior*, M. R. Denny, ed., Wiley, New York, pp. 153-167.

Ratner, S. C., and R. Boice, 1975, Effects of Domestication on Behavior, in *The Behavior of Domestic Animals*, E. S. E. Hafez, ed., Williams & Wilkins, Baltimore, pp. 3-19.

Ratner, S. C., and M. R. Denny, 1964, *Comparative Psychology: Research in Animal Behavior*, Dorsey, Homewood, Ill.

Ratner, S. C., and K. R. Miller, 1959, Classical Conditioning in Earthworms, *Limbricus terrestris*, *Journal of Comparative and Physiological Psychology* 52:102-105.

Razran, G., 1961, Recent Soviet Phyletic Comparisons of Classical and of Operant Conditioning: Experimental Designs, *Journal of Comparative and Physiological Psychology* 54:357-365.

Razran, G., 1971, *Mind in Evolution: An East-West Synthesis of Learned Behavior and Cognition*, Houghton Mifflin, Boston.

Reed, C. A., 1946, The Copulatory Behavior of Small Mammals, *Journal of Comparative Psychology* 39:185-206.

Reed, C. A., and R. Reed, 1946, The Copulatory Behavior of the Golden Hamster, *Journal of Comparative Psychology* **39**:7-12.

Remley, N. R., 1980, J. B. Watson and J. J. B. Morgan: The Original Drive Theory of Motivation, *Bulletin of the Psychonomic Society* **16**:314-316.

Rheingold, H. L., ed., 1963, *Maternal Behavior in Mammals*, Wiley, New York.

Rheingold, H. L., and E. H. Hess, 1957, The Chick's "Preference" for Some Visual Properties of Water, *Journal of Comparative and Physiological Psychology* **50**:417-421.

Rhine, J. B., and W. McDougall, 1933, Third Report of a Lamarckian Experiment, *British Journal of Psychology* **24**:213-235.

Rice, G. E., and P. Gainer, 1962, "Altruism" in the Albino Rat, *Journal of Comparative and Physiological Psychology* **55**:123-125.

Richards, R. J., 1977, Lloyd Morgan's Theory of Instinct: From Darwinism to Neo-Darwinism, *Journal of the History of the Behavioral Sciences* **13**:12-32.

Richmond, G. and B. D. Sachs, 1980, Grooming in Norway Rats: The Development and Adult Expression of a Complex Motor Pattern, *Behaviour* **75**:82-96.

Richter, C. P., 1922, A Behavioristic Study of the Activity of the Rat, *Comparative Psychology Monographs* **1**(2):1-55.

Richter, C. P., 1927, Animal Behavior and Internal Drives, *The Quarterly Review of Biology* **2**:307-343.

Richter, C. P., 1947, Biology of Drives, *Journal of Comparative and Physiological Psychology* **40**:129-134.

Richter, C. P., 1949, Domestication of the Norway Rat and Its Implications for the Problems of Stress, *Proceedings of the Association for Research in Nervous and Mental Diseases* **29**:19-47.

Richter, C. P., 1954, The Effects of Domestication and Selection on the Behavior of the Norway Rat, *Journal of the National Cancer Institute* **15**:727-738.

Richter, C. P., 1971, Inborn Nature of the Rat's 24-hour Clock, *Journal of Comparative and Physiological Psychology* **75**:1-4.

Riesen, A. H., 1940, Delayed Reward in Discrimination Learning by Chimpanzees, *Comparative Psychology Monographs* **15**(77):1-54.

Riesen, A. H., 1958a, Plasticity of Behavior: Psychological Aspects, in *Biological and Biochemical Bases of Behavior*, H. F. Harlow and C. N. Woolsey, eds., University of Wisconsin Press, Madison, pp. 425-450.

Riesen, A. H., 1958b, Henry Wieghorst Nissen: 1901-1958, *American Journal of Psychology* **71**:795-798.

Riesen, A. H., 1971, Nissen's Observations on the Development of Sexual Behavior in Captive-born, Nursery-reared Chimpanzees, *The Chimpanzee* **4**:1-18.

Riesen, A. H., and L. Aarons, 1959, Visual Movement and Intensity Discrimination in Cats after Early Deprivation of Patterned Vision, *Journal of Comparative and Physiological Psychology* **52**:142-149.

Riess, B. F., 1954, The Effect of Altered Environment and of Age on Mother-Young Relationships among Animals, *Annals of the New York Academy of Sciences* **57**:606-610.

Riley, D. A., and M. R. Rosenzweig, 1957, Echolocation in Rats, *Journal of Comparative and Physiological Psychology* **50**:323-328.

Riopelle, A. J., and C. W. Hill, 1973, Complex Processes, in *Comparative Psychology: A Modern Survey,* D. A. Dewsbury and D. A. Rethlingshafer, eds, McGraw-Hill, New York, pp. 510-546.

Ristau, C. A., and D. Robbins, 1982, Language in the Great Apes: A Critical Review, in *Advances in the Study of Behavior,* vol. 12, J. S. Rosenblatt, R. A. Hinde, C. Beer, and M. C. Busnel, eds., Academic Press, New York, pp. 141-255.

Robinson, D. N., 1977, Preface, in *Seminal Research Papers,* D. N. Robinson, ed., University Publications of America, Washington, D.C., pp. xxi-xxxv.

Robinson, E. W., 1933, A Preliminary Experiment on Abstraction in a Monkey, *Journal of Comparative Psychology* 16:231-236.

Robinson, J. S., 1953, Stimulus Substitution and Response Learning in the Earthworm, *Journal of Comparative and Physiological Psychology* 46:262-266.

Rockett, F. C., 1955, A Note on "An Experimental Test of an Alleged Innate Sign Stimulus" by Hirsch, Lindley, and Tolman, *Perceptual and Motor Skills* 5:155-156.

Roe, A., and G. G. Simpson, eds., 1958, *Behavior and Evolution,* Yale University Press, New Haven.

Rogers, W. W., 1932, Controlled Observations on the Behavior of Kittens toward Rats from Birth to Five Months of Age, *Journal of Comparative Psychology* 13:107-127.

Rohles, F. H., Jr., M. E. Grunzke, and H. H. Reynolds, 1963, Chimpanzee Performance during the Ballistic and Orbital Project Mercury Flights, *Journal of Comparative and Physiological Psychology* 56:2-10.

Rollin, B. E., 1981, *Animal Rights and Human Morality,* Prometheus, Buffalo, N.Y.

Romanes, G. J., 1882, *Animal Intelligence,* Appleton, New York.

Romanes, G. J., 1883, *Mental Evolution in Animals,* K. Paul, London.

Romanes, G. J., 1885, *Jelly-fish, Star-fish, and Sea-urchins Being a Research in Primitive Nervous Systems,* Appleton, New York.

Romanes, G. J., 1888, *Mental Evolution in Man,* Appleton, New York.

Rose, D., 1947, Comparisons of Fetal Development in Normal and Hyperthyroid Rats, *Journal of Comparative and Physiological Psychology* 40:87-105.

Rosenblatt, J. S., 1982, Personal communication, May 27.

Rosenblatt, J. S., and B. R. Komisaruk, 1977, *Reproductive Behavior and Evolution,* Plenum, New York.

Rosenblatt, J. S., G. Turkewitz, and T. C. Schneirla, 1969, Development of Home Orientation in Newly Born Kittens, *Transactions of the New York Academy of Sciences* 31:231-250.

Rosenblum, L. A., 1971, The Ontogeny of Mother-Infant Relations in Macaques, in *The Ontogeny of Vertebrate Behavior,* H. Moltz, ed., Academic Press, New York, pp. 315-367.

Rosenkoetter, J. S., and R. Boice, 1975, Earthworm Pheromones and T-maze Performance, *Journal of Comparative and Physiological Psychology,* 88:904-910.

Rosenthal, R., 1965, Introduction, Clever Hans: A Case Study of Scientific Method, in *O. Pfungst's Clever Hans (The Horse of Mr. Von Osten),* R. Rosenthal, ed., Reprinted edition, Holt, New York, pp. ix-xxxix.

Ross, S., and J. P. Scott, 1949, Relationship between Dominance and Control of

Movement in Goats, *Journal of Comparative and Physiological Psychology* 42:75-80.

Ross, S., W. I. Smith, and B. L. Woessner, 1955, Hoarding: An Analysis of Experiments and Trends, *Journal of General Psychology* 52:307-326.

Rosvold, H. E., 1955, Calvin Perry Stone, *American Journal of Psychology* 68:326-329.

Rumbaugh, D. M., and T. V. Gill, 1976, Language and the Acquisition of Language-type Skills by a Chimpanzee *(Pan)*. *Annals of the New York Academy of Sciences* 270:90-123.

Rundquist, E. A., 1933, Inheritance of Spontaneous Activity in Rats, *Journal of Comparative Psychology* 16:415-438.

Rusak, B., and I. Zucker, 1975, Biological Rhythms and Animal Behavior, *Annual Review of Psychology* 26:137-171.

Russell, R. W., 1954, Comparative Psychology, *Annual Review of Psychology* 5:229-246.

Samelson, F., 1980a, E. G. Boring and His *History of Experimental Psychology, American Psychologist* 35:467-470.

Samelson, F. 1980b, J. B. Watson's Little Albert, Cyril Burt's Twins, and the Need for a Critical Science, *American Psychologist* 35:619-625.

Samelson, F., 1981, Hero Worship Squared, *Contemporary Psychology* 26:63-64.

Sanborn, H. C., 1932, The Inheritance of Song in Birds, *Journal of Comparative Psychology* 13:345-364.

Savage-Rumbaugh, E. S., D. M., Rumbaugh, and S. Boysen, 1978, Linguistically Mediated Tool Use and Exchange by Chimpanzees (*Pan troglodytes*), *Behavioral and Brain Sciences* 4:539-554.

Schaffner, B., ed., 1955, *Group Processes,* Josiah Macy Foundation, New York.

Schiller, C. H., ed., 1957, *Instinctive Behavior: The Development of a Modern Concept,* International Universities Press, New York.

Schiller, P. H., 1948a, Delayed Response in the Minnow, *Journal of Comparative and Physiological Psychology* 41:233-238.

Schiller, P. H., 1948b, Delayed Detour Response in the Octopus, *Journal of Comparative and Physiological Psychology* 42:220-225.

Schiller, P. H., 1952, Innate Constituents of Complex Responses in Primates, *Psychological Review* 59:177-191.

Schiller, P. H., 1957, Innate Motor Action as a Basis of Learning, in *Instinctive Behavior: The Development of a Modern Concept,* C. H. Schiller, ed., International Universities Press, New York, pp. 264-287.

Schlosberg, H., 1947, The Concept of Play, *Psychological Review* 54:229-231.

Schmidt, K. P., 1957, Warder Clyde Allee, *Biographical Memoirs of the National Academy of Sciences,* 30:2-40.

Schneck, M. R., and C. J. Warden, 1929, A Comprehensive Survey of the Experimental Literture on Animal Retention, *Journal of Genetic Psychology* 36:1-20.

Schneirla, T. C., 1929, Learning and Orientation in Ants Studied by Means of the Maze Method, *Comparative Psychology Monographs* 6(30):1-143.

Schneirla, T. C., 1933, Motivation and Efficiency in Ant Learning, *Journal of Comparative Psychology* 15:243-266.

Schneirla, T. C., 1938, A Theory of Army-Ant Behavior Based upon the Analysis of Activities in a Representative Species, *Journal of Comparative Psychology* 25:51-90.

Schneirla, T. C., 1939, A Theoretical Consideration of the Basis for Approach-Withdrawal Adjustments in Behavior, *Psychological Bulletin* 37:501-502.

Schneirla, T. C., 1942, "Cruel" ants—and Occam's razor, *Journal of Comparative Psychology* 34:79-83.

Schneirla, T. C., 1943, Postscript to "Cruel Ants," *Journal of Comparative Psychology* 35:233-235.

Schneirla, T. C., 1946a, Contemporary American Animal Psychology in Perspective, in *Twentieth Century Psychology,* P. L. Harriman, ed., Philosophical Library, New York, pp. 306-316.

Schneirla, T. C., 1946b, Problems in the Biopsychology of Social Organizations, *Journal of Abnormal and Social Psychology* 41:385-402.

Schneirla, T. C., 1946c, Ant Learning as a Problem in Comparative Psychology, in *Twentieth Century Psychology,* P. L. Harriman, ed., Philosophical Library, New York, pp. 276-305.

Schneirla, T. C., 1947, Herbert Spencer Jennings: 1868-1947, *American Journal of Psychology* 60:447-450.

Schneirla, T. C., 1949, Levels in the Psychological Capacities of Animals, in *Philosophy for the future,* R. W. Sellars, V. J. McGill, and M. Farber, eds., MacMillan, New York, pp. 243-286.

Schneirla, T. C., 1950, The Relationship between Observation and Experimentation in the Field Study of Behavior, *Annals of the New York Academy of Sciences* 51:1022-1044.

Schneirla, T. C., 1951, The "Levels" Concept in the Study of Social Organization in Animals, in *Social Psychology at the Crossroads,* M. Sherif and J. N. Rohrer, eds., Harper, New York, pp. 83-120.

Schneirla, T. C. , 1952, A Consideration of Some Conceptual Trends in Comparative Psychology, *Psychological Bulletin* 49:559-597.

Schneirla, T. C., 1953a, The Concept of Levels in the Study of Social Phenomena, in *Groups in Harmony and Tension,* M. Sherif and C. Sherif, eds., Harper, New York, pp. 54-75.

Schneirla, T. C., 1953b, Insect Behavior in Relation to its Setting, in *Insect Physiology,* K. Roeder, ed., Wiley, New York, pp. 685-722.

Schneirla, T. C., 1954a, Problems and Results in the study of Ant Orientation, in *Proceedings of a Conference on Orientation in Animals,* T. C. Schneirla, ed., Office of Naval Research, Washington, D.C., pp. 30-52.

Schneirla, T. C., 1954b, Psychological Problems in the Orientation of Mammals, in *Proceedings of a Conference on Orientation in Animals,* T. C. Schneirla, ed., Office of Naval Research, Washington, D.C., pp. 193-200.

Schneirla, T. C., 1956, Interrelationships of the "Innate" and the "Acquired" in Instinctive Behavior, in *L'Instinct dans le Comportement des Animaux et de l'Homme,* Masson, Paris, pp. 387-452.

Schneirla, T. C., 1957a, The Concept of Development in Comparative Psychology, in *The Concept of Development,* D. B. Harris, ed., University of Minnesota Press, Minneapolis, pp. 78-108.

Schneirla, T. C., 1957*b*, Theoretical Considerations of Cyclic Processes in Doryline Ants, *Proceedings of the American Philosophical Society* 191:106-133.

Schneirla, T. C., 1958, The Study of Animal Behavior: Its History and Relation to the Museum: I, *Curator* 1:17-35.

Schneirla, T. C., 1959*a*, An Evolutionary and Developmental Theory of Biphasic Processes Underlying Approach and Withdrawal, in *Nebraska Symposium on Motivation 7*, M. R. Jones, ed., University of Nebraska Press, Lincoln, pp. 1-42.

Schneirla, T. C., 1959*b*, The Study of Animal Behavior: Its History and Relation to the Museum: II, *Curator* 2:27-48.

Schneirla, T. C., 1962, Psychology, Comparative, *Encyclopaedia Britanica* 18:690-703.

Schneirla, T. C., and N. R. F. Maier, 1940, Concerning the Status of the Starfish, *Journal of Comparative Psychology* 30:103-110.

Schneirla, T. C., and G. Piel, 1948, The Army Ant, *Scientific American* 178:16-23.

Schneirla, T. C., and J. S. Rosenblatt, 1961, Behavioral Organization and Genesis of the Social Bond in Insects and Mammals, *Amerian Journal of Orthopsychiatry* 31:223-253.

Schneirla, T. C., and J. S. Rosenblatt, 1973, "Critical Periods" in the Development of Behavior, *Science* 139:1110-1115.

Schneirla, T. C., J. S. Rosenblatt, and E. Tobach, 1983, Maternal Behavior in the Cat, in *Maternal Behavior in Mammals*, H. L. Rheingold, ed., Wiley, New York, pp. 122-148.

Schorger, A. W., 1954, Wallace Craig, *Auk* 71:496.

Schrier, A. M., 1969, *Rattus* Revisited, *American Psychologist* 24:681-682.

Scott, J. P., ed., 1950, Methodology and Techniques for the Study of Animal Societies, *Annals of the New York Academy of Sciences* 51:1001-1122.

Scott, J. P., 1962, Critical Periods in Behavioral Development, *Science* 138:949-958.

Scott, J. P., 1963, Reply to Schneirla and Rosenblatt, *Science* 139:1115-1116.

Scott, J. P., 1967, Comparative Psychology and Ethology, 18:65-86.

Scott, J. P., 1973, The Organization of Comparative Psychology, *Annals of the New York Academy of Sciences* 223:7-40.

Scott, J. P., 1976, Animal Behavior and Social Organization, Paper presented at meetings of the Animal Behavior Society, Boulder, Colo., June.

Searle, L. V., 1949, The Organization of Hereditary Maze-Brightness and Maze-Dullness, *Genetic Psychology Monographs* 39:279-325.

Sears, R. R., 1982, Harry Frederick Harlow (1905-1981), *American Psychologist* 37:1280-1281.

Sebeok, T. A., and J. Umiker-Sebeok, 1979, Performing Animals: Secrets of the Trade, *Psychology Today* 13(6):78-91.

Sebeok, T. A., and J. Umiker-Sebeok, 1980, *Speaking of Apes*, Plenum, New York.

Seligman, M. E. P., 1970, On the Generality of the Laws of Learning, *Psychological Review* 77:406-418.

Seligman, M. E. P., 1980, Harris on Selective Misrepresentation: A Selective Misrepresentation of Seligman, *American Psychologist* 35:214-219.

Seligman, M. E. P., and J. L. Hager, 1972, *Biological Boundaries of Learning*, Appleton-Century-Crofts, New York.

Seward, G. H., 1940, Studies of the Reproductive Activities of the Guinea Pig. II. The Role of Hunger in Filial Behavior, *Journal of Comparative Psychology* 29:25-41.

Seward, J. P., 1940, Studies on the Reproductive Activities of the Guinea Pig. III. The Effect of Androgenic Hormone on Sex Drive in Males and Females, *Journal of Comparative Psychology* 30:435-449.

Seward, J. P., and G. H. Seward, 1940, Studies on the Reproductive Activities of the Guinea Pig. I. Factors in Maternal Behavior, *Journal of Comparative Psychology* 29:1-24.

Sheffield, F. D., J. J. Wulff, and R. Backer, 1951, Reward Value of Copulation without Drive Reduction, *Journal of Comparative and Physiological Psychology* 44:3-8.

Shepard J. F., 1911, Some Results in Comparative Psychology, *Psychological Bulletin* 8:41-42.

Shepard, J. F., 1914, Types of Learning in Animals and Man, *Psychological Bulletin* 11:58.

Shepard, J. F., and F. S. Breed, 1913, Maturation and Use in the Development of an Instinct, *Journal of Animal Behavior* 3:274-285.

Shepherd, W. T., 1911, Imitation in Raccoons, *American Journal of Psychology* 22:583-585.

Shepherd, W. T., 1915a, Tests on Adaptive Intelligence in Dogs and Cats, as Compared with Adaptive Intelligence in Rhesus Monkeys, *American Journal of Psychology* 26:211-216.

Shepherd, W. T., 1915b, Some Observations on the Intelligence of the Chimpanzee, *Journal of Animal Behavior* 5:391-396.

Shepherd, W. T., 1923, Some Observations and Experiments of the Intelligence of the Chimpanzee and Ourang, *American Journal of Psychology* 34:590-591.

Siegel, A. I., 1953, Deprivation of Visual Form Definition in the Ring Dove. I. Discrimination Learning, *Journal of Comparative and Physiological Psychology* 46:115-123.

Siegel, P. S., and H. L. Stuckey, 1947, The Diurnal Course of Water and Food Intake in the Normal Mature Rat, *Journal of Comparative and Physiological Psychology* 40:365-370.

Simpson, G. G., 1953, The Baldwin Effect, *Evolution* 7:110-117.

Singer, B., 1981, History of the Study of Animal Behavior, in *The Oxford Companion to Animal Behaviour,* D. McFarland, ed., Oxford University Press, Oxford, pp. 255-272.

Skinner, B. F., 1930, On the Inheritance of Maze Behavior, *Journal of General Psychology* 4:342-346.

Skinner, B. F., 1959, John Broadus Watson, Behaviorist, *Science* 129:197-198.

Skinner, B. F., 1963, Behaviorism at Fifty, *Science* 140:951-958.

Skinner, B. F., 1966, The Phylogeny and Ontogeny of Behavior, *Science* **153**:1205-1213.

Skinner, B. F., 1974, *About Behaviorism*, Knopf, New York.

Skiner, B. F., 1975, The Shaping of Phylogenic Behavior, *Journal of the Experimental Analysis of Behavior*, **24**:117-120.

Skinner, B. F., 1977, Herrnstein and the Evolution of Behaviorism, *American Psychologist* **32**:1006-1012.

Small, W. S., 1899, Notes on the Psychic Development of the Young White Rat, *American Journal of Psychology* **11**:80-100.

Small, W. S., 1900, An Experimental Study of the Mental Processes of the Rat, *American Journal of Psychology* **11**:133-165.

Small, W. S., 1901, Experimental Study of the Mental Processes of the Rat. II, *American Journal of Psychology* **12**:206-239.

Smith, J. C., and H. D. Baker, 1960, Conditioning in the Horsehoe Crab, *Journal of Comparative and Physiological Psychology* **53**:279-281.

Smith, W. I., and E. B. Hale, 1959, Modification of Social Rank in the Domestic Fowl, *Journal of Comparative and Physiological Psychology* **52**:373-375.

Smith, W. I., and S. Ross, 1950, Hoarding behavior in the golden hamster *(Mesocricetus auratus auratus)*, *Journal of Genetic Psychology* **77**: 211-215.

Snowden, C. T., 1982, Not All Our Snarks Are Boojums, *Comparative Psychology Newsletter* **2**(1):5-6.

Snowden, C. T., and A. Hodun, 1981, Acoustic Adaptations in Pygmy Marmoset Contact Calls: Locational Cues Vary with Distances Between Conspecifics, *Behavioral Ecology and Sociobiology* **9**:295-300.

Solem, A., and W. J. McKeachie, 1979, Norman R. F. Maier (1900-1977), *American Psychologist* **34**:266-267.

Spalding, D. A., 1873, Instinct with Original Observations on Young Animals, *MacMillan's Magazine* **27**:282-293. (Reprinted *British Journal of Animal Behavior* **2**(1954):1-11.

Spalding, D. A., 1875, Instinct and Acquisition, *Nature* **12**:507-508.

Spear, N. E., and B. A. Campbell, 1979, *Ontogeny of Learning and Memory*, Lawrence Erlbaum, Hillsdale, N.J.

Spence, K. W., 1939, The Solution of Multiple Choice Problems by Chimpanzees, *Comparative Psychology Monographs* **15**(75):1-54.

Spragg, S. D. S., 1940, Morphine Addiction in Chimpanzees, *Comparative Psychology Monographs* **15**(79):1-132.

Sprott, R. L., and J. Staats, 1975, Behavioral Studies Using Genetically Defined Mice—A Bibliography, *Behavior Genetics* **5**:27-82.

Stamm, J. S., 1956, Genetics of Hoarding: II. Hoarding Behavior of Hybrid and Backcrossed Strains of Rats, *Journal of Comparative and Physiological Psychology* **49**:349-352.

Stellar, E., and G. Lindzey, 1978, Clifford T. Morgan: 1915-1976, *American Journal of Psychology* **91**:343-348.

Stevens, H. C., 1913, Acquired Specific Reactions to Color (Chromotropism) in *Oregonia gracilis*, *Journal of Animal Behavior* **3**:149-178.

Stevens, S. S., 1951, *Handbook of Experimental Psychology,* Wiley, New York.

Stevenson, H. W., E. H. Hess, and H. L. Rheingold, 1967, *Early Behavior: Comparative and Developmental Approaches,* Wiley, New York.

Stone, C. P., 1922, The Congenital Sexual Behavior of the Young Male Albino Rat, *Journal of Comparative Psychology* 2:95-153.

Stone, C. P., 1923, Further Study of Sensory Functions in the Activation of Sexual Behavior in the Young Male Albino Rat, *Journal of Comparative Psychology* 3:469-473.

Stone, C. P., 1924a, Delay in the Awakening of Copulatory Ability in the Male Albino Rat Incurred by Defective Diets, *Journal of Comparative Psychology* 4:195-224.

Stone, C. P., 1924b, A Note on "Feminine" Behavior in Adult Male Rats, *American Journal of Physiology* 68:39-41.

Stone, C. P., 1927a, Recent Contributions to the Experimental Literature on Native or Congential Behavior, *Psychological Bulletin* 24:36-61.

Stone, C. P., 1927b, The Retention of Copulatory Ability in Male Rats Following Castration, *Journal of Comparative Psychology* 7:369-387.

Stone, C. P., 1932a, The Retention of Copulatory Ability in Male Rabbits following Castration, *Journal of Genetic Psychology* 40:296-305.

Stone, C. P., 1932b, Wildness and Savageness in Rats of Different Strains, in *Studies in the Dynamics of Behavior,* K. S. Lashley, ed., University of Chicago Press, Chicago, pp. 1-55.

Stone, C. P., 1935, Sex Differences in the Running Ability of Thoroughbred Horses, *Journal of Comparative Psychology* 19:59-67.

Stone, C. P., 1940, Precocious Copulatory Activity Induced in Male Rats by Subcutaneous Injections of Testosterone Propionate, *Endocrinology* 26:511-515.

Stone, C. P., 1943, Multiply, Vary, Let the Stongest Live and the Weakest Die—Charles Darwin, *Psychological Bulletin* 40:1-24.

Stone, C. P., 1947, Methodological Resources for the Experimental Study of Innate Behavior as Related to Environmental Factors, *Psychological Review* 54:342-347.

Stone, C. P., ed., 1951, *Comparative Psychology,* 3rd ed., Prentice-Hall, Englewood Cliffs, N.J.

Stone, C. P., and L. W. Ferguson, 1940, Temporal Relationships in the Copulatory Acts of Adult Male Rats, *Journal of Comparative Psychology* 30:419-433.

Stone, C. P., M. I. Tomlin, and R. G. Barker, 1935, A Comparative Study of Sexual Drive in Adult Male Rats as Measured by Direct Copulatory Tests and by the Columbia Obstruction Apparatus, *Journal of Comparative Psychology* 19:215-241.

Stout, A. K., 1967, Hobhouse, Leonard Trelawney, in *The Encyclopedia of Philosophy,* P. Edwards, ed., Macmillan, New York, p. 46.

Sturman-Hulbe, M., and C. P. Stone, 1929, Maternal Behavior in the Albino Rat, *Journal of Comparative Psychology* 9:203-237.

Suomi, S. J., and H. A. Leroy, 1982, In Memoriam: Harry F. Harlow (1905-1981), *American Journal of Primatology* 2:319-342.

Sutherland, N. S., 1959, A Test of a Theory of Shape Discrimination in *Octopus vulgaris* Lamarck, *Journal of Comparative and Physiological Psychology* **52**:135-141.

Swindle, P. F., 1917, The Biological Significance of the Eye Appendages of Organisms, *American Journal of Psychology* **28**:486-496.

Swindle, P. F., 1919a, Analysis of Nesting Activities, *American Journal of Psychology* **30**:173-186.

Swindle, P. F., 1919b, Some Forms of Natural Training to which Certain Birds are Subjected, *American Journal of Psychology* **30**:165-172.

Tavolga, W. N., 1969, *Principles of Animal Behavior*, Harper & Row, New York.

Tavolga, W. N., 1970, Levels of Interaction in Animal Communication, in *Development and Evolution of Behavior*, L. R. Aronson, E. Tobach, D. S. Lehrman, and J. S. Rosenblatt, eds., San Francisco, pp. 281-302.

Teleki, G., 1981, C. Raymond Carpenter, 1905-1975, *American Journal of Physical Anthropology* **56**:383-385.

Terrace, H. S., 1979a, *Nim: A Chimpanzee Who Learned Sign Language*, Knopf, New York.

Terrace, H. S., 1979b, How Nim Chimpsky Changed My Mind, *Psychology Today* **13**(6):65-76.

Thiessen, D. D., 1972, *Gene Organization and Behavior*, Random House, New York.

Thiessen, D. D., and M. Rice, 1976, Mammalian Scent Gland Marking and Social Behavior, *Psychological Bulletin* **83**:505-539.

Thiessen, D. D., and D. A. Rodgers, 1961, Population Density and Endocrine Function, *Psychological Bulletin* **58**:441-451.

Thomas, G., 1975, Editorial, *Journal of Comparative and Physiological Psychology* **89**:1-4.

Thompson, R., and J. V. McConnell, 1955, Classical Conditioning in the Planarian, *Dugesia dorotocephala*, *Journal of Comparative and Physiological Psychology* **48**:65-68.

Thompson, W. R., 1953a, Exploratory Behavior as a Function of Hunger in "Bright" and "Dull" Rats, *Journal of Comparative and Physiological Psychology* **46**:323-326.

Thompson, W. R., 1953b, The Inheritance of Behavior: Behavioral Differences in Fifteen Mouse Strains, *Canadian Journal of Psychology* **7**:145-155.

Thompson, W. R., 1958, Social Behavior, in *Behavior and Evolution*, A. Roe and G. G. Simpson, eds., Yale University Press, New Haven, pp. 291-310.

Thompson, W. R., and W. Heron, 1954, The Effects of Early Restriction on Activity in Dogs, *Journal of Comparative and Physiological Psychology* **47**:77-82.

Thorndike, E. L., 1898a, Animal Intelligence: An Experimental Study of the Associative Process in Animals, *Psychological Review Monograph Supplement* **2**(4):1-109.

Thorndike, E. L., 1898b, Some Experiments on Animal Intelligence, *Science* **7**:818-824.

Thorndike, E. L., 1898c, Review of W. Mills', *Animal Intelligence*, *Science* **8**:520.

Thorndike, E. L., 1899a, The Instinctive Reaction of Young Chicks, *Psychological Review* **6**:282-291.

Thorndike, E. L., 1899*b*, Do Animals Reason? *Popular Science Monthly* **55**:480-490.

Thorndike, E. L., 1899*c*, A Note on the Psychology of Fishes, *American Naturalist* **33**:923-926.

Thorndike, E. L., 1899*d*, A Reply to "The Nature of Animal Intelligence and the Methods of Investigating It," *Psychological Review* **6**:412-420.

Thorndike, E. L., 1901*a*, The Mental Life of the Monkeys, *Psychological Review Monograph Supplement* **3**(5):1-57.

Thorndike, E. L., 1910*b*, The Evolution of the Human Intellect, *Popular Science Monthly* **60**:58-65.

Thorndike, E. L., 1901*c*, The Intelligence of Monkeys, *Popular Science Monthly* **59**:273-279.

Thorndike, E. L., 1911, *Animal Intelligence*, MacMillan, New York.

Thorndike, E. L., 1915, Watson's "Behavior," *Journal of Animal Behavior* **5**:462-467.

Thorndike, E. L., 1936, Edward Lee Thorndike, in *A History of Psychology in Autobiography*, vol. 3, C. Murchison, ed., Clark University Press, Worcester, Mass., pp. 263-270.

Thorpe, W. H., 1953, Editorial, *British Journal of Animal Behaviour* **1**:3-4.

Thorpe, W. H., 1956, Ethology as a New Branch of Biology, in *Perspectives in Marine Biology*, A. A. Buzzati-Traverso, ed., University of California Press, Berkeley, pp. 411-428.

Thorpe, W. H., 1961, Comparative Psychology, *Annual Review of Psychology* **12**:27-50.

Thorpe, W. H., 1973, Is There a Comparative Psychology? The Relevance of Inherited and Acquired Constraints in the Action Patterns and Perceptions of Animals, *Annals of the New York Academy of Sciences* **223**:89-112.

Thorpe, W. H., 1979, *The Origins and Rise of Ethology* Praeger, New York.

Thorpe, W. H., and D. Davenport, eds., 1965, Learning and Associated Phenomena in Invertebrates, *Animal Behaviour*, Suppl. 1.

Thorpe, W. H., and O. L. Zangwill, 1963, *Current Problems in Animal Behavior*, Cambridge University Press, Cambridge.

Timberlake, W., 1980, A Molar Equilibrim Theory of Learned Performance, in *The Psychology of Learning and Motivation*, vol. 14, G. M. Bower, ed., Academic Press, New York, pp. 1-58.

Timberlake, W., 1983, The Functional Organization of Appetitive Behavior: Behavior Systems and Learning, in *Advances in Analysis of Behavior: Biological Factors in Learning*, vol. 3, M. D. Zeiler and P. Harzem, eds., Wiley, Chichester, pp. 173-217.

Tinbergen, N., 1948, Social Releasers and the Experimental Method Required for Their Study, *Wilson Bulletin* **60**:6-51.

Tinbergen, N., 1951, *The Study of Instinct*, Oxford University Press, Oxford.

Tinbergen, N., 1955, Psychology and Ethology as Supplementary Parts of a Science of Behavior, in *Group Processes*, B. Schaffner, ed., Foundation, J. Macy, Jr., New York, pp. 75-167.

Tinbergen, N., 1957, On Anti-predator Responses in Certain Birds—A Reply, *Journal of Comparative and Physiological Psychology* **50**:412-414.

Tinbergen, N., 1958, *Curious Naturalists*, Basic Books, New York.

Tinbergen, N., 1963, On Aims and Methods of Ethology, *Zeitschrift für Tierpsychologie* **20**:410-429.

Tinklepaugh, O. L., 1928, An Experimental Study of Representative Factors in Monkeys, *Journal of Comparative Psychology* 8:197-236.

Tinklepaugh, O. L., 1932*a*, Maze Learning of a Turtle, *Journal of Comparative Psychology* 13:201-206.

Tinklepaugh, O. L., 1932*b*, Multiple Delayed Reactions with Chimpanzees and Monkeys, *Journal of Comparative Psychology* 13:207-243.

Tinklepaugh, O. L., and C. G. Hartman, 1930, Behavioral Aspects of Parturition in the Monkey *(Macaca rhesus)*, *Journal of Comparative Psychology* 11:63-98.

Tobach, E., 1970, Some Guidelines to the Study of the Evolution and Development of Emotion, in *Development and Evolution of Behavior*, L. R. Aronson, E. Tobach , D. S. Lehrman, and J. S. Rosenblatt, eds., Freeman, San Francisco, pp. 238-253.

Tobach, E., 1978, The Methodology of Sociobiology from the Viewpoint of a Comparative Psychologist, in *The Sociobiology Debate*, A. L. Caplan, ed., Harper, New York, pp. 411-423.

Tobach, E., and L. R. Aronson, 1970, T. C. Schneirla: A Biographical Note, in *Development and Evolution of Behavior*, L. R. Aronson, E. Tobach, D. S. Lehrman, and H. S. Rosenblatt, eds., Freeman, San Francisco, pp. xi-xviii.

Tobach, E., and T. C. Schneirla, 1968, The Biopsychology of Social Behavior of Animals, in *Biologic Basis of Pediatric Practice*, R. E. Cooke and S. Levin, eds., McGraw-Hill, New York, pp. 68-82.

Tobach, E., L. R. Aronson, and E. Shaw, 1971, *The Biopsychology of Development*, Academic Press, New York.

Tobach, E., H. E. Adler, and L. L. Adler, eds., 1973, Comparative Psychology at Issue, *Annals of the New York Academy of Sciences* 223:1-198.

Tolman, E. C., 1920, Instinct and Purpose, *Psychological Review* 27:217-233.

Tolman, E. C., 1922, Can Instincts Be Given Up in Psychology? *Journal of Abnormal and Social Psychology* 17:139-152.

Tolman, E. C., 1923, The Nature of Instinct, *Psychological Bulletin* 20:200-216.

Tolman, E. C., 1924, The Inheritance of Maze-Learning Ability in Rats, *Journal of Comparative Psychology* 4:1-18.

Tomlin, M. I., and R. M. Yerkes, 1935, Chimpanzee Twins: Behavioral Relations and Development, *Journal of Genetic Psychology* 46:237-263.

Topoff, H., 1976, The Social Organization of Army Ants: Integration of Field and Laboratory Research, in *Psychological Research: The Inside Story*, M. H. Siegel and H. P. Ziegler, eds., Harper & Row, New York, pp. 50-75.

Towe, A. L., 1954, A Study of Figural Equivalence in the Pigeon, *Journal of Comparative and Physiological Psychology* 47:183-287.

Triplett, N., 1898, The Dynamogenic Factors in Pacemaking and Competition, *American Journal of Psychology* 9:507-533.

Triplett, N., 1901, The Educability of the Perch, *American Journal of Psychology* 12:354-360.

Tryon, R. C., 1930, Studies in Individual Differences in Maze Ability: I. The Measurement of the Reliability of Individual Differences, *Journal of Comparative Psychology* 11:145-170.

Tryon, R. C., 1940, Genetic Differences in Maze-Learning Ability in Rats, in *The Yearbook of the National Society for the Study of Education*, vol. 39, G. M. Whipple, ed., Public School Publishing Company, Bloomington, Ill., pp. 111-118.

Tsai, C., 1925, The Relative Strength of Sex and Hunger Motives in the Albino Rat, *Journal of Comparative Psychology* 5:407-415.

Tsai, L. H., 1931, Sucking Preference in Nursing Young Rats, *Journal of Comparative Psychology* 12:251-256.

Twitmyer, E. B., 1905, Knee-jerks without Stimulation of the Patellar Tendon, *Psychological Bulletin* 2:43-45.

Ulrich, R. E., and N. H. Azrin, 1962, Reflexive Fighting in Response to Aversive Stimulation, *Journal of the Experimental Analysis of Behavior* 5:511-520.

Urban, W. M., 1935, James Mark Baldwin: Co-editor, *Psychological Review,* 1894-1909, *Psychological Review* 42:303-306.

Utsurikawa, N., 1917, Temperamental Differences between Outbred and Inbred Strains of the Albino Rat, *Journal of Animal Behavior* 7:111-129.

Uytman, J. D., 1967, McDougall, William, in *The Encyclopedia of Philosophy,* P. Edwards, ed., Macmillan, New York, pp. 226-227.

Vale, J. R., 1980, *Genes, Environment, and Behavior: An Interactionist Approach,* Harper & Row, New York.

Vale, J. R. and C. A. Vale, 1969, Individual Differences and General Laws in Psychology, *American Psychologist* 24:1093-1108.

Verplanck, W. S., 1955, Since Learned Behavior is Innate, and Vice Versa, What Now? *Psychological Review* 62:139-144.

Verplanck, W. S., 1957, A Glossary of Some Terms Used in the Objective Science of Behavior, *Psychological Review Supplement,* vol 64, 42p.

Verplanck, W. S., 1958, Comparative Psychology, *Annual Review of Psychology* 9:99-118.

Voronin, L. G., 1962, Some Results of Comparative Physiological Investigations of Higher Nervous Activity, *Psychological Bulletin,* 59:161-195.

Waddington, C. H., 1953, Genetic Assimilation of an Acquired Character, *Evolution* 7:118-126.

Wade, N., 1980, Does Man Alone Have Language? Apes Reply in Riddles, and a Horse Says Neigh, *Science* 208:1349-1351.

Wallace, R. A., 1973, *The Ecology and Evolution of Animal Behavior,* Goodyear, Pacific Palisades, Calif.

Wang, G. H., 1923, The Relation Between "Spontaneous" Activity and Oestrous Cycle in the White Rat, *Comparative Psychology Monographs* 2(6):1-27.

Wang, G. H., 1924, A Sexual Activity Rhythm in the Female Rat, *American Naturalist* 58:36-42.

Wapner, S. and B. Kaplan, 1964, Heinz Werner: 1890-1964, *American Journal of Psychology* 77:513-517.

Warden, C. J., 1927a, The Historical Development of Comparative Psychology, *Psychological Review* 34:57-85, 135-168.

Warden, C. J., 1927b, *A Short Outline of Comparative Psychology,* Norton, New York.

Warden, C. J., 1927c, Is Intelligence Adaptive? *New Republic* 50:346-347.

Warden, C. J., 1928, The Development of Modern Comparative Psychology, *Quarterly Review of Biology* 3:486-522.

Warden, C. J., 1930, A Note on the Early History of Experimental Methods in Comparative Psychology, *Journal of Genetic Psychology* 38:466-471.

Warden, C. J. and J. Baar, 1929, The Müller-Lyer Illusion in the Ring Dove, *Turtur risorius, Journal of Comparative Psychology* 9:275-292.

Warden, C. J., and R. A. Jackson, 1935, Imitative Behavior in the Rhesus Monkey, *Journal of Genetic Psychology* 46:103-125.

Warden, C. J., and J. B. Rowley, 1929, The Discrimination of Absolute Versus Relative Brightness in the Ring Dove, *Turtur risorius, Journal of Comparative Psychology* 9:317-337.

Warden, C. J., and L. H. Warner, 1927, The Development of Animal Psychology in the United States during the Past Three Decades, *Psychological Review* 34:196-205.

Warden, C. J., and L. H. Warner, 1928, The Sensory Capacities and Intelligence of Dogs, with a Report on the Ability of the Noted Dog "Fellow" to Respond to Verbal Stimuli, *Quarterly Review of Biology* 3:1-28.

Warden, C. J., T. N. Jenkins, and L. H. Warner, 1935, *Comparative Psychology: A Comprehensive Treatise,* vol. 1, *Principles and Methods,* Ronald, New York.

Warden, C. J., H. A. Fjeld, and A. M. Koch, 1940a, Imitative Behavior in Cebus and Rhesus Monkeys, *Journal of Genetic Psychology* 56:311-322.

Warden, C. J., T. N. Jenkins, and L. H. Warner, 1940b, *Comparative Psychology: A Comprehensive Treatise,* vol. 2, *Plants and Invertebrates,* Ronald, New York.

Warden, C. J., T. N. Jenkins, and L. H. Warner, 1940c, *Comparative Psychology: A Comprehensive Treatise,* vol. 3, *Vertebrates,* Ronald, New York.

Warkentin, J., and L. Carmichael, 1939, A Study of the Development of the Air-Righting Reflex in Cats and Rabbits, *Journal of Genetic Psychology* 55:67-80.

Warner, L. H., 1927, A Study of Sex Behavior in the White Rat by Means of the Obstruction Method, *Journal of Comparative Psychology* 4(22), 68p.

Warner, L. H., 1928, Facts and Theories of Bird Flight, *Quarterly Review of Biology* 3:84-98.

Warner, L. H., 1931a, The Present Status of the Problems of Orientation and Homing Birds, *Quarterly Review of Biology* 6:208-214.

Warner, L. H., 1931b, The Problem of Color Vision in Fishes, *Quarterly Review of Biology* 6:329-348.

Warren, J. M., n.d., Evolution and Intelligence, Pennsylvania State University, unpublished manuscript.

Warren, J. M., 1959, Solution of Object and Positional Discriminations by Rhesus Monkeys, *Journal of Comparative and Physiological Psychology* 52:92-93.

Warren, J. M., 1960, Reversal Learning by Paradise Fish *(Macropodus opercularis), Journal of Comparative and Physiological Psychology* 53:376-378.

Warren, J. M., 1961, The Effect of Telencephalic Injuries on Learning by Paradise Fish, *Macropodus opercularis, Journal of Comparative and Physiological Psychology* 54:130-132.

Warren, J. M., 1965*a*, Comparative Psychology of Learning, *Annual Review of Psychology* **16**:95-118.

Warren, J. M., 1965*b*, Primate Learning in Comparative Perspective, in *Behavior of Nonhuman Primates: Modern Research Trends*, A. M. Schrier, H. F. Harlow, and F. Stollnitz, eds., Academic Press, New York, pp. 249-281.

Warren, J. M., 1973, Learning in Vertebrates, in *Comparative Psychology: A Modern Survey*, D. A. Dewsbury and D. A. Rethlingshafer, eds., McGraw-Hill, New York, pp. 471-509.

Warren, J. M., 1976, Tool Use in Mammals, in *Evolution of Brain and Behavior in Vertebrates*, R. B. Masterton, M. E. Bitterman, C. B. G. Campbell, and N. Hotton, eds., Lawrence Erlbaum, New York, pp. 407-424.

Warren, J. M., and A. Baron, 1956, The Formation of Learning Sets by Cats, *Journal of Comparative and Physiological Psychology* **49**:227-231.

Washburn, M. F., 1904, The Genetic Methods in Psychology, *Journal of Philosophy, Psychology and Scientific Methods* **1**:491-494.

Washburn, M. F., 1935, James Mark Baldwin: 1861-1934, *American Journal of Psychology* **47**:168-169.

Washburn, M. F., 1908*a*, The Animal Mind: A Text-book of Comparative Psychology, MacMillan, New York.

Washburn, M. F., 1908*b*, "The Animal Mind", *Psychological Bulletin* **5**:345-346.

Washburn, M. F., 1908*c*, French Work in Comparative Psychology for the Past Two Years, *Journal of Comparative Neurology and Psychology* **8**:511-520.

Washburn, M. F., 1911, A Discussion of Instinct, *Journal of Animal Behavior* **1**:456-460.

Washburn, M. F., 1923, A Questionary Study of Certain National Differences in Emotional Traits, *Journal of Comparative Psychology* **3**:413-430.

Washburn, M. F., 1932, Margaret Floy Washburn, in *A History of Psychology in Autobiography*, C. Murchison, ed., Clark University Press, Worcester, Mass., pp. 333-358.

Washburn, M. F., and I. M. Bentley, 1906, The Establishment of an Association Involving Color-discrimination in the Creek Chub, *Semotilus atromaculatus*, *Journal of Comparative Neurology and Psychology* **16**:113-125.

Waters, R. H., 1939, Morgan's Canon and Anthropomorphism, *Psychological Review* **46**:534-540.

Waters, R. H., D. A. Rethlingshafer, and W. E. Caldwell, 1960, *Principles of Comparative Psychology*, McGraw-Hill, New York.

Watson, J. B., 1903, *Animal Education*, University of Chicago, Chicago.

Watson, J. B., 1904, Some Unemphasized Aspects of Comparative Psychology, *Journal of Comparative Neurology and Psychology* **14**:360-363.

Watson, J. B., 1906, The Need of an Experimental Station for the Study of Certain Problems in Animal Behavior, *Psychological Bulletin,* **3**:149-156.

Watson, J. B., 1907*a*, Report of John B. Watson on the Condition of the Noddy and Sooty Tern Colony on Bird Key, Tortugas, Florida, *Bird-Lore* **9**:307-316.

Watson, J. B., 1907*b*, Psychological Literature, *Psychological Bulletin* **4**:288-296.

Watson, J. B., 1908*a*, Imitation in Monkeys, *Psychological Bulletin* **5**:169-178.

Watson, J. B., 1908*b*, The Behavior of Noddy and Sooty Terns, *Publications of the Carnegie Institution* **2**(103):187-255.

Watson, J. B., 1908c, Recent Literature on Mammalian Behavior, *Psychological Bulletin* **5**:195-205.

Watson, J. B., 1910a, Further Data on the Homing Sense of Noddy and Sooty Terns, *Science* **32**:470-474.

Watson, J. B., 1910b, The New Science of Animal Behavior, *Harper's Magazine* **120**:346-353.

Watson, J. B., 1911, Literature for 1910 on the Behavior of Vertebrates, *Journal of Animal Behavior* **1**:430-447.

Watson, J. B., 1912a, Instinctive Activity in Animals, *Harper's Magazine* **124**:376-382.

Watson, J. B., 1912b, Literature for 1911 on the Behavior of Vertebrates, *Journal of Animal Behavior* **2**:421-440.

Watson, J. B., 1913, Psychology as the Behavorist Views It, *Psychological Review* **20**:158-177.

Watson, J. B., 1914, *Behavior: An Introduction to Comparative Psychology*, Holt, New York.

Watson, J. B., 1915, Recent Experiments with Homing Birds, *Harper's Magazine* **131**:457-464.

Watson, J. B., 1919, *Psychology from the Standpoint of a Behaviorist*, Lippincott, Philadelphia.

Watson, J. B., 1923, Professor McDougall Returns to Religion, *New Republic* **34**(II):11-14.

Watson, J. B., 1926, What is Behaviorism? *Harper's Magazine* **152**:723-729.

Watson, J. B., 1927, The Behaviorist Looks at Instincts, *Harper's Magazine* **155**:228-235.

Watson, J. B., 1930, *Behaviorism*, 2nd ed., University of Chicago Press, Chicago.

Watson, J. B., 1936, John Broadus Watson, in *A History of Psychology in Autobiography*, vol. 3, C. Murchison, ed., University Press, Worcester, Mass., pp. 271-281.

Watson, J. B., and K. S. Lashley, 1915, Homing and Related Activities of Birds, *Publications of the Carnegie Institution* **7**(211):1-104.

Watson, J. B., and W. McDougall, 1929, *The Battle of Behaviorism*, Norton, New York.

Watson, J. B., and J. J. B. Morgan, 1917, Emotional Reactions and Psychological Experimentation, *American Journal of Psychology* **28**:163-174.

Watson, J. B., and R. Rayner, 1920, Conditioned Emotional Reactions, *Journal of Experimental Psychology* **3**:1-14.

Waugh, K. T., 1908, The Animal Mind, *Psychological Bulletin* **5**:205-209.

Wayner, M. J., and D. K. Zellner, 1957, The Role of the Suprapharyngeal Ganglion in Spontaneous Alternation and Negative Movements in *Lumbricus terretris* L., *Journal of Comparative and Physiological Psychology* **50**:282-287.

Webb, W. B., 1974, Sleep as an Adaptive Response, *Perceptual and Motor Skills* **38**:1023-1027.

Welker, W. I., 1959, Genesis of Exploratory and Play Behavior in Infant Raccoons, *Psychological Reports* **5**:764.

Whalen, R. E., 1961*a*, Comparative Psychology, *American Psychologist* 16:84.

Whalen, R. E., 1961*b*, Strain Difference in Sexual Behavior of the Male Rat, *Behaviour* 18:199-204.

Whalen, R. E., 1963, Sexual Behavior of Cats, *Behaviour* 20:321-342.

Wheeler, O. A., 1916, The Basis of Comparative Psychology, *Sociological Review* 6:338-347.

Whitman, C. O., 1898/1899, Myths in Animal Psychology, *The Monist* 9:524-537.

Whitney, G., 1976, Genetic Substrates for the Initial Evolution of Human Sociality. I. Sex Chromosome Mechanism, *American Naturalist* 110:867-875.

Wilcock, J., 1972, Comparative Psychology Lives on Under an Assumed Name—Psychogenetics! *American Psychologist* 27:531-538.

Wilson, E. O., 1975*a*, *Sociobiology: The New Synthesis,* Harvard University Press, Cambridge, Mass.

Wilson, E. O., 1975*b*, Slavery in Ants, *Scientific American* 232(6):32-36.

Wilson, J. R., N. Adler, and B. LeBoeuf, 1965, The Effects of Intromission Frequency on Successful Pregnancy in the Female Rat, *Proceedings of the National Academy of Sciences* 53:1392-1395.

Windle, W. F., 1980, The Cayo Santiago Primate Colony, *Science* 209:1486-1491.

Winslow, C. N., 1940, A Study of Experimentally Induced Competitive Behavior in the White Rat, *Comparative Psychology Monographs* 15(78):1-35.

Winslow, C. N., 1944*a*, The Social Behavior of Cats. I. Competitive and Aggressive Behavior in an Experimental Runway Situation, *Journal of Comparative Psychology* 37:297-313.

Winslow, C. N., 1944*b*, The Social Behavior of Cats. II. Competitive, Aggressive, and Food-Sharing Behavior When Both Competitors Have Access to the Goal, *Journal of Comparative Psychology* 37:315-326.

Witkin, H. A., 1975, Heinz Werner: 1890-1964, *Child Development* 36:307-328.

Witmer, L., 1909, A Monkey With a Mind, *Psychological Clinic* 3:179-205.

Witmer, L., 1910, Intelligent Imitation and Curiosity in a Monkey, *Psychological Clinic* 3:225-227.

Witt, G., and C. S. Hall, 1949, The Genetics of Audiogenic Seizures in the House Mouse, *Journal of Comparative and Physiological Psychology* 42:58-63.

Wolfe, J. B., 1936, Effectiveness of Token-Rewards for Chimpanzees, *Comparative Psychology Monographs* 12(60):1-72.

Wolfe, J. B., 1939, An Exploratory Study of Food Storing in Rats, *Journal of Comparative Psychology* 28:97-108.

Wood, D. C., 1973, Stimulus Specific Habituation in a Protozoan, *Physiology and Behavior* 11:349-354.

Wood-Gush, D. G. M., 1963, Comparative Psychology and Ethology, *Annual Review of Psychology* 14:175-200.

Woodworth, R. S., 1918, *Dynamic Psychology,* Columbia University Press, New York.

Woodworth, R. S., 1952, Edward Lee Thorndike, *Biographical Memoirs of the National Academy of Sciences* 27:208-237.

Woodworth, R. S., 1959, John Broadus Watson: 1878-1958, *American Journal of Psychology* 72:301-310.

The Writer of the Note, 1896, Prof. C. Lloyd Morgan on Instinct, *Science* 3:356.

Wundt, W., 1894, *Lectures on Human and Animal Psychology*, J. E. Creighton and E. B. Titchener, trans., Swan Sonnenschein, London.

Wyers, E. J., and E. W. Menzel, 1980, Behavior and Reality, *American Psychologist* 35:968-970.

Wyers, E. J., G. E. Smith, and I. Dinkes, 1974, Passive Avoidance Learning in the Earthworm (*Lumbricus terrestris*), *Journal of Comparative and Physiological Psychology* 86:157-163.

Wyers, E. J., H. E. Adler, K. Carpen, D. Chiszar, J. Demarest, O. J. Flanagan, E. vonGlasersfeld, S. E. Glickman, W. A. Mason, E. W. Menzel, and E. Tobach, 1980, The Sociobiological Challenge to Psychology: On the Proposal to "Cannibalize" Comparative Psychology, *American Psychologist* 35:955-979.

Yarczower, M., and L. Hazlett, 1977, Evolutionary Scales and Anagenesis, *Psychological Bulletin* 84:1088-1097.

Yeager, D. L., 1973, Comparative Psychology? *American Psychologist* 28:181-184.

Yerkes, A. W., 1916, Comparison of the Behavior of Stock and Inbred Albino Rats, *Journal of Animal Behavior* 6:294-296.

Yerkes, R. M., 1901, The Formation of Habits in the Turtle, *Popular Science Monthly* 58:519-525.

Yerkes, R. M., 1902, Habit-Formation in the Green Crab, *Carcinus granulatus*, *Biological Bulletin* 3:241-244.

Yerkes, R. M., 1903, The Instincts, Habits, and Reactions of the Frog, *Psychological Review Monograph Supplement* 17:579-638.

Yerkes, R. M., 1904a, Physiology and Psychology, *Journal of Comparative Neurology and Psychology* 14:511-514.

Yerkes, R. M., 1904b, Animal Education, *Journal of Comparative Neurology and Psychology* 14:70-71.

Yerkes, R. M., 1905, Animal Psychology and Criteria of the Psychic, *Journal of Philosophy Psychology and Scientific Methods* 2:141-149.

Yerkes, R. M., 1906, Objective Nomenclature, Comparative Psychology and Animal Behavior, *Journal of Comparative Neurology and Psychology* 16:380-389.

Yerkes, R. M., 1907, *The Dancing Mouse. A Study in Animal Behavior*, Macmillan, New York.

Yerkes, R. M., 1908, Recent Progress and Present Tendencies in Comparative Psychology, *Journal of Abnormal Psychology* 2:271-279.

Yerkes, R. M., 1910, Psychology in Its Relations to Biology, *Journal of Philosophy, Psychology, and Scientific Methods* 7:113-124.

Yerkes, R. M., 1912, The Intelligence of Earthworms, *Journal of Animal Behavior* 2:332-352.

Yerkes, R. M., 1913a, Comparative Psychology: A Question of Definitions, *Journal of Philosophy, Psychology, and Scientific Methods* 10:580-582.

Yerkes, R. M., 1913b, The Heredity of Savageness and Wildness in Rats, *Journal of Animal Behavior* 3:286-296.

Yerkes, R. M., 1913c, A Society for Animal Psychology, *Journal of Animal Behavior* 3:303-304.

Yerkes, R. M., 1914, The Harvard Laboratory of Animal Psychology and the Franklin Field Station, *Journal of Animal Behavior* 4:176-184.

Yerkes, R. M., 1915*a*, Maternal Instinct in a Monkey, *Journal of Animal Behavior* 5:403-405.

Yerkes, R. M., 1915*b*, The Role of the Experimenter in Comparative Psychology, *Journal of Animal Behavior* 5:258.

Yerkes, R. M., 1916*a*, The Mental Life of Monkeys and Apes: A Study of Ideational Behavior, *Behavior Monographs* 3(12):1-145.

Yerkes, R. M., 1916*b*, Provision for the Study of Monkeys and Apes, *Science* 43:231-234.

Yerkes, R. M., 1917*a*, Methods of Exhibiting Reactive Tendencies Characteristic of Ontogenetic and Phylogenentic Stages, *Journal of Animal Behavior* 7:11-28.

Yerkes, R. M., 1917*b*, Behaviorism and Genetic Psychology, *Journal of Philosophy, Psychology and Scientific Methods* 14:154-161.

Yerkes, R. M., 1925, *Almost Human*, Jonathan Cape, London.

Yerkes, R. M., 1927*a*, The Mind of the Gorilla, *Genetic Psychology Monographs* 2(1 and 2):178-187.

Yerkes, R. M., 1927*b*, The Mind of a Gorilla: Part II. Mental Development, *Genetic Psychology Monographs* 2(6):526-532.

Yerkes, R. M., 1928, The Mind of a Gorilla. Part III. Memory, *Comparative Psychology Monographs* 5(24):1-92.

Yerkes, R. M., 1932*a*, Robert M. Yerkes, in *A History of Psychology in Autobiography*, vol. 2, C. Murchison, ed., Clark University Press, Worcester, Mass., pp. 381-407.

Yerkes, R. M., 1932*b*, Yale Laboratories of Comparative Psychobiology, *Comparative Psychology Monographs* 8(38):1-33.

Yerkes, R. M., 1933*a*, Genetic Aspects of Grooming, a Socially Important Primate Behavior Pattern, *Journal of Social Psychology* 4:3-25.

Yerkes, R. M., 1933*b*, Discussion Concerning the Anthropocentrism of Psychology, *Psychological Review* 40:209-212.

Yerkes, R. M., 1936, A Chimpanzee Family, *Journal of Genetic Psychology* 48:362-370.

Yerkes, R. M., 1939, Sexual Behavior in the Chimpanzee, *Human Biology* 11:78-111.

Yerkes, R. M., 1940, Social Behavior of Chimpanzees: Dominance between Mates in Relation to Sexual Status, *Journal of Comparative Psychology* 38:147-186.

Yerkes, R. M., 1941, Conjugal Contrasts Among Chimpanzees, *Journal of Abnormal and Social Psychology* 36:175-199.

Yerkes, R. M., 1943*a*, Early Days of Comparative Psychology, *Psychological Review* 50:74-76.

Yerkes, R. M., 1943*b*, Chimpanzees: A Laboratory Colony, Yale University Press, New Haven.

Yerkes, R. M., and D. Bloomfield, 1910, Do Kittens Instinctively Kill Mice? *Psychological Bulletin* 7:253-263.

Yerkes, R. M., and C. A. Coburn, 1915, A Study of the Behavior of the Pig *Sus scrofa* by the Multiple Choice Method, *Journal of Animal Behavior* 5:185-225.

Yerkes, R. M., and J. D. Dodson, 1908, The Relation of Strength of Stimulus to Rapidity of Habit-Formation, *Journal of Comparative Neurology and Psychology* 18:459-482.

Yerkes, R. M., and A. M. Eisenberg, 1915, Preliminaries to a Study of Color Vision in the Ring-Dove *Turtur risorius, Journal of Animal Behavior* 5:25-43.

Yerkes, R. M., and J. H. Elder, 1936, Oestrus, Receptivity, and Mating in the Chimpanzee, *Comparative Psychology Monographs* 13(65):1-39.

Yerkes, R. M., and G. E. Huggins, 1903, Habit Formation in the Crawfish *Cambarus affinis, Psychological Review Monograph Supplement* 17:565-577.

Yerkes, R. M., and S. Morgulis, 1909, The Method of Pawlow in Animal Psychology, *Psychological Bulletin* 6:257-273.

Yerkes, R. M., and H. W. Nissen, 1939, Pre-linguistic Sign Behavior in Chimpanzee, *Science* 89:585-587.

Yerkes, R. M., and J. B. Watson, 1911, Methods of Studying Vision in Animals, *Behavior Monographs* 1(2):1-90.

Yerkes, R. M., and A. W. Yerkes, 1929, *The Great Apes: A Study of Anthropoid Life,* Yale University Press, New Haven.

Yerkes, R. M., and A. W. Yerkes, 1936, Nature and Conditions of Avoidance (Fear) Responses in Chimpanzees, *Journal of Comparative Psychology* 21:53-66.

Yoakum, C. S., 1909, Some Experiments Upon the Behavior of Squirrels, *Journal of Comparative Neurology and Psychology* 19:565-568.

Young, P. T., 1928, Precautions in Animal Experimentation, *Psychological Bulletin* 25:487-489.

Young, P. T., 1930, Precautions in Animal Experimentation, *Psychological Bulletin* 27:119-120.

Young, P. T., 1932, Relative Food Preferences of the White Rat, *Journal of Comparative Psychology* 14:297-319.

Zajonc, R. B., 1965, Social Facilitation, *Science* 149:269-274.

Zajonc, R. B., ed., 1969, *Animal Social Psychology,* Wiley, New York.

Zuckerman, C. B., and H. Wallach, 1968, Wolfgang Köhler, in *International Encyclopedia of the Social Sciences,* D. L. Sills, ed., Macmillan, New York, pp. 438-443.

Zusne, L., 1975, *Names in the History of Psychology,* Wiley, New York.

Index

Boldface numerals following the names of individuals indicate biographical material.

About the Author

DONALD ALLEN DEWSBURY is a professor of psychology at the University of Florida. His research interests relate to comparative animal behavior with emphasis on the study of adaptive significance, reproductive behavior, the use of the comparative method, and the behavior of rodents.

Dr. Dewsbury received the A.B. degree from Bucknell University in 1961 and the Ph.D degree from the University of Michigan in 1965. He was an N.S.F. post-doctoral fellow in the laboratory of Dr. Frank A. Beach at the University of California, Berkeley in 1965-1966. His published scientific papers number over 140. Dr. Dewsbury's books include *Comparative Psychology: A Modern Survey* (co-edited with D. A. Rethlingshafer, McGraw-Hill, 1973), *Comparative Animal Behavior* (McGraw-Hill, 1978), *Sex and Behavior: Status and Prospectus* (co-edited with T. E. McGill and B. D. Sachs, Plenum, 1978), and *Mammalian Sexual Behavior* (Hutchinson Ross, 1981). He is a member of a dozen scientific organizations and has served as treasurer and president of the Animal Behavior Society.